CRIME SCENE
INVESTIGATION
A Step-by-Step Procedure Manual

Real-World
CRIME SCENE
INVESTIGATION
A Step-by-Step Procedure Manual

Gabriele Suboch, PhD

Northcentral University
Prescott Valley, Arizona, USA

Colorado State University-Global Campus
Greenwood Village, Colorado, USA

Lee County Sheriff's Office (Retired)
Fort Myers, Florida, USA

CRC Press
Taylor & Francis Group
Boca Raton London New York

CRC Press is an imprint of the
Taylor & Francis Group, an **informa** business

CRC Press
Taylor & Francis Group
6000 Broken Sound Parkway NW, Suite 300
Boca Raton, FL 33487-2742

First issued in paperback 2020

ISBN-13: 978-1-4987-0744-2 (hbk)
ISBN-13: 978-0-367-77910-8 (pbk)

Visit the Taylor & Francis Web site at
http://www.taylorandfrancis.com

and the CRC Press Web site at
http://www.crcpress.com

This book is dedicated to my parents, Helmut and Johanna Kruppa, and especially to my husband, Alexander Suboch, who always supported and encouraged me in my endeavors.

This book is also dedicated to the men and women in law enforcement who risk their lives to protect and serve our communities.

Contents

Preface   **xvii**
Author   **xix**

1   **Tools of the Trade**   **1**

   1.1   Introduction   1
       1.1.1   The Duties of the Crime Scene Investigator   1
   1.2   Forensic Tools to Document the Crime Scene   1
       1.2.1   Scene Documentation   1
       1.2.2   Note Taking   2
       1.2.3   Crime Scene Sketching   2
       1.2.4   Photographic Documentation   3
   1.3   Evidence Collection   4
       1.3.1   Crime Scene Contamination and Protective Gear   4
       1.3.2   Markers for Identifying Physical Evidence   6
       1.3.3   Evidence Measuring Devices   7
       1.3.4   Packaging Materials   7
       1.3.5   Blood Evidence Collection Kit   8
       1.3.6   Entomology Evidence Collection Kit   9
       1.3.7   Trace Evidence Collection   10
       1.3.8   Drug Testing Kit   11
       1.3.9   Sexual Assault Evidence Collection Kit   11
       1.3.10   Gunshot Residue Kit   14
       1.3.11   Semen Testing Kit (Acid Phosphatase Kit)   15
   1.4   Tools to Develop Evidence   16
       1.4.1   Fingerprint Detection Kit   16
       1.4.2   Bloodstain Pattern Analysis Kit   17
       1.4.3   Blood Detection Kit   18
          1.4.3.1   Kastle Myers Test Kit   18
          1.4.3.2   Hexagon OBTI Presumptive Blood Test   19
          1.4.3.3   Luminol   20
          1.4.3.4   Bluestar   22
          1.4.3.5   Amido Black   23
          1.4.3.6   ZAR-PRO™   23
   1.5   Additional Tools for Evidence Recovery   23
       1.5.1   Toolbox   24

	1.5.2	Metal Detector	24
	1.5.3	Excavation Kit	25
	1.5.4	Accessory Lights	25
	1.5.5	Laser Trajectory Kit	25
	1.5.6	Shoe and Tire Impression Casting	26
1.6	Summary		27
References			27

2 Forensic Photography   29

2.1	Camera Equipment		29
	2.1.1	Digital Cameras	29
	2.1.2	Lenses	30
	2.1.3	Filters	31
	2.1.4	Storage Media	32
2.2	Photography Basics		33
	2.2.1	Light and Photography	33
		2.2.1.1 Daylight	33
		2.2.1.2 Night Photography	34
	2.2.2	Capture an Image	35
		2.2.2.1 Fill the Frame	35
		2.2.2.2 Depth of Field	36
		2.2.2.3 Shutter Speed and Shutter Priority	37
		2.2.2.4 Keep the Film Plane Parallel	38
		2.2.2.5 Aperture Priority	38
		2.2.2.6 Flash Photography	39
		2.2.2.7 Effect of Flash Angle	39
2.3	Specialized Photography on Scene and in the Laboratory		39
	2.3.1	Luminol and Bluestar Photography	39
		2.3.1.1 Steps for Luminol Photography	39
	2.3.2	Bluestar Photography	41
	2.3.3	Ultraviolet and Infrared Photography	41
		2.3.3.1 Applications for Ultraviolet Photography	43
	2.3.4	Infrared Photography	43
	2.3.5	Identification Photographs	44
2.4	Crime Scene Photography		45
	2.4.1	Document the Photos	45
		2.4.1.1 Photo Identifier	45
		2.4.1.2 Photo Log	47
	2.4.2	Scene Photography	48
		2.4.2.1 Overall Photography	48
		2.4.2.2 Methods of Exterior and Interior Overall Photography	51

		2.4.2.3	Midrange Photographs	54
		2.4.2.4	Close-Up Photographs	55
	2.4.3	Photographing a Body on Scene		58
		2.4.3.1	Body Panorama Photos	58
		2.4.3.2	Photographing the Victim's Injuries	59
		2.4.3.3	Photographing an Accident Scene	60
	2.4.4	Footwear Impressions		62
2.5	The Expert Witness			63
2.6	Legal Challenges of Forensic Photography			64
	2.6.1	Murder Trial in Florida		64
2.7	Checklist for Crime Scene Photography			65
2.8	Conclusion			66
References				66

3   Impression Pattern Evidence   67

3.1	Fingerprints			67
	3.1.1	Fingerprint Patterns		67
		3.1.1.1	Arch	67
		3.1.1.2	Whorl	67
		3.1.1.3	Loop	67
	3.1.2	Elimination Fingerprints		69
		3.1.2.1	Suspect Fingerprints	70
		3.1.2.2	Inked Fingerprints from Deceased	70
	3.1.3	Categories of Fingerprints		72
	3.1.4	Methods to Develop Latent Fingerprints		73
		3.1.4.1	Stabilizing the Fingerprint on Nonporous Surfaces with Cyanoacrylate Fuming	73
		3.1.4.2	Different Applications of the Cyanoacrylate Fuming Methods	76
	3.1.5	Powder Processing of Fingerprints		78
		3.1.5.1	Fingerprint Powders	78
	3.1.6	Chemical Processing of Fingerprints on Porous Surfaces		81
		3.1.6.1	Iodine Fuming	81
		3.1.6.2	Ninhydrin	82
		3.1.6.3	Physical Developer	83
		3.1.6.4	DFO	84
	3.1.7	Fingerprints in Blood		84
		3.1.7.1	Amido Black	84
	3.1.8	Special Processing Methods		85
		3.1.8.1	Small Particle Reagent	85

		3.1.8.2	Wetwop	86
		3.1.8.3	Enhancing Latent Fingerprints on Metal Surfaces	86
		3.1.8.4	RUVIS System	88
3.2	Shoe and Tire Impressions			89
	3.2.1	Classification of Shoe and Tire Impressions		90
	3.2.2	Processing Methods for Shoe and Tire Impressions		90
		3.2.2.1	Developing Latent Shoe Impressions	90
		3.2.2.2	Three-Dimensional Shoe Impressions	93
		3.2.2.3	Casting Tire Impression in Dirt and Sand	97
		3.2.2.4	Impression Lifted from a Tire	98
	3.2.3	Identification of Shoe and Tire Impressions		99
3.3	Tool Mark Impressions			99
References				100

4   Arriving at the Crime Scene   103

4.1	Introduction			103
	4.1.1	The First Responder		103
		4.1.1.1	Officer Safety	103
		4.1.1.2	Securing the Scene	104
		4.1.1.3	Crime Scene Contamination	104
		4.1.1.4	Setting the Inner and Outer Perimeter	105
		4.1.1.5	Crime Scene Log	106
	4.1.2	The Initial Call for the CSI		107
	4.1.3	Arriving on Scene		108
	4.1.4	Legalities for Entering the Crime Scene		108
		4.1.4.1	Legal Searches and the Fourth Amendment	108
		4.1.4.2	Justification of Reasonable Searches	111
		4.1.4.3	The Search Warrant	112
		4.1.4.4	Searches with Consent	118
		4.1.4.5	Exigent Circumstances	119
	4.1.5	Walk-Through of the Scene		120
	4.1.6	Crime Scene Process		121
		4.1.6.1	Steps of a Typical Crime Scene Investigation	121
4.2	Documenting the Scene			121
	4.2.1	Photographing the Scene		123
	4.2.2	Sketching the Crime Scene		124
		4.2.2.1	Types of Sketches	124
	4.2.3	Crime Scene Mapping		128
		4.2.3.1	Baseline Mapping	131

	4.2.3.2	Rectangular Coordinate Mapping	133
	4.2.3.3	Triangulation Method	133
	4.2.3.4	Polar/Grid Coordinate Mapping	134
	4.2.3.5	Use of GPS	134
4.3	Searching for Additional Evidence		135
	4.3.1	Indoor Crime Scene Searches	135
		4.3.1.1 Spiral Search Pattern	136
		4.3.1.2 Pie or Wheel Search Pattern	136
		4.3.1.3 Zone Search Pattern	136
		4.3.1.4 Elevation Zone Search Pattern	138
	4.3.2	Outdoor Crime Scene Searches	138
		4.3.2.1 Line, Strip, or Parallel Search Pattern	138
		4.3.2.2 Grid Search Pattern	139
4.4	Managing Crime Scene Searches		139
	4.4.1	Outdoor Searches	139
	4.4.2	Indoor Searches	143
	4.4.3	Where to Find Evidence	143
	4.4.4	Officer Safety during Crime Scene Searches	144
4.5	Developing, Analyzing, and Reconstructing the Scene of a Crime		144
4.6	Evidence Collection, Packaging, and Preservation		145
	4.6.1	Paper or Plastic or Other Containers?	145
		4.6.1.1 Paper Bags and Cardboard Boxes	145
		4.6.1.2 Plastic Bags	147
		4.6.1.3 Plastic and Metal Containers	147
		4.6.1.4 Optional Packaging	148
	4.6.2	Labeling Evidence	148
	4.6.3	Sequence of Collecting Evidence	149
		4.6.3.1 Property Receipt	150
		4.6.3.2 Chain of Custody	150
4.7	Motor Vehicles Involved in a Crime		151
	4.7.1	General Vehicle Crime Scene Procedures	152
		4.7.1.1 Documentation of the Vehicle	152
		4.7.1.2 Photographing the Vehicle	152
		4.7.1.3 Sketching the Vehicle	155
		4.7.1.4 Transporting the Vehicle	156
		4.7.1.5 Searching the Vehicle	157
		4.7.1.6 Developing and Recovering Additional Evidence	157
4.8	Final Walk-Through		158
	4.8.1	Releasing the Scene/Vehicle	159
References			159

5   Excavation, Bones, Bugs, and Botany   161

5.1   Excavations   161
   5.1.1   Legal Implications   161
       5.1.1.1   Basic Crime Scene Rules   161
   5.1.2   Excavation Equipment   161
   5.1.3   Information about the Site   163
   5.1.4   Arriving at the Crime Scene   163
       5.1.4.1   Managing the Crime Scene Team   163
   5.1.5   Clandestine Graves   164
       5.1.5.1   Searching for the Clandestine Gravesite 164
       5.1.5.2   Determining the Outer and Inner
               Perimeter of the Scene   165
       5.1.5.3   Surface Evidence Collection   165
       5.1.5.4   Setting Up a Grid   167
       5.1.5.5   Beginning to Excavate   167
       5.1.5.6   Recovery of the Body   168
       5.1.5.7   Condition of the Body   173
       5.1.5.8   Transport of the Body   173
       5.1.5.9   Bugs, Insects, and Plant Material
               inside the Gravesite   174
       5.1.5.10 Clearing from the Gravesite   174
   5.1.6   Surface Skeletal Scattered Remains   174
       5.1.6.1   Leading the Crime Scene Team   174
       5.1.6.2   Determine the Grid and Search
               for More Bones   175
       5.1.6.3   Jurisdiction of the Medical Examiner   175
       5.1.6.4   Searching for Additional Evidence   175
5.2   Identification of the Remains through Forensic
   Anthropology   177
   5.2.1   Taphonomic Assessment   177
   5.2.2   Methods of Identification of the Victim   178
   5.2.3   Estimating the Victim's Age   178
       5.2.3.1   Skeletal Development   178
       5.2.3.2   Teeth Development   179
       5.2.3.3   Sexual Dimorphism   179
       5.2.3.4   Estimation of Stature   180
       5.2.3.5   Evidence for Cause and Manner
               of Death   180
       5.2.3.6   The Forensic Anthropology Report   180
5.3   Facial Reconstruction   181

5.4 Identification of the Victim through Forensic Odontology 181
5.4.1 Grin Line Identification 182
5.4.1.1 Creating the Images 182
5.4.1.2 Comparing the Images 182
5.5 Entomology 183
5.5.1 Time of Death Estimation 183
5.5.2 Life Cycle 185
5.5.3 Toxicology and Insects 186
5.5.4 Bugs Tell More Stories... 186
5.5.5 Collection of Entomology Samples on Scene 187
5.5.6 Note Taking at a Death Scene with Insect Activity 187
5.6 Botany 190
5.6.1 What Can Plants Tell Us? 190
5.6.2 Proper Collection of Plant Material 191
References 192

6 Crime Scene Reconstruction 195

6.1 What Is Bloodstain Pattern Analysis? 195
6.1.1 Anatomical Aspects of Blood 196
6.1.1.1 Medical Conditions Causing Blood Loss 196
6.1.2 Physical Properties of Blood 197
6.1.3 The Levels of Bloodstain Pattern Analysis 198
6.1.4 Classification of Bloodstains 198
6.1.5 Passive Bloodstains 198
6.1.5.1 Passive/Gravity Stain Patterns 200
6.1.5.2 Spatter Patterns 202
6.1.5.3 Altered Bloodstain Patterns 207
6.1.6 Target Surface Differences 209
6.1.7 Directionality and Angle of Impact 209
6.1.8 Areas of Origin 212
6.1.9 Documenting Bloodstains at the Crime Scene 212
6.1.9.1 Investigator/Bloodstain Pattern Analyst Safety 212
6.1.9.2 Procedure for Determining the Area of Convergence 212
6.1.9.3 Stringing Method to Determine the Area of Origin 214
6.1.9.4 Roadmapping 216
6.1.9.5 Applying the Road Mapping Method 216
6.1.10 Computerized Bloodstain Pattern Analysis 217
6.1.10.1 HemoSpat 217

6.2   Firearms and Shooting Reconstruction   218
       6.2.1   Firearms   218
                6.2.1.1   Revolver   218
                6.2.1.2   Semi-Automatic Handgun   219
                6.2.1.3   Rifles and Shotguns   220
                6.2.1.4   Cartridges and Shotgun Shells   221
                6.2.1.5   Bullet and Cartridge Comparison   222
       6.2.2   Firearm Safety   222
                6.2.2.1   Clearing a Firearm   222
       6.2.3   Identifying a Firearm   224
       6.2.4   Identification Markings on Live and Spent
                Cartridges   224
       6.2.5   Collection and Preservation of Firearms   224
       6.2.6   Serial Number Restoration   227
       6.2.7   Shooter to Target Distance Determination   227
                6.2.7.1   Characteristics of a Gunshot Fired
                           at a Distance of 1 inch or Less   228
                6.2.7.2   Characteristics of a Gunshot Fired
                           at a Distance of 12 to 18 inches 228
                6.2.7.3   Characteristics of a Gunshot Fired
                           at a Distance over 3 feet   228
                6.2.7.4   Distance Determination of Shotguns 228
                6.2.7.5   Collection of Clothing with Powder
                           Residues   230
       6.2.8   Gunshot Residue Kit   230
                6.2.8.1   ISid2—Gunshot Residue SEM Test Kit
                           and Instant Shooter Kit   231
       6.2.9   Trajectory Reconstruction   231
6.3   Glass Fracture Match   235
       6.3.1   Glass Fractures   235
       6.3.2   Glass Fractures Associated with a Gunshot   235
       6.3.3   The 3R Rule   236
       6.3.4   Sequencing Bullet Holes   236
References   237

7   Death Investigation   239

7.1   What Is a Death Investigation?   239
       7.1.1   Criminal Investigator versus Medico-Legal
                Death Investigator   239
       7.1.2   Coroner versus Medical Examiner   239
                7.1.2.1   The Coroner   240
                7.1.2.2   The Medical Examiner   240

7.2   Autopsy   241
        7.2.1   What Is an Autopsy?   241
                7.2.1.1   Cause, Manner, and Mechanism of Death   241
                7.2.1.2   The Mortis Brothers—The Chemistry
                          of Death   242
                7.2.1.3   Time of Death   244
        7.2.2   Purpose of the Autopsy   248
                7.2.2.1   The Duties of the Medical Examiner
                          and the Medico-Legal Death Investigator   249
                7.2.2.2   Autopsy at the Medical Examiner's Office   252
                7.2.2.3   Internal Autopsy   268
                7.2.2.4   Evidence Collection from the Victim   270
        7.2.3   Lab Submission for Evidence from the Autopsy   272
7.3   Death Investigations   274
        7.3.1   Response to Death Investigations   274
                7.3.1.1   Possible Cover-Up Attempt   275
        7.3.2   Suicide   275
                7.3.2.1   Suicide through Asphyxiant Gas   277
                7.3.2.2   Death Investigation: Asphyxia
                          by Hanging   278
                7.3.2.3   Death by Power Tools   280
                7.3.2.4   Death Investigation: Gunshot   282
                7.3.2.5   Death Investigation: Poisoning
                          and Overdose   283
                7.3.2.6   Death Investigation: Drowning   285
        7.3.3   Sudden Infant Death Syndrome   289
                7.3.3.1   Reconstruction of the Scene   297
        References   297

8   Mixed Cases   299

8.1   Multi-Agency Investigations   299
        8.1.1   Drug Investigations   299
                8.1.1.1   Marijuana Grow Operations   299
                8.1.1.2   Crime Scene Response   303
                8.1.1.3   Maintenance for the Seized Live Plants   304
                8.1.1.4   Methamphetamine   308
        8.1.2   Aviation Accidents   312
                8.1.2.1   The National Transportation
                          and Safety Board (NTSB)   312
                8.1.2.2   Local Response to an Aviation Accident
                          Site   314
        8.1.3   Human Trafficking and Human Smuggling   321

		8.1.3.1	Human Trafficking	322
		8.1.3.2	Human Smuggling	322
		8.1.3.3	Crime Scene Response to Human Trafficking and Human Smuggling	325
	8.1.4		Officer-Involved Shooting	326
		8.1.4.1	Who Should Investigate the Officer-Involved Shooting?	327
		8.1.4.2	CSI Response to Officer-Involved Shooting	327

Appendix A: Forensic Databases   **339**

Appendix B: Violent Crimes and Homicide Field Notes   **345**

Index   **375**

Preface

Welcome to *Real-World Crime Scene Investigation*, a procedural manual for crime scene investigators. This book is designed to provide you with hands-on information and guidance on how to investigate different types of crime scenes. Modern forensic equipment, processing procedures, techniques, and methods will be introduced.

This book differs from other crime scene and forensic textbooks as it is written by a crime scene investigator for readers beginning a career or who are already working in the field of law enforcement, especially in crime scene investigation. It is designed as a field guide providing step-by-step instructions on how to document a crime scene, sketch, map, search, collect, and preserve physical evidence.

Many college students graduate with an associate's or bachelor's degree in forensics or criminal justice. The newly hired college-educated crime scene investigator (CSI) possesses theoretical knowledge about different forensic disciplines, but lacks practical application. In many cases, the CSI responds to a crime scene and is lost, not knowing what steps to perform first and why. This book provides step-at-a-time instructions that can be easily followed. Field note templates for different types of cases, for example, vehicle processing, autopsy, and boat and airplane identification, are provided.

The chapters in the book range from introducing the basic crime scene tools and their application to crime scene reconstruction with bloodstain pattern analysis and firearm trajectory, how to document plane crashes, methamphetamine laboratories, and officer-involved shootings. Throughout the chapters, **hints** and **cautions** are included providing information on how to easily accomplish a task and/or warn about common errors.

Many people helped me in the preparation of this book. I thank my friend, Phil Sanfilippo, and the team from Tritech Forensics for their assistance in providing me with images of forensic equipment. Special thanks to my friend Ron Mueller, Crime Scene Unit Supervisor at the Charlotte County Sheriff's Office in Punta Gorda, Florida, for providing me with crime scene sketches and photos. Thank you to my friend and retired FBI Photography Instructor Michael Brooks for his assistance.

Special thanks go to my coworker and longtime friend Randolph Eubanks for his contribution of crime scene templates to my book. I also thank Nick from 3rd Tech., and Ken E. Boots from Factual/Diagrams.com for their assistance.

Author

Dr. Gabriele Suboch is a professor in criminal justice studies, after retiring from a career in law enforcement. She possesses more than 25 years of experience in law enforcement with the Bavarian State Police in Germany, the Lee County Sheriff's Office in Fort Myers, Florida, and is currently volunteering as an auxiliary deputy with Hendry County Sheriff's Office in Labelle, Florida.

She obtained more than 1,200 hours of specialized forensic training and more than 650 hours of law enforcement/correction training. She is a certified bloodstain pattern analyst.

Dr. Suboch testified as an expert witness in fingerprint technology, crime scene investigation, crime scene photography, and bloodstain pattern analysis. She was the lead crime scene investigator and testified in high profile cases such as the Gateway double murder, Juan Mendez double murder in Lehigh Acres, Florida, and the murder of Mrs. Lame, which was broadcast live on Court TV and on the Internet.

Her formal education includes a master's degree in business administration with specialization in public administration from Impac University (2003), a master's degree in business administration with specialization in criminal justice from Northcentral University (2007), and a PhD in business administration and specialization in criminal justice from Northcentral University in 2009. Her dissertation topic was assessing the use of bloodstain pattern analysis by department, location, and officer factors. The dissertation is published in ProQuest and in book format.

Currently, she is a professor in criminal justice studies at Northcentral University teaching and developing criminal justice and forensics courses at the graduate and doctoral level. Dr. Suboch is the lead criminal justice instructor at Colorado State University Global Campus teaching and developing criminal justice and forensics courses.

Dr. Suboch is a member of the subcommittee for Bloodstain Pattern Analysis of the Organization of Scientific Area Committees (OSAC). OSAC is part of an initiative by National Institute for Standard and Technology (NIST) and the Department of Justice to strengthen forensic science in the United States.

Tools of the Trade

1

1.1 Introduction

1.1.1 The Duties of the Crime Scene Investigator

Crime scene investigation consists of the documentation, development, collection, and preservation of physical evidence at the scene of a crime. The duties of the crime scene investigator (CSI) are manifold. Crime scene investigators are experts in one or more forensic disciplines such as DNA analysis, bloodstain pattern analysis, toxicology, chemistry, and impression evidence (footwear, tire and tool marks, and fingerprint technology).

Criminalists are employed with municipal, state, or federal law enforcement agencies. While some criminalists work primarily in the laboratory, others respond to crime scenes. The investigator's duties at the crime scene include the thorough documentation of the characteristics and specifics of the scene via notes, photographs, and drawing a sketch of the scene as well as including physical evidence, and marking, measuring, collecting, and preserving evidence. Some physical evidence is not always visible to the naked eye, such as latent fingerprints, and often involves additional processing. Casting shoe and tire tracks and analysis of bloodstain patterns provide information about the events that led to the bloodshed. Bullet trajectory provides information about the location of the shooter and the victim during the incident. Special equipment is required to perform those special tasks. Professionalism in the handling and application of the forensic tools, whether it is a trajectory laser or chemicals to detect blood, is imperative for a thorough crime scene investigation.

1.2 Forensic Tools to Document the Crime Scene

1.2.1 Scene Documentation

Documenting the crime scene *in situ*, as seen, can be conducted in different ways. Note taking is the most common form. After the crime scene investigation is concluded, a final crime scene report will be established from the notes taken during the investigation. Photographs, video recording, and crime scene sketches provide visual documentation of the scene that may be presented to the jurors in a later trial. Commonly, it may take one or two years before a crime will be prosecuted in court and the crime scene investigator is required to testify to the documentation, detection, collection, and preservation of evidence from the crime scene, as well as analysis of physical evidence at the crime scene such as bloodstain pattern analysis. The crime scene investigator testifies under oath and all presented information must be factual and accurate; otherwise, the investigator could face criminal charges for perjury or wrongful testimony.

1.2.2 Note Taking

Documentation at the crime scene can be performed in different ways. Even with electronic devices such as digital audio recorders, the old paper and pencil note taking is still valid. Many agencies have developed templates and documentation packages to ensure uniform documentation of all crime scenes by all personnel. Several samples of templates for autopsies, vehicle processing, and felony crime processing can be found throughout the book and in the appendix.

The basic crime scene documentation kit consists of

- Notepad
- Pencil and eraser
- Pen and permanent markers
- Digital voice recorder

Weather conditions can change while working an outside crime scene and documenting a crime scene in the rain can create difficulties. An all-weather notebook with an all-weather pen and notepad will allow note taking even in the rain.

1.2.3 Crime Scene Sketching

A crime scene sketch is a layout of the crime scene. In the crime scene sketch, the location of the victim and physical evidence is documented. In most cases, the prosecutor will introduce the crime scene sketch as a visual aid to demonstrate the relationship between the location of the recovered physical evidence and the victim.

A basic crime scene sketching kit, as illustrated in Figure 1.1, consists of

1. Gridded notepad
2. Specialized grid boards that allow for easier sketching
3. Pencil and eraser
4. Ruler
5. Compass
6. GPS if available to determine the coordinates

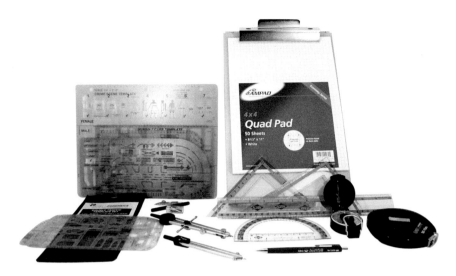

Figure 1.1 Basic crime scene sketching kit. (With permission from Tritech Forensics.)

1.2.4 Photographic Documentation

Pictures are worth a thousand words. This saying is especially valid in crime scene documentation. Photos and video of the crime scene provide the investigator, the prosecutor, the defense attorney, and the juror in the courtroom with a true depiction of the characteristics and specifics of the scene.

A basic camera kit, as shown in Figure 1.2, for forensic investigative photography should contain:

- Digital camera, preferably 14 plus megapixels
- Lenses 50 to 100 mm
- Lenses 100 to 300 mm
- Flash
- Tripod
- Storage media
- Scales in different sizes
- Skylight filters
- Antiglare filters
- Special filters for ultraviolet (UV) and infrared (IR) photography
- Additional batteries and car charger
- Universal serial bus (USB) cable to download photos to computer on scene if necessary
- Camera backpack for easy transport of the photo equipment

Figure 1.2 Basic camera kit.

1.3 Evidence Collection

After photographs and notes are taken, the evidence collection phase begins. Contamination can jeopardize the integrity of evidence on scene and must be avoided. Before the evidence can be collected, every piece of evidence is marked, measured, and then packaged and sealed. Different evidence—such as blood, saliva, semen, or shoe and tire impressions—requires specific collection and preservation methods.

1.3.1 Crime Scene Contamination and Protective Gear

What is crime scene contamination, what causes it, and why is it important? Based on Locard's principle of exchange, every time two items come into contact, there is an exchange of some form of trace evidence. Every person entering and leaving a crime scene brings some form of trace evidence such as hairs, fibers, soil, or blood on the soles of the shoes into the scene, and removes trace evidence from the scene. Cross-contamination can occur if the crime consists of several scenes and the CSI moves from one scene to the next.

As an example, in the O.J. Simpson double murder investigation, detectives from the Los Angeles Police Department (LAPD) responded to the crime scene at Bundy Drive where the bodies of Nicole Brown Simpson and Ronald Goldman had been recovered. The scene contained biological evidence. The detectives did not wear protective booties over their shoes and without changing shoes, continued to the O.J. Simpson residence in Brentwood.

There is a chance that blood and DNA evidence had been transferred from the Bundy Drive scene to the Brentwood home, thus cross-contamination between the two scenes.

There are several ways to prevent crime scene contamination and cross-contamination between multiple scenes.

- Limit the access to the scene and only allow investigative personnel and CSI personnel into the inner circle of the scene. The first responder on the scene or the patrol personnel maintaining the crime scene log is responsible for the entry of all investigative personnel to the scene.
- However, the most common means of eliminating contamination is by wearing protective gear.

Every crime scene investigator and detective should be equipped with the basic protective gear such as

- Gloves
- Booties
- Face mask
- Hairnet
- TyVac suit

Protective Gear

At no time should the CSI or any investigative personnel be allowed in the inner circle of a crime scene without wearing booties and gloves. Booties will prevent the transfer of trace evidence from the soles of the shoes, while the gloves not only prevent the destruction of fingerprint evidence and touch DNA, but also protect the CSI from contact with biohazard materials such as blood, saliva, or any other biological liquids. A face mask is important because DNA can be transmitted through saliva, sneezing, or coughing onto the items of evidence present at the crime scene. Wearing a hairnet will minimize the transfer of hair from the investigative personnel onto the crime scene. Hair contains mitochondrial DNA and the hair root can be used for nuclear DNA testing to establish a complete DNA profile.

If the shoes or any equipment have accidentally been exposed to biological hazards such as blood, saliva, or other body fluids, wash the contaminated area with a 10% solution of bleach and water. At no time should protective gear be recycled for future uses. Gloves should be changed after the collection of each item of evidence, especially biological evidence to avoid cross-contamination. Booties need to be discarded on leaving the scene and new booties need to be worn every time entering the scene. At no time should the CSI or any investigative personnel walk in and out of the scene wearing the same set of booties as illustrated in Figure 1.3.

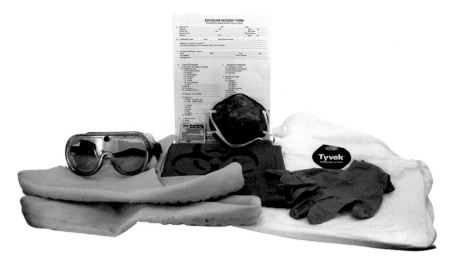

Figure 1.3 Protective gear for the crime scene investigator. (With permission from Tritech Forensics.)

1.3.2 Markers for Identifying Physical Evidence

Individually marking physical evidence with continuous numbers or letters is essential to separate and identify each item and pinpoint the location of recovery. The location of the evidence might provide information about the sequence of events. Yellow markers with numbers, letters, or compass directions are commonly used, as shown in Figure 1.4. Markers with American Board of Orthodontics (ABO) scales allow showing the size of the evidence such as a projectile or a spent cartridge.

Figure 1.4 Yellow evidence marker. (With permission from Tritech Forensics.)

Every evidence marking kit should contain: *Evidence Kit*

- Yellow marker numbers 1 through 99
- Yellow marker letters
- Yellow markers North, South, East, West
- First response evidence markers
- Photo-reflecting chalk to outline evidence or the body
- Luminescent marker numbers for night scenes

1.3.3 Evidence Measuring Devices

After marking, sketching, and photographing the evidence, triangulated or baseline measurements of the location of the evidence in relation to a fixed point will be attained. Different kinds of measuring devices are available, such as

- Multiple measuring tapes (25 ft, 100 ft, and 300 ft)   *Measuring Devices*
- Measuring wheel
- Magnetic rulers
- Laser measuring device if available

1.3.4 Packaging Materials

The proper packaging of physical evidence preserves the quality of the evidence and thus ensures the value for further forensic testing. Any biological evidence should be packaged in paper as plastic packaging would result in molding and degrading or destruction of DNA. Since physical evidence can be anything from a hair to a tire, the CSI has the need of a variety of different packaging materials, as shown in Figure 1.5, such as

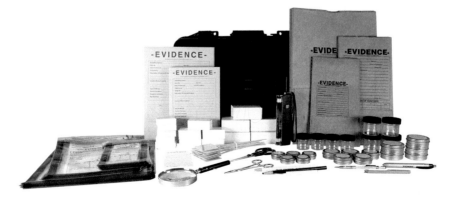

Figure 1.5 Packing material. (With permission from Tritech Forensics.)

Packaging materials [handwritten annotation]

- Paper bags in different sizes (S, M, L, XL)
- Coin envelopes for trace evidence such as hairs and fibers
- Cardboard boxes for firearms and rifles
- Cardboard boxes or plastic containers for knives
- Metal pill boxes for small items
- Cardboard boxes for small trace evidence
- Plastic bags in different sizes
- Roll of butcher paper for large items of evidence
- Metal arson collection cans
- Nylon arson collection bags
- Syringe/sharps evidence collection tubers
- Hand preservation bags for deceased
- Antistatic evidence bags for electronic devices
- Evidence sealing tape
- Biohazard stickers
- Body bags
- Body blanket for large items
- Biological swab collection boxes

1.3.5 Blood Evidence Collection Kit

Blood is a biological fluid that can be found at most crime scenes. Blood can be present on the floor of a business or house when a burglar cuts himself while breaking a window, the scene of an aggravated battery, or at a homicide or suicide scene when weapons such as knives or firearms have been used. The documentation of the presence of blood on the scheme through photography, notes, and sketches is significant. Blood is an excellent source for DNA.

The following equipment is necessary to collect bloodstains at the crime scene:

Blood kit [handwritten annotation]

- Sterile water
- Sterile cotton swabs
- Cardboard containers to store the blood sample
- Blood vials

These basic steps are required when collecting blood samples.

Steps collecting blood [handwritten annotation]

- Visually examine and determine if the bloodstain is wet or dry.
- If the stain is wet,
  - Saturate the tip of the sterile swab with blood.
  - Air-dry the swab (the back of the cardboard collection box has a small hole to position the swab for drying).
  - Avoid contamination between multiple samples.

Figure 1.6 Blood evidence collection kit. (With permission from Tritech Forensics.)

- After air-dried, place the swab in the cardboard box.
- Write the following information on the outside of the box:
  - Case number
  - Kind of crime
  - Date and time of collection
  - Name of the collector
  - Area the swab was collected from
  - Add biohazard sticker
  - Seal with evidence tape, initial and date
  - Prepare property receipt and maintain chain of custody
- If the stain is dry,
  - Saturate a sterile swab with sterile water.
  - Swab the dried bloodstain until a sufficient sample is obtained.
  - Air-dry and follow the procedures of preserving and packaging.

A bloodstain evidence collection kit containing all necessary equipment is commercially available as illustrated in Figure 1.6.

1.3.6 Entomology Evidence Collection Kit

Forensic entomology is the application of entomology involving the invasion of insects on the body after death. Different species of insects such as flies, ants, beetles, wasps, and especially the blowfly, will invade a body shortly after death. Based on the insect succession, the entomologist can determine the approximate

Figure 1.7 Entomology evidence kit. (With permission from Tritech Forensics.)

time of death (Siegel and Houck, 2007). Therefore, it is important to collect any insect samples at the crime scene.

The basic entomology evidence collection kit, as illustrated in Figure 1.7, consists of

- Aerial or swap net
- Kill jar (glass jar with screw-on lid containing fingernail polish remover, cotton balls, or paper towels)
- Four to six disposable plastic containers
- Aluminum foil
- Digital or dial top thermometer
- Ethyl alcohol
- Small toolbox
- Forceps and/or small plastic spoons
- Nonadhesive heavy bond paper and adhesive paper labels

At crime scenes with multiple victims, or if the responding CSI is not trained in the collection of entomological evidence, a forensic entomologist may be consulted to respond to the scene. Also, in some cases where the time of death determination is critical, the medical examiner may consult a forensic entomologist.

1.3.7 Trace Evidence Collection

Trace evidence consists of hairs, fibers, glass, paint chips, and any other minutiae item that can be left by the suspect, the victim, or any other person present at the crime scene. A forensic evidence vacuum is used to collect trace evidence such as hairs and fibers from the crime scene. Trace evidence is not always visible with the naked eye and needs to be examined under a microscope. The

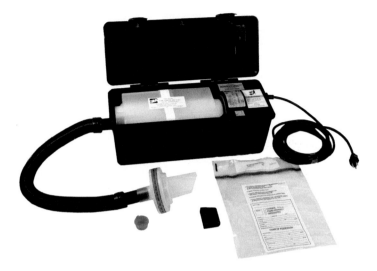

Figure 1.8 Trace evidence vacuum. (With permission from Tritech Forensics.)

vacuum has a filter to eliminate cross-contamination from individual crime scenes; see Figure 1.8. Evidence vacuuming is used in sexual assault investigations as well as on the seats and floorboard inside a vehicle. The filter with the trace evidence will be sent to the laboratory for examination and identification.

1.3.8 Drug Testing Kit

Drugs, especially illegal drugs, come in different shapes such as pills, powder, liquids, or in plant material. Presumptive chemical drug tests will allow the crime scene investigator to determine what the unknown substance contains. A chemical drug testing kit consists of different test kits, one for each kind of drug, such as marijuana, methamphetamine, cocaine, LSD, and morphine as illustrated in Figure 1.9. These drug tests are presumptive tests and the drug evidence still has to be tested with gas chromatograph for purity and components in the laboratory. The crime scene investigator should be very careful when handling unknown substances as some of the drugs such as LSD can be absorbed through the skin.

1.3.9 Sexual Assault Evidence Collection Kit

In cases of sexual abuse or sexual assault, the detective will require the victim to visit a medical facility for evidence collection. Depending on the agency's arrangements with the hospital or women's centers, the victim will meet a forensic nurse who will perform the evidence collection of hairs, swabs, and bodily fluids. There are two types of sexual assault evidence collection kits: the suspect's sexual assault evidence collection kit and the victim's sexual assault evidence collection kit; see Figure 1.10.

Figure 1.9 Master narcotics kit. (With permission from Tritech Forensics.)

Figure 1.10 Sexual assault evidence collection kit. (With permission from Tritech Forensics.)

The suspect's evidence collection kit contains

Suspect's Kit

- Instruction sheet
- Outer clothing collection bags
- Paper bag for underpants
- Envelope for the collection of scrapes and foreign materials
- Envelope with towel for collection of pubic hair
- Comb
- Envelope for pulled pubic hair
- Envelope for pulled head hair
- Envelope with swab for saliva sample
- Blood tube or bloodstain card for collection of blood sample
- Packaging materials such as evidence seal and biohazard sticker

The victim's sexual assault evidence collection kit contains

Victim's Kit

- Instructions of evidence collection procedures
- Authorization for collection and release form
- Victim's medical history and assault information form
- Bag and paper sheets for the collection of foreign materials
- Bags for outer clothing
- Envelope for debris collection including paper, swab box, and nail scraper
- Envelope for pubic hair combings including towel and plastic comb
- Envelope for pulled pubic hairs
- Envelope for pulled head hair
- Envelope with slides, sterile swabs, and boxes for vaginal swabs and smears
- Envelope with slides, sterile swabs, and boxes for rectal swabs and smears
- Envelope with specimen disc for known saliva sample collection
- Envelope with blood tubes and/or bloodstain cards for known blood sample
- Packaging materials such as biohazard labels, integrity seals

Many state laboratories provide sexual assault evidence collection kits free of charge for law enforcement agencies in their jurisdiction. Therefore, the content of the sexual assault kits may vary. Some kits might include a property receipt to maintain the chain of custody, while others request the agency to provide its own property receipt. In every case, however, the forensic nurse will seal the collection evidence bags and sign the chain of custody over to the crime scene investigator or the detective present.

1.3.10 Gunshot Residue Kit

When a handgun is fired, gunpowder and primer residues such as lead, barium, and antimony are propelled toward the target, but vaporous powders are also blown back toward the hand of the shooter. Traces of these residues are often deposited on the firing hand of the shooter. The detection of residues does not necessarily indicate that the person had fired the weapon, but merely that the person had been in the environment where a weapon had been fired. The scanning electron microscope (SEM) gunshot residue kit is used to collect the gunshot residue from the suspect's and victim's hands for further examination under the SEM in the laboratory.

An SEM gunshot residue kit, as shown in Figure 1.11, requires to perform the following steps:

- Instructions
- Plastic gloves
- Fill in the information sheet about the suspect/victim.
- Use the two sticky stubs to swab the palm and the inner right hand.
- Use the two sticky stubs to swab the palm and the inner left hand.
- Close the tabs and place in the evidence bag.
- Seal and initial, write property receipt with chain of custody for the transport to the laboratory.

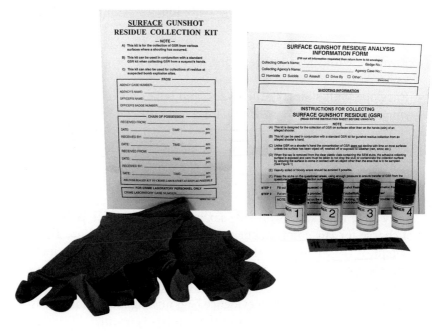

Figure 1.11 Gunshot residue kit. (With permission from Tritech Forensics.)

In addition, the new ISid-2 gunshot residue kit contains the conventional SEM gunshot residue collection kit to be tested in the laboratory and an additional instant shooter kit.

- Swab the suspect's right and left hand with the L.E.T. swab.
- Apply a chemical agent.
- A blue reaction on the swab indicates the presence of nitrocellulose.

This presumptive test indicates a high probability that the suspect had recently fired a weapon or at least was in the environment where a weapon had been fired.

1.3.11 Semen Testing Kit (Acid Phosphatase Kit)

Acid phosphatase (AP) is an enzyme that is secreted by the prostate gland into the seminal fluid. The presence of this enzyme can easily be detected when it comes in contact with an acidic solution of sodium alpha napththylphosphate and Fast Blue dye. This testing method is used to examine garments for seminal stains and to determine if a stain found on a bedsheet is in fact semen. The test kit contains AP test strips for presumptive testing at the crime scene as illustrated in Figure 1.12 (Saferstein, 2011). However, this is only a presumptive test and further testing in the laboratory is necessary to establish a DNA profile.

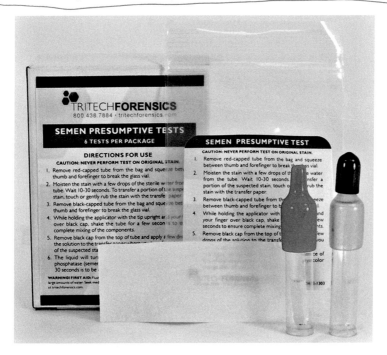

Figure 1.12 Acid phosphatase kit. (With permission from Tritech Forensics.)

1.4 Tools to Develop Evidence

Latent evidence is evidence that is not visible with the naked eye such as fingerprints, cleaned up blood, and shoe impressions in dust. A variety of processing techniques ranging from chemical processing to casting are necessary to recover the evidence.

1.4.1 Fingerprint Detection Kit

Fingerprints are found at most crime scenes when the offender touches the point of entry, the point of exit, or moves items in the residence or business. Fingerprints can also be obtained from the skin of a person, such as in strangulation.

The basic fingerprint kit as shown in Figure 1.13 contains

- Standard black powder
- Fiber brushes
- Magnetic powder
- Magnetic powder applicator
- 1 ½ in. clear lifting tape
- 4 in. clear lifting tape
- Clear lifting pads
- Gel lifting tape
- White fingerprint cards in different sizes

Figure 1.13 Fingerprint kit. (With permission from Tritech Forensics.)

- Large fingerprint cards for palm prints
- Different color powders for processing of dark, light, and colored surfaces
- Fluorescent fingerprint powders
- Handheld black light

In addition to a fingerprint kit, every crime scene vehicle should be equipped with a fingerprint elimination kit. The elimination kit will be used to obtain fingerprints from victims or witnesses who had been inside the crime scene allowing the latent print examiner to eliminate the victim or witness as a possible suspect. A fingerprint elimination kit consists of

- Fingerprint elimination cards
- Black ink
- Ink cleaning material

1.4.2 Bloodstain Pattern Analysis Kit

Bloodstain pattern analysis is the examination of the size, shape, and distribution pattern of bloodstains at the crime scene to reconstruct the occurrences that led to the bloodshed. A technique of stringing together selected bloodstains to see where they converge is one way to determine the area of convergence—the source of the blood. For the stringing method, the following items are required as the bare minimum for each bloodstain pattern analysis kit as illustrated in Figure 1.14.

Figure 1.14 Bloodstain pattern kit. (With permission from Tritech Forensics.)

- Adhesive vertical and horizontal scales
- Elastic string in different colors
- Protractor/angle finder
- Scientific calculator
- Mity Loupe 7×
- Mity Loupe 10×
- Adhesive photo scales
- ABFO photomicrography scale
- Metric ruler
- Yard stick
- Scissors
- Clear scotch tape or wax clips
- Magic marker

[handwritten note: Bloodstain Pattern kit]

More detailed information about bloodstain pattern analysis is presented in Chapter 6.

1.4.3 Blood Detection Kit

A blood detection kit consists of different chemicals to perform presumptive tests at the crime scene to determine if the reddish brown stain found at the scene is blood or any other substance. Several forms of presumptive tests for the presence of blood can be performed at the crime scene, such as the Kastle Meyer test, Hexagon OBTI test, etc.

1.4.3.1 Kastle Meyer Test Kit

As shown in Figure 1.15, the Kastle Meyer test kit contains

[handwritten note: all blood (animal or human)]

- Alcohol
- Phenolphthalein chemical
- Hydrogen peroxide
- Filter papers
- Blood standard

The Kastle Meyer test is a five-step test. The steps consist of

1. Perform a field test to ensure the chemicals properly react.
   a. Swab the sample blood standard provided in the kit with the filter paper.
   b. Add the chemicals in the appropriate order.
   c. Check the test results in the form of a pink reaction.
2. Swab the suspected stain with the filter paper.

Figure 1.15 Phenolphthalein kit. (With permission from Tritech Forensics.)

3. Add a drop of alcohol to the swabbed area.
4. Add a drop of phenolphthalein.
5. Add a drop of hydrogen peroxide.

Bright pink = positive

If the stain turns into a bright pink color, it is a positive test result for the presence of blood. However, the Kastle Meyer test can only determine the presence of blood, which can be human blood, animal blood, or a false reaction to iron, chocolate, bleach, or other components.

1.4.3.2 Hexagon OBTI Presumptive Blood Test *= human blood*

The Hexagon OBTI presumptive test allows testing for the presence of human blood versus the Kastle Meyer test, which only determines the presence of blood, either animal or human. In the investigation of a crime scene, it might be crucial to know right away that the stain consists of human blood. For example, if there are dogs and cats on scene, it is important to determine if the stain on the suspect's shirt is human blood or the blood of a cat as the suspect stated. The Hexagon OBTI test kit uses the presence of human hemoglobin from the sample blood to determine the presence of human blood. Since the only animal blood that reacted positive for human blood was weasel, gorilla, and badger blood, the false positives of this blood detection method are relatively minimal.

The Hexagon OBTI test, as illustrated in Figure 1.16, consists of

- Collection tube
- Test bar

Figure 1.16 Hexagon OBTI test. (With permission from Tritech Forensics.)

The test will be performed as follows:

1. Unscrew the red cap of the tube.
2. Collect samples of the presumed blood from various areas.
3. Immerse into the tube, close and shake gently.
4. Pour three drops from the tube onto the test.
5. Wait 3 to 5 minutes for test results.

On the test, there are two lines such as C and T. If a red line appears across the C line, it indicates that the test had been performed properly and that the chemical reactions were functioning. A second red line at the letter T indicates a positive test result for the presence of human blood. Even a faint line at the letter T indicates the presence of human blood. No control line indicates that the chemicals are not working properly and the entire test procedure should be repeated to ensure the test results are valid.

1.4.3.3 *Luminol*

Luminol is a blood-detecting chemical that can be used in the visualization of cleaned-up bloodstains and blood patterns. In other words, stains and patterns which in some cases may otherwise not be visible to the naked eye. Luminol reacts with the iron from the hemoglobin in blood serving as a catalyst for the chemiluminescence reaction causing a blue glow when the solution is sprayed on a surface with blood. The glow lasts for about 30 seconds allowing sufficient time for photography.

Luminol is available in a powder form and will be mixed with water (15 mg of Luminol mixed with 8 ounces of water makes about 8 ounces of workable solution); see Figure 1.17. The solution should be applied immediately

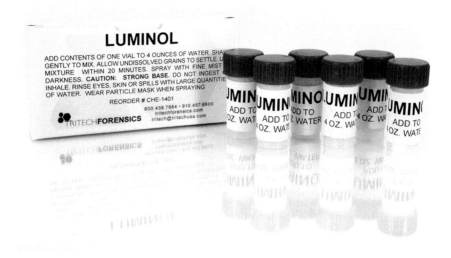

Figure 1.17 Luminol. (With permission from Tritech Forensics.)

as the mixed solution does not have a shelf life. The chemiluminescence will fade within 30 seconds. However, more solution can be reapplied if necessary. Consider that every time additional solution is applied, the original sample is diluted.

Luminol processing requires a darkening of the entire room to properly see the chemiluminescence. This can become a problem, especially in outdoor scenes. It may be necessary to wait until the night hours to process with Luminol in large outdoor areas. However, some areas are lighted with streetlights and the use of a tent or a large tarp may come in handy to darken the area for Luminol photography.

Several false positive reactions have been recorded with Luminol solution including: chocolate, bleach, and any kind of household cleaner containing bleach, chlorine, metals such as nails, copper-containing material and certain food items such as horseradish. Research has shown that the application of Luminol does not destroy DNA and a DNA profile can be established after Luminol has been applied.

1.4.3.3.1 Processing a Scene with Luminol
This process requires two people, one for the photography and one person to apply the working solution.

- Ensure the room is dark (close blinds or tape trash bags on the window to avoid light entering the room).
- Set up the camera on a tripod.
- Set the camera to 400 or higher.

- Place an identifier in the area such as a yellow marker or a placard with the words living room, bedroom, or hallway so you can identify the photos.
- Mix the chemicals according to the manufacturer.
- The photographer should be ready to take a photo.
- Camera in focus.
- Fill the entire frame.
- Ensure depth of field.
- After carefully shaking the solution, spray the area to be examined.
- If a blue chemiluminescence appears, take the photo using long-term exposure.
- Use a flashlight and provide a flash of one second resulting in the photo showing the interior of the room and the luminescence from Luminol.

After a positive reaction from Luminol has been achieved, the crime scene investigator should perform a presumptive blood test, either a Kastle Meyer test with phenolphthalein or a Hexagon OBTI test to confirm the presence of blood.

After the positive presumptive blood test, it is important to mark, photograph, and collect the area showing chemiluminescence for future DNA testing in the laboratory. If it is not possible to collect the physical item such as a concrete floor, it is recommended to swab the areas with a sterile swab and sterile water as explained in the collection of blood samples.

1.4.3.4 *Bluestar*

Bluestar is a blood-visualizing agency containing the Luminol molecule. Bluestar can be applied to detect blood that has been diluted to 1:10,000 and is not visible to the naked eye. The chemical reactions between Bluestar and blood result in luminescence that can be photographed. Contrary to Luminol, Bluestar does not require total darkness and the luminescence lasts longer and is more intensive in color. Bluestar is a more efficient choice for processing outdoor scenes as it does not require darkness and can be applied during the daytime hours. Bluestar allows detecting cleaned up blood, fingerprints in blood, or shoe impressions in blood. Luminol reacts with common household cleaners that contain bleach. Bluestar reacts with cleaners as well; however, the color is different than the positive luminescence for the presence of blood. No chemical residues remain on the evidence and DNA testing can be performed after the application of Bluestar. Bluestar chemical tablets are available in a kit with a fine mist atomizer or as tablets only. The preparation for the working solution consists of mixing a pair of tablets (white and beige) in 4 ounces of distilled water in a plastic bottle with a fine mist atomizer. The solution is workable right away and has a shelf life of several days.

Steps for Bluestar application:

1. Prepare the working solution.
2. Spray the solution at a distance of 20 in. onto the surface.
3. The chemical reaction with the presence of blood will react with a luminescence.
4. Spraying onto a surface that does not contain any blood to ensure the chemicals are working properly should perform a negative control test.
5. Photograph the luminescence with and without scale.
6. If the luminescence weakens, the chemical can be reapplied to strengthen the chemical reaction for better contrast in the photographs.
7. Always perform a presumptive blood test such as the Kastle Meyer test or Hexagon OBTI test.

1.4.3.5 *Amido Black*

Amido Black is a chemical used to enhance fingerprints, footprints, or shoe impressions in blood. Amido Black consists of two solutions: the staining solution and the rinsing solution. The staining solution, which is already pre-mixed in a spray bottle, will be applied to the surface. After a developing time of 1 minute, the rinsing solution will be applied to remove the stain from the nonimpression area. Several rinses with distilled water will provide a clear view of the fingerprint, shoe, or tire impression.

1.4.3.6 *ZAR-PRO*™

ZAR-PRO is a fluorescent blood-lifting strip allowing quick and easy lifting of a bloody fingerprint from virtually any surface, even fabric. The lifts are permanent and cannot smear or smudge. These strips are excellent for lifting impressions from items that are too large to collect and photography does not always provide the necessary clarity for comparison or scanning into the Automated Fingerprint Identification System (AFIS) database. See ZAR-PRO in Figure 1.18 (zar-pro.com).

1.5 Additional Tools for Evidence Recovery

Every crime scene is unique and requires distinct processing methods. Shovels, buckets, and sifters are a necessity for an excavation. Hammer and saws are needed to remove a projectile from drywall and a trajectory laser kit defines the flight path of the projectile.

Figure 1.18 ZAR-PRO™. (With permission from Tritech Forensics.)

1.5.1 Toolbox

Every crime scene vehicle should be equipped with a toolbox containing basic hand tools such as

Toolbox
Kit

- Hammer
- Screwdrivers
- Socket set
- Saw
- Battery powered drill
- Battery powered saw or rotary tool

These tools are necessary to remove projectiles out of the wall, the floor, or the ceiling. If a projectile passed through a screen door, the CSI might decide to collect the entire door as evidence and the tools are necessary to remove the door hinges. A projectile might be lodged in the wall and the CSI needs to cut the plasterboard to recover the projectile. The rotary tool or the battery-powered saw will be essential.

1.5.2 Metal Detector

A metal detector, commonly used for recreational purposes to find old coins or silver, also has application in crime scene investigations. Spent casings are made of brass and can be detected with a metal detector. An underwater metal detector can also be used by a dive team when searching for a knife or a firearm.

1.5.3 Excavation Kit

Unfortunately, not all crime scenes are above ground. In many cases, the offender buries the victim in a shallow or deep grave requiring an excavation to recover the victim and evidence that may lead to the suspect. The basic excavation equipment consists of

Excavation Kit

- Shovels
- Rakes
- Buckets
- Sifters
- Wooden or plastic horses
- Wooden stakes and rope to mark the quadrants
- Yellow marks with numbers, letters, and compass directions
- Compass
- Tarps in different sizes
- Sun tent to cover the scene from the elements
- Auxiliary lights

At large crime scenes with multiple victims, a forensic anthropologist may be consulted to assist in the excavation of the skeletal remains. Unfortunately, a forensic anthropologist may not be available and the crime scene may have to be held and secured awaiting the anthropologist's arrival.

1.5.4 Accessory Lights

Unfortunately, most crimes occur during evening hours or at night. Most CSI units work different shifts including evening and night shifts to cover 24 hours. Many scenes are outside of town or in rural areas without any streetlights or other light sources. Therefore, it is recommended to have an accessory light kit in the crime scene vehicle to ensure the detection of all evidence from the crime scene. Portable accessory light kits are powered by a battery pack allowing usage in any location necessary such as in the field or in the woods.

1.5.5 Laser Trajectory Kit

With laser projection, the crime scene investigator can determine the projectile trajectories at the crime scene. The laser is attached to a penetration rod that is inserted into the bullet hole in the wall, door, floor, or ceiling and the laser beam allows us to determine the direction and angle of the source. This method can also be used to determine the direction and angle of the projectile exit to determine possible impact sites. Projection lasers can also be applied in the determination of the point of convergence in bloodstain pattern analysis. See the laser trajectory kit illustrated in Figure 1.19.

Figure 1.19 Laser trajectory kit. (With permission from Tritech Forensics.)

A trajectory kit consists of

Trajectory Kit

- Ballistic angle finder
- Set of two stringing tips
- Laser pointer
- Center cones
- O-rings
- Bullet penetration rods
- Tripod mount
- Multicolored photographic rods
- Roll of colored trajectory string
- Rod connectors
- Bullet tips

1.5.6 Shoe and Tire Impression Casting

Footwear impressions are evidence that is easily overlooked or destroyed due to lack of training or education in the proper detection, collection, and preservation methods (Dutelle, 2014). The shoe impressions can be in dirt or snow, on tiled or wooden floors inside a residence or a business, or outside on a landing or walkway. The method of documentation with photography and sketching is the same if indoors or outdoors; however, the casting and lifting methods differ (Hildebrand, 2013). A three-dimensional cast will be used to collect the shoe impression in dirt, sand, or even snow.

Figure 1.20 Impression evidence kit. (With permission from Tritech Forensics.)

A shoe/tire impression evidence kit, as shown in Figure 1.20, contains

Impression Kit

- Plastic mixing bowl
- Bag of dental stone mixture
- Container with water
- A flexible metal form to adjust to the size of the shoe impression
- Wooden sticks for pouring the mixture without destroying the impression
- Permanent mark and ruler
- Gel lifting material is used for shoe impressions in dust inside a building

Caution: The CSI is responsible for the maintenance of the equipment in the assigned crime scene vehicle. It is absolutely significant that the vehicle is always restocked and all devices are charged and extra batteries and memory cards are available.

1.6 Summary

In this chapter, the basic tools of the trade for crime scene investigations were introduced and explained. However, no two crime scenes are alike and not all tools are used at every scene. On the contrary, additional tools or the assistance of other agencies may be required. For example, the fire department uses the jaws of life to cut out a door of an accident vehicle or the bomb squad defuses a pipe bomb.

Let's see the procedures and applications of such tools in the next chapter.

References

Dutelle, A. (2014). *An Introduction to Crime Scene Investigation*. Jones Bartlett Learning. James Bartlett Learning, Burlington, MA.

Hildebrand, D. (2013). *Footwear, the Missing Evidence.* Retrieved from http://www
    .crime-scene-investigator.net/footwear.html.
Saferstein, R. (2011). *Criminalistics: An Introduction to Forensic Science*, 10th ed.,
    Prentice-Hall, Upper Saddle River, NJ.
Siegel, J. and Houck, M. (2007). *Fundamentals of Forensic Science.* Academic Press,
    Fletcher, NC.
ZAR-PRO™ Fluorescent Blood Lifting Strips (n.d.). Retrieved from http://tritech
    forensics.com/store/product/fluorescent-blood-lifting-strips-zar-protm/.

Forensic Photography 2

The purpose of forensic photography is to capture quality, representative photographic images of the crime scene at the given time when the investigator entered the crime scene. Still photography is a way to capture an instant of time. Photographs of a scene, interior or exterior, should be taken from a natural perspective such as the photographer's view standing at full height (Robinson, 2007). However, there are exceptions to the rule; for example, if the item of evidence is housed under a cabinet, a deck, or in a confined space, requiring other solutions. It is recommended to note the different circumstances if questions should arise later in trial. Forensic photography also includes photography of evidence in the crime laboratory after chemical processing or examination with alternate light sources. Scene photography is an underestimated aspect of crime scene processing. You only have one chance to capture the scene *in situ*, just as you have only one shot to collect evidence at the outset. The photos, along with any crime scene drawings and videography, will be the only visual record of the crime scene for the entire life cycle of a given case. Occasionally, evidence overlooked at the scene can be discovered or seen from photos days, weeks, or even years later, that may be relevant to a case.

2.1 Camera Equipment

2.1.1 Digital Cameras

For most of the crime scene photography and accident photography, a digital single lens reflex camera is recommended. There are many different cameras on the market and prices can vary from a couple of hundred of dollars to thousands of dollars. The recommendation is to purchase a camera that should

1. Be a digital single lens reflex camera (DSLR).
2. Have the capability to change to manual settings.
3. Be able to use a wide variety of interchangeable lenses.
4. Be lightweight, and easy to transport and store.
5. Have at least 14 megapixels and more.

Figure 2.1 Camera equipment.

Since cameras are exposed to different temperatures, rain, snow, and other rugged weather conditions, it is recommended to always carry a backup camera. Batteries are another area of concern, and it is important to always carry extra batteries. It is important to have adequate storage media such as SD cards with at least 16 megabytes. Cameras with high resolutions, 14 or higher megapixels, require more storage for every image; therefore, multiple media cards should be available. Silicone rubber cases, called Camera Armor, snuggle over the camera protecting it from scratching or damaging from knock, bumps, and falls. See Figure 2.1 for camera equipment necessary to document crime scenes.

2.1.2 Lenses

A lens is an optical device that captures light from a subject and focuses onto a digital sensor. *Normal lenses* measure a focal length of 4 in. and may be 1/2 in. in diameter. The normal lens is standard equipment with most cameras and is an intermediator between a wide-angle and telephoto lens. A *wide-angle lens* has a shorter focal length and can cover a picture angle wider than 60 degrees. The wide-angle lens is recommended for photographing buildings, streets, and interior crime scenes. The *telephoto lens* has a longer focal length and allows capturing close-up photos from a distant subject. The telephoto lens is often used for surveillance photography. The commonly used telephoto lens has an 85–135 mm focal length. *Autofocus equipped cameras* use an infrared sensing module to determine the distance to the object with high-speed motor-driven focusing. The AF lens gives the photographer the freedom to concentrate on the exposure and framing. *Macro lenses* are used for close-up photography of evidence. The macro lenses are 50–55 mm. Macro lenses are used to photograph small items of evidence such as hair and fibers. Macro lenses are often used in the laboratory environment to document trace evidence (Miller and Marin, 2015).

2.1.3 Filters

A filter is a transparent colored media used to regulate the color or the intensity of light used to expose the image. A filter will allow the photographer to filter out one color that would distract the image of a fingerprint, for example, photographing a fingerprint on a red Coca Cola soda can could be a challenge. Using a red filter number 24 or 25 (red filter) is used for color separation allowing a better image of the fingerprint. Polarizing filters are used in photographing a vehicle identification number (VIN) of a vehicle parked in the sunlight or parked in a garage with neon overhead lights to avoid the reflection, as shown in Figure 2.2. Blue filters are used for photographing blood in black and white (Miller and Marin, 2015).

Hint: Always use an orange filter while photographing and searching for evidence at a crime scene with an alternate light source or laser. The orange filter emits blue light and allows photographing fluorescence.

Figure 2.2 Photo of VIN taken by Suboch at FBI.

Hint: Always use a red filter while photographing and searching for evidence at a crime scene with an alternate light source or laser. The red filter emits green light and allows photographing fluorescence.

2.1.4 Storage Media

Digital cameras store the captured image on a memory card. There are several different formats of memory cards, as shown in Figure 2.3.

- Secure Digital (SD) memory card
  This card is the most commonly used memory card and is compatible with the majority of digital cameras.
- Secure Digital High Capacity (SDHC) memory card
  This card is identical to the SD card; however, it has a higher storage capacity ranging from 2–32 MB. However, some early model digital cameras may not be compatible.
- Secure Digital 'Xtra Capacity (SDXC) memory card
  These SD cards provide a higher capacity and faster processing speed. The maximum storage capacity is 2TB (Terabytes). Always check if your camera is compatible to recognize this new technology.

Figure 2.3 Image of memory cards.

The computer used to download the images needs to be able to read exFAT file systems to be compatible with SDXC such as Linux, Windows 7, and Mac OSX (Snow Leopard).

- Compact Flash (CF) memory card

    The CF card provides high storage capacities and fast processing. This card was introduced by Scandisk in 1994 and had been widely used in Sony cameras. Today, this card is only used in highly advanced DSLRs. Compact Flash cards are used as recording media for Canon's new line of professional high definition video cameras.

- Micro SD memory cards

    The Micro SD card was used for storing images in cell phones. It is a very small memory card with a capacity of 2 GB. The Micro SDHC edition can record files from 4–32 GB and is used in GPS systems and MP3 players.

2.2 Photography Basics

2.2.1 Light and Photography

What is light and why is it so important in photography? Light triggers a reaction on the computer chip/sensor in a digital camera to record an image. The light that is necessary to form images can be supplied by a variety of light sources such as natural and manufactured light sources. The sun emits a variety of energies, which form the electromagnetic spectrum. Within this electromagnetic spectrum is a variety of energies that include visible light, infrared light, and ultraviolet light.

In photography, several types of light sources can be used to create a qualitative good image. Each light source has a unique characteristic such as the type of light (quality) and the intensity of light (quantity) that will affect the quality of the image. The common types of lighting at crime scenes and in the laboratory are

- Daylight
- Electronic flash
- Fluorescent
- Tungsten
- Nightlight

2.2.1.1 Daylight

The most common lighting situation is daylight, which equals sunlight. Sunlight consists of a variety of lighting situations and the photographer's adapting to these different conditions is paramount to successfully record a quality image. Light conditions can change quickly, especially in the morning or afternoon hours. Large clouds bringing shade, as well as bright sunlight require the photographer to continuously adapt to those changes. The time of the day changes the appearances of the images; for example, in the morning when it is cool, bluish colors are more prevalent, whereas at sunrise, white light becomes predominant on a clear day. As the sun sets, reddish colors begin to appear caused by atmospheric haze. Rain, overcast, and snow present different lighting conditions; however, the color shift is not as dramatic.

2.2.1.2 Night Photography

Unfortunately, many crimes occur at night in poorly lit areas. The built-in flash in the camera or the exterior flash unit will not provide adequate light for quality images. Some agencies have mobile light sources with generators, but those resources may not be available at all scenes. Smaller law enforcement agencies may not have portable light sources and can ask the local fire department for assistance. Also, every county emergency operations center (EOC) has portable light sources that may be available to light large crime scenes, for example, a plane crash in a large field. Another option to provide additional light to a poorly lit outdoor crime scene would be to position police vehicles to shine the headlights inside the perimeter of the scene. Painting with light is the photographic technique to be used whenever a single flash would be inadequate for the size of a large dimly lit scene.

2.2.1.2.1 Painting with Light A technique called painting with light can be applied in night photography of a crime scene in a dark alley or in an area without any lighting, as shown in Figure 2.4. This technique requires multiple flashes but only one flash unit.

- One person remains at the camera while the other walks around with a strobe unit.
- The shutter of the camera is locked open (T or B setting on the camera), f/22 while the photographer holds his hand over the camera lens to keep out stray light.
- The person with the strobe walks to the first position, tells the photographer to remove his hand from the camera lens, and fires the flash.
- The photographer covers the lens with his hands again.
- The person with the strobe walks to the second position and repeats the process until the entire area to be photographed has been illuminated (Miller and Marin, 2015).

Figure 2.4 Painting with light.

2.2.2 Capture an Image

The photography of a crime scene is founded on the basic rules of photography. One of such basic rules is the cardinal rule stating

1. Fill the frame
2. Maximize depth of field
3. Keep the film plane parallel (Robinson, 2014)

2.2.2.1 *Fill the Frame*

A basic rule states that if an item is valuable enough to photograph it, be sure to have at least one photograph where you fill the frame with it. The primary object can easily get lost in the background; therefore, it is important to put as many pixels as possible over the principal object. Zoom in or get closer to the item to eliminate unwanted areas around the primary object. Filling the frame is important for close-up images of evidence; for example, when photographing a firearm, ensure that the entire frame is filled with the firearm and not the floor where the firearm had been found. In some occasions, however, it is necessary to take a larger/broader photograph of the evidence to be able to place the item within its original location within the scene. For example, a photograph of a bullet hole in the wall should be photographed with a fill-the-frame exposure but also with an additional image showing the location of the bullet hole in the crime scene.

2.2.2.2 *Depth of Field*

The depth of field is a range from the closest clear object to the farthest clear object appearing in acceptable focus, as shown in Figure 2.5.

The depth of field is affected by

- Choice of f/stop
- Choice of lens
- Distance between subject and camera

The f/stop is a camera control and directly affects the depth of field. F/stops range from f/2 to f/22. F/2 provides the shortest depth of field range, increasing when moving toward the lens opening of f/22. The f/stop number is related to the focal length of the lens. This relationship can be demonstrated in the following formula:

FFL/f/stop = Depth of Field

FFL - focal length of the lens

f/stop – particular f/stop

Depth of Field—diameter of the diaphragm or the size of the lens opening

Figure 2.5 Depth of field.

Robinson (2007) explained, "Because wide-angle lenses produce smaller lens openings than 'normal' and telephoto lenses, the resultant DOF range will be greater. Because 'normal' lenses produce smaller lens openings than telephoto lenses, their resultant DOF range will be greater" (p. 163).

The distance between the objects is important in the choice of the f/stop. F/22 provides a depth of field at a range of 6 ft to infinity when hyper focal focusing. F/22 has less than a 1/4 ft depth of field range when taken in extreme close-up photos. Hyper focal focus is applied when taking photos of large outdoor crime scenes with infinity in the background. Zone focus is taking photographs of large crime scenes without infinity in the background, requiring a depth of field scale.

2.2.2.3 *Shutter Speed and Shutter Priority*

The shutter priority mode allows the photographer to control the length of exposure by dictating the time during which the shutter of the camera will remain open. Shutter speed is the time the camera exposes the sensor to light from the scene.

Shutter speed is measured in seconds, and in factions of seconds; for example, the bigger the denominator, the faster the speed, such as 1/1000 is much faster than 1/30. The most commonly used shutter speed is 1/60 of a second or faster, as slower speeds are difficult to use without getting camera shake. Camera shake is when the camera is moving while the shutter is open resulting in blurred photos.

Hint: Use a tripod when shooting photos at lower shutter speeds (lower than 1/60 s) to avoid camera shake.

The shutter speed available on the camera settings doubles with each setting, for example, 1/500, 1/250, 1/125, 1/60, 1/30, 1/15, 1/8. Always keep in mind that doubling the aperture setting doubles the amount of light reaching the sensor. Therefore, increasing the shutter speed by 1 stop requires decreasing the aperture by one stop to achieve a similar exposure.

Some cameras offer the options for very slow shutter speeds such as 1 s, 10 s, 30 s, or bulb. The "B" setting allows the shutter to remain open as long as wanted. This setting is used when photographing luminescent chemical processing such as Luminol or Bluestar, as explained later in the chapter.

When choosing the shutter speed, the photographer has to determine if there is movement in the scene, to freeze the motion or letting the moving object blur the photo. Freezing movement requires a faster shutter speed such as 1/60 s and faster. Slower shutter speeds will result in blurred photos; see Figure 2.6. This kind of decision can be important in surveillance photography when taking photos of drug deals trying to capture the license plate of the vehicles.

Figure 2.6 Stop motion.

2.2.2.4 *Keep the Film Plane Parallel*

In overall photography of exterior buildings, facades, and walls, it is crucial to hold the film plane parallel to the surfaces. The photographer holding the film plane parallel to the building results in the lens being perpendicular to the wall. That can create a problem if a window or a mirror is on the wall, as the flash will reflect in the glass and the photographer can see him or herself. In this scenario, it is necessary for the photographer to capture the image while standing at a light diagonal angle from the mirror to avoid taking a self-portrait. In close-up photography of evidence such as fingerprints, it is very critical that the film plane is parallel; otherwise, the image cannot be used for comparison.

2.2.2.5 *Aperture Priority*

The aperture priority allows the crime scene photographer control over the depth of field of each exposure and in automatic cameras, the shutter speed is automatically set to 1/60 s. The aperture is the physical diaphragm in the lens element of the camera and the camera operator can control the opening of the diaphragm. The degree at which the diaphragm is opened or closed is determined in f/numbers, whereas the smallest number represents the largest opening of the diaphragm (Miller and Marin, 2015). Aperture priority is useful in overall scene photography; a narrow aperture such as f/16 or f/22 is necessary to capture a quality image of the objects in the foreground, middle distance, and background. Often, the shutter speed is immaterial. In portrait photography such as mug shots or mid-range photographs, a wide aperture such as f/1.4 or f/2.8 increases the object in the forefront while the background is out of focus and is less distracting.

2.2.2.6 Flash Photography

Most DSLR digital cameras have a built-in pop-up flash unit; however, external flash units can still be attached through the hot shoe of the camera. It might seem unreasonable to use a flash for an outdoor photo in the sunlight; however, using the flash can sometimes result in a higher quality of the image.

2.2.2.7 Effect of Flash Angle

Flash units can be used to increase and control the level of detail seen in an exposure. For example, holding a flashlight at a 45-degree angle to the surface of a document can expose indented writing. When photographing a shoe or tire impression in dirt, a flashlight held at a 45-degree angle will increase the detail visible in the tire track. A fingerprint impression can be detected and the image can be enhanced with a flashlight at a 45-degree angle.

2.3 Specialized Photography on Scene and in the Laboratory

2.3.1 Luminol and Bluestar Photography

Luminol and Bluestar are blood detection agents that react with the iron in the blood causing an illuminescent effect. Luminol is applied in liquid form with a spray bottle to the area of interest.

Luminol is a chemiluminescence reagent commonly applied to detect blood and bloody impressions that are not visible to the naked eye, such as cleaned up blood. A mixture of Luminol and sterile water is applied to the suspected area. To capture images of the chemical reaction of Luminol, the area has to be darkened. Luminol is very sensitive and can detect the presence of blood at dilutions of up to 1:1,000,000, or in other words, one part of blood per one million parts of water or other liquid.

A blue-colored luminescence is an indication of a positive test result for blood. The luminescence lasts only for approximately 2 min before the intensity begins to fade. Setting up the camera equipment prior to administering Luminol is essential to capturing the image while the chemical reaction occurs. Every additional spray of Luminol will dilute the blood sample. See the example of Luminol photography in Figure 2.7.

2.3.1.1 Steps for Luminol Photography

Luminol photography is a team effort of a photographer capturing the images, an assistant applying the chemical, and a second assistant controlling the room lighting and a flashlight or an additional exterior flash unit.

Figure 2.7 Luminol photography.

 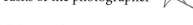 Tasks of the photographer

- Mounts the camera onto a tripod
- Places the camera perpendicular over the region to be processed
- Captures overall images of the area to be processed for the presence of blood
- Places yellow marker numbers or a placard close to the area to be photographed for orientation. Yellow letter markers A, B, C, are beneficial when multiple areas are processed with Luminol
- Sets the ISO/ASA to 400
- Removes or disables the flash
- Adjusts the camera to manual setting and partially depresses the release
- Examines through the viewfinder if the object/floor/area to be captured is in focus, if necessary adjusts
- Captures the images

First assistant

- Shuts the blinds; if necessary covers the window with black plastic material or a blanket to avoid any incoming light
- Combines distilled water with Luminol chemical and applies to the area of concern

Photographer

- Reconfirms that the image is in focus

Second assistant

- Turns off the lights

Photographer

- Presses the release and allows the camera to determine the exposure time, how long the lens should be open to capture a quality image

Tip: When photographing Luminol, ask the additional person to flash a light with a flashlight for less than a second and the photo will not only show the Luminol luminescent but also the surrounding area as shown in Figure 2.7.

2.3.2 Bluestar Photography

Photographing chemical processing with BlueStar requires the same basic photography methods; however, it is not necessary to totally darken the room. Bluestar luminescences in a blue color. Also, the chemical effect lasts for about 2 to 3 s allowing time to capture the images. A noticeable difference between Luminol and Bluestar is the shelf life. Whereas Luminol once mixed does not have a shelf life, Bluestar can be stored for about 1 or 2 weeks. When using previously mixed Bluestar, it is important to pay attention to the chemical reaction time and the brightness of the luminescence as a slower reaction time and a lighter luminescence point to the end of the shelf life.

2.3.3 Ultraviolet and Infrared Photography

Without light, the computer chip in the digital camera does not have the capability to create an image. Images are affected differently by natural light and manufactured light. The electromagnetic spectrum consists of a variety of energies emitted by the sun. These energies travel in the form of wavelengths varying in size or length and can be measured in nanometers (nm). With the human eye, we can only see a limited amount. The human eye can only capture a small percentage of wavelengths, also called the visible spectrum. The visible spectrum is between 400 nm and 700 nm. The three primary colors are red, green, and blue and when mixed together, produce white light, as illustrated in Figure 2.8.

Ultraviolet light is subdivided into three bands: long wave UV (320–400 nm), medium wave UV (280–320 nm) and short wave UV (200–280 nm).

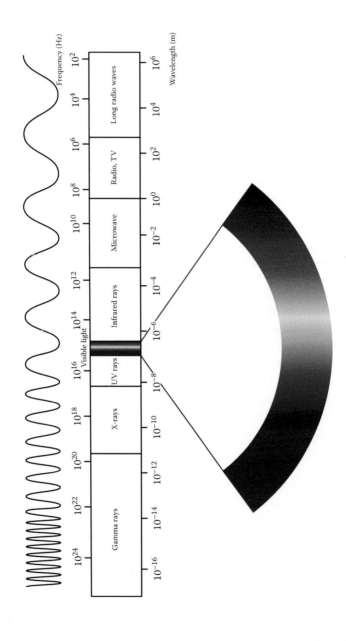

Figure 2.8 Electromagnetic spectrum.

Through ultraviolet radiation, latent evidence such as trace evidence of hairs and fibers but also biological evidence such as semen, saliva, or blood not readily visible to the naked eye can be detected. To capture the image of such evidence, it is necessary to place a barrier filter over the camera lens to block all visible light. The Wratten 18A filter is commonly used as it allows transmission of high levels of ultraviolet radiation.

2.3.3.1 Applications for Ultraviolet Photography

Bite marks, tattoos, and bruises can be visualized and captured as evidence with reflective UV photography.

According to Cochran (n.d.), several easy steps are required for this technique:

1. Mount the camera on a tripod and place parallel to the subject to be photographed.
2. Ensure that the camera/film plane and bite mark plane are parallel and the victim should be situated about 12–14 in. from the camera lens.
3. Capture an unfiltered photo at visible light of the bite mark before taking the UV photo. It is recommended to take additional general orientation photos of the location as well.
4. After examining through the viewfinder that the image is in focus, instruct the victim to stand still and **keep their movement to a minimum while you take a series of 3–4 photos**. Always situate an ABO ruler next to the bite mark without covering the injury itself.
5. Turn on the alternate light source and set to UV light.
6. After rechecking the camera focus, mount the UV filter onto the camera and capture several exposures using f-stops f-5.6, f-8, and f-11.
7. In order to achieve high quality images, it is recommended to point the flash or the light source at different angles at the injury and reshoot the images using the same f-stops. **Lots of light is the key to good photos**. Make sure the flash is pointed in the direction of the injury.

2.3.4 Infrared Photography

Infrared (IR) energy, present beyond the visible spectrum, affects photography. Infrared energy begins at a wavelength at 700 nm and expands to approximately 200,000 nm. Unfortunately, a camera can only capture the range between 700 and 1350 nm. As in ultraviolet photography, a barrier filter is required to block all visible light when photographing in the IR ranges. Commonly used filters are filter numbers 25, 29, 70, 87, 87B, and 87C. Infrared photography can be used in document examination to determine alterations in checks or other handwritten documents such as contracts or last will and testaments. Even if the ink on a document appears to be identical under visible light, certain frequencies of infrared light will show the differences in the inks used allowing a comparison between the original and the ink used in the alteration.

Gunshot residue patterns on dark surfaces such as blue denim material or black velvet are not easily noticeable with visible light due to the lack of contrast with the background. The use of infrared light provides a significant increase in contrast, making the gunshot residue visible and photographically documentable.

2.3.5 Identification Photographs

Identification photographs have multiple applications in criminal investigations. Identification photographs, also called mug shots, are needed for a

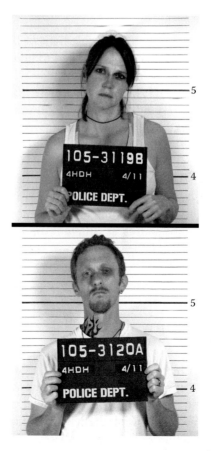

Figure 2.9 Mug shots.

photo lineup to show the witness to identify the offender, or for identification cards of inmates in jails and prisons. An identification photo can also be used as an investigative tool to locate a suspect or for neighborhood canvassing.

The crime scene investigator (CSI) will take the following basic identification photographs:

1. Front view of the person
2. Side view of the person
3. Front image including two 3/4 views of the face
4. Front view of the standing person
5. Side view of the standing person

Color photos should be taken to capture the skin, hair, and eye color of the person; see illustration in Figure 2.9. Digital cameras allow for uploading the images into the computer to use for a digital photo lineup.

2.4 Crime Scene Photography

Photography is one of the most important parts in the documentation process of the scene of a crime. The crime scene photos are physical evidence and can be admitted in trial to

1. Record the condition and location of the scene.
2. Document the original position, location, and condition of physical evidence.
3. Show the original position, location, and condition of any body or bodies in potential homicide cases.
4. Provide a realistic depiction of the crime scene to the jurors in the courtroom.

To accomplish these goals, it is necessary to capture a series of photographs taken at different angles and distances. Those photos are referred to as aerial, overall, midrange, and close-up photographs. There are several steps that have to be followed to ensure the proper photographic documentation of the scene of a crime.

2.4.1 Document the Photos

2.4.1.1 Photo Identifier
The first photo taken at every crime scene or documenting an incident or a piece of physical evidence is the photo identifier. The photo identifier contains significant information about the scene, as shown in Figure 2.10. It is

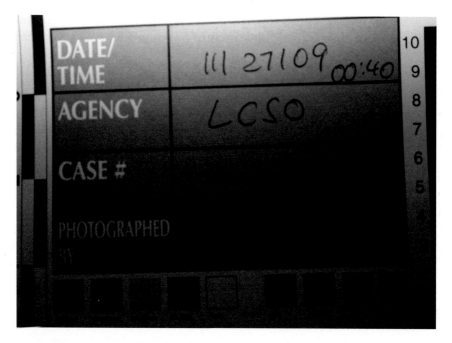

Figure 2.10 Photo identifier.

important to fill the frame with the photo identifier when taking this photograph. The photo identifier contains information such as

- Case number
- Location (physical address)
- Date and time
- Name of photographer and ID number

If the crime scene documentation with photographs exceeds more than one day, than a new photo identifier is necessary for each new date. For example, on May 21, 2014, crime scene photographer Smith takes images at a bank robbery at the Bank of America on Main Street in Miami, Florida. On May 22, 2014, the vehicle used in the bank robbery is found set on fire at a dirt road off Beach Drive in Homestead, Florida. Crime scene photographer Smith responds to the scene of the recovered vehicle and has to create a new photo identifier for the new location and date. The suspect has been arrested and is transported to the police station for interrogation and photos. An additional photo identifier is necessary when crime scene photographer Smith takes the photos of the suspect at the police station. If questions should arise in court, the photo identifier links the photos to the different locations and times.

Back when film was used for crime scene photography, it was important to create a new photo identifier for each roll of film. Today, digital storage media can capture over 1000 photos; however, large crime scenes may require use of more than one storage media. Therefore, it is recommended to add a number of storage media.

If no photo identifier template is available, write the information on a blank piece of paper and capture the information in the first image.

Hint: Always use a new photo identifier for change of date, photographer, location, or additional crime scenes.

2.4.1.2 Photo Log

Many crime scene photography textbooks recommend that every image should be logged in a photo log; however, the digital photo contains the information of time and date when the photo was taken, as well as the technical information such as ISO, f-stop, and aperture setting if necessary. Almost every law enforcement agency and laboratory has changed from film photography to digital photography and, consequently, often do not require a photo log. Always check with the agency's policy and follow the standards.

2.4.1.2.1 Labeled Scale Each item of evidence should be photographed with several close-up photographs, with and without a labeled scale. What is the difference between a photo scale and a labeled scale and why is the labeled scale important? Some crime scene investigators may argue that a scale is to show the measurement of the item, and that no label is necessary as long as the yellow evidence marker is next to the evidence for identification. Remember that the photo will be presented in court and it should tell the judge, the jury, and the attorneys about the image. During the trial, the prosecutor or defense attorney can ask the crime scene photographer to identify the crime scene photos. The attorneys can ask questions such as, "Do you recognize the photo? How do you recognize the photo? Did you take the photo? What does the photo depict? Is this photo an accurate depiction of the scene/evidence that you saw that day when you documented the crime scene? What time did you take the photo? What were the lighting conditions when you took the photo? What camera, lens, filter, and storage media did you use? What f-stop, manual or automatic settings on the camera did you use to take this image?"

Using a labeled scale makes the image self-documenting and easily admissible in trial. The label should include the same information as the photo identifier, such as case number, date, physical address, and name and ID number of the photographer. Slash marks can be used to show the evidence marker number and allow for multiple use of the ruler, as illustrated in Figure 2.11.

Rulers come in different colors and it is important to choose the color that best contrasts the background surface. Always ensure that the evidence and

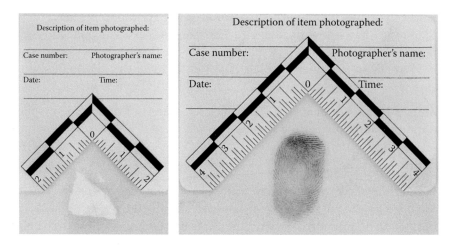

Figure 2.11 Labeled scale.

the scale are in focus. When photographing the victim's injuries, add the victim's name and the location of the injury to the information on the label.

Rule of thumb: Always place the scales at the same plane as the evidence.

2.4.2 Scene Photography

Documenting a crime scene through photographs is accomplished through:

- Overall photography
- Midrange or medium range photography
- Close-up photography

Each of these categories provides a different perspective of the scene, and combined, an excellent realistic depiction of the scene as experienced when the crime scene photographer arrived.

2.4.2.1 Overall Photography

Overall photographs provide a general overview of the scene, interior and exterior, and the surrounding areas of the scene—for example, a two-story residence, the vehicle in the driveway, and the stop sign at the end of the lawn. Overall photos are taken from the natural perspective, the photographer's viewpoint of the scene when standing at full height. There are exceptions to the rules. For example, at an accident scene, the photographer takes photos from the driver's perspective sitting inside the accident vehicle showing a restricted view as reason for not seeing the other vehicle causing the accident. Another example is a victim found underneath a boardwalk or underneath a mobile home. The photographer should note that he took the photos while sitting in the driver's seat of the vehicle, or crawling underneath the board-walk or mobile home, to avoid later confusion in court.

2.4.2.1.1 Exterior Overall Photos   Overall photos are usually taken with a wide-angle camera lens to cover a large area or the entire scene if possible. Nearby roads, street signs, road signs, highways, and other landmarks should be included in overall photos to provide the future juror with a realistic depiction of the area where the crime occurred. When photographing exterior scenes, the photographer should be taking photos at the nearest intersection walking toward the scene, in other words, from the exterior perimeter to the inner perimeter, as shown in Figure 2.12.

If a building is included in the crime scene, it is required to take overall photos of the following:

- Capture all sides of the building including garages and other structures.
- Include the street view and the backyard view of the residence.
- Photograph the residence from all four compass views (North, South, East, and West).
- Photograph the closed intersection including the street names.
- Capture names and special characteristics of the building for identification.
- Views toward the home from both directions of the street.
- Views of possible escape routes.
- Views from the street toward the building.
- Any vehicles parked in the driveway and on the nearby street.

It is important to choose the best lens for overall photos. A 55-mm lens will provide the true distance between the photographer and the building, whereas the photo taken from the same position with a 35-mm lens appears to show a greater distance. Photos taken with a 24-mm lens showed an even larger distance to the building. Therefore, crime scene photos should be taken with a 50-mm lens to provide the most realistic image for court; see Figure 2.12.

At almost every crime scene such as violent crimes, or multiple scenes, aerial photographs are required to provide the jurors in court with a true depiction of the scene. Large law enforcement agencies maintain an aviation unit enabling the crime scene investigator to record aerial images from the department helicopter or fixed wing airplane. In aerial photography, it is important to capture images in 360 degrees. Document the date, time, type of plane, weather condition, and the elevation from which the photos have been taken. The photographs should depict an overview of the area and medium range photos of the crime scene. A wide-angle lens is recommended for aerial photography.

(a)

(b)

(c)

Figure 2.12 Exterior views of a residence: front (a), side (b), back (c) views.

Hint: Use a shutter speed of 1/500 s or 1/1000 s when taking aerial photographs.

Drones equipped with a digital camera have increasingly become used for aerial photographs of a crime scene, especially if the agency does not maintain an aviation unit. Drones are more cost-effective than a manned helicopter, considering the needed manpower and jet fuel cost.

2.4.2.1.2 Interior Overall Photos   The crime scene photographer has to ensure that he enters the residence legally, meaning that

1. No search warrant is required.
2. A search warrant has been read and served.
3. The owner gave consent to search.

Interior overall photos are important as they show the scene as discovered and before anything has been moved. The 50-mm lens is recommended for interior overall photos as it shows the scene as seen by the photographer. Always photograph doors and windows as they appear, open, partially open, or closed. Do not turn on lights or ceiling fans.

The interior overall photos of a residence include:

- Photos of the hallways
- Closets in the hallways
- Each room in the residence
- Swimming pool and recreation areas
- Garage
- Attic
- Basement

Taking the photos when walking through the residence will create a series of photos in the natural view of the photographer.

2.4.2.2 Methods of Exterior and Interior Overall Photography

There are three different methods to take overall photographs of an area: the 360-degree method, the wall-to-wall method, and the four corners or compass method.

2.4.2.2.1 360-Degree Method   In the 360-degree method, the photographer takes overlying images of the scene. The photographer is placed in the center of the scene. The camera is mounted on a tripod. Photos will be exposed while rotating at 45 degrees, ensuring that the photos overlap by 10%. It is important to continue the motion until returning to the starting point to ensure full 360-degree imaging. It is recommended to use a tripod with a degree meter.

Figure 2.13 300-degree with permission from Mike Brooks.

The 360-degree method shown in Figure 2.13 is mostly applied in outdoor scenes; however, it can also be used in indoor scenes. A tripod is necessary for scenes during sundown or at night when higher ISO levels are required for better image quality. Photographing an indoor scene with this method results in the recording of the area at eye level without a view of the ceiling and the floor of the room. This method lacks the capability to provide a wide-angle view of the scene.

2.4.2.2.1.1 Newest Technology   Many law enforcement agencies have replaced traditional photography, crime scene sketching, and mapping methods with laser scanners to document the scene. The laser scanner accurately documents the entire scene in only minutes for a 360-degree scan of a room versus the photographer selecting the images. Lasers create, annotate, and present multiple panoramic images of the scene. Some lasers record the images on DVDs for distribution to attorneys and prosecutors. The laser records millions of data points including measurements. The laser scanner can be used for indoor and outdoor crime scenes. At accident scenes, the 3D laser scanner creates a digital accident reconstruction with 3D simulations. These 3D laser images provide excellent visual aids for the jurors in court, as illustrated in Figure 2.14.

2.4.2.2.2 Wall-to-Wall Method   Robinson (2007) stated that when the film plane is held parallel to the wall, the right side of the wall would appear as large as the left side of the wall. Doors, pictures, electric outlets, and

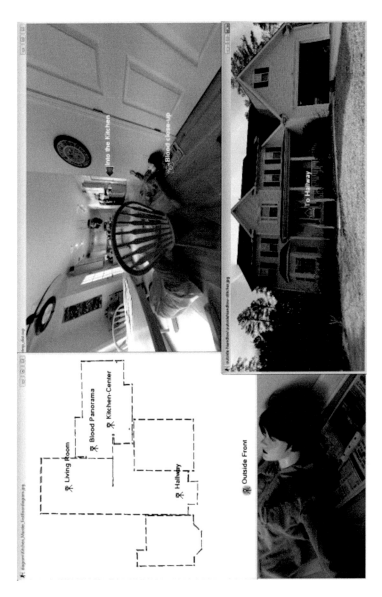

Figure 2.14 360-degree exposure. (With permission from 3rd Tech.)

Figure 2.15 Wall-to-wall method.

other fixtures on the walls will be easier to see and identify, as they are closer to the camera. The photographer has to take six images to capture a 360-degree view of the room; however, the left and right sides of the walls are uniform and the size of the room is not distracted. This method creates a realistic view of the room and the photographer can unequivocally state in court that the photo is a realistic depiction of the room, as shown in Figure 2.15.

2.4.2.2.3 Four Corners or Compass Method   Photographing the scene from the four corners, also called four compass points (North, East, South, and West) of each room or area that relates to the crimes is the most efficient method. The photographer will use a wide-angle photo lens. While standing in one corner, the camera is aimed straight across the room at the opposite corner. It is important to aim it level to minimize the effects of converging vertical lines. The wide-angle lens allows for the ability to show the floor, the midrange, and the ceiling of the room, whereas the 360-degree method will only allow exposure at eye level, thus eliminating the exposure of the ceiling and the floor in the photograph—see Figure 2.16. Always be sure to capture images of all points of entry, stairwells, and hallways.

2.4.2.3 Midrange Photographs
Midrange or medium distance photos are used to relate significant evidence relative to its location and other elements and fixtures at the scene. The

Figure 2.16 Four-corner method.

photographer takes one set of midrange photos without scales and yellow evidence number markers and captures a second set of images that include yellow evidence number markers and labeled scales. Always include a reference point to allow orientation where the evidence had been located. Rulers and yardsticks can be used to show the distance between different items of evidence. Always photograph the point of entry and exit from the offender and victim's perspective such as capturing an image of the exterior view into the residence and the view from the residence to the outside.

A midrange photo contains two items: a fixed point and the item of evidence, as shown in Figure 2.17. Take, for example, a gun lying on the floor in front of the bathtub in the master bathroom. The gun is the evidence and the bathtub is the fixed point. The photographer captures the image from a point in the bathroom where both items are parallel to the film plane. Another option is to look for a diagonal line while one item will be in the forefront and the other item in the background of the image. In our example, the firearm would be in the forefront and the bathtub in the background of the image.

2.4.2.4 Close-Up Photographs

Close-up photographs, also called macro photography, or identification photographs should be taken in addition to overall and intermediate photos to further clarify the scene. Always take a close-up photograph of the evidence as found on scene without any scale, marker, or being moved or altered.

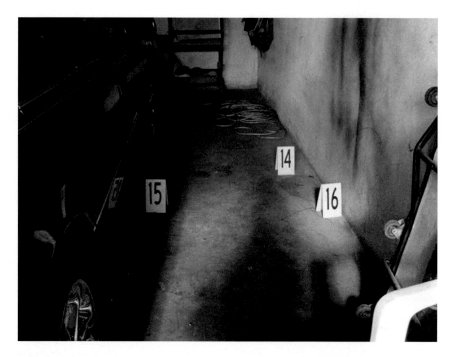

Figure 2.17 Location of evidence captured with a midrange photo.

These photos provide a further means of showing the evidence in the natural state of discovery. Evidence should always be documented and preserved *in situ*, as found.

To ensure a proper capture of the evidence, f/11 stop should be used if the photo will be used to compare it with another item of evidence as this f-stop provides a good depth of field and avoids image softness creating distraction.

As stated previously, two photographs should be taken of each item, one photograph depicting the item as it appears and an identical photo with a labeled scale. The film plane has to be parallel to the object. Filling the frame is important in close-up photography, especially if the evidence is minutiae such as a piece of lead from a projectile or a hair or fiber. The labeled scale at the film plane will allow for a true 1:1 enlargement for comparison such as for fingerprint comparison. If the camera is held at an oblique angle, the measurement of the object will be depreciated and is inaccurate: for example, the size of a knife blade or a spent projectile or cartridge. Therefore, the camera must always be placed directly above the object so that the photo can be reproduced to scale, a factor that is essential to fingerprint photography; see Figure 2.18. While macro lenses are recommended, however, newer digital

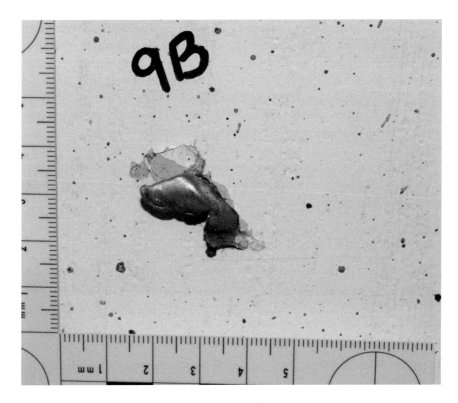

Figure 2.18 Close-up photo with labeled scale.

cameras have a built in macro function. Always ensure that the item of evidence photographed in a macro setting is identifiable. This can be accomplished with a labeled scale.

Warning: Adobe Photoshop can be used to correct images that are not properly captured; however, these programs do not guarantee to accurately produce a true presentation of the physical evidence. And, all steps used to modify any image must be able to be explained and/or reproduced in court.

2.4.2.4.1 Altered Close-Up Photographs   The evidence is photographed at the scene *as found*. In some instances, evidence may be present that was not apparent when the item was photographed at the scene. For example, a gun may have a bloody fingerprint on the bottom side that was not apparent when the original "as found" close-up photo was taken. The crime scene photographer will take an "altered" close-up photo as soon as possible as packaging the evidence and transport to the laboratory may destroy the fingerprint. This additional close-up photo may be the only opportunity to obtain a quality image of the critical fingerprint.

Another scenario when "altered" close-up photographs are required is when the "as is" background does not allow for a clear identification of the evidence. For example, a spent projectile found on a brown multi-colored carpet may be difficult to identify in the "as found" photograph. The crime scene photographer can change the background the evidence is on to capture a better image of the evidence for later comparison. A brown paper bag or a piece of paper provides excellent backgrounds for altered close-up photographs.

Rule of thumb: If the photographer alters an image, the alteration has to be easily recognizable to avoid confusion with the image depicting the item of evidence in its original state.

2.4.3 Photographing a Body on Scene

At a homicide, suicide, or accident scene, the deceased is considered the main piece of evidence and has to be fully documented with photographs, notes, measurements, and sketching. A series of mid-range photographs is most suited to show the victim in relation to fixed features such as a building, a street sign, a door, a driveway or any other fixture.

Warning: In most states, the body is under the jurisdiction of the medical examiner or coroner, and the crime scene investigator or investigative personnel is not permitted to move, roll, or search the deceased without the presence of the medical examiner or personnel from the medical examiner's office such as a medico-legal death investigator. Check with your local medical examiner's office to verify.

2.4.3.1 *Body Panorama Photos*

After the midrange photographs have been concluded, a body panorama should be shot by taking a series of photographs showing all four sides of the victim. A full face shot, taken while standing over the victim, should be included for later identification of the body. A tripod placed 90 degrees over the victim's face should be used to take this image. Standing over the body holding the camera does not result in the film plane being parallel to the victim's face. Depending on the light conditions at the scene, the photographer may change the ISO from 100 or 200 during daytime to ISO 400 for evening and night photography. F/22 provides the best images within a 10 ft distance between the photographer and body. Always fill the frame when taking the full-face photo to achieve a high quality image.

At some scenes, it may not be possible to move far enough away to capture the entire body with one image. No problem. Take two images and explain how the images overlap. You are documenting the body at the scene as found. Using a 50-mm lens when taking the head-to-toe and toe-to-head photos avoids the body appearing stretched or compressed. Any lens will work for left and right side photos of the body.

For full body shots, place a tripod directly above the midpoint of the body to ensure that the film plane is parallel to the body. A shutter release cable may be used to take the image. Always make sure to fill the frame. Depending on the light conditions, indoors, outdoors, daytime, or nighttime, flash assist may be required. Most digital cameras automatically adjust to the lighting conditions.

2.4.3.2 *Photographing the Victim's Injuries*

After all photographs of the entire body have been concluded, the next set of photographs will document the injuries and wounds on the body. Wounds are evidence, and as with any other types of evidence, the documentation starts by taking a set of midrange photos. It is important to capture the wound and its location in relation to a fixed point such as a knee, the hand, elbow, or any joint. Next, the crime scene photographer will take close-up photos of the wound with a labeled scale. After all wounds have been documented, the body will be moved and the medico-legal death investigator or the medical examiner can search the body for any form of identification such as a wallet, driver's license, jewelry with initials, etc. See Figure 2.19. Take a photo of the items being discovered and note where they have been found on the subject.

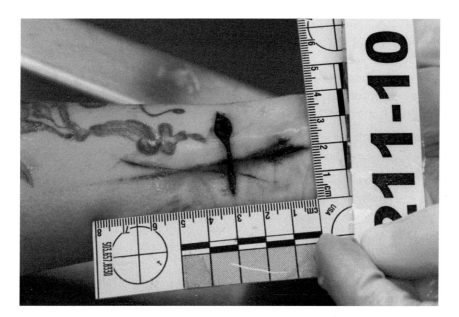

Figure 2.19 Close-up photo of injury.

2.4.3.3 *Photographing an Accident Scene*

A five-step procedure is applied to capture adequate photographic documentation of most automobile and vehicular accidents, that is, trucks, recreational vehicles, all terrain vehicles or motorcycles. This procedure is most applicable to an accident scene at an intersection: however, it can be applied to any automobile or vehicular accident.

The CSI performs the following steps to take overall photos of the accident scene:

- Apply the basic photographic rules:
  - Create a photo identifier.
  - Take a shot of the photo identifier.
  - Maintain photo log.
- Take the first photograph from a distance of approximately 100 ft from the intersection to show the Driver 1 viewpoint.
- From the same location, take shots toward the direction of the second vehicle.
  - Include any obstacles that could have obstructed the drivers' views.
- Take photos from the possible point of impact from a distance of 25 ft.
  - Include all traffic controls and skid marks.
- Capture photos from Driver 2 viewpoint.
  - 25 ft from the possible point of impact.
  - Basic shots from a distance of 100 ft (identical Driver 1 photos).
- Photograph three photos each of Driver 1 and 2's viewpoints.

These images provide sufficient documentation of the scene and the possible point of impact, as well as the final position of the vehicles and/or persons.

Caution: Watch out for oncoming traffic if the road is not completely blocked off by police cars and officers redirecting traffic.

Try to accomplish the overall photography as fast as possible to clear the road and continue traffic.

The next steps of the documentation of the accident scene include

- Midrange photos of each involved vehicle illustrating the damages
- Capture close-up photographs of
  - All compass directions of each vehicle
  - Paint transfers between vehicles
  - Existing damage and rust areas

- Vehicle Identification Number (VIN) in the dashboard and in the driver's doorframe
- License plate
- Soles of the occupants of both vehicles (look for accelerator or brake pedal impressions)
- Bloodstains or bloodstain patterns (if occupants are injured to determine the driver and passenger)
- Capture images of any skid marks and tire tracks including
  - Direction of travel
  - Length of the track (make sure to capture the entire length of the track)
    - Use a ruler to show the length of the marks
    - Place a ruler across the skid mark to show the width of the impression
    - Use f-stop f/22 or f/32 for best depth of field when photographing the entire length of the impression

After the CSI clears from the accident scene, he or she maintains the chain of custody and other requirements in the standard operating procedure manual for crime scene photography (Robinson, 2010).

2.4.3.3.1 Hit-and-Run Accident Photography   In a hit-and-run accident scene, after following the basic accident procedures, additional photography is required to document any kind of physical evidence that could lead to the identification of the suspect's vehicles.

The CSI performs the following steps to document a hit and run accident:

- Always take mid-range and close-up photographs.
  - Paint transfers on all involved vehicles
  - Place a scale to the paint transfer to show the size
  - Use a yardstick or ruler to show the distance from the ground or any other fixed point to the paint transfer
  - Any cloth transfer, especially in accidents with injuries
  - Any debris around the accident scene
  - Skid and tire marks
  - Any bloodstains or stain patterns
    - Use a color filter to enhance the contrast of the blood on a black steering wheel and take a black and white image.
- Always photograph the blood trails as the bloodstain pattern analyst can determine the direction of travel based on the shape of the bloodstain.

Hint: Change the setting on the digital camera to black and white or monochrome mode and use a Wratten 25 (red) filter creating a better contrast by lightening the blood from the background. Alternatively, a Wratten 47 filter makes the blood appear darker (Robinson, 2010).

2.4.4 Footwear Impressions

Footwear impression in sand, dirt, or even snow can be found at the point of entry or exit of a crime scene. Before the crime scene investigator begins to reproduce the impression with dental stone, medium range and close-up photographs should be taken.

The photographer will perform the following steps to capture images of shoe impressions:

- Apply the basic photographic rules:
  - Create a photo identifier.
  - Take a shot of the photo identifier.
  - Maintain a photo log.
- Mount the camera on a tripod.
  - This ensures that the camera lens is parallel to the plane of the impression.
  - Check the level of the impression plane either
    - By placing a level next to the impression
    - Use the level built in the tripod
  - Mark the impression with a labeled ruler.
  - Hold a light source such as a flashlight or an off-shoe flash at a 45-degree angle at the side of the impression to create oblique lighting while creating a shadow in the ridges in the soil and highlighting the detail of the impression.
- Placing a handkerchief or a cloth over the flash, or using a bounce flash, reduces the intensity of a flash during night or indoor photography of a shoe or tire impression.
- Always fill the frame with the entire impression.
- A thin layer of contrasting colored spray paint enhances the ridge detail of the impression and allows for capturing a better quality image.
- After clearing from the scene, follow the basic photography rules such as maintaining the chain of custody and other requirements in the standard operating procedure manual for crime scene photography.

Hint: If a tire impression is too long to capture in one image, divide the tire impression into sections and capture several overlapping images of the entire impression. Overlap the images by about 10%. Place a labeled ruler

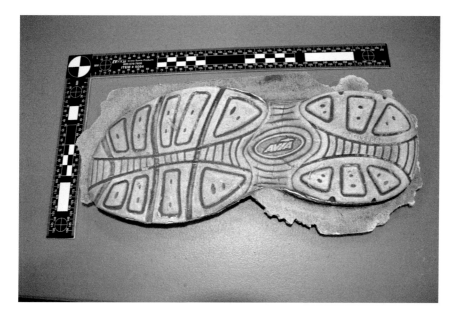

Figure 2.20 Footwear impression cast.

with the section number next to the impression for identification, as shown in Figure 2.20.

2.5 The Expert Witness

Under the discovery law, the defense attorney and the prosecutor have the same rights to both view physical evidence and to subpoena any and all investigative personnel to questioning in depositions.

The crime scene photographer is often requested by the courts to testify on details relative to the photos from the incident. The photographer can testify that he or she took the photos, when the photos were taken, what the photos depict, and the reason why the photo was taken (among other details). The photographer can also provide information about the camera equipment and photographic method applied to capture the image. Depending on the court proceedings, the judge may allow a detective or a crime scene investigator to identify a photo because the CSI is familiar with the scene, even if he or she did not personally take the photo. The line of questioning to authenticate the images is often along the lines of: Is the photo a fair and accurate representation of the scene as you saw it at the crime scene? What is depicted in the photograph? When did you take the photograph? It is common that photographs are challenged in court.

2.6 Legal Challenges of Forensic Photography

Videos, photos, and digital images are admissible in court if they

- Are relevant to the case
- Are a true and accurate representation of the scene
- Possess probative value not outweighed by their prejudicial effect

Digital images may be enhanced for more detail; however, the original unenhanced image has to be kept to maintain integrity (*Washington v. Hayden*, 1998).

Defense attorneys still continue to demonstrate in court how easily digital images can be manipulated.

2.6.1 Murder Trial in Florida

In 2002, law enforcement used a computer software program called More Hits to enhance a smudged palm print found on a piece of duct tape. The court allowed the evidence to be presented. The defense attorney argued that it was "junk science" and presented an expert witness, an art professor, who showed how easily images can be manipulated in Adobe Photoshop. The defendant was acquitted (*Florida v. Victor Reyes*, 17th Jud. Cir. Ct., Case 99-11535CF10A, Opinion and Order on Defendant's Motion in Limine, October 21, 2002).

Every law enforcement agency using digital imaging for criminal investigations has to ensure and maintain established rigid standard operating procedures (SOP). The minimum SOP should include

- Archive all camera original images in unaltered form as soon as the photographs are captured.
  - The use of serial numbered digital disks recorded in the case file is optional.
  - Make copies for any editing work.
- Maintain a photo log with information about every image, either
  - Handwritten log
  - Camera file including
    - Make
    - Model
    - Serial number
    - Date and time of each image
    - Camera settings

- Maintain the chain of custody.
  - Image files have to be secured and protected.
  - Maintain information about
    - Who had access to the images
    - Where the images are stored
    - Were the images altered and by whom
- Document enhancements and alterations.
  - Always use a copy of the original images for alterations.
  - Use the historical function in Adobe Photoshop to document alterations and enhancements.
  - Optional, the macro function in the computer allows recording and playback of all keystrokes.

2.7 Checklist for Crime Scene Photography

- Check your equipment to ensure you have what you need.
  - Batteries are charged
  - Spare batteries
  - Lenses
  - Filters
  - Flash is charged
  - Remote flash cord
  - Remote shutter release cable
  - Multiple storage media
  - Photo identifiers
  - Photo scales
  - Labels and rulers
  - Tripod
- Always take
  - Overall photos, aerial photos if available
  - Midrange photos
  - Close-up photos
- Remember
  - The first photo is the photo identifier.
  - Keep a photo log if required.
  - Use labeled scales.
- Legalities
  - Do you enter a scene legally or is a search warrant required?
  - Maintain the chain of custody for the recording media.
  - Ensure your photos depict the scene truly and accurately.

- Capturing images:
  - Always include scales and labeled scales, yellow evidence markers, street signs, landmarks, etc.
  - Fill the frame with the evidence or subjects.
  - Achieve maximum depth of field for quality photos.
  - Take a set of photos with and without scales and yellow evidence markers.
  - Fill in flash for greater detail in the image, such as shoe impressions.
- **Never delete digital images.**
- **Ensure that investigative personnel are not captured in the crime scene photos.**
- **Document, document, document. Note particularly who took photos on which day in which area of the scene.**

2.8 Conclusion

In this chapter, we learned about the importance of forensic photography at the crime scene as well as in the laboratory. Always remember, storage media is cheap and you can never capture too many images. Photography is applied throughout any forensic processing, may it be impression evidence, excavations, or crime scene reconstruction, as shown in the following chapters.

References

A Simplified Guide to Crime Scene Photography. (n.d.). Retrieved from http://www.forensicsciencesimplified.org/photo/why.html.

Cochran, P. (n.d.). Use of reflective ultraviolet photography to photo-document bruising to children. Retrieved from http://www.crime-scene-investigator.net/uvchildphoto.html.

Florida v. Victor Reyes, 17th Jud. Cir. Ct., Case 99-11535CF10A, Opinion and Order on Defendant's Motion in Limine. (October 21, 2002). Retrieved from http://caselaw.findlaw.com/fl-district-court-of-appeal/1134096.html.

Hak, J. (2003). The admissibility of digital evidence in criminal prosecutions. Retrieved from http://www.crime-scene-investigator.net/admissibilitydigitalevidencecriminalprosecutions.html.

Miller, L. and Marin, N. (2015). *Police Photography*, 7th ed. CRC Press, Boca Raton, FL.

Robinson, E. (2007). *Crime Scene Photography*. Academic Press, Burlington, MA.

Robinson, E. (2010). *Crime Scene Photography*, 2nd ed. Academic Press, Burlington, MA.

Robinson, E. (2014). *Crime Scene Photography*. Academic Press, Burlington, MA.

Washington v. Hayden. (1998). Retrieved from http://caselaw.findlaw.com/wa-court-of-appeals/1189825.html.

Impression Pattern Evidence

3

3.1 Fingerprints

Minutiae friction ridge patterns are present on the fingertips, palms, and soles of the feet. The skin's sebaceous glands produce natural oils, salt, and amino acids. Combined with water and sweat, this leaves an impression of the friction ridge formation on any object being touched. No two persons have the same arrangement of ridge patterns, making fingerprints unique. The human fetus develops fingerprints at three month's gestation. Throughout the lifetime of every person, the fingerprint pattern does not change. However, the quality of the ridge detail deteriorates with age.

3.1.1 Fingerprint Patterns

Fingerprint patterns are grouped into three general types of patterns: arch, loop, and whorl.

3.1.1.1 Arch

The arch fingerprint pattern is subdivided into pain arch and tented arch. Only 5% of all fingerprint patterns are arch. The basic arch fingerprint pattern consists of ridges centering from one side of the finger that rise in the center and flow outward to the other side as illustrated in Figure 3.1.

3.1.1.2 Whorl

Whorl fingerprint patterns are subdivided into plain whorl, the central pocket loop whorl, the double loop whorl, and the accidental whorl. Whorl patterns account for 30–35% of all fingerprint patterns. Every whorl pattern has two deltas with a recurve in front of each delta (see Figure 3.2).

3.1.1.3 Loop

Loop fingerprint patterns are divided into two types: the ulnar loop and the radial loop. Loop patterns account for 60–65% of all fingerprint patterns. Loop patterns can be identified by a sufficient recurve, one delta, and a ridge count across the looping ridge, shown in Figure 3.3.

Figure 3.1 Arch fingerprint pattern.

Figure 3.2 Whorl fingerprint pattern.

Figure 3.3 Loop fingerprint pattern.

3.1.2 Elimination Fingerprints

At almost every crime scene—whether it is a burglary, robbery, or a murder scene—the suspect touches one or more items or surfaces leaving the minutiae ridge impressions of his or her fingers or palms of the hand. Fingerprinting the scene will result in a wealth of fingerprint lifts and it is important for the latent examiner to be able to distinguish the victim's fingerprints and eliminate other legitimate prints (e.g., other residents of a household, etc.), from the suspect's prints found on the scene. Therefore, it is recommended to ask the victim and all people who live at a given residence, or work at a given workplace—wherever the crime scene is—to agree to be fingerprinted, to provide what are termed *elimination fingerprints*.

An elimination fingerprint kit is available that contains elimination fingerprint cards, black ink, and cleaning pads; see illustration in Figure 3.4.

The following steps have to be followed to take elimination fingerprints:

1. Ask for the photo ID of the person to be fingerprinted.
2. Verify that the photo ID and the person are identical.
3. Fill in the information on the fingerprint card such as
   a. First and last name
   b. Date of birth
   c. Address

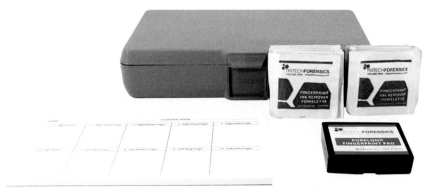

Figure 3.4 Elimination fingerprint kit. (With permission from Tritech Forensics.)

  4. Use the ink pad and roll the tip of each finger from side to side.
  5. Repeat for all ten fingers.
  6. Take notes if a finger is missing or if there are any other irregularities.

3.1.2.1 Suspect Fingerprints

Every suspect is asked to provide a set of inked and rolled fingerprint impressions. The inked fingerprints will be used for comparison to the latent fingerprints from the crime scene. If the suspect is charged with the crime, the fingerprint cards will be submitted to the state identification agency, such as the Florida Department of Law Enforcement in Florida, to establish a criminal history in the Florida Crime Information Center (FCIC). The state agency submits the digital images and arrest information to the FBI for entering into the National Crime Information Center (NCIC) database (Saferstein, 2015).

Inked suspect fingerprints include the inked impressions of all ten fingers as well as full palm print impressions and also from the sides of each finger and hand. The suspect fingerprints will be added to the criminal history (Fish et al., 2015).

3.1.2.2 Inked Fingerprints from Deceased

According to Fish et al. (2015), at every autopsy, a set of inked fingerprints is taken for identification purposes. The set of fingerprints will be secured as evidence while the chain of evidence is maintained. The victim's inked fingerprints can also be used as elimination fingerprints to exclude the victim's prints found at the scene. In Figure 3.5, the special equipment for taking inked fingerprints from a deceased is shown, such as

- Curved fingerprint card holder/spoon also called dead man's spoon
- Fingerprint cards cut in strips for each hand fitting the fingerprint card holder
- Ink pad

Figure 3.5 Decedent fingerprint spoon set. (With permission from Tritech Forensics.)

Processing Method. The CSI will perform the following steps to obtain a good quality fingerprint from the deceased's hands.

- Place a fingerprint strip in curved fingerprint spoon.
- Clean the fingers to be printed.
- Apply ink from the ink pad onto the fingertips.
- Holding the curved fingerprint spoon in one hand, press the deceased's finger into the curved spoon to obtain the impression.
- Fill in the information on the back of the fingerprint card.
  - Case number
  - Victim's name
  - Right or left hand
- Write a property receipt for the inked set of fingerprints and maintain the chain of custody.

Depending on the condition of the deceased, special methods may be applied to obtain sufficient inked fingerprints. Bodies submerged in water for a period of time lose the outer layer of skin, whereas extreme heat can result in mummification.

Different methods can be applied to enhance the fingerprints of the deceased.

3.1.2.2.1 Fluid Injection Method   Fingertips of decomposed bodies have distorted ridges, which require injections with tissue builder or saline solution. The following procedures are required to do this:

- Tying off the digit below the first joint with string.
- Injecting the fluid with a hypodermic needle under the skin to pump up the flesh.
- Applying the ink and using the fingerprint spoon to obtain the fingerprints.

 3.1.2.2.2 Boiling Water Method   This method requires boiling water to be placed on an examination table proficient to evacuate liquids.

- Place the deceased's hand on top of a sponge with the palms facing upward.
- Pour boiling water onto the friction ridges of the palms and fingertips.
- The flesh will plump up allowing obtaining inked or dusted and lifted fingerprints.

 3.1.2.2.3 Peeled Skin Method   When the victim is putrefied, the skin will peel off. The CSI will secure the peeled skin containing the victim's fingerprints. A method to recover the friction ridge impression from peeled skin requires the CSI to do the following:

- Double glove his or her hands.
- Slide the peeled fingerprints over the CSI's own finger.
- Ink and roll the fingerprint on a fingerprint card.

 ## 3.1.3 Categories of Fingerprints

Fingerprints found at a crime scene are classified into three categories:

- Latent fingerprints
- Patent fingerprints
- Plastic fingerprints

Latent fingerprints are not visible to the naked eye and require powder or chemical processing. Latent fingerprints represent the majority of fingerprints found at the crime scene.

Patent fingerprints are visible to the naked eye. Patent fingerprints are found in blood, paint, oil, grease, or dust as they contrast with the surface on which they are found, for example an oily fingerprint on a mirror or a bloody fingerprint on a tiled floor.

Plastic fingerprints are three-dimensional prints impressed into items such as soap, wax, silly putty, or other soft surface materials.

3.1.4 Methods to Develop Latent Fingerprints

At the crime scene, fingerprints can be found on almost any kind of surfaces, porous and nonporous. Contrary to porous surfaces, nonporous surfaces do not absorb liquids.

Nonporous surfaces are plastic, metal, glass, etc. Nonporous items can be processed at the crime scene with black powder or fluorescent powders. Porous items are wood, paper, cardboard, etc. Porous items require chemical processing, commonly performed in the laboratory.

3.1.4.1 Stabilizing the Fingerprint on Nonporous Surfaces with Cyanoacrylate Fuming

Why stabilize fingerprints?

Fingerprints are fragile evidence. If they are on nonporous metallic and nonmetallic surfaces such as soda cans, plastic bottles, a mirror or a window, touching or wiping over the surface smudges or even destroys the ridge detail. Collecting evidence without gloves adds the crime scene investigator's fingerprints to the evidence creating an overlay of two or more prints making it very difficult for the latent examiner to separate the ridge detail of the different fingerprints. Evidence packaged in a paper or plastic bag may rub against the bag or each other smudging the print. Extreme change in temperature from cold to heat or heat to cold may destroy ridge detail. Therefore, it is of the utmost importance to stabilize the ridge detail as soon as possible.

3.1.4.1.1 The Cyanoacrylate or Superglue Method The cyanoacrylate method, also called superglue method, stabilizes the ridge detail of the fingerprint and touch DNA that might be present in the print. The cyanoacrylate technique uses the vapors of superglue to develop latent fingerprints. Latent fingerprints are composed of sweat, amino acids, fatty acids, proteins, potassium, and sodium. Cyanoacrylate or superglue fuming works by having a high affinity or strong attraction to the amino acids, fatty acids, and proteins in a fingerprint and the vapors of the superglue adhere to these components, as illustrated in Figure 3.6.

The superglue fuming is mostly performed in the laboratory in a fuming chamber. The vapors created by heating superglue (cyanoacrylate) in a small aluminum container adhere to the ridge detail on the evidence, making it visible. Placing a small container with water helps to hydrate fresh and aged fingerprints. The superglue vapors adhere to the object's surface, which makes the fingerprint visible and semipermanent allowing the print to be

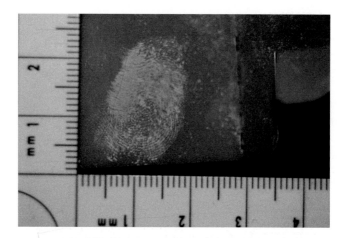

Figure 3.6 Fingerprints developed with cyanoacrylate fuming.

dusted with fingerprint powder and tape lifted several times without being disturbed or destroyed. See Figure 3.6 and the cyanoacrylate fuming chamber in Figure 3.7 (Cyanoacrylate fuming, n.d.).

There are two different ways of fuming for a fingerprint with superglue:

Superglue Method (handwritten)

Method 1

1. Inside the fuming chamber, place a few drops of superglue into a small, circular aluminum container and place onto a warming plate. A coffee cup warmer works very well.
2. Inside the fuming chamber, place water into a second small circular aluminum container and place onto a second warming plate.
3. Place the item of evidence into the fuming chamber.
4. Once the superglue heats up, fumes will develop, aggregating on the print.
5. Allow time for the fingerprints to develop on the evidence.
6. The fingerprint will be visible as a white film on the ridges, making the print visible.

Method 2

1. Prepare cotton balls by dipping into a solution of 1 lb baking soda dissolved in 1 gallon of water and thoroughly air-dry. The cotton balls can be prepared ahead and stored in a plastic bag for future use. The cotton balls will act as a catalyst and accelerate the reaction of the superglue.
2. Inside the fuming chamber, place several prepared cotton balls into a small circular aluminum container.
3. Place the items to be processed into the fuming chamber.
4. Drip several drops of superglue onto the cotton balls.

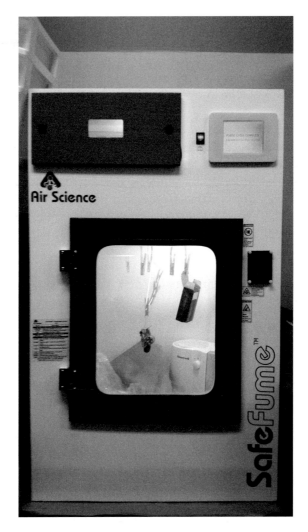

Figure 3.7 Cyanoacrylate fuming tank.

5. Within a few moments, the reaction is visible and the superglue begins to fume.
6. The fingerprints will be visible as a white film on the ridge detail of the fingerprint.
7. It is recommended to place a black fingerprint card with a sample fingerprint on its surface inside the fuming chamber to determine when the print is fully developed and to avoid overprocessing.

3.1.4.1.2 Research to Improve the Quality and Efficiency of Superglue Fuming Methods of Latent Fingerprints In May 2015, Dr. Mark D. Dadmun, an expert in polymer chemistry at the University of Tennessee, published a study explaining the importance of temperature on superglue fuming of aged fingerprints and temperature control in a forensic laboratory. The research revealed that fuming at lower temperatures increased the rate of polymerization during the fuming. The best temperature of fuming is between 10 and 15°C. The lowering in temperature improved the quality of aged latent prints.

Previously, it was suggested to place a small jar with water into the glue tank to rehydrate an aged fingermark for a successful development of latent prints by superglue fuming. Contrary to previous beliefs, "exposure to boiling water vapors harms prints by removing initiators by dissolving them into the steam and releasing them from the print before fuming." This current study revealed that rehydrating fresh or aged prints by maintaining room temperature or boiling water vapors are not sufficiently improving the print quality (Dadmun, 2015, p. 2).

3.1.4.2 Different Applications of the Cyanoacrylate Fuming Methods

3.1.4.2.1 Superglue a Vehicle   The superglue method can also be applied to the interior and exterior of vehicles. A fuming chamber can be constructed from plastic sprinkler pipes and large plastic tarps. Instead of using cotton swabs, prepare 100% cotton facial towels with the baking soda/water solution as catalyst (Figure 3.8).

- Place the prepared towels on aluminum foil on the front driver and passenger's floorboard, the rear floorboards, and in the trunk.
- Keep the doors of the vehicle open and the windows up.
- Place additional towels on pieces of aluminum foil on the floor around all four sides of the vehicle.
- Place superglue onto the towels and wait for the superglue to begin fuming and fingerprints will develop.
- **Caution** is required here as the large amount of superglue used in this method can cause irritation to the eyes and the throat. Ensure good ventilation before continuing to process with fingerprint powder. As in the fuming chamber, a black fingerprint card with a fingerprint on the surface can be used as a test card.

3.1.4.2.2 Superglue a Deceased   Before preparing to apply the superglue method to a deceased, it is important to obtain the permission from the medical examiner. The medical examiner has jurisdiction of the body. Fuming a body for latent fingerprints can be important in strangulation cases, sexual assault, and violent crimes where it is possible that the suspect's fingerprints are on the victim's skin.

Figure 3.8 Vehicle in homemade superglue tank.

Since there is no fuming chamber available for the size of a human body, a body box used for cremations can substitute for the fuming chamber. As in the vehicle superglue method, the cotton swabs should be substituted with 100% cotton towels and prepared in the baking soda/water solution. Place at least two towels on each side of the victim lying on the gurney. Add superglue to the towels and cover with the cardboard boxes. Ensure that the box is sealed as tight as possible. As on the surface of nonporous items, the fingerprints will appear in a white film over the ridge detail on the victim's skin. Additional processing with fingerprint powder and tape lifting will be required. As in the fuming chamber, a black fingerprint card with a fingerprint on the surface can be used as a test card.

3.1.4.2.3 Superglue at the Crime Scene   Fingerprints can be easily disturbed, especially if the particular piece of evidence is collected from the scene and transported to the laboratory for further processing. Rubbing against the packaging material can result in the loss of ridge detail. Therefore, it is recommended to use portable superglue fuming chambers to semipermanently fixate the fingerprint. If no portable superglue tank is available, a plastic bag, Rubbermaid bin, or a cardboard box can substitute for the fuming chamber.

3.1.4.2.4 Homemade Superglue Fuming Chamber Many small law enforcement agencies do not have the budget or the caseload to justify the purchase of superglue fuming chambers valued at $5,000 to $10,000. Crime scene investigators can get creative and develop their own crude fuming chambers out of a glass aquarium with a plastic lid. Several hooks attached to the lid allow for hanging items such as small handguns. However, these homemade fuming chambers do not have air filters and the user needs to be cautions to avoid inhalation of fumes.

3.1.4.2.5 Superglue Fuming Wand A fuming cartridge is attached to the Fume-A-Wand, a hand-held butane-powered portable heating appliance. A flameless catalytic heat source heats the CN pellet to generate polymerized superglue fumes. The handheld wand can be used inside a fuming chamber and provides sufficient heat to develop a fingerprint within 30 seconds. This wand can be used at the crime scene and is safe to be used on a deceased.

3.1.4.2.6 CN Cyanoacrylate CN is a photo-luminescent cyanoacrylate containing a dye blend specific to latent fingerprint residues. The CN is preserved inside a steel wool cartridge and dispersed with a butane torch with a flameless burner allowing for easy use at the crime scene. After a fuming time of about 5 minutes, the latent prints are almost immediately visible. CN developed prints are best visualized with an alternate light source between 450 and 515 nm. The prints are highly luminescent and stabilized.

3.1.5 Powder Processing of Fingerprints

3.1.5.1 Fingerprint Powders

Latent powders and magnetic powders are used to develop latent fingerprints on nonporous surfaces. Traditional fingerprint powder, also called black powder, is composed of fine carbon or charcoal. Latent powder is available in different colors such as black, white, fluorescent red, fluorescent green, and other colors. It is important to choose a color that contrasts the surface of the evidence, for example, white powder on a black surface or black powder on a light surface.

Traditional powder, also called carbon powder, is applied with a fingerprint brush onto any metallic or nonmetallic, nonporous surface. Magnetic powder is similar to traditional powder except that it contains minute magnetic particles such as iron dust. Magnetic powder is applied with a magnetic wand versus a fingerprint brush. Fluorescent powders can be applied with a feather brush or a magnetic wand. These powders fluoresce under ultraviolet light and filters are required to photograph the developed fingerprint impressions. Fluorescent powders work well on firearms, especially on the wooden rifle stock and paneling. Table 3.1 outlines the various powder types and surface types on which they are optimized.

Table 3.1   Regular versus Magnetic and Fluorescent Powder Types

Regular Powder	Magnetic Powder	Fluorescent Powder
Nonporous surfaces such as glass, mirror, painted surfaces, windows, wooden floors, and metal surfaces.	Nonporous surfaces such as plastic bottles, plastic dishes, wax-coated magazine covers, and any surface that is nonmetallic.	Nonporous surfaces such as untreated metal, stainless steel, firearms, and any dark nonporous surfaces.

3.1.5.1.1 Process of Powdering for Fingerprints   Many laboratories have a fingerprint station with a filter catching the loose fingerprint powder from cycling through the air in the entire room, as illustrated in Figure 3.9.

Here are the steps for powdering for fingerprints using traditional powder:

1. Identify the surface to process for latent fingerprints.
2. There is no difference if the surface has been stabilized with superglue.
3. There are three general options for latent powders:
   - Traditional powder for all metallic, nonporous surfaces
   - Magnetic powder for all nonmetallic, nonporous surfaces
   - Fluorescent powder for all dark and low contrast surfaces
4. Pour a small amount of latent powder on a small piece of paper. Always ensure that the powder is in contrast to the color of the surface to be processed. Latent powder is available in black, gray, and white. Fluorescent powders are available in different colors such as

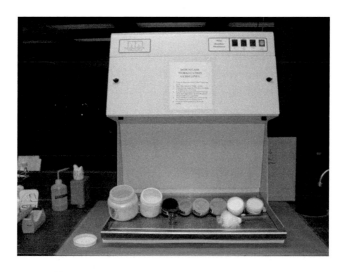

Figure 3.9 Fingerprint station.

green, pink, and red. The application and lifting methods of both powders are identical, except fluorescent powder lifts are placed on a fingerprint card with black photo paper, whereas white background fingerprint cards are used for latent prints developed with black fingerprint powder.

5. Load the fingerprint brush with latent powder and run the brush bristles over the surface in a circular motion.
6. If too much powder has been deployed, simply blow the powder off the surface.
7. Take a black and white photograph of the developed fingerprint.
8. Don't forget to add a scale next to the fingerprint to allow for a 1:1 enlargement required for later identification.
9. Apply fingerprint-lifting tape to the developed fingerprint. Using a piece of cloth or a plastic card to apply pressure to the surface of the lifting tape will help to minimize air bubbles.
10. Attach the lifting tape to the photo paper side of the fingerprint card.
11. Fill in the required information on the fingerprint card and draw a sketch of the area from where the print was recovered. Some agencies require adding measurements to the sketch.

3.1.5.1.2 Processing Latent Fingerprints with Magnetic Powder   The steps for processing latent prints using magnetic powder are as follows:

1. There is no difference in the powder processing method if the latent fingerprints on the surface of the item of evidence have been stabilized with cyanoacrylate.
2. Identify the surface to process for latent fingerprints to ensure it is nonporous and nonmetallic.
3. Pour a small amount of magnetic powder on a small piece of paper. Always ensure that the powder is in contrast to the color of the surface to be processed. Magnetic powder is available in black and light gray.
4. Load the magnetic wand with magnetic powder and hover the wand over the surface to be processed in a circular motion.
5. If too much powder has been deployed, collect the powder with the magnetic wand.
6. Take a black and white photograph of the developed fingerprint.
7. Don't forget to add a scale next to the fingerprint to allow for a 1:1 enlargement required for later identification.
8. Apply fingerprint-lifting tape to the developed fingerprint. Using a piece of cloth or a plastic card to apply pressure to the surface of the lifting tape will help to minimize air bubbles.
9. Attach the lifting tape to the photo paper side of the fingerprint card.

10. Fill in the required information on the fingerprint card and draw a
    sketch of the area from where the print was recovered. Some agencies
    require measurements in the sketch.

Every latent fingerprint, developed with magnetic (magna) powder or
with traditional fingerprint powder, lifted on a fingerprint card, becomes
physical evidence. The chain of evidence has to be maintained for every piece
of evidence including every lifted fingerprint. The chain of custody is maintained on the property receipt. The fingerprint card, packaged in either a plastic bag or in an envelope, sealed and initialed by the crime scene investigator,
who developed the latent, will be listed on the property receipt and the chain
of custody will be maintained on the bottom of the property receipt as well.

3.1.6 Chemical Processing of Fingerprints on Porous Surfaces

Porous surfaces are materials that absorb liquid such as raw wood, paper, and
cardboard. Chemical processing is required to visualize fingerprints on such
surfaces. Several different chemicals are available to develop latent fingerprints. Some of the chemicals react with the amino acids in the fingerprint while others react with the oil, salt, or water contained in the ridge detail.

3.1.6.1 Iodine Fuming

Iodine fuming is one of the oldest methods to develop latent fingerprints on
porous surfaces such as raw wood, paper, or cardboard. Iodine is inexpen-
sive, easy to use, and sensitive, but most important nondestructive because
the produced stains are ephemeral. Iodine should be the first method chosen
for detecting fingerprints on porous surfaces.

On the contrary, prints developed with iodine fuming disappear within
a few hours or days. Iodine fuming is used to detect fingerprints; however,
the developed prints are not permanent. One method to stabilize the print is
to treat it with a starch solution. The starch combines with iodine resulting
in dark blue-black complex, fixing the image for weeks and maybe months
depending on the storage conditions. Benzoflavone is an after treatment for
iodine-developed prints fixing the print permanently (Latent print development using iodine fuming, 2012).

Equipment needed for iodine fuming:

- Goggles, gloves, and protective gear
- Iodine fuming chamber (either professional chamber or homemade
  chamber)
- Magnifying glass or loupe to examine the developed fingerprint
- Camera to photograph the developed print
- Small spray bottle

- Iodine crystals
- Starch solution (approximately 1 g of starch like cornstarch in 25 mL water; if lumpy, filter to achieve a clear liquid)
- Evidence to be processed

Iodine fuming can be performed at the laboratory and at the crime scene. At the crime scene, a Ziploc bag can be used as a fuming chamber.

Processing Method. Iodine fuming requires the following steps:

- Place several iodine crystals in a Ziploc bag.
- Add the item to be processed.
- Close tightly.
- Apply heat by cubing one hand over the crystals for 15 seconds. Body heat will activate the sublimation process converting the solid crystals into a purple gas.
- Wear goggles, gloves, and a respirator for personal safety.
- Photograph the developed prints.
- Fix the developed prints with the starch solution or benzoflavone.

3.1.6.2 Ninhydrin

Ninhydrin is a chemical that reacts with amino acids and small particles of water in the latent print. The chemical reaction results in visualizing the fingerprints in a purple color as illustrated in Figure 3.10. Ninhydrin is available in aerosol form, which can be used at the crime scene or as a liquid used in the laboratory. The fingerprints appear within 24 to 48 hours of processing.

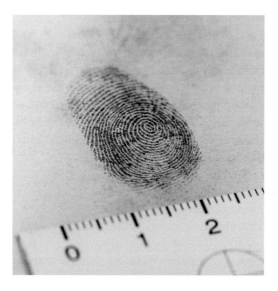

Figure 3.10 Fingerprints developed with ninhydrin.

Processing method in the laboratory requires the following steps:

1. Place ninhydrin chemical in a clean glass pie plate or casserole dish.
2. Dip the porous item to be processed into the chemical.
3. Rinse and hang up to dry.
4. Avoid contamination between items.
5. Developing finalizes within 24 to 48 hours.
6. Spray the processed item with fixative (purchased in aerosol form).
7. Photograph the fingerprint with scale.

Hint: To accelerate the developing process, a steam iron or a heating plate at a temperature of 80–100°C can be used to hasten the processing time of the treated item.

3.1.6.3 Physical Developer

Physical developer is a silver-nitrate based chemical that washes away all proteins from the surface of the evidence to develop a latent fingerprint. Physical developer can be used after iodine fuming or processing with ninhydrin, but has to be used as the last resort. Physical developer has been very successful on visualizing fingerprints on money.

Physical developer consists of a prewash and a working solution. The chemicals can be mixed for each processing or can be purchased premixed.

Several steps are required in this processing method:

1. Prepare the prewash and the working solution:
   - Prewash: In a clean glass container, dissolve 50 g of maleic acid powder in 2 L of distilled water.
   - Commercial working solution: Combine 1 part of solution A (5 ml, 10 ml, 15 ml) with 18 parts of solution B (90 ml, 180 ml, 270 ml).
2. Pour the prewash and working solution in a clean glass container.
3. Using plastic forceps, submerge the item to be processed in the prewash solution.
4. Place the containers on a mechanical rocker to keep the reagent mixed and to ensure the item is thoroughly washed.
5. Leave item in the prewash for 10 minutes.
6. Using plastic forceps, submerge in the working solution for 20 minutes.
7. Using plastic forceps, rinse twice for 5 minutes each.
8. Air-dry the item on a clean flat surface.
9. Photograph the developed fingerprints.

Hint: Setting the time on an alarm clock avoids chemically overprocessing the evidence.

3.1.6.4 *DFO*

DFO is a chemical that reacts with the amino acids in the body's proteins. DFO is used as a substitute for ninhydrin and works best on visualizing fingerprints on paper. The DFO processing method consists of the following:

1. Place DFO chemical in a clean glass container.
2. Using plastic forceps, submerge the item to be processed in the chemical.
3. Using a hot plate or a coffee warmer, heat the item for about 10 minutes at 100°C (212°F).
4. Wearing orange goggles, examine the fluorescence with an alternate light source at 450, 485, 525, and/or 530 nm for best fluorescence (570–590 nm for brown and yellow paper).
5. Photograph the developed latent prints with scale.

Hint: When later processing with ninhydrin or physical developer should be performed, process with DFO first to achieve fluorescence.

3.1.7 Fingerprints in Blood

Patent and latent fingerprints in blood are found on surfaces such as walls, floors, and ceilings. The fingerprints should be photographed *in situ*, as seen, before enhancing with chemicals. Several chemical processing methods are available for detecting and enhancing fingerprints in blood.

3.1.7.1 *Amido Black*

Amido Black is a protein dye reacting with the protein in the blood resulting in a bluish-black color while enhancing the detail and the contrast between the print and the surface. Additional processing with physical developer can be used to further enhance the ridge detail, as illustrated in Figure 3.11.

Caution: Amido Black is not a blood detection chemical.

The processing method of Amido Black requires the following:

1. Photograph the area to be processed with scale. Use a yellow marker or placard to identify the area if there is more than one region to be processed.
2. Apply Amido Black working solution to the area. The working solution is blue-black in color and commercially available in premixed form.
3. Spray all areas adjacent to the visible stain since additional bloody prints or shoe impressions not visible to the naked eye might develop.

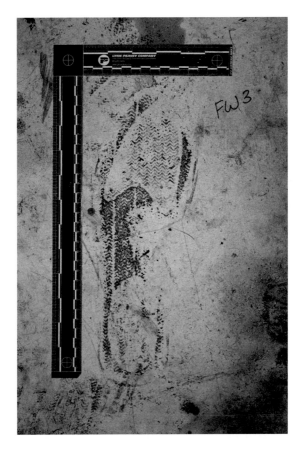

Figure 3.11 Shoe impression processed with Amido Black.

4. Spray the areas with the rinse solution until the background is clean and developed patterns are visible.
5. Photograph the developed prints/shoe impressions with scale.

3.1.8 Special Processing Methods

In this subsection, we are introducing special processing methods including small particle reagent (SPR), Wetwop, and how to enhance fingerprints on metal surfaces.

3.1.8.1 Small Particle Reagent

SPR consists of molybdenum disulfide. In this developing technique, small black particles adhere to the fatty substances in the fingerprint residue. SPR can be used on different surfaces and can develop latent prints on wet surfaces such as vehicles after the rain, in snow, or with morning dew, or even under water.

To process a vehicle with SPR, the following steps are required:

1. Using a plastic spray bottle, apply SPR to the wet surface.
2. Repeat after 1 minute.
3. Rinse with clean water.
4. Photograph the developed ridge detail with scale.
5. Let dry and attempt to lift the print.

3.1.8.2 Wetwop

Wetwop is a chemical processing method to develop fingerprints on the sticky side of tape such as Scotch tape, masking tape, duct tape, brown packaging, and nylon reinforced strapping tapes. Fingerprints on the sticky side of the tape can lead to the suspect in kidnapping cases or when the victim has been bound.

When processing with Wetwop, the CSI will do the following:

1. Place the tape with the sticky side up on a flat surface.
2. With a camel hairbrush or fine paintbrush, apply Wetwop chemical to the sticky side of the tape.
3. Rinse with clear water.
4. The latent print develops almost immediately.
5. Photograph the latent print with scale.

3.1.8.3 Enhancing Latent Fingerprints on Metal Surfaces

There are several methods to develop latent fingerprints on metal surfaces through oxidation; 1% Gun Blue solution is the most common method. Different metal surfaces such as copper, steel, and aluminum, just to mention a few, can be found at a crime scene such as on spent cartridges. The cyanoacrylate method and dusting with black powder may not result in sufficient ridge detail for identification purposes. The problem of enhancing latent fingerprints on metal surfaces can be reduced by using a mixture of commercial brass blackening and distilled water or a solution of commercial aluminum blackening and distilled water. Experiments have shown that those solutions are more effective in developing ridge detail than a 1% Gun Blue solution (Smith and Kauffman, 2009).

3.1.8.3.1 Reason for the Reaction of Metal with Birchwood Casey Brass Black/Aluminum Black Solutions   Birchwood Casey Brass Black is a chemical oxidizing agent commonly used to blacken brass, bronze, and copper surfaces such as the surfaces on firearms. The active component selenium dioxide or selenious acid causes the oxidation of metal surfaces. When a metal surface is submerged in a Brass Black or Aluminum Black solution (Brass Black and distilled water; Aluminum Black and distilled water), the contaminants

on the metal surface such as sebaceous deposits and oils from the ridge skin protect the metal surface and prevent the oxidation causing the ridges of the print to remain white while the surrounding surface becomes darkened.

These processing solutions are very cost effective; a bottle of Brass Black or Aluminum Black can be found at Walmart and hardware stores for about $6 and a gallon of distilled water sells for about $1. Both mixed solutions have an almost infinitive shelf life and provide an excellent asset to police departments with limited budgets.

3.1.8.3.2 Processing Metal Surfaces with Brass Black Solution and Aluminum Black Solution   The processing of metal surfaces such as spent cartridges can be performed in the laboratory as well as at the crime scene.

Required equipment for processing:

- Container large enough to submerge the items to be processed. (A glass pie plate or a glass baking dish works very well.)
- Safety equipment such as safety glasses, gloves, and vented area.
- Measuring cup with fluid ounces indicators.
- Stop watch, stopwatch function in a wristwatch, or stop watch function in smartphone.
- Distilled water.
- Brass Black or Aluminum Black.

Processing method. The following steps are required for this processing method:

1. In a clean container mix one part Brass Black or Aluminum Black with 4 parts distilled water, for example, 2 ounces of Brass Black and 8 ounces of distilled water.
2. Determine the metal surface of the evidence.
3. Refer to Table 3.2 to determine the processing time for that specific metal.
4. Submerge the item to be processed.
5. Check for developing prints. If prints develop before the expected exposure time, remove from solution, rinse with tap water or distilled water, and let air-dry.
6. After the processing time is expired, rinse the item with tap water or distilled water and let air-dry.
7. After the print is dried, it will be very difficult to smudge the print.
8. If the print is overexposed and the evidence is too oxidized, submerge the item in ethanol or methanol.

Hint: Brass metal surfaces processed with Brass Black solutions can be submerged in bleach to darken the surface and to lighten the friction ridges.

Table 3.2 Approximate Time for Enhancement with Brass Black Solution

Metal Surface	Brass Black Solution
Brass	1.45 to 2.30 minutes
Copper	30 to 45 seconds
Galvanized steel	20 seconds
Galvanized iron	20 seconds
Aluminum	1.30 to 1.45 minutes
Hardened steel	12 seconds
Stainless steel	72 hours
	Submerged in the solution for 2 hours and air-dried. It can take up to 72 hours before ridge detail develops. This method is not recommended for stainless steel.

Table 3.3 Test Results for Aluminum Black and Brass Black Solution on Various Metals

Metal Surface	Aluminum Black Solution	Brass Black Solution
Brass	Acceptable	Best
Copper	Acceptable	Best
Galvanized steel	Good	Best
Galvanized Iron	Good	Best
Aluminum	Best	Acceptable
Hardened steel	Acceptable	Best
Stainless steel	Unacceptable	Unacceptable

Approximate time for enhancement. Table 3.2 illustrates the approximate time for enhancement for various metal surfaces with Brass Black solution.

Caution: Different alloys may require increased or decreased processing time.

Comparison of Aluminum Black and Brass Black solution. Table 3.3 illustrates the test results of Aluminum Black and Brass Black solution for enhancement for various metal surfaces.

3.1.8.4 RUVIS System

Reflected ultraviolet imaging system (RUVIS) is an ultraviolet image converter to detect latent fingerprints. RUVIS detects fingerprints on nonporous surfaces without the application of any kind of powders. A UV light is aimed at the surface with the supposed fingerprint. Once the UV light strikes the fingerprint, the light reflects back to the viewer separating the fingerprint from the background. The image intensifier will convert the UV light to visible light. The located fingerprint can be processed with powder for further development.

Fingerprint on Champagne Bottle Led to Killer

In September 2006, the fire department and sheriff's deputies responded to a single-family home in North Fort Myers, Florida. Part of the house had been on fire. First responders discovered two deceased elderly females inside the residence, later identified as the homeowner and her sister. Both females had been beaten to death. The perpetrator tried to set the house on fire to cover up the murder; however, the fire only spread from the master bedroom to the bathroom and the hallway. One victim was found lying on the ground at the front door while the other victim was lying in a pool of blood between the living room and the hallway. Open food boxes in the kitchen indicated that the perpetrator helped himself to food and drinks. The CSI team fingerprinted any items in the residence that the perpetrator could have touched including an empty champagne bottle on the living room floor. A fingerprint with good ridge detail was developed and lifted. During the interview with family members, the lead detective asked about the champagne bottle. Family members stated that the victim would have never opened that bottle because of its sentimental value. The fingerprint was scanned into automated fingerprint identification system (AFIS) and the search identified the suspect, David Richard Patton. An arrest warrant was issued and law enforcement issued a statewide BOLO (be on the lookout), as the perpetrator had stolen the victim's car. He abandoned the vehicle in Fort Lauderdale, Florida. The perpetrator had contacted his family and advised that he was on his way to Topeka, Kansas in a Greyhound bus. Law enforcement officers arrested Patton at the Greyhound station. He was arrested and pleaded guilty to the double murder.

3.2 Shoe and Tire Impressions

From time to time, impression evidence in the form of shoe, tire, or tool impressions is present at the crime scene. Fabric impressions can also be found particularly on a vehicle involved in a hit-and-run accident. Shoe and tire impressions are among the physical evidence that is easily overlooked due to lack of training and education in the proper search, documentation with photographs, collection and preservation of the evidence, or undervalued as being important.

Shoe impressions can be found in the dirt next to the point of entry or exit at a burglary scene, on the tiled floor in a bank, or bloody shoe impressions on a wooden floor next to the murdered victim. Tire impressions can be found on dirt roads, in sand, snow, tiled driveways, and paved roads. The primary concern for impression evidence is the preservation of the impression for later reproduction and identification in the laboratory.

3.2.1 Classification of Shoe and Tire Impressions

Shoe and tire impressions can be subdivided into categories just as fingerprints:

- *Visible impressions*: Shoe impression created when a person steps into a foreign substance and contaminated the soles of the shoes that come in contact with a clean surface. The impression is visible with the naked eye. Most visible impressions are found on tiled, wood, or vinyl floors. Shoe and tire impressions can also consist of oil, grease, or blood on different surfaces, such as tire marks on paved roads or blood shoe impressions on a cement floor in a garage.
- *Plastic impressions*: Impressions created by stepping into a soft surface such as mud, snow, dirt, or sand creating a three-dimensional impression. The impression is three-dimensional as it shows the length, width, and depth of the impression. These impressions can be preserved with a cast made of dental stone.
- *Latent impressions*: Latent impressions are most overlooked, as they are not visible to the naked eye. Most banks have tiled floors and shoe impressions can be obtained from this surface. The developing process is the same as for latent fingerprints.

3.2.2 Processing Methods for Shoe and Tire Impressions

Depending on the surface of the suspected shoe impression, different processing methods can be applied from dusting for latent shoe impressions to casting with dental stone for shoe and tire impressions in dirt or soil.

3.2.2.1 Developing Latent Shoe Impressions

Smooth surfaces such as tiled, wooden, and vinyl floors are best suited for the powder method. The tiled floors at most banks and convenience stores allow for best results.

3.2.2.1.1 **Black/Magna Powder Method**   Black powder and magnetic powder used to develop latent fingerprints on metallic surfaces are also used to develop latent shoe impressions on smooth surfaces such as tiled floors, lacquered wood, or marble floors, as shown in Figure 3.12.

Figure 3.12 Shoe impression developed with magnetic powder.

Processing method. The CSI will perform the following processing steps:

1. Photograph the area to be processed with midrange and close-up photographs.
2. Required material:
   - Fingerprint brush or magna brush
   - Black fingerprint powder or magna (magnetic) fingerprint powder
   - Lifting tape
   - Fingerprint card
3. Apply black powder to the tiled surface.
4. The shoe impression will develop as the powder adheres to the oil, grease, or other component on the soles of the shoes that created the impression.
5. Place a labeled scale next to the developed shoe impression and accomplish midrange and close-up photos. Make sure to capture a fixture in the room for orientation.
6. Lift the impression with fingerprint lifting tape. Sometimes, the impression is larger in size than the lifting tape and overlapping of several layers of tape is necessary to cover the entire impression.
7. Transfer the lifting tape to the fingerprint card. (Fingerprint cards come in different sizes; however, several smaller cards can be over-lapped to cover the entire impression.)

8. Fill in the information in the fingerprint card. If one fingerprint card is not large enough, overlap multiple cards.
9. Draw a sketch of the location where you developed the shoe impression.

3.2.2.1.2 Inked Impression from the Sole of a Shoe   Shoe impressions can provide valuable evidence linking a suspect to the scene of the crime. During the interview, the detective pays attention to the type of footwear worn by the suspect. If the impression at the crime scene is consistent with a sneaker and the suspect wears a pair of sneakers, the detective will ask for the sneakers for comparison of the sole impressions. The detective issues a property receipt maintaining the chain of custody of the evidence and submits a processing request to the crime scene unit.

Processing method. The CSI, after maintaining the chain of custody and receiving the pair of sneakers from the evidence custodian, will perform the following examination:

- Photograph the soles of the shoes from different angles including all sides and a bird's eye view of the sole pattern. Place a scale next to visible defects and take close-up photos. If necessary, add a small plastic arrow in a contrasting color pointing to the defect so it is easily identifiable in the image.
- Lifting the impression pattern from the soles of the shoes requires the following steps:
  - Material required:
    – Clean fabric rag
    – Fingerprint ink or a commercial ink pad
    – Piece of brown paper
  - Using the clean rag, remove any dirt and small rocks from the soles of the shoe.
  - Lightly coat the sole of the shoes with fingerprint ink or press the commercial inkpad against the sole of the shoe.
  - Press the sole of the shoe onto the brown butcher paper. If too much ink distorts the impression, remove with clean rag and redo.
  - Let dry and add information such as
    – Case number
    – Date and time impression printed
    – Initial of the crime scene investigator
    – Describe the shoe:
      – Left foot
      – Right foot

- Brand name
- Size
- Material
- Color
- Defects if visible

Caution: This method is intrusive as the ink may remain on the soles of the shoes for a longer period of time requiring intensive cleaning.

3.2.2.1.3 Electrostatic Dust Print Lifting Device   Crime scenes are not sterile, especially at the scene of a robbery at a convenience store or a bank robbery, or the carpet or upholstery in the living room of a residence. Everybody walking through the scene transfers dust and other particles from their shoes to the surface walked upon. Side lighting with a flashlight at a 45-degree angle can more easily show the presence of a shoe impression in dust. The electrostatic dust print-lifting device allows enhancing, collecting, and preserving such prints.

The electrostatic dust print-lifting device consists of a metalized lifting film, a grounding plate, and a battery-operated charging device, as illustrated in Figure 3.13. The processing and collection requires the following steps:

1. Place the metalized lifting film over the dust print.
2. Place the ground plate approximately 8 in. next to the film.
3. Connect the two metal prongs of the charging device to the ground plate and to the probe on the lifting film.
4. Turn on the charging device electrostatically charging the film.
5. The film will suction over the print causing the dust particles to adhere to the film.
6. Ensure removal of all air bubbles before lifting the film.
7. The print impression will be visible on the film.

Electrostatic dust lifting (ESDL) can also be used on concrete driveways. Ron Mueller (2012) wrote an article about the use of ESDL on tire impressions on a driveway. After the basic overall, midrange, and close-up photos of the tire tracks had been taken, he used the ESDL to enhance the tire impression. Surprisingly, he discovered additional shoe impressions that were not visible to the naked eye, not being captured in the digital photographs.

3.2.2.2 Three-Dimensional Shoe Impressions

The best method to preserve a three-dimensional shoe impression in dirt, sand, or snow is to cast the impression with dental stone. Specialized snow wax is used to cast impressions in snow. The shoe cast is depicted in Figure 3.14.

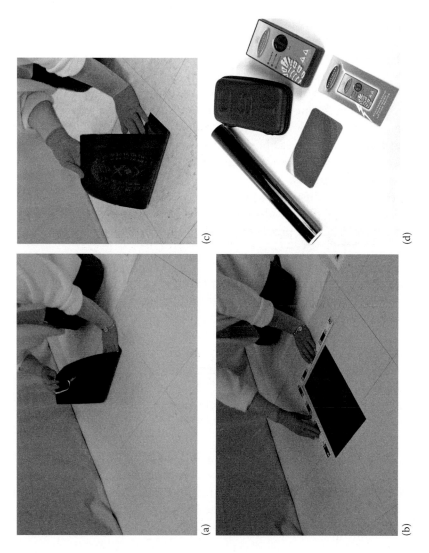

Figure 3.13 Electrostatic lifter steps 1 (a), 2 (b), 3 (c), and equipment (d). (With permission from Tritech Forensics.)

Figure 3.14 Photo of shoe impression cast.

Required equipment:

- Dental stone powder (2 lb of powdered material).
- 16 ounces of water.
- Plastic mixing bowl. A Ziploc bag can substitute the mixing bowl.
- Spray paint in a bright color such as neon pink, or any color that will provide a contrast to the surface of the impression, or a can of hairspray.
- Rectangular expandable metal frame.
- Spoon or tong depressor.
- Permanent marker.
- Packaging material such as a cardboard box.

Processing method. The CSI will perform the following steps necessary to cast a shoe impression:

1. The first step in documenting a shoe impression in dirt, sand, or snow is to obtain medium range and close-up photographs with and without scale.
2. Mark the shoe impression with a yellow evidence marker.
3. Draw a crime scene sketch including all shoe impressions (identified by the yellow evidence marker numbers).
4. Carefully spray a thick coat of lacquer or hairspray over the impression without disturbing the pattern of the impression.
5. In the mixing bowl or in the Ziploc bag, combine 16 ounces of clean water with 2 lb of dental stone. Mix thoroughly to avoid lumps. The consistence of the mixture should be similar to pancake batter.
6. Expand and place the rectangular metal frame around the shoe impression. Ensure that the entire impression is inside the frame.
7. Using the tong depressor or spoon, carefully pour the dental stone mixture inside the metal frame. The cast should have a thickness of at least 1 in.
8. Let the cast dry thoroughly. The drying time varies depending on weather conditions, temperature, and humidity.
9. Using a permanent marker, write the following information on the outside of the cast:
   - Compass direction North
   - Case number
   - Date and time when casted
   - Initial of the crime scene investigator casting the impression
   - Item number and yellow marker number (if applicable)
   - Short description where the cast was taken (cast of shoe impression in dirt underneath the window at the north side of the residence at marker 6)
10. When the cast is dried, carefully remove from the dirt. Do not clean the cast and collect all dirt, grass, and other components that adhered to the cast.
11. Place the cast in a cardboard box, seal with evidence tape, initial and date across the evidence tape, and fill in a property receipt for the item.

A cast of a shoe impression is three-dimensional. To compare the cast to the sole pattern of the suspect's or the victim's shoe, it is necessary to develop a cast of the suspect's shoe to be able to compare it with the cast from the scene. Three-dimensional impressions cannot be compared to two-dimensional impressions.

Figure 3.15 Bio foam for shoe impressions. (With permission from Tritech Forensics.)

Bio-Foam is a compressible foam material allowing capturing and reproducing sole impressions as shown in Figure 3.15. Bio-Foam has a closed cell structure and moisture-proof preventing contamination and distortion. By simply pressing the known shoe into the foam, an impression with accurate detail of the shoe's soil is created. The Bio-Foam impression is like a mold and can be casted with dental stone in the same manner as described above.

3.2.2.3 Casting Tire Impression in Dirt and Sand

Tire impressions are cast in the same method and with the same material as shoe impressions. Always cast at least two to three feet of tire impression. Extreme temperature affects the drying time of the casting. During the summer, in extreme heat, it is recommended to make the solution thinner to achieve better detail in the casting.

In winter conditions of extreme cold, it is recommended to add a tablespoon of potassium sulfate to the mixtures of two cups of dental stone. The potassium sulfate helps to accelerate the curing process. In snow and ice, it is possible to freeze the cast and then thaw it in the laboratory.

3.2.2.4 Impression Lifted from a Tire

The basic method used to collect inked impressions from the sole of a shoe can also be applied to lift inked impressions from tires. It is not necessary to remove the tire from the vehicle. The CSI will perform the following steps:

1. Photograph the tire from different angles including the imprint on the outside of the tire and the tread pattern. Place a scale next to visible defects and take close-up photos. If necessary, add a small plastic arrow in a contrasting color pointing to the defect so it is easily identifiable in the image.
2. Material required:
   - Clean fabric rag
   - Piece of white chalk
   - WD40 spray or aerosolized oil
   - Piece of brown paper
3. Using the clean rag, remove any dirt and small rocks from the tire.
4. Using white chalk, place a white line on the tire to ensure you ink an entire tire rotation.
5. Apply a light coat of WD40 or any other aerosolized oil onto the tire, making sure to cover the entire tire.
6. Cut a long piece of butcher paper and lay on the floor in front of the tire. Ensure that the butcher paper is at least 8 ft long to ensure capture of the complete tire rotation.
7. Slowly, drive the vehicle over the paper. A second person should tell the driver when the marked line is on the butcher paper.
8. Repeat the process of spraying oil onto the reminder of the tire.
9. Slowly drive over the end of the butcher paper. A complete rotation of an inked tire impression has been captured. The imprint should be between 6 and 8 ft long depending on the size of the tire.
10. If too much oil distorts the impression, remove the access ink with a clean rag and drive over a new piece of butcher paper.
11. Using a magna brush, apply a thin layer of magnetic fingerprint powder to visualize the impression.
12. Let dry and add information such as
    - Case number
    - Date and time impression printed
    - Initial of the crime scene investigator
    - Describe the tire:
      - Right front/left front/right rear/left rear tire
      - Tire manufacturer
      - Tire size
      - Defects if visible

Another method to obtain an impression of a tire while on the vehicle is to apply a layer of black ink onto the tire instead of WD40 or aerosolized oil.

Caution: When using the ink method, ink will remain on the vehicle for quite a while and not only stain the floor of the Police Impoundment Bay but also leave marks on the owner's driveway and garage.

3.2.3 Identification of Shoe and Tire Impressions

The shoe or tire examiner has three options to identify and match a shoe or tire impression obtained from the crime scene:

- Search the Sole Mate database for sole impressions.
- Search the Threadmate database for tire impressions.
- Compare with a standard obtained from the suspect's shoes or from a suspected vehicle. For this comparison, an inked lift of the impression is necessary to compare the defects of the soles of the shoes or the wear pattern of the tires on the vehicle to the impressions found on scene.

3.3 Tool Mark Impressions

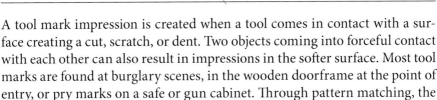

A tool mark impression is created when a tool comes in contact with a surface creating a cut, scratch, or dent. Two objects coming into forceful contact with each other can also result in impressions in the softer surface. Most tool marks are found at burglary scenes, in the wooden doorframe at the point of entry, or pry marks on a safe or gun cabinet. Through pattern matching, the visual comparative examination of the topographical features of two different tool marks, the height or depth, width, and curvature can be defined for one tool mark and be compared to other tool marks.

During the manufacturing process, random marks are placed on work pieces such as screwdriver blades and the surfaces of common tools. Tool wear and chemical erosion can also create distinguished marks. The size and the shape of the impression can identify the tool such as a hammer, a crowbar, chisel, or screwdriver. These tools can be identified by microscopic irregularities such as ridges and valleys created during the machining and finishing process (Forensic analysis of tool mark impressions, n.d.).

At the laboratory, the tool mark examiner uses a comparison microscope to compare the crime scene tool marks with the test impressions made with the suspected tool. That is why it is important to collect the tool mark bearing object and send it to the laboratory with the suspected tool.

Caution: Under no circumstances must the crime scene investigator attempt to fit the suspected tool into the tool mark. The contact between the tool and the marked surface may alter the impression.

Always obtain midrange and close-up photographs of the pry marks or tool impressions. Make sure to capture the location of the pry mark in regard to a fixture. Depending on the crime scene, using a ruler to show the distance from the floor or the ceiling to the pry mark may provide additional important information. Whenever possible, the entire object containing the tool impression, such as a doorframe or a window frame, should be cut out and collected.

The tool impression can be casted with a silicone-based putty material commercially known as Mikrosil.

Processing method. The CSI will perform the following steps to document and cast a tool mark impression:

1. Thoroughly photograph the tool impression with and without scale with medium range and close-up photographs.
2. Mikrosil silicone kit consists of hardener, mixing card, Mikrosil silicone, and mixing sticks. Using the wooden sticks, combine hardener and Mikrosil silicone on the mixing card.
3. Apply to the tool impression. The Mikrosil mixture will dry almost immediately into a rubbery consistence and can be removed.
4. The negative image of the tool impression is captured in the plastic mold.
5. Collect the mold as evidence and place in a small cardboard box to avoid additional scratching.

Mikrosil casting can also be performed on wounds of live and deceased victims to determine and match possible murder weapons. Mikrosil is available in different colors.

An alternative to Mikrosil is the Accutrans casting system, an extruder gun used to create casts of tool marks. Often, tool marks are small and applying Mikrosil with a spatula is not possible. The extruder gun dispenses a small amount of silicone directly on the tool mark upon pressing the trigger. Within a short time, the silicone dries creating a cast that can be removed and collected as evidence, as well as be compared to possible tools in the laboratory.

References

Cyanoacrylate (super glue) fuming (n.d.). Retrieved from http://www.personal.psu.edu/msp5018/blogs/english_202c/the-development-of-fingerprints-with-cyanoacrylate-super-glue-fuming.html.

Dadmun, M. (2015). Developing methods to improve the quality and efficiency of latent fingermark development by superglue fuming. Retrieved from https://www.ncjrs.gov/App/Search/SearchResults.aspx?txtKeywordSearch=dadmun&fromSearch=1.

Fish, J.T., Miller, L.S., Braswell, M.C., and Wallace Jr., E.W. (2015). *Crime Scene Investigation*. 3rd ed., Taylor & Francis, Boca Raton, FL.

Forensic analysis of tool mark impressions (n.d.). Retrieved from http://resource.rockyview.ab.ca/t4t/forensicscience35-5cr/Module09/L3/M9L3P02-ToolMarkImpressionEvidence.html.

Latent print development using iodine fuming (2012). Retrieved from http://www.csitechblog.com/2012/02/printips02-iodine-fuming-.html.

Mueller, R. (2012). Utilizing an electro static dust lifter to lift tire impressions of concrete driveways. Retrieved from http://www.swgtread.org/news/non-peer-reviewed/225-utilizing-an-electrostatic-dust-lifter-to-lift-tire-impressions-off-of-concrete-drive-ways.

Saferstein, R. (2015). *Criminalistics: An Introduction to Forensic Science*. 11th ed. Prentice Hall, Upper Saddle River, NJ.

Smith, K. and Kauffman, C. (2009). Enhancement of latent prints on metal surfaces. Retrieved from FDIAI News, Jan–March 2009, https://www.fdiai.org/resources/newsletter/.

Arriving at the Crime Scene

4

4.1 Introduction

No two crime scenes are alike. The crime scene investigator receives basic information during the initial notification from either the detective on scene or the communications supervisor and should mentally prepare him or herself before arriving on scene. This is mainly due to differences in environmental conditions, settings, the victim, and the condition of the crime itself. A homicide will require more equipment and specialized analysis than a burglary. Multiple victims or multiple crime scenes will require more crime scene personnel. Nonetheless, the basic process and procedures of investigating any crime scene such as documenting, photographing, developing, measuring, sketching, collecting, and preserving evidence will always be the same.

4.1.1 The First Responder

Commonly, the first responders are police, firefighters, and emergency medical personnel responding to the emergency call. Upon arrival, the police officer will determine if a crime has been committed. Even before the officer can perform lifesaving measures, he or she will conduct a protective sweep of the scene to ensure that the area is safe, that the suspect is not lurking around or hiding.

4.1.1.1 Officer Safety

The police officer will evaluate the scene to ensure it is safe from biohazardous dangers such as chemical spills or structural dangers at fire scenes. The presence of a suspect on scene creates a danger for every first responding officer. Securing the scene includes searching the premises to ensure that the offender is not hiding in the attic, the trunk of a vehicle, in a closet, or in the basement. Officers find themselves in dangerous encounters with possible suspects, for example, a woman covered in blood approaching from a spare bedroom at a domestic assault. The officer has to control the woman while figuring out the scenario. The woman may be later identified as a witness or victim rather than the perpetrator. However, the officer should never take a situation for granted and the safety for all parties is of the utmost importance.

Another important aspect of scene security is that criminals might leave loaded firearms, biohazards, or chemical hazards behind.

Important: The three main safety considerations of the first responding officer are

- Is the crime in progress and is the offender on scene?
- Are there natural hazards that inhibit danger for first responders?
- Are there man-made hazards that could endanger the first responders?

Burglar in the Attic

In the summer months in a rural community in Florida, a crime scene investigator was called to the scene of a burglary of a single-family home. The patrol officer searched and secured the scene. Upon arrival, the CSI met with the patrol officer who briefed the CSI about the specifics of the scene during the walk-through of the home. The patrol officer returned to his patrol vehicle parked on the road in front of the residence to type the incident report. While taking overall photographs of the scene, the CSI heard some noise coming from the ceiling in the living room. He left the residence and notified the patrol officer. The CSI, who was also an auxiliary certified deputy sheriff, and the patrol officer searched each room in the residence and found the attic entrance. The deputy entered the attic and found the burglar hiding in the attic.

This scenario shows the importance of searching and securing the scene to ensure that the offender is not present on scene.

4.1.1.2 Securing the Scene

As soon as possible, the officer will exclude all unauthorized personnel from the scene. Homicide scenes can attract large crowds of onlookers, neighbors, and the press, requiring additional officers to maintain scene security. It is extremely important to limit the access to the scene to avoid contamination.

4.1.1.3 Crime Scene Contamination

Crime scene contamination is based on the Locard principle that every time when two objects come into contact, there is a transfer. Every person walking into a scene deposits trace evidence from the sole of the shoes, as well as removes trace evidence when leaving the scene. Commonly, homicide scenes attract detectives from other than homicide units as well as patrol officers who "want to see the scene." It is the first officer's duty to ensure that the crime scene remains in its original stage. To properly control access to the crime scene, the officer assigned to maintain scene security must have proper authority to exclude fellow police officers, and even higher-ranking officers and supervisors, who have no business inside the scene.

Lack of controlling the access to a crime scene allows loss of the opportunity to collect valuable evidentiary materials and allows for valuable evidentiary material to become contaminated, thus rendering them invalid for testing.

Curious Officer

In a small town in Southwest Florida, a man had been found beaten to death in his single family home. Inside the residence, the floor in the living room was saturated in blood and bloody shoe impressions and other trace evidence was visible. While the CSI team documented and photographed the scene, a district sergeant knocked on the door requesting to enter the scene. The CSI asked in a friendly tone, "Sir, what is the reason that you need to come inside the scene?" The officer answered, " I just want to see the scene." The CSI refused stating, "Sir, we have bloody shoe impressions on the floor and cannot let you come inside as your entry would contaminate the scene and we may lose important evidence." The officer's complaint to his supervisor that the civilian CSI's refused entry to the inner perimeter of the scene resulted in a verbal warning for the officer as the CSI did as he was supposed to in following department policy and minimizing the contamination of the scene. The officer should have known better based on his training in law enforcement; however, sometimes curiosity can override common sense.

4.1.1.4 Setting the Inner and Outer Perimeter

Every crime scene contains an outer and inner perimeter. The inner perimeter is the immediate area where the crime occurred. For example, a body is found in the living room of a residence. The inner perimeter would be the living room. The outer perimeter would be the borders of the entire property. Upon arrival on scene, the focal point of the officer is the body lying in the kitchen, spent casings in the driveway, or broken windows at the convenience store.

The officer cordons off the premises in proper proportion using yellow barrier tape "Crime Scene—Do Not Cross," as illustrated in Figure 4.1. The boundaries of the scene should include the area where the crime occurred and exit and entry paths as well as any areas where evidence could have been discarded. Securing a larger area versus a smaller area is

Figure 4.1 Crime scene secured with yellow barrier tape.

recommended as any evidence outside the boundaries might be destroyed. Any unauthorized person will be asked to leave the cordoned off area. The patrol officer will note the names and contact information of witnesses and transmit this information to the lead investigator. The officer will also take notes of any fixtures that have been moved during securing the scene or rendering first aid to the victim. A victim may be trapped under a fallen chair or table or the officer has to break a window to get entry to the residence. The front door was locked or unlocked, the lights were on, and ceiling fans were on are circumstances that may become important later in the investigation.

4.1.1.5 Crime Scene Log

The officer will initiate a crime scene log listing the time, name, agency, and reason for any person crossing the barrier tape entering the crime scene, as illustrated in Document 4.1. The patrol officer securing the scene will maintain the scene log. The log is maintained until all personnel clear from the scene and the property is released to the owner, as shown in Document 4.1. A copy of the crime scene log should be filed with the case folder and a copy with the crime scene report. The prosecutor and defense attorney may review the crime scene log to determine who entered the scene and can request a written statement from every person inside the crime scene.

Crime Scene Entry Log

All personnel entering the crime scene must sign this sheet.

Agency Case number ....

Date...

Scene location..

....

Scene Security Officer.........................……..…...**Badge #**...........................

Rank/Name	ID #	Agency	Time In	Time Out	Deputy ID logging entry	Reason for Entry	Statement Obtain Y/N
Smith, R.		EMS	14:15	14:45		First Aid to Victim	
CSI Jones, D.		Metro Dade Police	14:18	14:35		CSI Investigation	
CSI Hall, B.		Metro Dade Police	15.05			CSI Investigation	

Date/Time scene released..........................**to**...

Document 4.1 Crime scene log.

4.1.2 The Initial Call for the CSI

The crime scene investigation begins with the notification call from the communication supervisor, crime scene manager, or major crimes detective. The call out procedures may vary from agency to agency. Most agencies maintain rotating on-call schedules. The CSI will note the date, time, name of the person making the initial call, location of the scene, and any preliminary information. A field note package assists in the note taking (see field note packages in Document 4.2). Most on-call CSI personnel have access to an assigned crime scene vehicle, either at the police station or as a take-home vehicle. The CSI is responsible for the maintenance of the vehicle and making sure that all basic forensic equipment is available at all times. Weekly inspections of supplies such as fingerprint powder, fingerprint cards, cotton swabs and other disposable material are recommended. Crime scene managers should perform monthly inspections of assigned crime scene vehicles to ensure the constant readiness.

4.1.3 Arriving on Scene

Upon arrival on scene, the CSI will observe the premises of the crime scene identified with yellow barrier tape, cones, or police officers positioned for additional scene security. In addition, a common entryway should be established to prevent personnel from entering or leaving a scene while trampling on uncollected evidence.

The crime scene vehicle should be parked in an area outside the yellow crime scene tape ensuring not to block the entryway for additional emergency personnel. The CSI talks to the officer securing the scene and signs in on the crime scene log. The CSI asks the first responder if a search warrant is necessary to ensure that legal entry to the scene is permitted.

Caution: At no time should the CSI enter the crime scene on her or his own without a walk-through of scene with the first responder or detective.

Note taking is a continuous effort during the entire crime scene investigation.

4.1.4 Legalities for Entering the Crime Scene

Entering the crime scene legally will determine if the collected evidence is admissible in trial. Illegally collected evidence is called the fruit of the poisonous tree.

The fruit of the poisonous tree is an extension of the exclusionary rule established in *Silverthorne Lumber Co. v. United States*, 251 U.S. 385 (1920). This doctrine holds that evidence gathered with the assistance of illegally obtained information must be excluded from trial.

4.1.4.1 Legal Searches and the Fourth Amendment

The Fourth Amendment to the Constitution of the United States reads:

Crime Scene Investigation
FIELD NOTES
PROPERTY CRIMES

CASE NUMBER ....

DATE...

CRIME..

TIME NOTIFIED.............................BY..

LOCATION OF CRIME SCENE..

....

CRIME SCENE INVESTIGATOR...

LEAD DETECTIVE...

FIRST OFFICER ON SCENE..

WALK-THROUGH GIVEN BY..

VICTIM

NAME..

ADDRESS..

DATE OF BIRTH...................GENDER:.....MALE.....FEMALE....................

DESCRIPTION OF THE BUILDING

STORIES......................DUPLEX............SINGLE FAMILY HOME............

BUSINESS............................CHURCH...

BLDG FACES...........NORTH.........EAST..........SOUTH.............WEST.....

ROOF:.....SHINGLES.....................TILES...

COLOR OF EXTERIOR....................................TRIM...........................

PHOTOGRAPHY

CAMERA.....................................STORAGE MEDIA..............................

TOTAL PHOTOS TAKEN...

SKETCH

NUMBER OF SKETCHES...

SKETCHED ON ....BY..

PROCESSING METHODS

FINGERPRINTS.............................DNA SWABS.....................................

TIRE IMPRESSION....................SHOE IMPRESSIONS...............................

NUMBER OF FINGERPRINTS LIFTS...

NUMBER OF DNA SWABS..

NUMBER OF TIRE IMPRESSION CASTS..

NUMBER OF SHOE IMPRESSION CASTS...

AREAS EVIDENCE RECOVERED FROM..

....

....

....

Document 4.2 Crime scene field note packages. (*Continued*)

MEASUREMENTS

MARKER	ITEM DESCRIPTION	POINT A	POINT B	POINT C	POINT D

POINT A ………………………..

POINT B ………………………..

POINT C………………………...

POINT D………………………...

POINT A TO B…………………..

POINT…………………………..

POINT…………………………..

POINT…………………………..

EVIDENCE COLLECTED

ITEM NUMBER	PACKAGED IN	ITEM DESCRIPTION	LOCATION RECOVERED FROM

SCENE CLEARED

DATE……………………………TIME……………………………………...…………..

EVIDENCE TRANSPORTED BY…………………………………………………..

DATE……………………………TIME…………………………………..

Document 4.2 (Continued) Crime scene field note packages.

The right of the people to be secure in their persons, houses, papers, and effects against unreasonable searches and seizures, shall not be violated, and no warrants shall issue, but upon probable cause, supported by oath or affirmation and particularly describing the place to be searched, and the person or things to be seized. (Orthmann and Hess, 2013, p. 96)

What does this mean for the crime scene investigator? To conduct a legal search, the crime scene investigator has to be aware and follow the legal requirements for searches, the areas and property to be searched, and the items to be collected based on the elements of the crime being investigated to be able to perform an organized, systematic, and thorough search of the premises. Searches should be narrow as general searches are unconstitutional. No illegally obtained evidence will be admissible in court based on the exclusionary rule. "The exclusionary rule established that courts may not accept evidence obtained by unreasonable search and seizure, regardless of its relevance for a case" (Orthmann and Hess, 2013, p. 96). The case *Weeks v. United States* in 1914 made the exclusionary rule valid in federal courts and *Mapp v. Ohio* in 1961 resulted in the adaptation in all courts. The exclusionary rule does not only apply to illegally seized evidence but also to any evidence obtained from illegally seized evidence, also called the fruit of the poisonous tree. For example, if an officer searches a vehicle illegally and finds a bag with cocaine, the cocaine would be the fruit of the poisonous tree as the search of the vehicle was not legal.

Wong v. United States

In the *Wong v. United States* case, the prosecution presented drugs into evidence against the defendant (371 US 471) (1963). The defendant had made a statement during arrest leading federal officers to a witness who had knowledge about drug deals. The Supreme Court ruled that the officer's discovery was a result of an illegal arrest and the fruit of the poisonous tree. The ruling did not only include the statement itself, but also the witness information and the actual drugs to which the witness had led them.

4.1.4.2 *Justification of Reasonable Searches*

The courts have provided guidelines for law enforcement personnel to ensure that the searches and seizures are reasonable and legal. For a search to be legal, the following conditions have to be met:

- A search warrant has been issued and signed by a judge.
- Consent in verbal or written form is given.
- The search is supplementary to a lawful arrest.

- A medical or other emergency exists.
- An officer's safety is at issue; for example, an officer stops a suspicious person and has reason to believe that the person is armed.
- The exception of the good faith doctrine stating that illegally obtained evidence is admissible in court if the officer was not aware that he was violating the suspect's Fourth Amendment rights.

4.1.4.3 The Search Warrant

A search warrant is always required to search the suspect's property including but not limited to a residence, vehicle, boat, plane, or any other property. The criminal investigator will appear before a judge and show probable cause that the location to be searched contains evidence pertaining to a crime. Probable cause is less than proof but more than a mere suspicion. A search warrant consists of the actual warrant and the affidavit.

The search warrant must contain the following information, as illustrated in the sample warrant in Documents 4.3 and 4.4:

- Reasons for the warrant
- The physical address of the location to be searched such as 1234 Main Street in Kings Town, AL
- The name of the owner of the property or renter, which can also be the suspect

4.1.4.3.1 Serving a Warrant   A search warrant has to be served by a certified law enforcement officer. Serving a warrant includes the officer reading the warrant out loud to either the person or the location to be served. The officer serving the warrant has to ensure that the description of the premises matches the description in the warrant. If there are any discrepancies, the warrant is invalid and the officer has to apply for a new warrant. The date, time, and name of the officer will be noted on the warrant. The officer will read the warrant to the person or to the property, for example, the police officer has to read the warrant to a vehicle. I know it sounds ridiculous, however, the law requires to read and serve the warrant. Serving a warrant should occur between 7 to 10 days after the judge signed it. A warrant should be served between the hours of 6:00 am and 9:00 pm. After the search is concluded and the physical evidence is collected, the officer will return the warrant accompanied with a detailed listing of all seized items to the issuing judge. At that point, the warrant is completed. If new witness or suspect statements result in the request for another search of the same premises, the investigator has to return to the judge to get a second warrant. The first warrant has been satisfied and is no longer valid for legally entering the premises.

**IN THE CIRCUIT COURT OF THE TWENTIETH JUDICIAL CIRCUIT IN AND
FOR HENDRY COUNTY, FLORIDA**

STATE OF FLORIDA
COUNTY OF Beach
AFFIDAVIT FOR SEARCH WARRANT

IN THE NAME OF THE STATE OF FLORIDA

BEFORE ME,..........................., Judge in and for Beach County, Florida,
personally appeared [Officers/Investigator's name], a sworn law enforcement officer for the
Beach County Sheriff's Office, Beach County, Florida, who being by me first duly sworn, on
oath, deposes and says that he has probable cause to believe and does believe that in or upon
Beach County, Florida, more particularly described as Island Coast Road, Beachtown, that the
laws of the State of Florida are currently being violated, to-wit:

F.S.S. 812.02 (4) Burglary of Conveyance
F.S.S. 812.014   Grand Theft

The evidence connected with this crime is currently secured/located within vehicle
registered to JOHN DOE (DOB 12/24/1985). Described as a 2006, white in color Ford F 250
Pickup truck, bearing a Florida license plate NAS 18, and a Vehicle Identification Number
(VIN) F120K5432893BTC2 , currently stored at the Sheriff's Office Impoundment Bay.

The following grounds for issuance of a Search Warrant, as required in Florida Statutes
Chapter 812 exists to wit: Burglary of a Conveyance and Grand Theft and that the following
property and/or evidence from reported burglary will be found inside the vehicle and/or
components with the vehicle, matching the documentation of the stolen items as declared by
the victim to Deputies of the Sheriff's Office.

That the facts tending to establish the grounds for this application and the probable
cause of your Affiant to believe that such facts exist are as follows:

Your affiant has probable cause to believe that the above named crime has been
committed and that the aforesaid property may be found inside the 2006, white in color Ford
F250 Pickup truck, bearing a Florida license plate NAS 18, and a Vehicle Identification Number
(VIN) F120K5432893BTC2, registered to John Doe, (DOB 12/24/1985) which is located at the
Sheriff's Office Impoundment Bay at 2345 Main Street in Beachtown, Florida.

On March 5, 2015, Detective James Watts responded to a reported past occurred
armed occupied burglary at 845 Island Coast Road in Beachtown, Florida. The ensuing
investigation revealed the following material facts:

1. On 3/4/2015, at approximately 02.15 hrs., Deputy Small, while patrolling the beach area
   in Beachtown, Florida, was dispatched to 845 Island Coast Road, in reference to a
   possible burglary in progress involving two armed suspects with knives.
   Communications dispatched the description of the suspects as having black hooded
   sweatshirts and black sweat pants, last seen heading southbound in Island Coast Road.

2. Deputy John Miles located two suspects matching the description of the suspected
   walking near the corner of Main Street and Market Street. This location is about 1 mile
   from the victims' home and the suspects had been discovered within 3 minutes from the
   incident occurring.

3. Both suspects identified themselves to Deputy Miles as James Black (DOB 4/5/1995)
   and John Doe (DOB 12/24/1985). Due to the call that the suspects are carrying knives,
   the officer pat down the suspects and discovered a knife on each suspect. James had a
   black folding knife with an approximately 6-inch blade in his left front pocket. John
   carried a silver double blade knife, about 6-inches in length in his right rear pocket.

Document 4.3 Affidavit.   *(Continued)*

4. Deputy Bill Warden assisted in a canvass of the area, where the suspects were encountered, revealed a one-gallon jug with loose US Currency, a pair of sneakers in a black plastic bag, a screwdriver and a flashlight.

5. Deputy Warden contacted the victim Mr. Jack Bauer and transported the victim to the location of the suspects. Mr. Bauer identified the suspects as the two who committed burglary to his residence and threatened him with a knife. Bauer stated to Deputy Warden that the two subjects were definitely the same people involved in the burglary at his residence. Suspects Black and Doe were both read Miranda rights and both agreed to speak with law enforcement. Both subjects stated that they did not know about the burglary and were just walking down to the beach. Mr. Bauer identified the property, (jug of money) as his property. Bauer also stated that the shoes Doe is wearing were his property as well.

6. Detective James Watts met with the victim, Mr. Bauer at the Sheriff's Office and obtained a sworn taped statement of the crime and his positive identification of the arrestees, as well as the identification of the property stolen from his residence.

7. Detective James Watts conducted a post-Miranda digitally taped statement of suspect John Doe. John Doe gave a full confession stating that he and Black burglarized Mr. Bauer's residence and vehicle and threatened Mr. Bauer, while armed, with bodily harm while armed with a knife. Doe stated that Black and him committed the crime as they desperately needed money. Doe stated that he did not want to make any more statements. Doe stated that his vehicle, a 2006 white in color Ford F250 pickup truck bearing a Florida license plate NAS 18, and a Vehicle Identification Number (VIN) F120K5432893BTC2 and James Black's 2005, blue in color Kia Sorrento, bearing the Florida license plate CRI ME2 and VIN K453CVT8475063K4, were parked at beach access number 4 along Island Coast Road.

8. In the meantime, Deputy Buchmann and Deputy Trout responded to the beach access and found Black's and Doe's vehicles in the parking lot. Deputy Buchmann saw a person, later identified as Jason Phillips (DOB 07/24/1986), standing by Black's vehicle and saw him crouching next to the vehicle when the Deputies approached. Deputies searched the area and Phillips was arrested for narcotics.
Deputy Buchmann looked inside Doe's vehicle and noticed several items that had been reported in previous burglaries along Island Coast Road. Deputy Buchmann contacted the victims and asked them to respond to the location of Black's vehicle. All victims made a positive identification of their property stolen from their vehicles while parked at their residence, as seen inside of Black's vehicle. Detective Watts requested both vehicles to be secured and towed the vehicle to the Sheriff's Office Impoundment area.

9. Mr. James Monroe, a victim of a vehicle burglary, stated that a .40 caliber silver and black Taurus handgun was stolen form his vehicle in the early morning hours of March 4, 2015. During a sworn post-Miranda statement, Jason Phillips stated that he had seen a handgun in the possession of Black and Doe that they just had stolen.

Document 4.3 (Continued) Affidavit.   *(Continued)*

As a result of the investigations, Detective Watts believes that Black and Doe committed the crimes of burglary and grand theft on Island Coast Road in Beachtown, Florida. This is evidenced in the belief/acknowledgement that the stolen items were recovered from inside Black's vehicle and Doe's vehicles. Both vehicles are located at the Sheriff's Office Impoundment Bay at 2345 Main Street in Beachtown, Florida.

ITEMS TO BE SEARCHED FOR:

The search is to include the above-described vehicle and all of its compartments. The probable cause being alleged and found that there is now being kept on said premise evidence which will link one person or person unknown to the crime of Burglary and Grand Theft. The evidence to be in the vehicle is to include but limited to

- .40 caliber Silver/black Taurus handgun
- United States coins
- Magnum flash light
- CD cases
- Sunglass cases
- Cellular phone
- Garmin GPS

10. **WHEREFORE,** your Affiant prays that a Search Warrant be issued according to the laws, commanding that the Sheriff of Hendry County, Florida, his Deputies and any other law enforcement officer in the State of Florida whom you direct, with such proper and necessary assistance, in the daytime or in the nighttime or on Sunday, as exigencies of the occasion may demand or require, to enter and search the aforesaid 2006, white in color Ford F 250 Pickup truck, bearing a Florida license plate NAS 18, and a Vehicle Identification Number (VIN) F120K5432893BTC2 and connected with the items being stolen from the victims' vehicles as described within this Search Warrant and any outbuildings and/or curtilage, as outlined in Florida State Statutes, and if the same or any part thereof be found, authorize the seizure and securing as evidence to be used in the prosecution of such person or persons unlawfully committing and/or possessing, or using the same in the violation of the laws of the State of Florida.

_____

[James Watts]
[Detective Sergeant]
Beach County Sheriff's Office

The foregoing instrument was acknowledged before me this **6th** day of March 2015, by [Name of Affiant] who is personally known to me and did take an oath.

_____

[Judge's Name]
County Judge
Twentieth Judicial Circuit for the State of Florida

Document 4.3 (Continued) Affidavit.

IN THE CIRCUIT COURT OF THE ....**JUDICIAL CIRCUIT IN AND FOR** ....**COUNTY, FLORIDA**

STATE OF FLORIDA
COUNTY OF ....

SEARCH WARRANT

IN THE NAME OF THE STATE OF FLORIDA

TO: The Sheriff/Police Chief of................., his Deputies/Officers , or any other law enforcement officer in the State of Florida whom you direct.

WHEREAS, complaint on oath and in writing, supported by Affidavit having been made before me by, Detective Joe Warrant, ID 2007 of the ....Sheriff's Office.

AND WHEREAS, said facts made known to me have caused me to certify and find that there is probable cause to believe certain laws have been and are being violated within

that the laws of the State of Florida are currently being violated, to-wit:
   F.S.S. 812.02 (4) Burglary of Conveyance
   F.S.S. 812.014   Grand Theft

The 2006 White Ford F 250 pickup truck, 2 door, King cab with an 8-feet extended truck bed bearing the Florida license plate NAS 18, Vehicle Identification number (VIN) F120K5432893BTC3, registered to John Doe, (DOB 12/24/1985) to be searched is currently secured/located at which is located at the Sheriff's Office Impoundment Bay at 2345 Main Street in Beach Town, Florida.

To reach the above described 2006 White Ford F 250 pickup truck, 2 door, King cab with an 8-feet extended truck bed bearing the Florida license plate NAS 18, Vehicle Identification number (VIN) F120K5432893BTC3, registered to John Doe, (DOB 12/24/1985) begin take exit 154 on Interstate 95 Southbound. Turn right on Fellow Land and continue to the intersection of Beach Plaza Blvd. Turn right on Beach Plaza Blvd and after 1.4 miles, turn left on Main Street. The Sheriff's Office Impoundment Bay is on the north side of the road. The above described 2006 White Ford F 250 pickup truck, 2 door, King cab with an 8-feet extended truck bed bearing the Florida license plate NAS 18, Vehicle Identification number (VIN) F120K5432893BTC3, had been in the control and custody of the evidence custodian employed with the Beach County Sheriff's Office, responsible for the chain of custody of vehicles in the Impoundment Bay.

And there is now being kept in the said Beach County Sheriff's Office Impoundment Bay at 2345 Main Street, Beach Town, Fl.
   The evidence believed to be within this vehicle is to include, but not limited to
   - Any container with loose US currency
   - Any music or video CDs and DVDs
   - Any firearm and ammunition
   - Any narcotics and paraphernalia
   - Any and all evidence connected to the listed crimes.
all of which is being kept and/or used in violation of the laws of the State of Florida to-wit:

   F.S.S. 812.02 (4) Burglary of Conveyance
   F.S.S. 812.014   Grand Theft

Document 4.4 Search warrant.   *(Continued)*

NOW THEREFORE, you are commanded with such proper and necessary assistance as may be necessary, in the daytime or in the nighttime or on Sunday, as exigencies of the occasion may demand or require, to enter and search the aforesaid 2006 White Ford F 250 pickup truck, 2 door, King cab with an 8-feet extended truck bed bearing the Florida license plate NAS 18, Vehicle Identification number (VIN) F120K5432893BTC3, connected with [Who the item belongs to or the location is controlled by registered to John Doe, (DOB 12/24/1985, currently impounded at the Beach County Sheriff's Office at 2345 Main Street in Beach Town, Fl, as described within this Search Warrant; as outlined in Florida State Statutes, and if the same or any part thereof be found, you are hereby authorized to seize and secure the same, given proper receipt thereof and delivering a duplicate copy of this Search Warrant to the person in charge of the property or in the absence of any such person, leaving a duplicate copy within said 2006 White Ford F 250 pickup truck, 2 door, King cab with an 8-feet extended truck bed bearing the Florida license plate NAS 18, Vehicle Identification number (VIN) F120K5432893BTC3 What is to be searched, and making a return of your doing under this Search Warrant within ten (10) days of the date hereof, and you are fully directed to bring said property so found and also the bodies of the persons in possession thereof before the Court that has jurisdiction of this offense to be disposed of according to law.

WITNESS my hand and seal this _____ day of _____, 20_____.

_____
[Judge's Name]
County Judge
.......................Judicial Circuit for the State of Florida

SW[Case Number]

Document 4.4 (Continued) Search warrant.

4.1.4.3.2 Serving the Warrant on a Vehicle The officer who serves the warrant compares the vehicle identification number (VIN) and license plate number of the vehicle to ensure the numbers match the search warrant. If the numbers do not match, the warrant cannot be served and the officer has to return to the judge to either apply for a new warrant or the judge might initial the changes in the existing warrant. Another interesting point is that the officer who requests the warrant does not have to be the same officer serving the warrant. For example, the criminal investigator might write the warrant and present it to the judge and the certified law enforcement crime scene investigator might serve the warrant.

4.1.4.3.3 Body Search Warrant In many violent crimes and sexual assault cases, physical evidence in the form of hairs, and body fluids such as semen, saliva, and blood are found on the victim. This evidence can place the suspect at the crime scene. If the suspect refuses to voluntarily provide a buccal swab for a DNA sample, a blood or hair sample, then the investigator can request a body search warrant from the judge. The requirements for the body search warrant are identical to the search warrant for any kind of property or premises. The judge will include the physical evidence to be collected such as

- Head hair
- Pubic hair
- Blood sample
- Saliva sample, also called buccal swab

The body search warrant will be read and served by a certified law enforcement officer; however, the physical evidence collection will be performed by a forensic nurse. The crime scene investigator is present and will take custody of the evidence that will be signed over on an evidence sheet from the nurse to the crime scene investigator. A missing link in the chain of custody will result in the inadmissibility of evidence. As with the general search warrant, a listing of the physical evidence collected will be returned to the judge within 7 to 10 days.

4.1.4.4 Searches with Consent

The police officer can search a property without a search warrant if the actual property owner gives consent to a search. This consent can be verbal or in written form, as illustrated in Document 4.5. Many law enforcement agencies require written consent with a signature to avoid possible legal issues that might arise at a later time. A third party can only give valid consent to government officials, if he or she has common authority over the premises, for example,

- Parent/child. A parent can give consent to search a child's room if the parents own the premises and the child lives at the premises.
- Employer/employee. The employer can only give consent to search for the employer's premises and areas used by the employee such as a desk or a locker room.
- Host/guest. A host can only give consent if he or she is the primary occupant of the premises for the area used by the guest.
- Spouses. If two people, such as a husband and wife, share the premises, either one can give consent to search.
- People living together can only give consent to the area that they occupy but not the private space of each other (Orthmann and Hess, 2013). Thus, the head of a condo association could not grant access to a unit within the complex.

The condo is rented long term by the owners, whereas a hotel room is a short-term rental. The manager or owner of a hotel can provide consent for search for a hotel room. However, depending on the state statutes and the crime committed, a search warrant may be required. For example, in a homicide investigation, if the suspect rented a hotel room and there is a mere

---

Your agency name here

WAIVERS / CONSENT   Complaint Number:

1. Type of Incident:

☐ Assault   ☐ Criminal Mischief   ☐ Other:
☐ Battery   ☐ Missing Person
☐ Misdemeanor   ☐ Felony   ☐ Burglary   ☐ Theft

2. Complainant/Victim/Owner/Subject:

I, (Name):_____ the undersigned,

☐ **CONSENT TO BE INTERVIEWED**   PERSON INTERVIEWED/INITIALS: [   ]

...hereby consent to being interviewed by the below listed Police/Sheriff's Office Official concerning the above shown Incident/Offense and I further understand that:

  I have the right to remain silent.
  Anything that I say can be used against me in court.
  I have the right to talk to a lawyer for advice before I am asked any questions and to have that lawyer with me during questioning.
  If I cannot afford a lawyer, one will be appointed for me before any questioning.
  If I decide to answer questions now without a lawyer present, I will still have the right to stop answering at any time. I also have the right to stop answering at any time until I talk to a lawyer.
  I understand each of my Constitutional Rights per Miranda.
  I have not previously requested any Law Enforcement Officer to allow me to speak to a lawyer.
  With these rights as stated above and by affixing my initials above and signature below, I now wish to make a voluntary statement and/or answer any questions asked me by any Official of the Sheriff's Office/Police Department.

☐ **CONSENT TO SEARCH/WAIVER OF SEARCH WARRANT**   OWNER/CUSTODIAN'S INITIALS: [   ]

...hereby give my full consent to Officials of Sheriff's Office/Police Department to search my:

☐ Residence   ☐ Vehicle/Vessel/Aircraft   ☐ Other: _____

further described as: _____

This consent extends throughout the main building, any enclosures and/or outhouses found on the property, and/or closed articles/packages. I further agree that anything or any article that may be found in this search, may be used at trial in any manner of which I may stand accused. I fully understand my Constitutional Rights in addition to giving this consent. I give this consent freely and voluntarily without compulsion, threat or coercion.

I have voluntarily signed this form as initialed above, on this _____ day of _____, at _____ .

Subject: _____   Witness: _____

Deputy Last Name/ID# (Printed): _____   Signature: _____

SIGNATURES

Document 4.5 Consent to search.

suspicion that the murder weapon is in the hotel room, the detective should obtain a search warrant to ensure that the evidence cannot be suppressed in trial. When in doubt, obtain a search warrant.

4.1.4.5 Exigent Circumstances

Exigent circumstances allow for the warrantless search without a lawful arrest or consent only in emergencies when probable cause exists and the search must be conducted immediately; for example, if police officers hear shots are fired and a person is screaming. In a crime scene investigation, exigent circumstances exist when physical evidence such as a tire track or blood can be destroyed due to environmental circumstances such as rain, flood, or snow. However, only the evidence in jeopardy can be collected and a warrant is required for additional searches. For example, weather can play a role in the summer in Florida where strong thunderstorms approach every afternoon.

Homicide in Bonita Springs, Florida

In Bonita Springs, Florida, a Hispanic man lived in a homemade shelter made out of cardboard boxes and plywood in the backyard of his son's nursery. He refused to move into his son's house and preferred to live outside. His friend, a homeless man, used to visit him and they would drink beer and talk. In August 2009, the two men were sitting in the backyard drinking beer. Suddenly, an argument broke out over the last bottle of beer. The argument turned into a physical confrontation and the Hispanic male stabbed his homeless guest who died on the way to the hospital. As the crime occurred on the property owned by the suspect's son and he lived at the premises, he had a legal standing at the property and a search warrant was necessary to legally enter the crime scene. The crime scene consisted of a small area where the two men had been sitting on white plastic chairs drinking beer. A pool of blood was in the dirt between the chairs. A sample of that blood would be important for further investigation. The detective wrote a search warrant request for the crime scene and was on the way to the courthouse for the judge's approval and signature when a thunderstorm was rapidly approaching the scene. Time-wise, it was impossible for the detective to return to the scene to serve the warrant before the thunderstorm. Due to the approaching storm, the crime scene investigator was allowed to apply the exigent circumstance rule and enter the crime scene and collect a blood sample that otherwise would have been washed away by the rain. The blood sample was legally obtained; however, the crime scene investigator had to leave the scene and wait until the search warrant was served to proceed with the full documentation and processing of the scene.

4.1.5 Walk-Through of the Scene

One of the best ways to learn about the specifics of an incident is to take notes during the initial walk-through. The first responder will point out which items had been moved during rendering first aid or securing a loaded firearm. The officer will provide information about his observations when he arrived on scene including smells, open doors, windows, and vehicles parked on the street or statements from eyewitnesses. The walk-through of the scene is a survey and the first orientation of the scene by the CSI. During the walk-through, the CSI will mentally begin to develop a hypothesis that can be changed during the course of the investigation. This is the time when the CSI has to determine if there is any physical evidence that needs immediate processing or protection. At outdoor scenes, always be aware of the weather conditions. Be aware of any alterations at the scene. The CSI will establish the perpetrator's path of entry and exit, the path through the crime scene, and observe and evaluate physical evidence present to develop a strategy for a methodical and thorough crime scene investigation. At this time, the CSI will determine if additional personnel are required for the investigation of the scene of the crime and notify the supervisor.

4.1.6 Crime Scene Process

Several procedures take place at a crime scene. Depending on the circumstances of the scene, all or only some procedures are required. For example, not every crime scene consists of bloodstain patterns, shoe impressions, or shots fired and does not require additional processing and analysis.

4.1.6.1 Steps of a Typical Crime Scene Investigation
Table 4.1 shows the steps of basic crime scene investigation from the detection of the crime to the crime scene reconstruction.

4.2 Documenting the Scene

Documenting a crime scene is performed through notes, photographs, video, and sketches. The note taking is a continuous effort throughout the entire investigation. After the investigation is concluded, the notes will be transferred into a crime scene report. The handwritten notes will be placed in the crime scene case folder. The handwritten notes should not be destroyed.

Important: The note taking begins with the initial notification.

- Upon arrival on scene
  - Note the time of arrival
  - Personnel present on scene
  - Names of lead detective and lead crime scene investigator
  - If necessary, mode of transportation such as CSI vehicle, boat, or helicopter
- Search warrant requirement
  - Who served the warrant
  - Date and time when warrant was served

Table 4.1 Sequence of Crime Scene Investigations

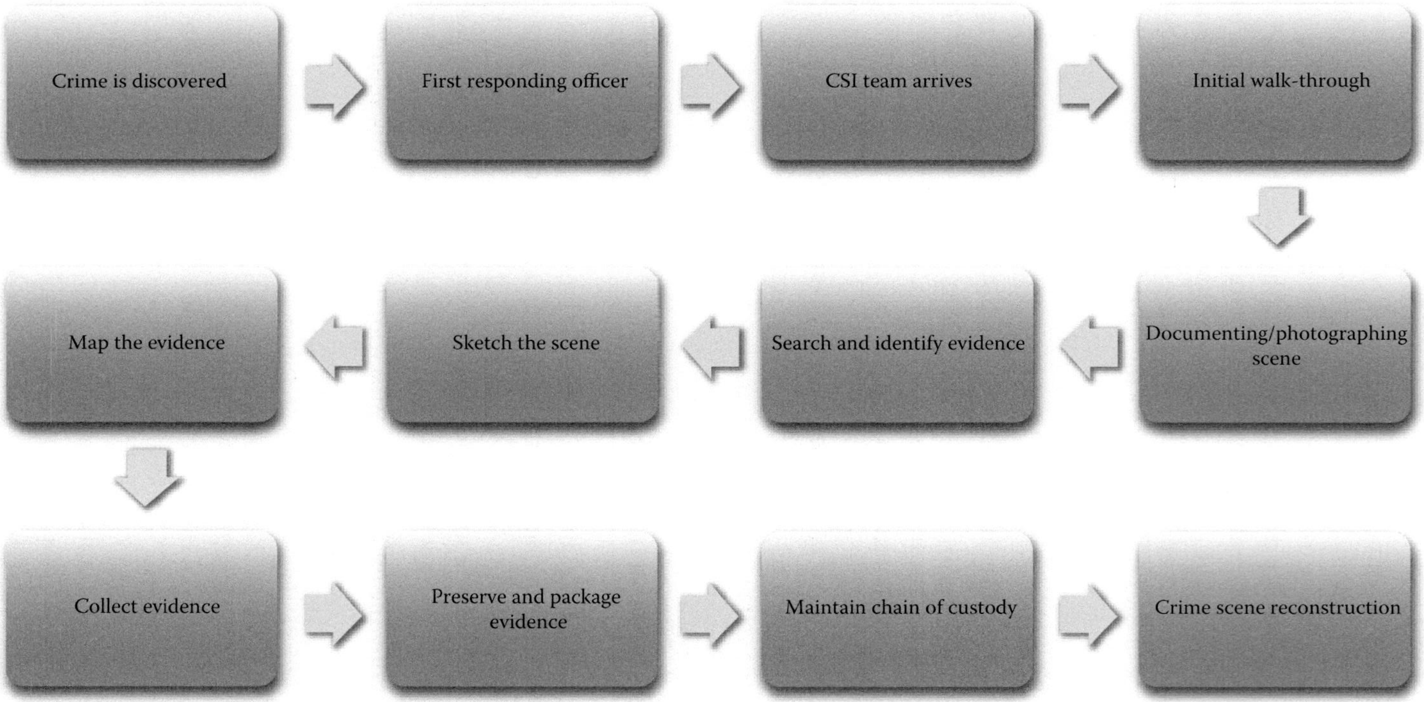

- Name of officer who conducted briefing and walk-through of scene
- Weather conditions
- Lighting conditions
- Scene description including
  - Location: city, rural, suburbs
  - Structure: private residence, apartment, business, church, school, warehouse
  - Description of the structure
    – Stories
    – Wood frame, mobile home, concrete block
    – Roof: tiled roof, shingles
    – Color and trim
    – Entrance faces north, south, east, west
    – Carport, garage
    – Window and door types
  - Surrounding of the structure
    – Fenced-in property
    – In-ground pool with pool cage
    – Above-ground pool
    – Shed on property
  - Vehicles parked on property
  - Victim description: position, clothing, wounds, jewelry (remember, the body is the jurisdiction of the medical examiner and cannot be altered)
  - Crime scene team, if several CSIs are present
    – Note time of briefing of each CSI
    – Assignment to each team member

Note taking is a continuous task throughout the entire investigation from the time of arrival to the time of conclusion and clearing from the scene. If the investigation continues for multiple days, always begin a new page with day, date, and time of arrival of the team and note if different tasks are assigned and which tasks have been concluded.

4.2.1 Photographing the Scene

Photographs are a permanent record of the crime scene in an untouched state. The images are valuable during the criminal investigation and for presentation at trial. The photographs are a permanent record of the condition of the scene and the location of physical evidence as perceived by the first responder and CSI team. The basic crime scene photography rules apply to photographically document every crime scene:

- Overall, medium range, and close-up photographs of the exterior and interior of the crime scene. If available, take aerial photographs of scenes of violent crimes or crime scenes that consist of more than one scene where the distance between the scenes may be crucial to the investigation.
- Any item of evidence should be photographed with and without yellow marker number and with and without a labeled scale.
- You can never have too many photos of a crime scene.

Most law enforcement agencies require videotaping of scenes of violent crimes such as homicides. Modern digital cameras have video capability allowing the CSI to video record the scene without additional equipment. Detailed information about crime scene photography is provided in Chapter 2.

4.2.2 Sketching the Crime Scene

Sketching the crime scene is an important part of documentation. The crime scene sketch is a layout of the indoor or outdoor crime scene and provides the investigator, prosecutor, defense attorney, judge, and jurors with a depiction of the precise location and relationship of objects and evidence on scene. The points of entry and exit, as well as the offender's movement through the scene, can be demonstrated in the sketch. In addition, "sketching the crime scene assigns units of measurement and provides a proper perspective of the overall scene and the relevant physical evidence identified within the scene" (Nordby, James, and Bell, 2014, p. 51). The crime scene sketch is a permanent record and admissible in court.

4.2.2.1 Types of Sketches

The CSI has to make a decision about which type of crime scene sketch will be required to provide a comprehensive view of the scene, what are the limits of each type of sketch to choose, and what to include and exclude in the sketch. The four commonly used types of sketches are

- Overview or bird's-eye view sketch. This sketch provides a floor plan of the scene and all items are depicted on a horizontal plane, as the viewer would look down at the scene, as illustrated in Sketch 4.1. This sketch can be used for indoor as well as outdoor scenes.
- Elevation sketch. This sketch exposes the vertical plane of the scene rather than the horizontal plane, as shown in Sketch 4.2. This sketch is suitable for documenting trajectory of bullets through windows, walls, and cabinets.

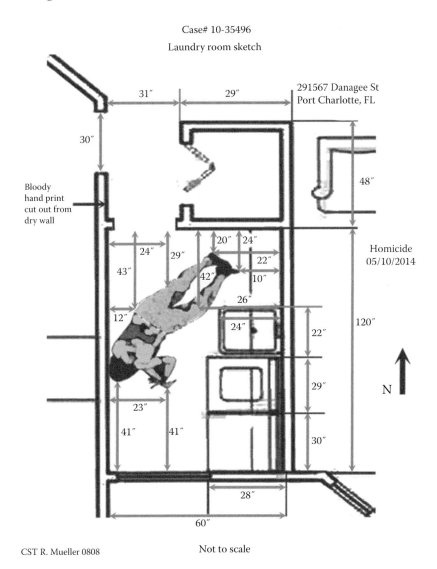

Sketch 4.1 Bird's-eye view sketch with evidence. (With permission from Ronald Mueller.)

- Exploded view or cross-protection sketch. This type of sketch is comparable to the bird's-eye view sketch (horizontal floor plan) except the walls are laid out flat, allowing showing objects in their relative position. This sketch is best suitable for bloodstain patterns on the ceiling, wall, and floor (Sketch 4.3).
- Perspective sketch. This sketch is a three-dimensional view of the scene depicting a special item of interest. This sketch is difficult to complete and requires artistic skills.

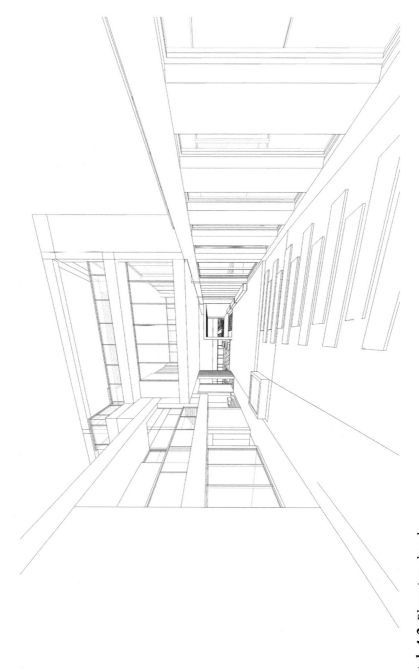

Sketch 4.2 Elevation sketch.

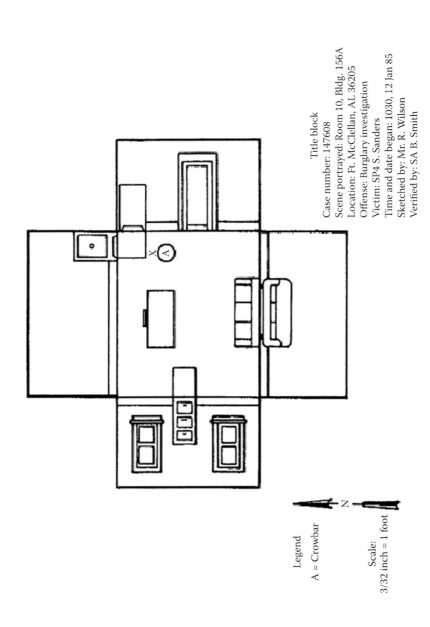

Title block

Case number: 147608
Scene portrayed: Room 10, Bldg. 156A
Location: Ft. McClellan, AL 36205
Offense: Burglary investigation
Victim: SP4 S. Sanders
Time and date began: 1030, 12 Jan 85
Sketched by: Mr. R. Wilson
Verified by: SA B. Smith

Legend
A = Crowbar

N

Scale:
3/32 inch = 1 foot

Sketch 4.3 Cross-projection sketch.

The CSI might not have the time or skill to create a sophisticated sketch and creates a rough sketch including all dimensions of the scene, all items of evidence in relation to other important features of the scene. The rough sketch is not drawn to scale and drawn by pencil. During the investigation, additional items of evidence and measurements will be added making the sketch a floating document. Measurements should be recorded in a chart for later inclusion in the final sketch. The rough sketch should be clearly marked "NOT TO SCALE."

A final or finished sketch will be prepared on conclusion of the crime scene investigation, as illustrated in Sketches 4.4 and 4.5. The final sketch can include measurements from two fixed points to the items of evidence. At large crime scenes with numerous items of evidence, it may be necessary to draw several rough sketches, for example, an overall sketch of the residence, and a sketch for the room where the crime occurred. To avoid clutter with symbols, numbers, and measurements, it may be necessary to create a sketch with measurements and an additional sketch showing the items of evidence.

Crime scene sketches are ordinarily not drawn to scale. Many computer programs are available to create finished crime scene sketches such as VISIO, Smart Draw, or CAD programs. Those programs allow creating sketches to scale and including components for crime scene sketches such as outlines of a body, weapons, drugs, etc.

Every crime scene sketch requires its own documentation, such as

- Case number
- Location (street address)
- Type of crime
- Name of sketcher
- Date and time of sketching
- Compass designation pointing north
- NOT TO SCALE, or the scale used if drawn to scale
- Legend for abbreviations, numbers, and symbols

All evidence present on scene is documented in the sketch, either by symbol, yellow marker number, or abbreviation.

4.2.3 Crime Scene Mapping

A CSI might sketch but not map a crime scene. Crime scene mapping is associated with crime scene measurements. A crime scene sketch does not include measurements or items of evidence, whereas a map includes symbols or numbers of the items of evidence and measurements. Rarely, measurements are recorded without any form of graphical representation of the

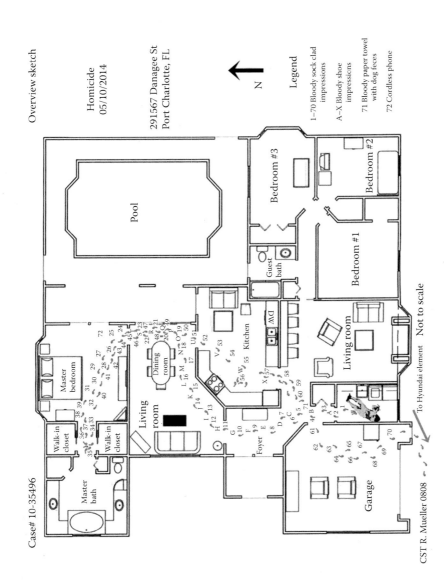

Sketch 4.4 Sketch with marked evidence. (With permission from Ronald Mueller.)

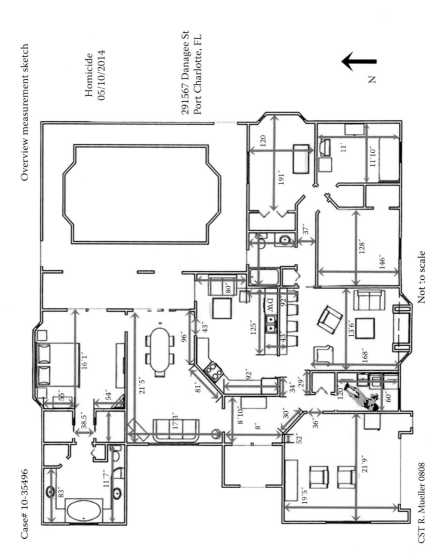

Sketch 4.5 Sketch with measurements. (With permission from Ronald Mueller.)

measurements. The mapping of a scene can be significant if the judge orders the jurors to the crime scene and requires the lead CSI to place every item of evidence in the location where found, especially in high profile cases or officer-involved shootings.

There are several techniques used to obtained measurements: baseline mapping, rectangular coordinate, triangulation, and polar/grid coordinates. The CSI determines which method is best suited for the circumstances of the crime scenes, for example, the triangulation method is suitable for indoor scenes; the baseline method is suitable for large outdoor scenes; and the polar coordination methods are used for outdoor scenes without any fixed location. Note in the report and in the sketch that all measurements are approximate and never documented or testified as 100% accurate.

4.2.3.1 Baseline Mapping

Baseline mapping is a basic form of crime scene mapping but is the least accurate. The baseline mapping is particularly useful for large outdoor scenes without two fixed points in the immediate vicinity of the evidence at the crime scene, as illustrated in Sketch 4.6 and Figure 4.2.

Steps to obtain baseline measurements include

1. Develop a baseline from which to conduct measurements. The baseline can be a roadway, a fence, or along a wall of a created baseline with a tape measure in the center of a road or field. Ensure it crosses/ covers the entire crime scene.

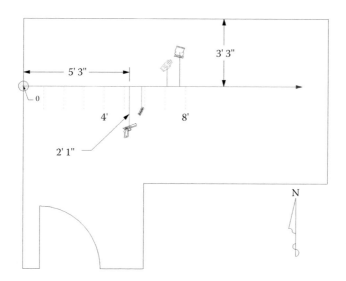

Sketch 4.6 Baseline mapping. (With permission from Kent Boots, Factual Diagrams.com.)

(a)

(b)

Figure 4.2 Baseline mapping at (a) outdoor and (b) indoor scene. (With permission from Kent Boots, FactualDiagrams.com.)

2. Locate two fixed points at the scene, for example, an intersection of a road as point A and an electro pole as point B. (Note the numbers on the electro pole for reconstruction if the pole has been removed.)
3. Measure the distance from the baseline to the center mass of the evidence at a 90-degree angle. If the angle is less or more than 90 degrees, the measurements will be inaccurate.
4. Note the distance from point A (beginning of the baseline) to the point of intersection (90 degrees) to the evidence.

4.2.3.2 Rectangular Coordinate Mapping

The rectangular coordinate mapping method is similar to the baseline method, except it utilizes two baselines, for example, one baseline is along the south wall and the second baseline is along the west wall, as shown in Sketch 4.7. A measurement is taken from both baselines to the center mass of the evidence. Due to the measurements taken from the two baselines, the accuracy is greater than the single baseline method. This method is suitable for small interior scenes such as hallways.

4.2.3.3 Triangulation Method

The triangulation method is the most accurate method without the use of technology. The accuracy is based on the application of two fixed points, as illustrated in Sketch 4.8. In the triangulation method, the CSI identifies two fixed points as measuring point A and B. Those points can be corners of a room, a doorframe, or a south and north side of a window. A table or a couch

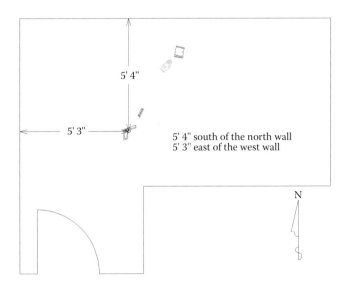

Sketch 4.7 Rectangular coordinate mapping. (With permission from Ken Boots, FactualDiagrams.com.)

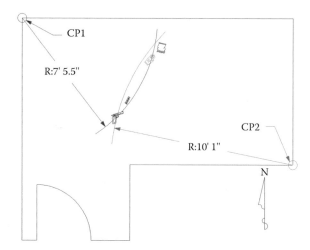

Sketch 4.8 Triangulation mapping method. (With permission from Kent Boots, FactualDiagrams.com.)

is not suitable as a fixed point because it can be easily moved. The CSI obtains the following measurements:

- Point A (SW corner of the room) to center mass of the evidence
- Point B (SE corner of the room) to center mass of the evidence
- Distance between A and B

4.2.3.4 Polar/Grid Coordinate Mapping

The crime mapping method is a two-dimensional system that employs the angle and distance from a fixed point to the location of the evidence, as shown in Sketch 4.9. A compass is required for this method to measure the angles and polar direction. This method is suited for large outdoor scenes with no, or only a few, landmarks, for example, a body found in the woods or in a large field.

4.2.3.5 Use of GPS

Global positioning system (GPS) is a satellite-based navigation system. The Department of Defense had placed 24 satellites in the Earth's orbit to create the network. Originally, the mean of GPS was for military purposes; however, the government made it available for civilian use in 1983. The satellites orbit the Earth twice a day and transmit signal information. The GPS receiver gathers these signals and uses triangulation to calculate the GPS's location. To calculate the two-dimensional position (longitude and latitude) of the user, the GPS has to lock on to the position of a minimum of three satellites.

Commercially available GPS receivers are accurate to approximately 12 m, sufficient for large crime scenes without fixed landmarks.

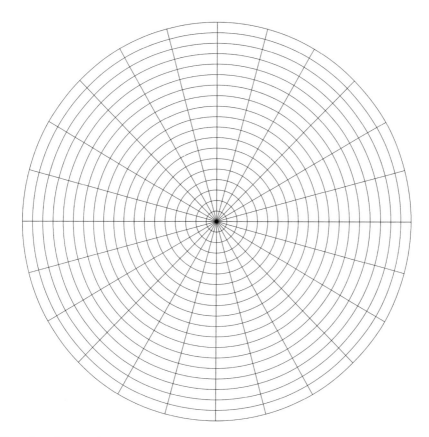

Sketch 4.9 Polar/grid coordinate mapping. (With permission from Kent Boots, FactualDiagrams.com.)

4.3 Searching for Additional Evidence

After all visible evidence at the scene is documented, photographed, sketched, collected, and preserved, the crime scene investigator will perform additional searches to discover further items of interest for the investigation. The crime scene should be searched in a systematic and methodical manner while avoiding missing or destroying evidence. The crime scene investigator will choose a search pattern that fits the characteristics of the crime and the crime scene. The location of the scene, indoor or outdoor, the size of the scene, and the available personnel are factors in the determination of the search pattern.

4.3.1 Indoor Crime Scene Searches

Several search patterns are available for indoor crime scene searches as well as vehicle searches. The crime scene investigator makes a decision of which method is most effective based on the circumstances of the scene. Some search patterns are more sufficient in indoor scenes or outdoor scenes, while others can be applied either indoors or outdoors.

4.3.1.1 Spiral Search Pattern

This search pattern can be subdivided into the inward and outward spiral search patterns, as illustrated in Sketch 4.10. In the inward spiral search, the crime scene investigator begins the search at the outer perimeter working toward the center of the scene. One person can successfully perform this search.

In the outward spiral search, the crime scene investigator begins searches from the center of the scene outward toward the outer perimeter, for example, from the body in a room toward the walls of the room, as shown in Sketch 4.10. One person can also successfully perform this search.

4.3.1.2 Pie or Wheel Search Pattern

The crime scene investigator begins to search from a critical point and travels outward in straight lines; for example, the search begins at the location of the body and travels outward in rays or straight lines to the outer perimeters of the scene, as shown in Sketch 4.11. This method is not very common and is used only under special circumstances.

4.3.1.3 Zone Search Pattern

When applying the zone search pattern, additional manpower is required. The lead crime scene investigator will separate the indoor scene into different zones and assign additional personnel to search a specific zone, as illustrated

Sketch 4.10 Spiral search pattern.

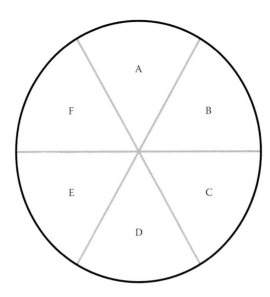

Sketch 4.11 Pie or wheel search pattern.

in Sketch 4.12. If enough manpower were available, it would be recommended to assign two CSIs to each zone to avoid missing physical evidence. This method can also be used in outdoor scenes when the specific zones are marked, such as in excavations. The zone search pattern is mostly applied at excavation scenes on skeleton remains. The zone search pattern is very efficient when searching a vehicle. The vehicle can be subdivided into zones such as trunk, rear bench seat, rear floorboard, etc.

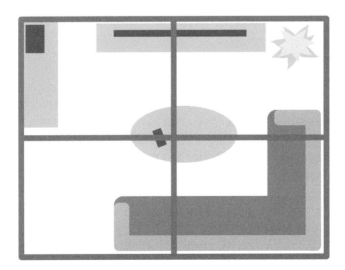

Sketch 4.12 Zone search pattern.

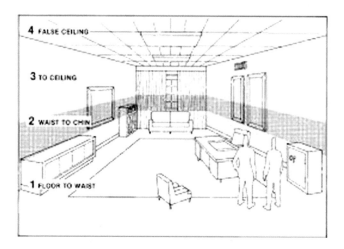

Sketch 4.13 Elevation zone search pattern.

4.3.1.4 Elevation Zone Search Pattern

This type of search is used with indoor crime scenes when searching for bullet holes, bloodstain patterns, or any kind of physical evidence that could be present on the walls or ceiling, as shown in Sketch 4.13. The CSI will search each elevation separately such as

1. Floor to waistline
2. Waistline to chin level
3. Chin level to ceiling
4. Ceiling

4.3.2 Outdoor Crime Scene Searches

Outdoor crime scene searches are mostly accomplished for the recovery of discarded weapons, projectiles, or spent cartridges. Outdoor searches require more manpower and cannot be accomplished by one person.

4.3.2.1 Line, Strip, or Parallel Search Pattern

A line, strip, or parallel search can be performed at outdoor and indoor crime scenes. At outdoor scenes, a minimum of one or two crime scene investigators line up shoulder width apart walking in straight lines across the crime scene. This method is applied when searching a grassy or wooded area. When applied at an indoor scene, the crime scene investigator will search the room or building in a linear pattern making sure to overlap the previous search line, as illustrated in Sketch 4.14.

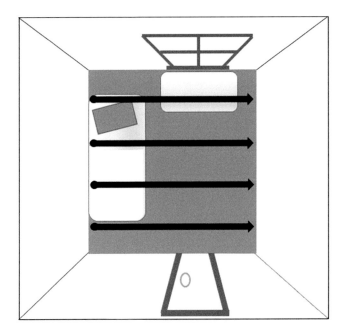

Sketch 4.14 Line, strip search pattern.

4.3.2.2 Grid Search Pattern

The grid search pattern is similar to the strip search pattern but the search is also performed in the opposite direction. The grid search pattern can also be used in large indoor crime scenes such as a warehouse, a school, or an office building. The grid search method is the most thorough search pattern, see Sketch 4.15. While it is time consuming, it can be more efficient when additional personnel are available to assist in the search.

4.4 Managing Crime Scene Searches

4.4.1 Outdoor Searches

Searching outdoor crime scenes is a team effort and requires additional personnel. Many law enforcement agencies ask for recruits from the police academy for assistance when searching large wooded areas. It is an excellent practice for the recruits and helps the agency to implement added resources and often find additional evidence.

If additional outside assistance is provided, the lead CSI will be in charge and assign a crime scene investigator to each group of recruits. The CSI will lead the team and flag all detected evidence.

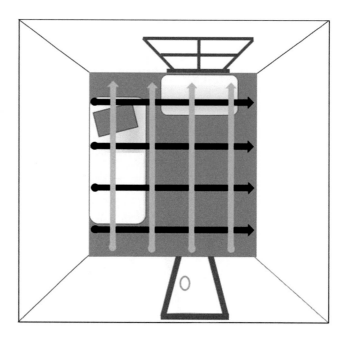

Sketch 4.15 Grid search pattern.

The lead crime scene investigator notes

- Applied search pattern
- Names of the search personnel and crime scene personnel in charge of each team
- Assigned zones

Depending on the dimensions of the area to be searched, the team CSI will assign an assistant to obtain overall, medium range, and close-up photos of each item of evidence being marked by the search teams. The lead CSI is responsible for ensuring that every item of recovered evidence is included in the crime scene sketch. The general evidence collection procedures such as measurements, packaging, and preservation apply.

Double Murder in Florida

On a Monday in July 9 of 2006, the bodies of a mother and her daughter were found in the mother's home. The mother, the daughter, and the daughter's infant son lived in the apartment on the east side of the duplex. Neighbors had noticed that the front door was open and the baby was in the high chair in the doorway and called 911. The first officer on scene found the front door open and discovered the mother stabbed to death in the master bedroom and the daughter stabbed to death in her bedroom. The screen of the porch at the southeast side of the duplex was torn, a cut was detected in the screen next to the door handle and the lock mechanism was missing. No signs of forced entry were visible on the south side door leading from the porch inside the residence. Bloodstain patterns indicated a struggle in the hallway as well as in the master bedroom where the mother had been stabbed. Different bloodstain patterns were found in the daughter's bedroom where she laid in a pool of blood. Bloody shoe prints were found on the tiled entry and blood transfer pattern on the northeast doorframe of the south bedroom, consistent with the perpetrator exiting the residence through the front door. Similar shoe impressions had been found in the master bedroom next to the mother.

On Thursday of the same week, students/cadets of the 109th Basic Law Enforcement Class had been recruited from the South West Florida Public Service Academy to assist in the search. The recruits were lined up, shoulder width apart, and walked in a straight line eastward from the residence. A crime scene investigator accompanied the group and marked any item with a yellow flag. A second crime scene investigator photographed the flagged items with and without yellow evidence markers. The teams had been searching the lots around the duplex for additional items of evidentiary value, and two items of interest had been located and flagged with yellow, numbered evidence markers.

One cadet found the first item at approximately 8:10. It was a pellet gun near an adjacent roadway, approximately 31 ft northeast from the northeast edge of the road and approximately 33 ft southeast from the southeast side of the duplex. A yellow evidence Marker #1 had been placed next to the item, as shown in Figure 4.3. The CSI photographer

Figure 4.3 Pellet gun.

photographed the pellet gun in its original place with and without a marker. The item was added to the crime scene sketch, and measurements were obtained before the evidence was collected and preserved.

The second item was a large butcher knife that was found at approximately 8:16 by another cadet. The butcher knife was located east of the residence, approximately 119 ft northeast from the northeast edge of the roadway and approximately 47 ft southeast from the southeast side of the duplex. A yellow evidence Marker #2 had been placed next to the item. The knife was photographed as found and additional close-up images have been captured, see Figure 4.4. A portion of the black handle was missing, as was one of the small silver rivets that had held the handle in place. The blade of the knife was bowed and the tip was bent sharply upward. The blade was stained with a possible mixture of blood and rust. Both items were photographed on brown paper, with and without scale, prior to packaging.

The Academy students were instructed to search the vacant lot directly across the street for additional items of evidentiary value. Two additional items of interest were located. One cadet located the top portion of a cell phone at a nearby intersection, at approximately 8:55. Its place was marked with a yellow evidence Marker #3. Another cadet located what appeared to be the bottom portion of the same cell phone just a few feet away from the top portion of the cell phone at approximately 8:57. It was marked with a yellow Evidence Marker #4. Photographs, measurements, and a sketch were drawn to document the evidence. No other items of interest were found. Statements were obtained from each of the cadets that had found items of interest that were collected as evidence. The Academy students cleared the scene shortly thereafter, around 9:28.

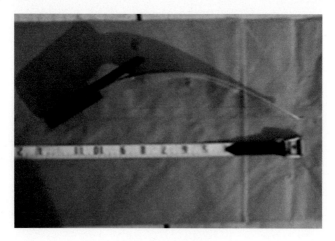

Figure 4.4 Knife recovered in the empty field.

Additional indoor searches were then performed at the double murder scene. The residence was subdivided into zones such as kitchen, living room, master bedroom, child's room, and spare bedroom. Zone searches were performed in each room after all visible evidence had been documented, photographed, sketched, and measured. A grid pattern was applied to ensure that all evidence was discovered. In the mother's master bedroom, the CSI recovered a broken knife handle on top of a bloodstained piece of newspaper on the floor next to her body. The CSI assigned to search the master bedroom captured photographs, documented the zone, drew a rough sketch, and measured the evidence prior to collection and preservation. In the daughter's bedroom, a knife blade was found on the floor next to the door. The zone "kitchen" revealed several knives in the kitchen consistent with the knife handle and the knife blade found in the victims' bedrooms.

4.4.2 Indoor Searches

Indoor searches can also be time consuming; however, due to the confined locations in a house or business, additional search teams are not required. Based on the search pattern, the lead CSI will assign a CSI to each room to be searched. The CSI will be responsible for the search and mark any item of evidence with a yellow marker or a placard. Each item of evidence will be photographed with overall, medium range, and close-up photos, added to the crime scene sketch, and measured before collection and preservation.

Working in the same area for several hours can lead to oversight of additional evidence. Upon completion of the search and collection of the evidence, it is recommended to use a fresh set of eyes, another CSI or officer, to ensure that all evidence is detected.

4.4.3 Where to Find Evidence

Evidence can be found in the most unusual places such as inside shoes, in the toilet water tank, or even inside the toilet, as illustrated in Figure 4.5. Always check curtain rods, the top of curtains, ceiling tiles, under rugs, under sofa seat cushions, underneath the mattress, and flip the mattress to ensure there is no blood. Always examine the ceiling and walls for bloodstain patterns or additional bullet holes. Every time, look for signs of attempted clean up of the scene such as fresh paint or the smell of strong cleaning solutions such as bleach. Check buckets and underneath the sink for heavy and excessive amounts of cleaning materials. Crime scenes are three-dimensional, always

Figure 4.5 Gun recovered in toilet.

look up and check the ceiling for bloodstains, bullet holes, or any other form of disturbance.

4.4.4 Officer Safety during Crime Scene Searches

Crime scene safety is important for the investigator's safety but also for the integrity of the evidence. Never use bare hands when searching for evidence. Always wear special protective gloves, such as Kevlar-coated gloves, when searching underneath furniture or in areas you cannot see. Especially in narcotics cases, syringes, razor blades, and other sharp materials can be hidden underneath car seats or underneath the spare tire in the trunk.

4.5 Developing, Analyzing, and Reconstructing the Scene of a Crime

Crime scene investigation consists of the documentation, sketching, mapping, collection, and preservation of physical evidence, but also requires implementing the use of forensic disciplines to develop latent evidence. Crime scene reconstruction consists of the use of bloodstain pattern analysis, trajectory examination, and the use of other forensic disciplines to determine the cause and manner of a crime. Several different methods of forensics are applied such as fingerprints, DNA, bite marks, shoe or tire impressions, as well as digital forensics for recovering data from electronic storage devices.

4.6 Evidence Collection, Packaging, and Preservation

After all evidence has been documented, photographed, sketched, and measured, the next step will be to physically collect each item. If a crime scene team is investigating the scene, it is recommended that one CSI will be assigned for the evidence collection. The packaging and preservation of evidence is significant to maintain the quality of the evidence for further testing in the laboratory.

In Table 4.2, the steps of evidence collection are illustrated. Those steps should be applied in the collection of every item of evidence.

Caution: Always package every item of evidence separately.

4.6.1 Paper or Plastic or Other Containers?

The packaging material used to preserve the evidence depends on the type of evidence. Evidence comes in all different shapes and sizes and the packaging methods have to be flexible, however, following the basic preservation guidelines. Proper packaging will minimize the risk of contamination.

4.6.1.1 Paper Bags and Cardboard Boxes

Any kinds of body fluids have to be packaged in paper bags. Blood, semen, and saliva should be air dried before packaging. Firearms should be collected in specialized gun boxes whereas long rifles should be packaged in rifle bags. Paper bags come in different sizes and provide excellent preservation for any

Table 4.2 Steps of Evidence Collection

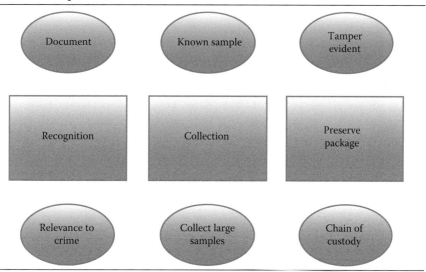

type of evidence. Boxes are also an excellent choice for biological evidence from bloody clothing, underwear from a sexual assault victim, to clothing from a victim involved in an aggravated assault. Remember the Locard principle: it also applies to biological evidence. Every time further biological forensic testing of the evidence is required, package the items in paper to avoid mold building and the effects of humidity diminishing the quality of the evidence for further DNA testing. That is the reason why most of the submission manuals for local, private, state, and federal laboratories require preservation of biological evidence in paper bags.

Caution: Never place any organic material such as live marijuana plants in plastic bags or containers, as the plants will deteriorate.

Experiment: This writer performed an experiment and placed a sample of live plant material in a plastic Ziploc bag and sealed it. Another sample of the same plant material was placed in a cardboard box and sealed with Scotch tape. Both containers were placed on a table in an air-conditioned room. After several days, the plant material in the Ziploc bag had begun to deteriorate and rot. The plant material inside the cardboard box dried and remained in a preserved condition. That is what would happen if marijuana or any other live plant evidence would be packaged in plastic instead of a breathable container such as a paper bag or in a cardboard box. See Figure 4.6 for packaging options.

Firearms should be packaged in cardboard boxes. Large gun boxes are recommended for rifles and smaller boxes for handguns. Always ensure that the weapon is not sliding within the box. Packaging material such as brown paper, cotton, or tightening the weapon with a zip tie block movement within the box.

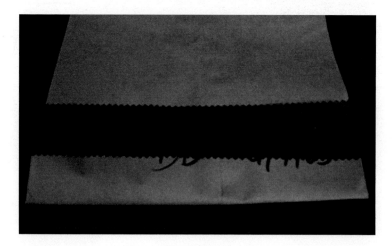

Figure 4.6 Sealed paper evidence bag.

Caution: Do not zip tie through the barrel or cylinder, as it would destroy the striation of the weapon. Live and spent cartridges should be packaged separate from the weapon. Shoe and tire casts can also be packaged in gun boxes if the size fits the cast. Always ensure that the evidence will not rub against the container and bolster with cotton or paper. Small cardboard boxes are suitable for jewelry or small items. Spent projectiles should be wrapped in cotton and then placed in a small cardboard box.

4.6.1.2 *Plastic Bags*

All dry and nonbiological evidence can be placed in plastic bags. Dried marijuana can be packaged in plastic, as can cocaine and other drugs. Plastic bags are excellent for any kind of metallic and nonmetallic evidence and are available in different sizes, as illustrated in Figure 4.7. Commercially purchased plastic evidence bags are self-sealing by removing a piece of plastic. Depending on the agency's policy, no additional seal with evidence tape is required and the CSI can initial and date the plastic fold.

4.6.1.3 *Plastic and Metal Containers*

Knives, glass, and syringes are sharp-edged items requiring special packaging. Syringes and knives should be placed inside a plastic container with Styrofoam blocks at each end. Glass pieces should be placed in plastic jars to ensure that anybody who handles the evidence does not become injured,

Figure 4.7 Evidence packaging materials.

thus contaminating the evidence. Evidence from fire and arson scenes may contain accelerants such as gasoline that have to be placed into an unlined metal paint can to preserve the vapors of the accelerants for later testing in the laboratory. Cell phones and other electronic storage devices should also be placed in an antistatic bag or placed inside an unlined paint can to avoid the signal from the cell tower to reach the device and possibly delete the last location or data on the hard drive if remote deleting programs are downloaded. Any kind of unknown liquid should be placed in a plastic container or metal container. Always ensure that chemicals do not come into contact with each other as it could result in possible ignition or explosions. Small metal boxes are an excellent container for pills and loose medication.

4.6.1.4 Optional Packaging

Larger items of evidence may not fit in a paper bag; even they are available in very large sizes. A roll of brown butcher paper can be used to wrap larger items such as a chair or a table. Originally packed loose fitting bedsheets can also be used to package large items such as a carpet or a larger piece of furniture. Additional wrapping in paper is required. Body boxes used for cremation provide excellent packaging for live marijuana plants and roots.

4.6.2 Labeling Evidence

Each item of evidence has to be labeled. Commercially purchased plastic bags contain a standard printed template for evidence information and chain of custody. Paper bags, metal containers, and plastic containers require writing the information onto the surface, such as

- Case number
- Item number
- Description of the item inside the container
- Location of recovery
- Date and time of collection
- Initials of the person collecting the evidence

An example of handwritten information on a paper bag would look like this:

Case number 15-0354
Item 1
One pair of white Nike Tennis Shoes in size 12, recovered from underneath the south
    side of the single bed along the north wall in the master bedroom, at marker 1
3/3/2015
GS (initial of the CSI)

Plastic bags with imprinted evidence information are available for sale from major forensic suppliers and can be customized for each agency. The CSI will fill in the information using a permanent marker.

Casts of shoe and tire impressions require adding the case number, north arrow, date, time of collection, and the initials of the CSI onto the smooth surface of the impression.

Caution: Never clean dirt, soil, roots, or plant material from the casted impression. Always package as is.

A short description of the area from where the impression was obtained should be included such as "Shoe impression from front yard east of the front door on the west side of the residence."
Firearms: When collecting a firearm, always include the following information:

- Make and model of firearm
- Caliber
- Serial number
- Information about national or international importer
- Include if there was a live round in the barrel
- Identify make and caliber of the live round

Caution: Always package ammunition separately from the firearm.

4.6.3 Sequence of Collecting Evidence

It is recommended to begin the collection of physical evidence at Marker 1 and to continue in numerical order. Always note the time when each item was collected on the outside of the container. One CSI of the team should be assigned to collect the evidence. He or she will immediately seal each package with evidence tape and initial and date across the seal. This system eliminates having several CSI collecting evidence and be subpoenaed to testify in court. The CSI assigned to collect the evidence will be able to testify to the integrity and chain of custody for all evidence from the scene.

Collecting known samples is as important as collecting unknown samples. For example, fingerprints are visible on the broken window at the point of entry to the convenience store. The CSI will obtain elimination fingerprints from the store clerk and manager who work in the store as standard fingerprints. The fingerprints lifted from the window will be the unknown scene prints and the latent examiner can compare the known to the unknown prints for a possible match. This principle also refers to shoe impressions, tire impressions, DNA, bite marks, and most forensic disciplines using comparisons.

4.6.3.1 Property Receipt

After all evidence is collected, the CSI will write a property receipt listing every item of evidence that is removed from the scene. Every property receipt contains information such as

- Case number
- If the item is evidence, found property, to be destroyed or kept safe
- Location where recovered
- Information of the victim, suspect, and name of the detective (including badge number)
- Continues item number
- Amount and description of the evidence
- Chain of custody

If a search warrant had been issued for the search, a copy of the search warrant and a listing of the seized items have to remain on scene. The listing of the collected evidence can be a paper listing or a copy of the property receipt, as shown in Document 4.6. It is recommended to photograph the listing and the search warrant left at the scene to avoid later issues about the seized items at the trial. The listing of the seized evidence protects the officer and the CSI personnel showing what items have been removed. Additional overall photos of the scene will evidence what high-end electronics such as large TV screens have been seized and what remained in the residence. In many cases, the owners of searched residences claimed that electronics had been seized that were not listed on the property receipt, claiming the officers or CSI personnel stole the items. An additional set of photographs provides a safety net for the officers and CSI showing what items remained on scene. In addition, the judge will also receive a listing of the seized items as an attachment with the return of the search warrant.

4.6.3.2 Chain of Custody

The chain of custody is a timeline beginning at the crime scene listing the date, times, and names of every person who handled the evidence. A chain of custody has to be maintained for every type of evidence. A missing link in the chain can lead to the inadmissibility of evidence in trial, if it goes missing or unaccounted for any period of time. The chain of custody has to show that the item is still in the same condition as recovered from the scene. The prosecutor will present the witness testifying in trial that

- The evidence presented in court is the same as they collected and preserved from the scene.
- The date and time lists when the evidence was received or transferred to another provider.
- There was no tampering with the evidence while in their custody.

Your Agency Name here...

Case #_____Evidence _____ Date _____

Check One Only ❑ Physical Evidence ❑ Found ❑ Destroy ❑ Safekeeping

Charges_____

❑ Suspect Name_____DOB_____

Address   _____

Victim(s) Name_____DOB_____

Address   _____

Address/Location where property is located/impounded

_____Date/Time:_____

Deputy's printed name_____

ID number _____District and Unit_____

Detective (if different)_____

❑ Owner   ❑ Finder   ❑ Victim

Bag #	Item	Qty	Full Description of Property

Chain of custody

Item	Date	Time	Released by	Received by	Location of Property

Document 4.6 Property receipt.

4.7 Motor Vehicles Involved in a Crime

The usage of vehicles varies from personal cars, delivery trucks, semi-tractor trailers, motorcycles, pickup trucks, motorboats or even airplanes are present at almost every crime scene. Whether it be the victim's vehicle or the suspect's vehicle, it should be searched for additional evidence.

Caution: If the vehicle is parked in the driveway at the crime scene and a search warrant is read, the vehicle will be included in the search warrant.

Note that motor vehicles can be a challenge due to restricted spaces in the interior and exterior, hidden compartments, and the undercarriage.

4.7.1 General Vehicle Crime Scene Procedures

Any kind of motorized or nonmotorized vehicle, ranging from a bicycle to a semitruck, can be involved in a criminal activity or even be the weapon used to kill a person. For instance, a man who just robbed a bank flees on a bicycle. A woman purposely runs her husband over with the family sedan. A murderer flees in the victim's vehicle from the scene of the crime. In any scenario, the vehicle is of evidentiary value for fingerprints, blood, and DNA leading to the identification of the suspect.

4.7.1.1 Documentation of the Vehicle

As at any other crime scene, documentation is essential. The CSI assigned to process and search the vehicle should note:

- Year, make, and model
- Color of exterior and interior of the vehicle
- Special features such as sunroof, moonroof, etc.
- VIN number and license plate including state and expiration date
- Owner of the vehicle from the registration and insurance documents
- Windows and doors are open, locked, or unlocked
- Any signs of forced entry
- Any interior and exterior damage such as dents and scratches
- Brand, size, and condition of tires
- Specialized equipment such as TV, DVD player, GPS system, movie system
- Any stickers or other identification markers
- Mileage reading of the odometer
- Radio station setting and A/C settings

The VIN plate of the vehicle is on the dashboard at the driver's side and is visible from the outside looking through the windshield. A metal plate with additional vehicle information is mounted on the driver's front doorframe.

In addition, many agencies use templates to document vehicles, as illustrated in Document 4.7.

4.7.1.2 Photographing the Vehicle

Motor vehicles can be the crime scene, an accessory to the crime, or a weapon of a crime. In any case, the basic crime scene photography methods apply,

Crime Scene Investigation
FIELD NOTES
VEHICLE PROCESSING

CASE NUMBER ....
DATE ....
CRIME..
TIME NOTIFIED...BY...
LOCATION OF CRIME SCENE..
....
CRIME SCENE INVESTIGATOR..
LEAD DETECTIVE..
FIRST OFFICER ON SCENE...
WALK-THROUGH GIVEN BY..

VEHICLE

MAKE..MODEL.............................YEAR..
SEDAN.........PICKUP TRUCK.....................VAN......................JEEP.....................SUV................
VEHICLE IDENTIFICATION NUMBER...
LICENSE PLATE..STATE..................EXPIRATION.............................
STICKERS/LABELS..
COLOR: EXTERIOR...INTERIOR...
SUNROOF...........................MOONROOF.............................CONVERTIBLE.............................
DOORS LOCKED........YES.........NO.......WINDOWS..CLOSED..................OPEN..........................
KEYS.........................IGNITION PUNCHED................YES.............NO.....................................
VEHICLE REGISTERED TO..
ADDRESS:...
....
EXTERIOR DAMAGE...
....
....
INTERIOR DAMAGE..
....
....

SEARCH WARRANT

SEARCH WARRANT REQUIRED:......................................YES....................NO........................
WARRANT READ ON....................TIME.................BY...
VEHICLE SEARCHED BY..
DATE..TIME..
PHOTOGRAPHY
CAMERA...STORAGE MEDIA...
TOTOAL PHOTOS TAKEN...

INVENTORY OF THE VEHICLE

ITEM DESCRIPTION	LOCATION RECOVERED
	DRIVER'S SIDE
	PASSENGER'S SIDE
	REAR DRIVER'S SIDE
	REAR PASSENGER'S SIDE
	TRUNK
	GLOVE COMPARTMENT
	CENTER CONSOLE
	STORAGE COMPARTMENT

Document 4.7 Vehicle field notes. *(Continued)*

PROCESSING METHODS
FINGERPRINTS

FINGERPRINTS..........YES..........NO..........NUMBER OF FINGERPRINTS LIFTED..................
PROCESSING METHOD..................
AREAS PROCESSED FOR FINGERPRINTS..................
....
....

DNA SWABS

DNA SWABS..........YES..........NO..........NUMBER OF DNA SWABS..................
AREAS SWABBED:
STEERING WHEEL..........................YES..........NO..........# OF SWABS..........
INTERIOR DRIVER'S DOOR..........................YES..........NO..........# OF SWABS..........
EXTERIOR DRIVER'S DOOR..........................YES..........NO..........# OF SWABS..........
CENTER CONSOLE (RADIO, A/C)..........YES..........NO..........# OF SWABS..........
INTERIOR PASSENGER'S DOOR..........YES..........NO..........# OF SWABS..........
EXTERIOR PASSENGER'S DOOR..........YES..........NO..........# OF SWABS..........
TURN SIGNAL..........................YES..........NO..........# OF SWABS..........
EXT. REAR DRIVER'S DOOR..........YES..........NO..........# OF SWABS..........
INT. REAR DRIVER'S DOOR..........YES..........NO..........# OF SWABS..........
EXT. REAR PASS. DOOR..........YES..........NO..........# OF SWABS..........
INT. REAR PASS. DOOR..........YES..........NO..........# OF SWABS..........

VACUUMINGS

QUADRANT 1
DRIVER'S SIDE FLOORBOARD..........................YES..........................NO..........
DRIVER'S SEAT..........................YES..........................NO..........

QUADRANT 2
PASSENGER'S SIDE FLOORBOARD..........................YES..........................NO..........
PASSENGER'S SEAT..........................YES..........................NO..........

QUADRANT 3
REAR FLOORBOARDS..........................YES..........................NO..........
REAR BENCH SEAT..........................YES..........................NO..........

QUADRANT 4
TRUNK..........................YES..........................NO..........

ADDITIONAL CHEMICAL PROCESSING

PROCESSING CHEMICAL..................
AREAS PROCESSED..................

EVIDENCE DEVELOPED..................
....
....
....
....

EVIDENCE COLLECTED

ITEM NUMBER	PACKAGED IN	ITEM DESCRIPTION	LOCATION RECOVERED FROM

SCENE CLEARED

DATE..................TIME..................
EVIDENCE TRANSPORTED BY..................
DATE..................TIME..................

Document 4.7 (Continued) Vehicle field notes.

such as overall photographs, medium range photos, and close-up photographs. In the overall photographs, it is important to depict the exact location of the vehicle such as in a parking lot or in the driveway of the residence. Always include a landmark such as a street sign, house number, or any other landmark that can help to identify the exact location of the vehicle. After the overall photos have been completed, the CSI will capture a set of medium range photos of the following areas:

- All four corners of the vehicle
- The front and rear of the vehicle
- The license plate and VIN number on the dashboard (If the VIN plate is not readable, take a photo of the metal plate inside the driver's doorframe.)
- Interior of the vehicle
- Glove box and other storage compartments
- Trunk area
- Underneath the vehicle if possible
- Any exterior and interior damage
- Any items of evidence found inside or outside and around the vehicle

Close-up photos should be obtained from all items of evidence found inside the vehicle such as registration, insurance documents, VIN number, license plate, and any evidence that can lead to the offender. Any interior or exterior damage such as scratches, dents, broken mirrors, and broken glass should be photographed using adhesive photographic scales. Photograph any pry marks or points of forced entry with medium range and close-up photos with and without scale. If multiple pry marks or scratches are in the same location, use numbers or letters, like in the road mapping methods, to be able to identify the different images.

4.7.1.3 Sketching the Vehicle

The crime scene investigator will draw a rough sketch of the area of recovery. Triangulated measurements are most effective to document vehicles in a parking lot or in a driveway. It is recommended to document the following measurements from points A and B (e.g., point A can be the north corner of a business and point B the west corner of the same business) to

- Front bumper (driver's side)
- Front bumper (passenger's side)
- Rear bumper (driver's side)
- Rear bumper (passenger's side)
- Right front tire (driver's side)

- Right front tire (passenger's side)
- Rear tire (driver's side)
- Rear tire (passenger's side)
- Total length of vehicle
- Total width of vehicle
- Distance between point A and B

Besides the basic information such as case number, date, time, address, name of sketcher, north compass direction, NOT TO SCALE, and identifiers for the vehicle, the measurements could also be added to the sketch as well as the reference points A and B.

4.7.1.4 Transporting the Vehicle

After the CSI documents, photographs, and sketches the vehicle, if directly involved in the case, the vehicle should be towed to a secure area for additional processing and evidence collection in a controlled environment. Most law enforcement agencies maintain a vehicle impoundment area or contracted areas at local towing companies or other secure facilities for storage and processing of vehicle for evidence. Before the vehicle is towed

- Check for broken mirrors, headlights, turn signals, or window glass that could be lost during transport; immediately collect a sufficient sample or if possible the entire broken mirror or headlight.
- Many agencies require sealing the doors, trunk, and hood with evidence tape, and to initial and date across the tape, to prevent contamination and to guarantee the integrity of the evidence.
- Always check the vehicle for soil samples on the tires or in the wheel well. If soil is present, immediately collect a sample.
- In vehicles that have been involved in accidents or have been used to commit the crime, check for hairs, fibers, and other debris; always collect a sample.

The CSI will issue a property receipt for the vehicle listing the year, make, model, color, style, VIN number, and license plate of the vehicle. The CSI, or a certified officer, will follow the vehicle, which has been loaded on the tow truck from the crime scene to the impoundment area to maintain the chain of custody. The officer will sign custody of the vehicle over to the evidence custodian at the impoundment facility.

A lack of maintaining the chain of custody of a vehicle can result in the inadmissibility of all evidence recovered from the vehicle.

4.7.1.5 Searching the Vehicle

The zone search pattern is sufficient for most vehicle searches. The vehicle is subdivided into zones such as front driver's seat, front passenger's seat, and rear bench seat, trunk, glove box, and storage compartments. The CSI should create a detailed inventory of all items found inside the vehicle. In narcotics investigations, it is important to take the additional steps of removing the hub cabs from the tires, as well as opening the glove box and storage compartments for hidden compartments. Open the hood and trunks and search for hidden compartments in the motor area and in the lining of the fabric in the truck, respectively.

4.7.1.6 Developing and Recovering Additional Evidence

A vehicle is an excellent source for trace evidence. The driver touches the steering wheel, shifts into gear, and may change the A/C setting and radio station depositing fingerprints and touch DNA. Hairs and fibers on the seats, as well as soil on the floor mats, can become crucial evidence placing a suspect at the crime scene.

4.7.1.6.1 DNA Evidence In *sexual assault cases*, it may be important to recover any type of body fluids for further DNA testing, such as semen, blood, or saliva. The CSI will use an alternate light source to search the seats and the floorboard for body fluids. Remember, blood appears black in color under the black light. If stains are present, the CSI may cut out the piece of fabric or carpet from the floorboard to collect the sample. Another method is to swab the stain with sterile water and a sterile cotton swab, air-dry, package and preserve as evidence; this is the same procedure as collecting a dried blood sample.

In addition, DNA swabs should be obtained from every vehicle. Common areas such as the steering wheel, shifter, A/C control, radio controls, interior and exterior door handles, window bottoms, and manual window cranks are excellent suppliers for DNA. If stains are visible on the seats or carpet on the floorboard, it is important to perform presumptive blood tests to determine if the stain is actually blood. Hexagon OBTI tests allow differentiating between human and animal blood; however, the Kastle Myers test also depicts the presence of blood, animal or human. If uncertain, always collect a swab from the stain. In addition, chemical detection for the presence of blood should be performed with Luminol or Bluestar. If the chemiluminescence is positive for the presence of blood, an additional presumptive blood test should be performed to determine if the stain is blood or any other material that reacts positive with the blood reagent. After the phenophthalein or hexagon OBTI test reveals a positive result, either swab the area or collect the entire item if possible. The floorboards, floorboard mats, the brake, and gas and clutch pedals are potential sources of blood transferred from the perpetrator's shoes.

4.7.1.6.2 Hair and Fiber Evidence   Hairs and fibers can also be found on the seats and the floorboard of a vehicle. A forensic vacuum cleaner with filter paper is recommended; however, the tape method is also sufficient. The CSI will use a clean piece of adhesive tape, such as wide fingerprint tape, and dab along the seat to capture all hairs and fibers with the sticky side of the tape. The tape is then removed and packaged.

4.7.1.6.3 Fingerprint Evidence   Fingerprinting the interior and exterior of the vehicle is the last step of the vehicle search and evidence detection and recovery. Always fingerprint the common areas such as

- Exterior and interior of the vehicle including all doors, hood, trunk, roof, and quarter panels
- Exterior and interior door handles
- Exterior and interior mirrors including the rearview mirror and the mirrors in the sun visor
- Radio and A/C
- Turn signal and emergency brake, if you have not swabbed it for DNA
- Around the trunk lock
- Gas door and gas cap

If the exterior of the vehicle is wet from morning dew or recent rain, the CSI has two options for processing for fingerprints. Option 1 would be to wait until the surface is dried, which means that a patrol officer will have to secure the vehicle. Option 2 is to apply the small particle reagent (SPR), a processing method for wet surfaces.

Processing the exterior of a vehicle with a small brush and fingerprint powder can be cumbersome. Using a palm size piece of fiberfill material used for pillows can be used to apply fingerprint powder to the exterior of the vehicle. This method is faster than and as effective as the brush method.

4.8 Final Walk-Through

Depending on the extent of the crime scene, a thorough investigation may take anywhere from 5 hours to 10 days or more. Commonly, homicide investigations last anywhere from 3 to 10 days and consist of thousands of photos and hundreds of items of evidence.

After all evidence is packaged and the property receipt is issued, the CSI removes the evidence from the scene and secures it for transport in the crime scene vehicle. At major crime scenes, and depending on department policy, the lead detective will return to the crime scene and perform a final walk-through with the crime scene investigators. Days and countless hours of scene documentation, photographing, sketching, searching, and developing and collecting evidence are spent between the detection of the crime and the final walk-through. During this time, the lead detective conducted interviews with witnesses, family members, and possible suspects and information about additional items of interest could be developed. A set of new eyes walking through the crime scene is always essential to ensure that all possible items of interest are collected.

The crime scene team will check their equipment and ensure that all evidence markers and forensic equipment have been collected prior to leaving the scene.

If the crime scene is inside a residence, the lead detective may notify a family member to come to the scene to receive the keys to the residence. The CSI will issue a property receipt and sign over custody for the keys to the family member. Always verify with a picture identification card or driver's license the identity of the person receiving the keys to the residence. Document the number of the driver's license or the identification card on the property receipt.

If a search warrant had been issued, take another set of overall photographs of the scene, or the vehicle. In many cases, the homeowner/vehicle owner may argue, and later sue law enforcement agencies for missing property such as high-end electronic items not listed as being seized. Taking another set of overall photos is evidence that those items remained on scene. Also, capture a copy of the search warrant and the listing of seized items or property receipt. The photo is evidence to prevent any future arguments in trial.

4.8.1 Releasing the Scene/Vehicle

After the detective and the CSI have concluded that the investigation of the scene/vehicle is thoroughly accomplished, all investigative personnel will clear from the scene. The patrol officer will remove the yellow barrier tape from the scene and sign out all personnel in the crime scene log. The crime scene investigator will collect the crime scene log or a copy of the crime scene log for the case report and file it in the case folder.

The CSI will transport all evidence to headquarters and subsequently via property receipt, maintaining the chain of custody turn the items over to the evidence section for storage.

References

Hess Orthmann, C. and Hess, K.M. (2013). *Criminal Investigation.* 10th ed. Cengage Learning, Boston, MA.

Nordby, J., James, S., and Bell, S. (2014). *Forensic Science: An Introduction to Scientific and Investigative Techniques.* 4th ed. CRC Press/Taylor & Francis, Boca Raton, FL.

Silverthorne Lumber Co. Inc. v. United States, 251 U.S. 385 (1920). Retrieved from https://supreme.justia.com/cases/federal/us/251/385/case.html.

Wong v. United States. Retrieved from https://supreme.justia.com/cases/federal /us/371/471/case.html.

Excavation, Bones, Bugs, and Botany

5

5.1 Excavations

The disposal of a body can vary tremendously. Some offenders vacate the victim at the crime scene, while others drop the victim into the nearest river or ocean, in remote wooded areas, or dig a grave in the backyard. Serial killers sometimes use mass graves; desperate mothers can bury babies under floors and in postholes, while others deposit bodies in wells.

5.1.1 Legal Implications

All human remains can be classified in two categories—prehistoric and recent. Prehistoric remains such as Native Americans are protected under federal law in the Native American Grave Protection and Repatriation Act. Recent remains fall under the jurisdiction of the medical examiner, who empowers local law enforcement to recover the remains.

The reasons for recovering the remains are to identify the person, to collect and preserve any physical evidence, and to determine the cause and manner of death to verify whether a crime has been committed leading to the death of the person. In many cases, only bones are recovered from buried or surface remains and identification may have to be performed via dental impressions. Therefore, it is very important to recover all evidence and apply the appropriate methods of detection and collection without destroying any evidence.

5.1.1.1 Basic Crime Scene Rules

At every crime scene, an excavation scene is documented with notes, photographs, sketches, measurements, detection, collection, preservation, and packaging of every piece of physical evidence. It is important to document the scene *in situ*, as any collection of a piece of evidence will alter the scene.

Hint: There are never too many photographs and notes can never be too detailed.

5.1.2 Excavation Equipment

Specialized equipment is required for the basic surface collection and burial excavations. The equipment may change depending on the environment, weather conditions, or terrain where the scene is located.

Basic equipment list for excavations:

- Large, medium, and small paper bags
- Large, medium, and small plastic evidence bags
- Latex gloves
- Leather work gloves
- Toolbox with household tools such as hammer, screwdriver, etc.
- Compass
- Biohazard bags
- Evidence markers with letters and numbers
- Evidence marker with "North" indicator arrow
- Level
- Excavation flags in different colors
- Wooden or metal stakes
- 50 ft, 100 ft measuring tape
- Heavy gauge fluorescent string
- Assorted paintbrushes
- Whisk broom
- Sifting screens
- Sawhorses
- Prune sheers
- 5-gallon buckets
- Probe
- Shovel
- Small hand shovels and rakes
- Body bag
- Utility knife
- Plastic tarp
- Sunblock (depending on the weather condition)
- Water (to keep the CSI hydrated)
- Charcoal masks
- Protective gear (if necessary in biohazard environments)
- Body transport sheet
- Tarp or tent to cover the gravesite
- GPS device
- Metal detector
- Pick
- Rake
- Laser measuring device
- Generator (for night scenes)
- Halogen lights or portable light pole (for night scenes)
- Personal head lights (for night scenes)

Many law enforcement agencies maintain a ready excavation trailer with all excavation equipment. This enclosed trailer can easily be hooked up to any pickup truck, SUV, or van and allows for immediate responses.

5.1.3 Information about the Site

Most recoveries of buried bodies begin with someone reporting a partially uncovered gravesite such as hunters, hikers, or 4-wheelers. Prisoners try to make deals for lesser sentences if they tell the location of the gravesite where the victim of a murder is buried. Unfortunately, most of the information obtained from prisoners is not very reliable and CSI teams have searched wooded areas for possible gravesites, which were never found. It is important to conduct thorough interviews with the witnesses to determine the specifics of the grave location, the terrain, and the weather conditions. In winter months, the excavation may have to be delayed due to frozen grounds. Also, legal restraints such as the requirements of a search warrant or consent from a landowner have to be obtained before legally entering the scene.

5.1.4 Arriving at the Crime Scene

The recovery procedures for surface skeletal remains are very similar to those for buried remains. Excavation scenes are investigated like any other crime scene and the basic scene procedures such as note taking, maintaining a crime scene log of every person entering and leaving the scene, photography, sketching, and mapping as well as collecting and preservation of evidence apply.

5.1.4.1 Managing the Crime Scene Team

An excavation of a buried body or skeletal remains is a team effort. One crime scene investigator will be assigned as the lead investigator who will maintain all note taking and write the final crime scene report. The lead CSI will assign a CSI to take all photographs, while another CSI is responsible for evidence collection and preservation. Additional personnel will be needed for searching the area, as well as digging and sifting. When searching large areas, recruits from the police academy and additional patrol personnel can be requested for assistance.

5.1.4.1.1 Safety of the Excavation Team   The lead crime scene investigator is also responsible for the well-being of the CSI team. In summer, in hot climates, it is important to place a canopy over the sifting station and if possible over the gravesite. To avoid heat exhaustion, every CSI team member should take breaks and drink plenty of fluids. Dehydration occurs very fast during physical labor. Nutrition is as important as hydration. The lead CSI should require that the team takes a lunch break outside the outer perimeter and eats nutritious food.

Fresh water to freshen up and clean hands should be available in bottles or buckets. Sometimes, the fire department can provide water supply from a fire truck.

5.1.5 Clandestine Graves

A clandestine grave is a secret burial ground. The person buried is commonly the victim of a violent crime and hidden in a shallow or deep grave in the woods or in the desert.

5.1.5.1 Searching for the Clandestine Gravesite

The search for a clandestine gravesite differs from the search for skeletal remains. In both scenarios, it is helpful to ask the witness to accompany the CSI team to the location where the alleged gravesite was discovered. If the witness is a prisoner, arrangements have to be made with the Corrections Bureau to provide armed personnel escorting the inmate to the location to direct the CSI team to the alleged gravesite.

The CSI team and other available law enforcement personnel perform a line search in the area looking for

- Disturbances in the vegetation
- Dead or uprooted vegetation
- Missing vegetation
- A change in the color of the topsoil
- Intensive insect activity
- Loose branches, twigs, or piled up leaves
- Depressions in the soil due to settling of loose soil
- Metal detect for victim's jewelry, projectiles, or casings
- Anything that appears to be out of the ordinary

The settling of loose soil can resemble the outline of a grave, called primary depression; secondary impressions are located around the abdominal area of a body (Figure 5.1).

The CSI will use metal probes to determine the difference in the density of the soil in the suspected area and surrounding area. If a grave had been dug, the soil used to refill the grave will be softer than the surrounding earth that had been compounded for years. Once the grave has been located, the CSI will probe the area to determine the outline of the grave. Metal flags will be placed at the outline of the grave.

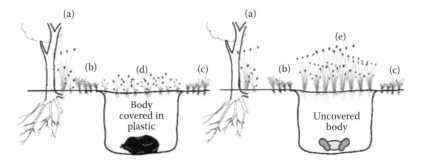

Figure 5.1 Plant growths in the vicinity of the remains. (a) Original vegetation; (b, c) different vegetation in the area trampled and disturbed during the original excavation of the grave; (d) area of new growth on the grave surface; (e) area of lush new growth on the grave surface due to the availability of nutrients from the decomposing body. (http://what-when-how.com/forensic-sciences /excavation-and-retrieval-of-forensic-remains/.)

5.1.5.2 Determining the Outer and Inner Perimeter of the Scene

After the area of the gravesite has been found and flagged, the outer and the inner perimeter will be determined. The inner perimeter is where the actual crime occurred or the location of the grave. The outer perimeter is the area surrounding the grave.

Before any additional search and processing can be started, the outer perimeter has to be established. If additional evidence should be discovered outside the outer perimeter, enlarge the perimeter to include all possible evidence.

Hint: The outer perimeter should include at least ¼ mile surrounding the potential burial area. Depending on the circumstances at the scene, enlarging the scene may be necessary. Too large is better than too small.

The gravesite is the inner perimeter and access to this area should be limited to CSI personnel involved in the actual excavation only. The lead CSI will establish a command post that can be as simple as a table or, at large scenes, a CSI vehicle. The lead CSI will establish an exit path from the outer to the inner perimeter to avoid destruction of possible evidence. Always search the area for the presence of any evidence before using it as an excess path (Figure 5.2).

5.1.5.3 Surface Evidence Collection

The crime scene team will perform line searches for surface evidence such as jewelry, shoe impressions, or tire tracks. Bloodstains can be found on branches or leaves, while broken branches and twigs may indicate somebody leaving the scene in a specific direction.

Figure 5.2 Excavation perimeter.

Surface Evidence Collection

- The photographer will take overall and midrange photos of the gravesite and the surrounding area.
- The lead CSI will note
  - Time when the gravesite was discovered
  - GPS and compass location of the grave
  - The names of the search team members
  - Sketches of the scene including
    - Overall sketch of the outer and inner perimeter
    - All recovered surface evidence
    - All recovered evidence from the gravesite
- The search team will mark the recovered evidence with metal flags.
- The photographer responds to the metal flags and captures overall, midrange, and close-up photos of each item. The metal flag will be replaced with a yellow evidence marker in a continuous numbering system.
- The evidence CSIs will obtain measurements of each piece of evidence. If no fixed objects are in the area, GPS readings of the compass method can be applied to determine the location of the evidence.
- The evidence CSI will collect and preserve the physical evidence and secure it in the locked CSI vehicle.

5.1.5.4 Setting Up a Grid

Prior to setting up a grid around the gravesite, the CSI will document (notes and photograph), examine, and remove every piece of debris. After all debris is removed, the CSI will

- Drive metal or wooden stakes in the ground around the gravesite.
- Create a square outline of the dig site.
- Place fluorescent string around the stakes at level height.
- Measure and note the height from the ground to the string.
- Determine the compass directions North and South to ensure that two stakes are north and two are south of the gravesite.
- The grid should be large enough that the excavating personnel can be within the grid without destroying the actual gravesite.
- Take additional photos of the grid.

An area close to the gravesite, after cleared of evidence, will be selected to set up the sifters. Placing the sifter on plastic horses allows for better working conditions. Placing a large tarp on the ground for storage of the sifted dirt allows for easier filling of the grave after the excavation.

5.1.5.5 Beginning to Excavate

After additional photos have been taken of the gravesite and the grid, and the debris of the surface has been removed, the CSI team can begin to breach the surface of the ground.

- Place a yellow marker number 1 for level 1 and "North direction marker" into the grid and photograph the first level of the excavation.
- Measure the length and width of the gravesite.
- The metal flags that had been used to mark the soft soil and the hard soil should remain in the ground as they mark the area most likely containing bones or other evidence.
- Always begin at the outer edge of the grave working toward the center.
- Use scoops, or small hand shovels can be used to remove the dirt while keeping the ground level parallel.
- Place the dirt into buckets and number the buckets.
- While one or two CSI remove soil from the gravesite, two or more CSI transport the buckets with soil to the examination area and sift the soil through the sifter for additional evidence such as hair, fingernails, teeth, bones, fragments, and other items such as jewelry.
- If the gravesite is in the mud, water screening may be necessary to recover the evidence.

Figure 5.3 Excavation inner perimeter.

- Any evidence recovered will be photographed with and without scale and collected as evidence.
- The evidence CSI will collect the evidence and note the excavation level, the bucket number, and the area from where the soil was removed.

Any evidence that is recovered within the gravesite should remain in place as long as possible and additional photos should be taken with and without scale, north arrow and marker depicting the excavation level. Overall photos allow depicting the location of all evidence in relation to each other. Triangulated measurements should be taken using the north and south stakes as fixed points A and B. The lead CSI will note the measurements and add the evidence to the sketch (Figure 5.3).

5.1.5.6 Recovery of the Body
When the body has been uncovered, continue to remove the soil around the remains to uncover as much as possible.

Caution: In most states, human remains fall under the jurisdiction of the medical examiner. Since the body is recovered, it is time to call the medical examiner's office and advise about the recovery. The medical examiner will determine if a medical legal death investigator or the medical examiner will respond to the scene or give permission for law enforcement to remove the remains.

Depending on the stage of decomposition of the remains and the level of expertise of the medico-legal death investigator and medical examiner in anthropology, a forensic anthropologist may be consulted.

The Rat House

In June 2010, in a city on the gulf coast of Florida, neighbors contacted the Lee County Sheriff's Office requesting a well-being check on an elderly female neighbor as they had not seen her in years. The neighbors also complained about trash, rats, cats, and bad odors coming from the residence. Deputies responded to the home and the daughter of the resident answered that her mother was in Connecticut visiting relatives. A week later, deputies of the Lee County Sheriff's Office and CSI personnel responded to the residence with a search warrant.

After the search warrant was read and served, the CSI team took exterior overall photos of the residence, the carport, and the vehicle parked in the carport as well as the entire property. It was difficult to open the front door of the residence as the floors were covered with trash piled 2 ft high, ranging from empty cans to paper bags, plastic containers, to deceased cats in carriers. Hundreds of rats had taken over and eaten the furniture and everything they could find, as shown in Figure 5.4. A strong ammonia odor was inside the house and the fire department was notified to check the air quality inside the residence before any investigative personnel began to excavate the scene.

The medico-legal death investigator and the CSI team searched through the rubbish in the sunroom, where the daughter had later stated her mother fell off a chair. She could not pick up her mother and let her lay on the floor. She comforted her with a blanket and pillow on the ground and her mother died two days later. She left the deceased on the floor and buried her with garbage.

Wearing Tivac Suits, booties, and breathing masks from the fire department, the medico-legal death investigator and a member from the CSI team searched the sunroom, where they discovered the skeletal remains of the woman's mother, as illustrated in Figure 5.5. The team could only remain for 20 minutes at a time inside the residence for health reasons. The skeletal remains were excavated from underneath the trash and transported to the local Medical Examiner's office by the professional services.

Numerous animal carriers with live cats and deceased and decomposed cats were found in the residence. Animal Control responded to the

(a)

(b)

Figure 5.4 Interior of the residence. (a) Excavation in residence and (b) the sunroom.

scene and took custody of the live animals, being so deathly sick that they had to be euthanized.

The daughter was arrested on charges of Social Security fraud. It was alleged that she lived with her dead mother from 2006 until 2010 and continued to cash her social security checks, totaling over $70,000.

Figure 5.5 Skeletal remains excavated in the sunroom.

The federal prosecutor could only indict her with embezzlement of more than $50,000 of retirement and survivor's benefits made to her mother between 2006 and July 2010 due to statute of limitations.

The daughter knew her mother was dead but did not alert the Social Security Administration and continued to cash the checks. A federal grand jury indicted her on charges of theft of public monies and Social Security fraud involving the death of her mother (Swift, 2011).

Once as much as possible of the body is exposed, place the body next to the gravesite and carefully lift the remains onto the bag. It may take two or three people to ensure that the body remains as intact as possible. After the body has been removed, continue to excavate for about 6 to 12 in. until you reach hard-packed soil, the true bottom of the grave. Evidence could have settled below the body due to gravity. Probing the bottom safeguards that it is the true hard-packed soil.

A second reason for excavating to the hard soil is to ensure that there isn't another grave under this grave.

Excavation of 7-Year-Old Boy

In Florida, the Lee County Sheriff's Office excavated the body of a 7-year-old boy in the yard of a residence. After probing the area, the CSI team discovered the clandestine grave. The grave was photographed, marked with flags, and wooden stakes outlined the gravesite. A rope connected

(a)

(b)

Figure 5.6 Excavation of a 7-year-old boy. (a) First discovery of the outline of the body. (b) Photo depicting the depth of the grave with the child's body.

to all stakes marked the actual gravesite. The excavation began in the late evening and lasted until midnight. Portable light poles powered by generators provided the necessary lighting. Each level of the excavation was set at 6 in.; level 1, 6 in. below ground level, level 2, 12 in. below ground level, etc. Every time a new excavation level approached, additional photographs with the concurrent level marker number were exposed; see Figure 5.6.

After the body was discovered, all dirt around the body was removed. The body was well preserved wearing pajamas. The body was transported to the medical examiner's office in Fort Myers, Florida.

5.1.5.7 *Condition of the Body*
The condition of the body depends on several factors such as

- Environmental conditions
- Time elapsed between death and discovery
- Stage of decomposition
- If the body was covered in plastic

If the body had been buried for a long period of time, the body may have decomposed to skeletal remains. The decomposition process depends on the way the body had been preserved. A body wrapped in a plastic tarp is preserved and protected from animal activity for a longer period of time than a body that is placed in a grave without any cover. Surface bodies or bodies in water attract scavengers such as insects and animals. The stages of decomposition are explained in Section 5.2.1.

A Good Day Fishing Gone Bad

In the summer of 1996, in Lee County, Florida, a grandfather, son, and grandson went on a fishing trip with their boat in the Caloosahatchee River. There are several small islands in the river used for overnight camping. The fishing crew decided to stay overnight at one of the little islands between Fort Myers and Cape Coral, Florida. During the evening, the father and the grandfather were drinking and got into an argument. The grandfather decided that he did not want to stay any longer and walked into the river to swim to land. The next morning, the son and grandson reported the grandfather missing. He never came home. The crime scene team of the Lee County Sheriff's Office responded to the island and searched for possible evidence and a clandestine grave. Examining the surface and vegetation, one area appeared to be disturbed. Probing resulted in loose soil consistent with a clandestine grave. The CSI team began to excavate the gravesite and recovered a blanket. Inside the blanket were the remains of a dog. The CSI team continued to excavate about 12 in. deeper to ensure that no additional body was buried underneath the dog. The crime scene team cleared the scene. Two days later, the grandfather's body floated in the river and was recovered. He died from drowning.

5.1.5.8 *Transport of the Body*
Most law enforcement agencies and medical examiners have annual contracts with professional body removal services for transport of the deceased from the scene to the medical examiner's office. The medico-legal death

investigator will notify the professional services to respond to the excavation scene for the transport of the remains.

Upon arrival on scene, the lead CSI will note

- Name of the professional service
- Employees of the professional service responding to the scene
- Date and time of arrival

The employee from the professional service places a numbered lock on the metal slider of the body bag. The CSI tapes evidence tape across the teeth of the zipper, dates, initials and takes photographs before transport.

5.1.5.9 Bugs, Insects, and Plant Material inside the Gravesite

After the body has been removed, the CSI will look for any kind of insects or bugs underneath the body or inside the gravesite. Photograph the insects or bugs, sketch and collect a sample in a glass container filled with methanol.

The CSI will also look at plant material inside the gravesite. Plant material inside the grave underneath the remains could have been transported with the body and provide information about the actual crime scene of the murder. Always photograph, sketch, and collect a sample of plant material in a paper bag.

5.1.5.10 Clearing from the Gravesite

After confirming that all evidence has been measured, collected, and preserved, it is time to fill the grave with the removed dirt. Placing a piece of rebar in the ground will allow reconstructing the grid for court if necessary. If the excavation site is on private property, the site should be returned to the original condition as best as possible.

A final walk-through of the inner and outer perimeter will guarantee that all evidence and crime scene equipment has been collected. The lead CSI will note the time in the field package.

5.1.6 Surface Skeletal Scattered Remains

The procedure for collecting surface scattered remains is very similar to the recovery of buried bodies. Both crime scenes are defined by an outer perimeter which should be ¼ mile surrounding the scatter area.

5.1.6.1 Leading the Crime Scene Team

Note taking, photographs, and crime scene sketches are required for both scenes. A lead crime scene investigator will be assigned to manage the crime scene team. The lead CSI will assign a CSI to take all photographs and another CSI will be responsible for collecting and preserving all evidence. The search and recovery of skeletal remains is a team effort and requires a minimum of four to five crime scene investigators/investigative personnel.

Even though the recovery of skeletal remains is not as labor intensive as the excavation of buried bodies, the CSI are exposed to the heat in the summer, and heat exhaustion, dehydration, and lack of nutrition are a concern for the lead CSI. Tarps and portable canopies can be placed in an area previously cleared for evidence to provide a shady place to take a break. Sufficient supply of water is a necessity.

5.1.6.2 Determine the Grid and Search for More Bones

Sometimes, the outer perimeter has to be extended due to bones and other evidence found outside the perimeter. Animal activity spreads bones in large areas. Jewelry can be found in bird's nests. Once the major portion of the bones has been discovered, overall, midrange, and close-up photographs of the skeletal remains will be captured. The lead CSI will draw a sketch of the scene including all bones recovered at the scene.

5.1.6.3 Jurisdiction of the Medical Examiner

In most states, the skeletal remains fall under the jurisdiction of the medical examiner/coroner. The CSI or criminal investigator notifies the medical examiner/coroner and reports the findings. The medical examiner/coroner will determine if a medico-legal death investigator will respond to the scene. When skeletal remains are recovered, the medical examiner/coroner or medico-legal death investigator responding to the scene will determine if the bones are human or animal. If the bones are of animal origin, no further collection of evidence is necessary and the CSI team can clear the scene.

5.1.6.4 Searching for Additional Evidence

The CSI team accompanied by the medico-legal death investigator continues the search for additional human remains and evidence. Cadaver dogs are excellent resources, as well as air searches with a helicopter in remote areas. In wooded areas, the line search method is most sufficient; however, it requires additional personnel to recover scattered remains and potential burial sites. The line search should be performed in an overlapping manner.

- All searching personnel walk shoulder-width apart in a straight line searching the area in front of them.
- A crime scene investigator will follow the search team placing metal flags by any recovered items of interest. It is recommended to use

different color flags for human remains and other items of evidentiary value.

- The photographer will follow and take overall, midrange, and close-
up photos of each item of evidence with and without yellow evidence
markers. The CSI will maintain a photo log. Always include a fixed
feature in the photos for orientation.
- The lead CSI notes the names of the search team, sketches the area
being searched, and notes all evidence recovered.
- The evidence collector will measure, collect, and preserve nonhu-
man evidence such as spent casings, knives, etc. GPS systems can
be used for measurements in remote areas. If the crime scene is
located close to a road, the manhole covers in the road contain
numbers that can be used for orientation. Placing a metal stake at
the scene can be used to reconstruct the scene at a later point as
the metal stake can be discovered with a metal detector and the
measurements and sketches allow for reconstructing the recovery
scene.

Warning: All biological evidence such as bones and body parts are photographed, measured, and sketched by the crime scene team, but collected by
the medical examiner's office or assigned professional services. Under no circumstances will the CSI team collect remains (Figure 5.7).

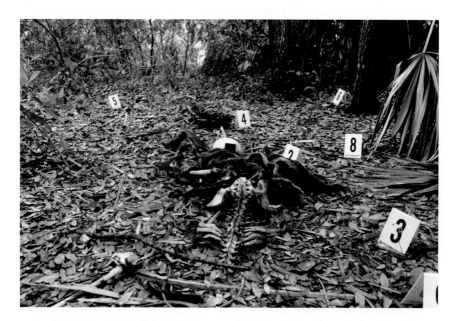

Figure 5.7 Skeletal remains.

5.2 Identification of the Remains through Forensic Anthropology

According to James and Nordby (2011), forensic anthropology is the application of the theory and methods of anthropology to forensic problems. The forensic anthropologist possesses extensive knowledge of the human skeleton complementing the forensic pathologist's understanding of soft tissue. Forensic anthropology is subdivided into four categories:

- Forensic taphonomy, the study of postmortem changes in the body due to environment, including decomposition, freezing, mummification, or scattering of skeletal remains by scavengers.
- Forensic archaeology, the recovery of scattered skeletal remains. Archaeologists use a variety of methods and techniques to recover and interpret material from prior events. The most common methods are
  - Aerial and infrared photography
  - Ground penetration radar
  - Metal detectors
- Extrapolation of soft tissue based on skeletal form.
- Biomechanical interpretation of sharp and blunt force injuries to the bone (James and Nordby, 2011).

The forensic anthropologist examines human remains focusing on

- Identifying the victim's age, sex, stature, ancestry, anomalies, pathology, and individual features.
- Providing information about the death and evidence of trauma.
- Assisting in the recovery of skeletal remains at gravesites.
- Reconstructing the postmortem period of the victim by analyzing the condition of the remains.

Osteology, the study of skeletal biology and odontology, the study of dental biology, are parts of the physical anthropology.

5.2.1 Taphonomic Assessment

The taphonomic assessment consists of several steps:

- Full inventory of the area of the gravesite/area of scattered remains such as
  - Distinguish the completeness of all skeletal remains found.

  - Determine if the skeletal remains are adult or adolescent.
  - X-rays should be taken if flesh is remaining.
- Evaluate the condition of the remains.
  - Determine the stage of decomposition.
  - Examine insect life cycles.
  - Look for weathering.
  - Are there any signs of scavenger activity?
  - Is there modification through sand, water, or geology?
- Examine soft tissues examination.
  - Examine fingerprints to determine viability.
  - Internal organ and tissues examination.
  - Inspect the bone formation in child victims.
  - Always screen for small bones or artifacts such as piece of a projectile, etc.
  - Consider X-ray to find additional evidence.
- Estimate the time of death.

5.2.2 Methods of Identification of the Victim

Most medical examiners and coroners require a positive identification of the remains. This can be accomplished by matching DNA, fingerprints, dental records, or X-rays. Surgical procedures can help to identify the victim, for example, breast implants contain a serial number. Bone changes can be based on occupations such as a tile layer or heavy construction worker.

5.2.3 Estimating the Victim's Age

The forensic physical anthropologist possesses extensive knowledge about the size of skeletons at every age. In diaphysis, the length of the long bone shafts of the victim are compared to the published tables of age identification, while epiphyses examines the two ends of the bones. The time formation, together with the growth and fusion of the diaphysis and epiphyses are patterned to create the age estimate. During the teen ages and twenties, the epiphysis of long bones fuses. The rates of the epiphyseal union are different and, therefore, all union sites should be examined.

5.2.3.1 Skeletal Development

The skeletal development of males and females differs; females develop earlier. The bone development sequence and timing also differ between populations. The bone development is different from person to person; therefore, the age estimates of skeletal remains should always be termed in ranges and not in exact years.

The bone density changes and it is not fixed until a person reaches adulthood. The bone density peaks in the twenties and declines in the forties. The bone density also varies based on age, hormonal status, exercise, weight, and nutrition. The bone density can be examined macroscopically, microscopically, and via bone densitometry. An onset of osteoarthritis is common in victims of 40 years of age and can help in the estimation of age.

The two most reliable indicators for adult age are the pelvic joint morphology.

- Pubic symphysis: measures the surface changes in pubic bones and compares to published standards.
- Iliac auricular surface: measures the joint surface changes to the auricular surface, the area where the ilium connects to the sacrum (James and Nordby, 2011).

Use-wear patterns on the hand identify whether the victim was right or left handed.

5.2.3.2 Teeth Development

Teeth can also help to determine the age and sex of a victim, as the tooth development also differs between gender and population. Unfortunately, there are only a few reference standards for the skeletons of children at various ages.

5.2.3.3 Sexual Dimorphism

Sexual dimorphism can be performed with DNA methods producing accurate determination of the victim's sex; other methods are genotype and phenotype. However, the determination of the biological sex of skeletal remains is not an exact science.

According to James and Nordby (2011), the female pelvis has

- Broader and increased depth of pelvic inlet and outlet
- Broad, shallow sciatic notch
- U-shaped subpubic angle
- Well-developed ventral arc
- Raised auricular surface

Males tend to have a larger skull and a more right-angled jaw. Men have larger joint surfaces, especially the mandibular and occipital condoyles. Men have larger weight-bearing joint surfaces such as the hip.

Variables that affect the sex determination are nutritional status, weight training, heavy chewing, and population affinity.

5.2.3.4 Estimation of Stature

The stature of a person is generally a fixed and accurate measurement; however, some people over- or underestimate the height when reporting a missing person. If the body is decomposed or skeletonized, the stature can be calculated based on the head, spine, and pelvis, and if at least one leg is present, the vertebral disc thickness and total stature can be estimated. Allometry is another method to estimate the stature based on the length of the long bone, however, the measurements differ from population to population (James and Nordby, 2011).

5.2.3.5 Evidence for Cause and Manner of Death

It is very difficult to differentiate between antemortem and perimortem injuries on bones. One sign of perimortem trauma is when a broken bone does not show any signs of healing as bones take several days before starting to heal. Blunt force trauma, however, produces impact marks and can fracture or fragment bones depending on the force of impact. A sharp force trauma with a knife or machete creates cuts or impact scars. Gunshot wounds create a specific pattern, especially in skulls. As in glass fracture matching, the fracture lines of a skull allow determining the sequence of the gunshot wounds.

5.2.3.6 The Forensic Anthropology Report

The basic forensic anthropology report contains information about

- Taphonomy
- Biological profile: age, sex, ancestry, stature, and pathology
- Individualization characteristic for identification
- Evidence of postmortem trauma

Bones Solve Cold Case

In 2010, in Porter, Texas, the charred remains of a 46-year-old woman were found in a garbage can. The victim was put in a garbage can and later set on fire. Forensic anthropologist Dr. Joan Bytheway is the lab director at the Southeast Texas Applied Forensic Science Facility, nicknamed the Body Farm, one of four facilities in the United States to examine the effects of climate, insects, animals, and soils on decomposition.

For months, Dr. Bytheway examined the victim's bones and discovered a triangular piece that was not burned at all and most likely dislodged before the body was burned. This piece of evidence showed that the skull was fractured before the body was set on fire. Further examination revealed a crack in the skull caused by a hammer. This was the kind of evidence that provided the sheriff's deputies leverage to question the suspect, 26-year-old Robert Hinton. Hinton confessed and was sentenced to 30 years in prison (KHOU, 2012).

5.3 Facial Reconstruction

The human skull provides clues to personal appearance such as the brow ridge, the distance between the eye orbits, the shape and size of the nasal chamber, the shape and projection of the nasal bones, the chin's form, and the overall profile of the facial bones. These all determine facial features in life. The forensic facial reconstructionist works together with the forensic anthropologist to determine the age, race, and gender of the skull.

The three-dimensional reconstruction process consists of several steps.

- Photographing the skull while in the Frankfort Horizontal position. (Frankfort Horizontal position is a reproducible position of a head where the upper margin of the ear and the lower margin of the orbit of the eyes are horizontal.)
- The victim's age, race, and gender determine the depth of the tissue when the reconstructionist places artificial eyes in the skull's eye sockets.
- Tissue markers for the depth of the tissue are glued to the skull before clay is applied following the tissue markers.
- The facial reconstructionist takes several measurements and notes the nose thickness and length, the width and thickness of the mouth, and eye placement.
- Any information about the victim's lifestyle or previous place of living helps to create an accurate reconstruction.
- A wig is used to represent hair. Other props such as eyeglasses, hats, or even facial hair may be used to accentuate the features of the individual.
- The facial reconstructionist photographs the sculpture and collects all notes and measurements in a document.

Three-dimensional facial reconstructions have been very successful in identifying unknown remains.

5.4 Identification of the Victim through Forensic Odontology

Forensic odontology is based on the comparison of unique features of a person's teeth. Dental identification is used in mass fatalities such as in plane crashes or decomposed bodies and skeletal remains. Dental identification was used to identify the victims of 9/11 and the hurricane victims in Haiti in 2008.

The creed of dental identification is the comparison of postmortem dental remains with antemortem dental records, X-rays, notes from the family dentist, and dental patterns such as missing or implanted teeth. Victims with complex dental records are easier to identify than victims with little or no restorative dental work. The comparison of the dental characteristics is one of the fastest methods of identification.

5.4.1 Grin Line Identification

In 2009, Drs. Susan A. Bollinger, Paula C. Brumit, Bruce A. Schrader, and David R. Senn introduced the grin line identification method. The research was published in the *Journal of the American Academy of Forensic Science* titled "Grin Line Identification Using Digital Imaging and Adobe Photoshop."

These forensic odontologists recognized a lack of antemortem dental records when asked to aid in identification. The grin line or GLID technique serves as another tool in forensic odontology. In this technique, grins seen in earlier or antemortem photographs are compared to images of postmortem anterior teeth taken by a forensic odontologist.

GLID requires the following steps.

5.4.1.1 Creating the Images
- Ask for a photo of the victim or missing person where he or she smiles and teeth are visible. The photo should have a quality of 300 dpi. If necessary, the photo quality can be digitally enhanced. The photo can either be scanned into the computer or a digital photograph can be taken of the original photo.
- Capture several digital close-up photographs of the dentures of the skeletal remains. Use different angles to ensure all views are captured.
- Import and archive the images into the computer.
- Crop the grin photos in the antemortem (AM) photos and create a file.
- Sharpen and enhance the images with the LEVELS tools.
- Size the AM images using common reference points and features from the postmortem (PM) images, creating an AM overlay.
- Compare the overlay to the PM image for matching features.
- Create a folder and archive all working images.

5.4.1.2 Comparing the Images
There are several steps of cropping the AM image and the PM image to the same size. It is important that the height and width of both images are identical. Use several tools in Adobe Photoshop to outline and isolate the teeth in the AM image. Dragging the AM overlay over the PM photograph performs the comparison.

Both maxillary and mandibular arches can be analyzed. The chance of a conclusion leading to identification is higher if the AM image depicts several individual characteristics. The GLID analysis can be applied using PM photographs of dental fragments if there is a sufficient amount of teeth, three or more, and those are the same teeth as in the AM image. One pitfall of this method is the possibility that anterior dentitions have been replaced with restoratives since the AM photo had been taken.

5.5 Entomology

Entomology is the study of insects whereas medico-legal entomology is the study of insects associated with a deceased. Through the study of insects, the forensic entomologist can estimate and determine the minimum time that the person has been dead and provide many other factors about the death. The study of the insects on the body can reveal if the body had been moved after death or whether the victim used drugs or was poisoned. Insects will also be present at wound sites and help determine the time frame of neglect or abuse of living victims. This information is important in the investigation of elderly abuse or child abuse.

5.5.1 Time of Death Estimation

Within minutes after death, blowflies, attracted by the gases from the newly deceased, arrive on the body starting to lay their eggs around the nasal and oral cavities, the areas where the gases from decomposition escape. In warm weather conditions, the eggs will hatch within 24 hours and the fly goes through three larval phases of development, called instars. The larvae develops into a young blowfly moving away from the corpse, burrows into the ground, forms pupae, and metamorphoses into a winged adult fly, crawling to the surface and flying away. The development of the blowfly depends on the environmental conditions and reference tables are available allowing use of this information for the determination of the approximate time of death.

There are two methods to estimate the approximate time since death. The first method is founded on the growth of larva Diptera, or flies such as the blowfly that will colonize the body shortly after death. The analysis is based on the known time passage between laying the first egg on the deceased until the first adult fly emerges from the puparial cases leaving the remains making it very valuable in estimating the minimum time since death (Nordby et al., 2014). This estimation of the time after death can be a couple of hours or several weeks. "The second method is based on the predictable successional colonization of the body by a sequence of

Figure 5.8 Maggots.

carrion insects" (Nordby et al., 2014, p. 174). The application of this method depends on the age of the remains and the type of insects collected from the remains (Figure 5.8).

Bugs Lead to the Suspect

Local police in a southeastern town in the United States received notification of a foul smelling odor coming from a single-family home. Police officers arrived on scene and found the decomposed body of a young female in a shallow grave in the basement of the residence. The preliminary cause of death was determined to be a single gunshot to the head, most likely from a small caliber rifle. The CSI team assisted a forensic entomologist in the excavation of the remains. The entomologist noticed numerous larvae and pupae of two different fly species in and around the gravesite.

The entomologist collected several specimens for further examination in the laboratory. He used weather data and soil temperature to reconstruct the climate conditions at the gravesite to determine the development stage of the fly species. He concluded that the specimens were in the fourth stage of development, which is consistent with a 28-day time interval and that the victim had been dead for 28 days.

This information was crucial for the investigators who now concentrated their investigation around the approximate time of death. Just a couple of days later, a female confessed that she had killed the woman 28 days prior to discovery by police.

5.5.2 Life Cycle

The life cycle of a fly is predictable and influenced by temperature, humidity, and nutrition. The following factors are important when determining the estimated time since death based on blowfly development:

1. Within 24 hours after death, the blowfly lays eggs on the remains.
2. The eggs hatch into maggots and feed from the organs and soft tissue of the remains.
3. The entomologist can determine the time after death based on the stages of development of the fly larvae.
4. Examining the most recent stage of larvae development permits determining the postmortem interval (PMI).
5. New flies and empty pupal cases found on the scene are evidence for a full cycle of fly development on the remains.

Time after death determinations based on the blowfly life cycle are not always straightforward due to the changes in the environment such as geological location, weather, humidity, climate, and presence of drugs. Cold weather will slow down the development of fly eggs into flies. Those conditions will be considered when determining the PMI (Saferstein, 2015) (Figure 5.9 and Document 5.1).

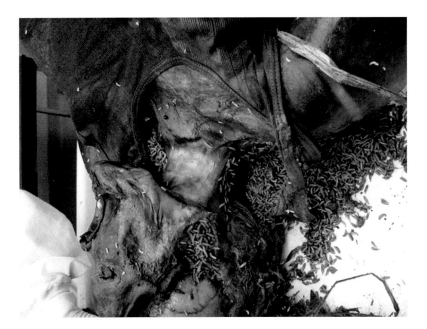

Figure 5.9 Maggot activity on body.

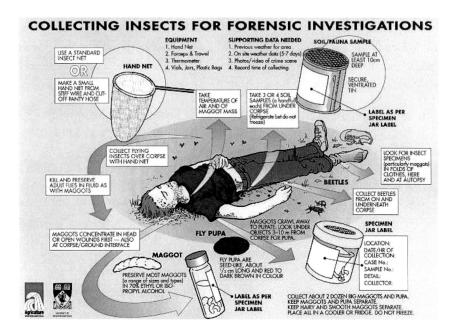

Document 5.1 Life cycle. (From www.nlm.nih.gov/visibleproofs/media/detailed /ll_a_216n.jpg.)

5.5.3 Toxicology and Insects

As the saying goes, "We are what we eat," and the same can be said of the insects on the remains. The insects eating from the body ingest all the toxins, poisons, and drugs present at the time of death. The metabolization of drugs or poison begins when the human body breaks down the chemicals called metabolites and later excretes them. The time elapsed between the drug usage and the time of death is significant when examining for the parent drug and metabolites. The toxicologist analyzes tissue and body samples to determine what toxins have been present during the time of death. This information can be crucial to determine the cause and manner of death.

5.5.4 Bugs Tell More Stories…

Other than the PMI, insects at the crime provide further information:

- Suspects can be linked to the scene of the crime if they are bitten by arthropods specific to the vicinity of the crime scene.
- Insects living in a specific area found on a body in a different vicinity indicate that the body has been moved.
- Blowfly larvae can be used to determine how long children have been neglected by their parents.

5.5.5 Collection of Entomology Samples on Scene

Whenever the crime scene investigator responds to a scene of a decomposed body, either indoors or outdoors, there is a presence of insects. It is important to collect a representative sample of the insects present on scene for the entomologist to determine the estimated time since death.

Every crime scene investigator on scene uses the entomological evidence collection kit to collect samples of the insects present on scene.

Steps to collect bug specimens:

- Collect a representative sample of each kind of adult insect (flies and beetles) present on scene and on the body. A representative sample is 50 plus insects.
- Collect samples of the eggs (live).
- Collect samples of the maggots from the trauma site and from other areas around the deceased (live and preserved).
- Collect samples of the beetles' grunts (preserved).
- Collect fly pupae (live).
- Collect any other insects around the body.

All preserved samples should be stored in a container with 70% ethyl alcohol solution.

All live samples should be placed in a "maggot motel," a folded pocket of foil with decomposition soaked soil or with vermiculate inside a plastic container with a layer of dry soil on the bottom.

5.5.6 Note Taking at a Death Scene with Insect Activity

Note taking is significant at a death scene with insect activity for later determination of the time and possible cause of death. These notes will provide the background information for the entomologist who is not present on scene. The entomology evidence collection work sheet in Document 5.2 provides an excellent guide for the necessary steps of documenting and collecting entomological evidence. The following steps are the minimum requirements for sufficient data for entomological examinations.

- Describe the scene in detail to rural, urban, aquatic, and vegetation
- Exposure to
  - Air
  - Buried
  - Clothing
  - Describe the debris on the body

Forensic Entomology Data Form

Date: _____	Collector: _____
Case Number: _____	Agency: _____
Location: (GPS coordinates, nearest physical address, city, state, country)	

Decedent: _____	Age: _____	Sex: _____
Last Seen Alive: _____	Date/Time Found: _____	
Date Reported Missing: _____	Time Insect Collection: _____	
Site Description:		

Condition of the remains: ☐ whole ☐ partial	If partial, what part is present:
Presence of trauma: ☐ yes ☐ no ☐ unknown	Evidence of scavenging: ☐ yes ☐ no ☐ unknown

Evidence of possible traumatic injury sites: (Comment and/or draw below)

Type of body/remains concealment:
☐ none ☐ plastic bag ☐ container, type: _____ ☐ burial, depth: _____
☐ other: _____

Location(s) of insect activity: (check all that apply)
☐ head ☐ mouth ☐ eyes ☐ ears ☐ anus ☐ genitals ☐ chest ☐ abdomen
☐ wound(s), location(s): _____ ☐ other: _____

Location on body of insect specimen collection: (check all that apply)
☐ head ☐ mouth ☐ eyes ☐ ears ☐ anus ☐ genitals ☐ chest ☐ abdomen
☐ wound(s), location(s): _____ ☐ other: _____

Approximate stage of decomposition:
☐ fresh ☐ bloated ☐ active decay ☐ advanced decay ☐ skeletonized
☐ saponification ☐ mummification ☐ dismemberment ☐ other: _____

Body exposure: (check all that apply)
☐ open air ☐ burial ☐ fully clothed ☐ partially clothed ☐ nude
☐ full sun ☐ partial shade ☐ full shade ☐ debris, type: _____
☐ other: _____
Portion of body clothed and description of clothing:

Document 5.2 Entomology specimen.   (Continued)

Forensic Entomology Data Form

Location of body and insect collection site: (check all that apply) □ indoor □ outdoor □ aquatic □ rural □urban/suburban	
Indoor: □ house □ shed or outbuilding Was structure closed to outside insect access? □ yes □ no □ unknown Was structure temperature controlled? □ yes, temperature: _____ □ no □unknown	Outdoor: (check all that apply) □ forest □ field □ pasture □ brush □ grass □ roadside □ pavement □ trash container □ vacant lot □ other: _____
Aquatic: (check all that apply) □ pond □ lake □creek □river □ canal □ditch □gulf □ swampy area □ salt water □ fresh water □ brackish water □ standing water □ running water □ other: _____ Water temperature: _____ Was the body floating on water surface? □ yes □no □unknown	Notes on the collection site or body condition:
Scene temperatures: (complete all that apply) ambient:_____ ambient (1 ft):_____ body surface:_____ ground surface:_____ under-body interface:_____ maggot mass:_____ soil temperature (1 inch):_____ soil temperature (3 inches):_____ A/C or Heat:_____ ceiling fan: on/off Note: Record all temperatures periodically each day at the site for 3-5 days after recovery.	
Method of insect preservation for soft-bodied specimens: □ hot water kill and 80% ethanol □ 80% ethanol □ other:_____	
Number of preserved samples:	Number of live samples:
How are live samples being maintained? □ room temperature at: _____ □ other: _____	Where were the specimens sent?

Dr. J.H. Byrd 2014.

Document 5.2 (Continued) Entomology specimen. (With permission from Dr. Jason Byrd.)

- Stage of decay (circle)
  - Fresh
  - Bloat
  - Active decay
  - Advanced decay
  - Skeletonized
  - Mummification
  - Dismemberment
- Look for evidence of scavengers
- Note the possible areas of dramatic injuries
- Document the scene temperature at outdoor scene

- • Ambient temperature 5 ft above the ground
- • Ambient temperature 1 ft above the ground
- • Body surface temperature
- • Ground surface temperature
- • Maggot mass temperature
- • Water temperature if the samples are in the water
- • Soil temperature (10 cm)
- • Soil temperature (20 cm)
- • Document scene temperature at indoor scene
  - • Note if air conditioner is on and what temperature it is set at
  - • Note if the ceiling fan is on or off
- • Always include the number of samples taken from the scene and separate into live and preserved samples
- • Always draw a sketch of the scene and note the insect activity on the body

Packing and shipping of samples to the entomology laboratory.

- • All containers should be labeled properly with the case number, agency name, date and time of recovery, and initials of collector.
- • A summarized case report should accompany the specimens.
- • Include the contact information of the investigating officer.
- • Include scene and autopsy photos of the deceased.

All specimens should be shipped overnight via FedEx or UPS to the nearest entomology laboratory.

5.6 Botany

Forensic botany is the application of plant science to solve crimes. Forensic botany is based on Locard's principle of exchange stating that a criminal always leaves something at the crime scene and takes something away. The first botanical testimony, an analysis of the wood grain of the ladder used in the Lindbergh kidnapping, was heard in a North American court in 1935, and led to the conviction of Bruno Hauptmann.

5.6.1 What Can Plants Tell Us?

Botanical evidence can be leaves, a branch, grass, a flower, or needles from a tree found at the crime scene, or even pollen. Leaves found on the deceased that are from a tree that is not natural to the geographical area where the victim is found will provide suggestions that the victim had been transported

and provide information about the possible whereabouts of the victim during the last days before death. It is important to collect any plant material
found on or around the deceased. Always air-dry the sample and package in
a paper bag to avoid molding and destruction of the plant DNA.

Seedpods Lead to Murderer

On May 2, 1990, a woman was killed and her body abandoned in the
Arizona desert. Even though police found a beeper next to the victim's
body that led to the offender, the key piece of evidence was the DNA
sequences from a few seedpods on the back of the suspect's truck. Judge
Susan Bolton of the Superior Court of Maricopa County ruled the admissibility of the DNA profile linking the seedpods to a Palo Verde tree present in the area where the body was discovered as evidence in the murder
trial. The judge's decision was a scientific and judicial first. While DNA
profiles from human blood and tissue are widely accepted in murder or
rape trials, this case was the first introduction of plant DNA in a criminal
trial.

When first approached by the Maricopa County, molecular geneticist
Tim Helentjaris of the University of Arizona, he questioned if such DNA
testing would be possible. Helentjaris questioned if he could obtain a sufficient sample from the seedpods and if there was enough genetic variation to identify an individual through its DNA. During the research, he
noticed that the Palo Verde tree has a high degree of genetic variation.
Helentjaris applied a technique known as randomly amplified polymorphic DNA, or RAPD, a method that involves the polymerized chain reaction (PCR) gene amplification. RAPD employs DNA primers containing
as few as 10 bases binding to many sites in the genome. If proper binding
conditions exist, each primer creates a reproducible profile of amplified
fragment. Using multiple primers makes it easy to identify the DNA of
individual trees.

Helentjaris matched the DNA of the seedpods from the suspect's
truck to the tree at the crime scene. He was able to distinguish the correct
tree from a lineup of 11 Palo Verde trees at the crime scene. Even though
the seedpods could not place the offender at the crime scene, they could
prove that his truck was at the scene (Yoon, 1993).

5.6.2 Proper Collection of Plant Material

As with any other item of physical evidence, the basic crime scene documentation process of notes, photographs, sketching, measurement, collection, and
preservation apply to the collection of plant material. Plants retain most of their

characteristics when dried. The color changes and shape changes after drying are known, measured and recorded allowing for testing dried materials.

- Always package plant material in paper.
- The best method to preserve green material is between two pages of newspaper in the center of a phone book.
- Record the color, size, and shape on the outside of the bag.
- Include the area where the item was found such as near the lake, major road, etc.
- If the plant material is soaked in fluids, collect in a plastic container and refrigerate immediately.
- A cooler can be used as temporary field storage, however, never place the sample on ice.
- Collect smaller plants in their entity (remove with shovel; remove dirt from roots before packaging in paper bag).
- 12 to 18 in. of a branch of a larger plant or tree are sufficient.
- Never place live plants in a plastic bag as the moisture and sugar in the plant material will degrade in plastic within 3 to 5 days.

Always maintain the chain of custody for every piece of evidence, even if it is only a seed, a root, or a leaf from a tree.

In this chapter, we learned about bones, bugs, and botany and how these forensic disciplines can provide excellent information leading to the suspect of a crime. In the next chapter, we will look at different methods of crime scene reconstruction.

References

Bollinger, S.A., Brumit, P.C., Schrader, B.A., and Senn, D.R. (2009). *Forensic Science*, 54 (2), doi: 10.1111/j.1556-4029.2008.00971.x.

Excavation and Retrieval of Forensic Remains. Retrieved from http://what-when-how.com/forensic-sciences/excavation-and-retrieval-of-forensic-remains.

Facial reconstruction. (n.d.). Retrieved from http://www.forensicartist.com/reconstruction.html.

James, S. and Nordby, J. (2011). *Forensic Science: Introduction to Scientific and Investigative Technology*, 2nd ed. CRC Press/Taylor & Francis; Boca Raton, FL.

KHOU. (2012). Bodies buried on a farm north of Houston help detectives solve crimes. (February 23, 2012). Retrieved from http://www.khou.com/story/news/2014/07/18/11673250/.

Nordby, J., James, S., and Bell, S. (2014). *Forensic Science: Introduction to Scientific and Investigative Technology*. 4th ed. CRC Press/Taylor & Francis; Boca Raton, FL.

Saferstein, R. (2015). *Criminalistics: An Introduction of Forensic Science*. 20th ed. Pearson Prentice Hall.

Swift, A. (2011). Feds indict Florida woman who kept her dead mom at home, cashed her Social Security checks. *Naples Daily News.* Retrieved from http://www .naplesnews.com/news/crime/gail-andrews-dead-mom-home-fort-myers.

Yoon, C.K. (1993). Botanical witness for the prosecution. America Association for the Advancement of Science. Retrieved from http://www.readabstracts.com /Science-and-technology/Botanical-witness-for-the-prosecution-What-might -cause-parasites-to-become-more-virulent.html#ixzz3j86RZGUL.

Crime Scene Reconstruction

6

Crime scene reconstruction is a reenactment of the events that took place during the commission of the crime. Saferstein (2011) stated, "Crime scene reconstruction is the method used to support a likely sequence of events at a crime scene by observing and evaluating physical evidence and statements made by individuals involved in the incident" (p. 299). Reconstructing a crime is a team effort and may involve the crime scene investigator, medical examiner, and law enforcement personnel. Information from the autopsy, evaluation of the evidence and witnesses, and victim and suspect statements are combined to answer the questions of who, how, where, and when. In homicide cases, the detective, crime scene investigator, and medical examiner who performed the autopsy and the medico-legal death investigator confer and examine all evidence to reconstruct the event that took place. In other cases, the judge can order the jury to visit the crime scene and ask the CSI to position all items of evidence in the location as originally found. That is one of the reasons why detailed documentation of the scene and mapping of the evidence is of utmost importance. In suicide cases, family members requested a reconstruction of the suicide as they could not believe that their loved ones killed themselves.

As an example, bloodstain pattern analysis can provide information about the weapon used in the bloodletting incident, answering how. Firearms trajectory determination allows determining location of the shooter and victim, answering where. The medical examiner determines the approximate time of death, answering when. Gunshot residue analysis determines who was on scene during the shooting, answering who.

6.1 What Is Bloodstain Pattern Analysis?

Bloodstain pattern analysis is the study of the shape, size, distribution pattern, location, and number of bloodstains to explain the physical events by which they were created. Bloodstain pattern analysis often provides information that cannot otherwise be obtained. Through the analysis of the bloodstains and bloodstain patterns, the analyst can determine

- Location of the victim and the offender during the bloodshed
- Number of perpetrators
- Movements and direction of a person or an object

195

- Possible weapon used in the bloodshed
- Type and direction of impact that produced the bloodshed
- Alteration of the scene after the bloodshed
- The position of the victim and/or objects during bloodshed

6.1.1 Anatomical Aspects of Blood

Blood counts as 8% of the total body weight; a man has between 5 and 6 L of blood, women between 4 and 5 L. The pressure of blood in our arteries is regulated by the pressure produced by the contraction of the heart and the status of the amount of dilation of the arterioles (James, Kish, and Sutton, 2005). Blood pressure is measured in millimeters of mercury (mm Hg). Blood pressure consists of two numbers, the systolic pressure during the contraction of the heart and the diastolic pressure when the heart relaxes. A blood pressure for humans of 115/75 is considered normal. To maintain blood supply to the brain and other organs in the body, the blood pressure must be maintained above 100/40. The brain is very sensitive to the reduction of blood supply and the blood circulation provides oxygen and nutrients to the organs.

Blood loss can be caused by injury or illness. Hemothorax (bleeding in the chest cavity) or hemopertoneum (bleeding in the abdominal cavity) can result in bleeding to death without any external loss of blood. External bleeding, however, allows the investigator to determine the what, where, and how the bloodletting occurred. Therefore, the first step in an investigation is to determine if the bleeding was caused by an injury or disease.

6.1.1.1 Medical Conditions Causing Blood Loss

Ruptured veins due to an illness can cause bleeding from the skin. Common causes for bleeding from the nose and mouth are lung cancer, tuberculosis, aortic aneurysm, or nasal cancer.

Caution: A gunshot into the victim's mouth with a small caliber firearm also causes bleeding from the mouth and nose and could be mistaken for disease bleeding. Always check for medical records, medications, and obtain autopsy confirmation before making a determination.

Trauma or damage to the respiratory system such as nose, mouth, airways, and lungs can result in depositing blood in the airway passages. Exhalation in the form of sneezing or coughing can forcefully project the blood from the nose or mouth. "If the bleeding started in the lung or the airways of the lung or if the blood is from the mouth, nose, or esophagus and is inhaled in the lung, the blood will be mixed with air" (James et al., 2005, p. 20). Abrasions and lacerations also produce bleeding. Incised wounds, commonly called cuts, from a sharp object such as a knife or machete may be fatal if a major artery is severed such as the femoral artery, brachial artery, or the carotid artery. While stab wounds are also created by sharp objects, they differ in the depth of tissue penetration. Stab wounds are deeper and may bleed less than lacerations as the surface of the skin may close up. Examining the stab wound on the skin, the medical examiner can determine if the sharp object had a single or double-edged blade.

6.1.2 Physical Properties of Blood

Human blood is unique and reacts like no other fluid, making it predictable when subjected to external forces. A cohesive force producing a surface tension within and on the exterior surface holds blood together. James, Nordby, and Bell (2014) explained, "Surface tension is defined as the force that pulls the surface molecules of a liquid toward the interior, decreasing the surface area and causing the liquid to resist penetration" (p. 71). The surface tension is articulated in force per unit length such as dynes per centimeter representing stored energy. A dyne equals 10^{-5} Newtons. A common example of surface tension is a water bug walking on a lake or pond. The surface tension of the water supports the bug's weight. James et al. (2005) showed that a razor blade floats on top of water, even though the weight of the steel razor blade is 7.8 times heavier than water. The razor blade has to be placed on the surface of the water without penetrating the skin of the surface tension to allow the blade to float. If the razor blade penetrates the skin of the surface tension, the blade will sink (Table 6.1).

The physical characteristics of a liquid are explained with terms such as cohesion, adhesion, and capillarity. Cohesion is the electrical attractive force between *like* molecules holding the molecules together resulting in strong cohesive forces at the surface of a liquid such as blood. Adhesion, in contrast, is the attractive forces of *unlike* molecules, for example, blood adhering to a knife. Capillarity is the phenomena when the surface tension causes a liquid to be drawn upward in a container opposing gravity (James et. al., 2005).

Table 6.1 Surface Tension of Common Fluids

Fluid	Dyne/cm at 20°C
Ethanol	22.3
Soap	25
Olive oil	32
Blood	50
Water	72.5
Mercury	465.0

Source: James, S., Kish, P., and Sutton, P. (2005). *Principles of Bloodstain Pattern Analysis: Theory and Practice* (Practical Aspects of Criminal & Forensic Investigations), 3rd ed. CRC Press, Boca Raton, FL, p. 52.

Blood spatter is created when the external force overcomes and penetrates the surface tension. "The shape of a blood drop in air is directly related to the molecular cohesive forces acting upon the surface of the drop. These forces cause the drop to assume the configuration of a spheroid" (James et al., 2014, p. 71). The shape of a falling drop of blood is slightly elongated when it breaks free. The effects of air resistance during the fall will slightly flatten the sphere. A drop of blood that propels through the air increases its velocity until the downward gravitational acceleration is equal to the friction of air resistance. The drop will cease to accelerate and maintain a constant velocity, also called the maximum terminal velocity. The maximum terminal velocity of a drop of blood is 25.1 ft/sec. This maximum terminal velocity can be achieved when a drop of blood falls from a height of 14 to 18 ft. Variables such as the size and weight of a drop may influence the time to reach terminal velocity.

Experiments show that a drop of blood falling from a distance of 6 in. on a piece of glass has a diameter of 13 mm, whereas a drop of blood falling from 7 ft onto a piece of glass has a diameter of 21 mm.

Caution: Do not attempt to determine the height from which the blood fell based on the diameter of stains, as the volume of the original blood is unknown.

6.1.3 The Levels of Bloodstain Pattern Analysis

On arrival on scene, the bloodstain pattern analyst visually examines and evaluates the characteristics of the bloodstains such as size, shape, and distribution patterns. Extensive knowledge of the physical characteristics of blood under known circumstances and experimentation is required to determine how the stains were created. The bloodstain pattern analyst must be able to identify the different mechanism used to create a stain pattern (James et al., 2005, p. 68). Table 6.2 illustrates the four levels of analysis in bloodstain pattern analysis.

6.1.4 Classification of Bloodstains

The physical characteristics of bloodstains allow categorizing them into three primary and multiple secondary categories (Table 6.3).

6.1.5 Passive Bloodstains

Passive bloodstain patterns are created by falling blood subjected to gravity and air resistance. Passive bloodstain patterns can also include transfer patterns such as wipe and swipe patterns, flow patterns, and blood drops in the form of single drops, a trail of drops, or multiple drops, and large volumes of blood such as pools of blood or materials such as clothing or carpets saturated in blood.

Table 6.2 | **The Four Levels of Analysis in Bloodstain Pattern Analysis**

Level 1	Level 2	Level 3	Level 4
Bloodshed event creates bloodstain pattern.	Utilize knowledge in bloodstain pattern analysis (BPA) to analyze and evaluate the physical characteristics of the bloodstain patterns.	Evaluate the specifics of the case and consider possible mechanism for BPA.	Reconstruct bloodletting events.

Table 6.3 | **Classification of Bloodstains**

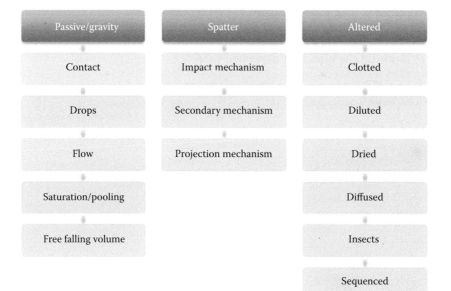

Passive/gravity	Spatter	Altered
Contact	Impact mechanism	Clotted
Drops	Secondary mechanism	Diluted
Flow	Projection mechanism	Dried
Saturation/pooling		Diffused
Free falling volume		Insects
		Sequenced
		Voids

Source: James, S., Kish, P., and Sutton, P. (2005). *Principles of Bloodstain Pattern Analysis: Theory and Practice* (Practical Aspects of Criminal & Forensic Investigations), 3rd ed. CRC Press, Boca Raton, FL, p. 62.

6.1.5.1 Passive/Gravity Stain Patterns

Drip trail blood patterns are created by free-falling blood from a force that is in horizontal motion. The blood impacts the surface at a 90-degree angle, for example, a bleeding person walking slowly. The distance of the trail depends on the amount of blood and if the person is actively bleeding, as illustrated in Figure 6.1.

Flow patterns are an accumulation of large volumes of blood moving across a surface from one point to another. Flow patterns can be found on the victim's body continuing to flow onto the floor or on a wall. An obstacle can detour the directionality of the flow pattern. Flow patterns on a body can also indicate the victim's movement in certain cases. Blood pools are buildups of large volumes of blood. The shape of the pool of blood depends on the surface contour. Extensive bleeding of the victim at one location or the intersection of several flow patterns commonly creates a pool of blood.

Saturation is the accumulation of blood that has been absorbed by a surface or material rather than depositing on top of the surface. Large saturations of blood are commonly found on carpets, carpet padding, rugs, and clothing and bedsheets.

It is important to always examine the victim's and the suspect's clothing. Two questions that are important to answer are

- Whose blood is it?
- How did the blood get deposited there?

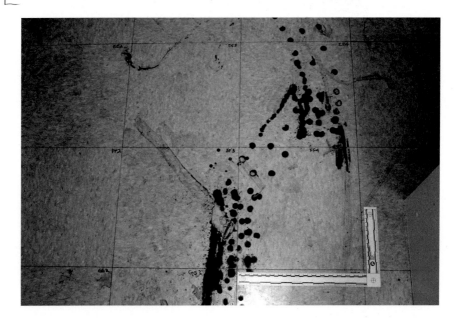

Figure 6.1 Drip trail pattern.

DNA testing can help to determine whose blood is present on the suspect's clothing. Alternatively, if there is an absence of blood on the suspect's clothing, some reasons for this may include

- The victim had been heavily clothed or covered with a blanket, minimizing the spatter patterns.
    1. The offender might have cleaned up the scene.
    2. The offender might have worn protective clothing, such as a painter's suit, that had been discarded.
    3. The assailant has changed clothing and discarded the clothes worn during the assault (James et al., 2014).

Transfer bloodstains are created when a wet, bloody surface, such as a bloodstained shirt or hand, comes in contact with a secondary surface, as illustrated in Figure 6.2. A recognizable image of all or a portion of the

Figure 6.2 Tire transfer pattern.

Figure 6.3 Wipe pattern.

original surface may be observed in the pattern, such as ridge detail from a fingerprint or palm print. Common transfer patterns are wipes, swipes, and transfer patterns of shoe imprints.

A wipe pattern is created when an object moves through a bloodstain. The feathered edge at the end of the wipe indicates the direction of travel, as illustrated in Figure 6.3.

A swipe pattern is created when a wet bloodied object contacts a secondary surface. Common swipe patterns are from hair, hands, and shoes transferred onto clothing, walls, and floors, as shown in Figure 6.4.

6.1.5.2 Spatter Patterns

Spatter patterns are a result of active events such as a shot, expiration, or cast-off from swinging a bloodstained object. James et al. (2005) defined spatter as a "dispersion of blood spots of varying size, created when a source of fluid blood is subjected to an external force" (p. 99). Spatter can be created by a variety of mechanisms. Spatter patterns are subdivided into three categories, as illustrated in Table 6.4.

Secondary spatter is created when the physical properties of blood undergo a secondary impact, for example, blood dripping into blood creates satellite spatter around the periphery of the parent stain, as shown in Figure 6.5.

Impact spatter is created when an object impacts a liquid blood source. Impact spatter is subdivided into three categories, as outlined in Table 6.5.

Figure 6.4 Swipe pattern.

Table 6.4   Spatter Patterns

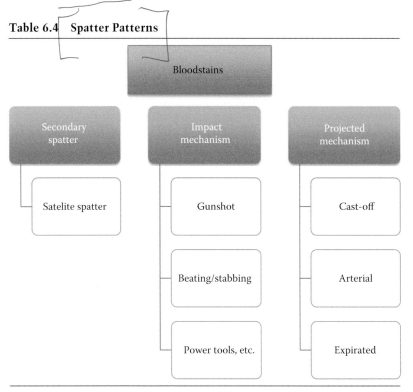

Source: James, S., Nordby, J., and Bell, S. (2014). _Forensic Science: An Introduction to Scientific and Investigative Techniques_, 4th ed. CRC Press, Boca Raton, FL.

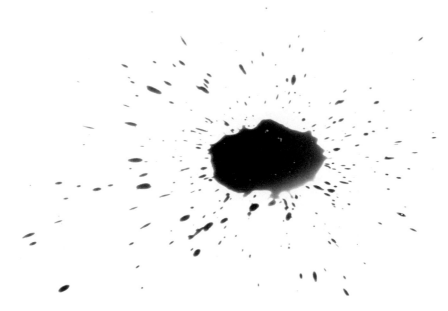

Figure 6.5 Blood dripping into blood.

Table 6.5 Impact Mechanism

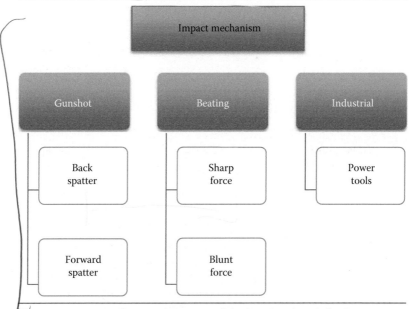

Source: James, S., Kish, P., and Sutton, P. (2005). *Principles of Bloodstain Pattern Analysis: Theory and Practice* (Practical Aspects of Criminal & Forensic Investigations), 3rd ed. CRC Press, Boca Raton, FL, p. 120.

Impact spatter is associated with a gunshot and produces small stains of less than 0.1 mm in diameter, in other words, a mist-like spatter. The weapon's caliber, the amount of blood, and the number of shots are variables that might create bloodstains with diameters of several millimeters.

- Back spatter patterns are blood drops that travel in the opposite direction of the external force applied. Back spatter is found on the suspect's clothing, hands, arms, and on the weapon, as shown in Figure 6.6.
- Forward spatter results from blood drops that travel in the same direction as the external force applied. Forward spatter patterns are only created when the projectile exits the victim.

Impact spatter is caused by beating and stabbing. The diameter of the bloodstains ranges between 1 and 3 mm. The size of the stains might vary due to the amount of blood and the force of impact. Exposed blood on a wound or a cut has to be present to create this impact pattern. The spatter pattern will be different depending on the weapon used in the assault such as a knife, a baseball bat, or a concrete block. In some situations, several different mechanisms might be present such as stabbing, expired blood, and a gunshot.

Figure 6.6 Back spatter on revolver.

James et al. (2005) concluded that the following variables affect the size, shape, and distribution of impact spatter:

- Shape, length, and weight of weapon
- Number of impacts
- Amount of force
- Direction of force applied
- Location of the wounds
- Movement of victim and assailant during the attack
- Amount of blood available for a given impact (p. 129)

Projection mechanism. James et al. (2014) explained, "Projection patterns result from the ejection of a volume of blood under pressure often related with a vascular breach" (p. 98). The projections mechanism is subdivided into three categories as illustrated in Table 6.6.

Projection patterns are created when a large volume of blood under pressure is propelled toward and strikes a surface. The most common projection pattern is the arterial spurt. Arterial spurt/gush results from blood exiting the body under pressure from a breached artery. These patterns are commonly found at burglary scenes when the offender cuts himself on broken glass, or at stabbing scenes (Figure 6.7).

The shape of the arterial spurt varies depending on

- The location of the severed artery
- The severity of the injury
- The blood volume
- If the victim was clothed
- Movement of the victim
- Position of the victim

Expiratory mechanism is created when blood accumulates in the lungs, the mouth, or in the nasal passages of the victim of a traumatic incident. The

Table 6.6 Projection Mechanism

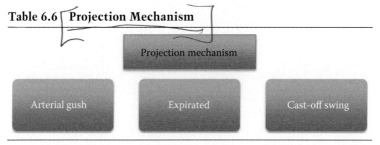

Source: James, S., Kish, P., and Sutton, P. (2005). *Principles of Bloodstain Pattern Analysis: Theory and Practice* (Practical Aspects of Criminal & Forensic Investigations), 3rd ed. CRC Press, Boca Raton, FL, p. 150.

Figure 6.7 Arterial spurt.

victim coughs, breaths out, or sneezes, relieving blood from the nasal passages and airways. The bloodstain is circular with an air bubble in the center, making it appear like a donut shape.

Cast-off bloodstain patterns are created during a beating with a blunt force object. However, blood does not accrue at the impact area at the first blow, as there is no blood to be spattered. Several blows create castoff patterns with an object in the general area of a wound and blood is present. Blood will stick to the object used in the bloodshed. Every time the assailant swings the object, it creates enough force to overcome the adhesive force holding the blood on the object, creating a linear castoff pattern. In this case, the blood will strike the surfaces of adjacent walls and ceilings. The analysis of the cast-off patterns can assist in the determination of the victim's and suspect's locations during the assault, especially when examining the vicinity of the 90-degree impact pattern.

6.1.5.3 Altered Bloodstain Patterns

There are different variables for the alteration of bloodstains and bloodstain patterns, ranging from environmental circumstances to decomposition, as illustrated in Table 6.7.

The aging of blood is visible and indicated through a change in color from red to reddish brown, to green and dark brown and blackish. As blood ages, it loses oxygen and color. This process will be accelerated in hot climates.

Table 6.7   Altered Bloodstains

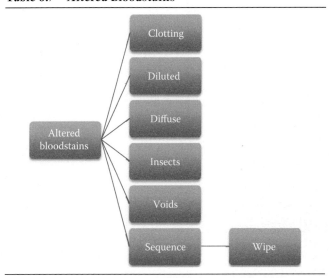

Source: James, S., Nordby, J., and Bell, S. (2014). *Forensic Science: An Introduction to Scientific and Investigative Techniques,* 4th ed. CRC Press, Boca Raton, FL.

Clotting of blood begins when the blood leaves the body and is exposed to the air and different surfaces. Depending on the surface and environmental circumstances, blood will clot within 3 to 15 min. The blood corpuscles are heavier and sink, while the scrum remains on the surface as a transparent liquid. The inexperienced analyst may interpret this phenomenon as a diluted stain, an attempt of a cleanup, or liquid added to the blood.

The center of the stain is dark whereas the surrounding area is lighter in color. Clot patterns may provide information about movement and drag patterns, as seen in Figure 6.8.

Diluted bloodstains may be present at scenes of extreme moisture such as rain, snow, or in tropical climates. Efforts to clean up the scene will also provide signs of dilution.

Caution: If you suspect cleanup of the crime scene, always perform preliminary blood tests with phenophthalein or OBTI, or check the area with Luminol or Bluestar for the presence of blood.

Insect activity at the crime scene can create small stains that are easily confused with impact blood spatter, especially in impact patterns such as gunshots. Bugs and insects will remain on scene with the blood as a food source for them. Flies ingest blood and regurgitate it onto surfaces allowing enzymes to break down the blood (James et al., 2005).

Void areas. A void area is the absence of blood in an area otherwise covered with bloodstain patterns, as shown in Figure 6.9. The void area is

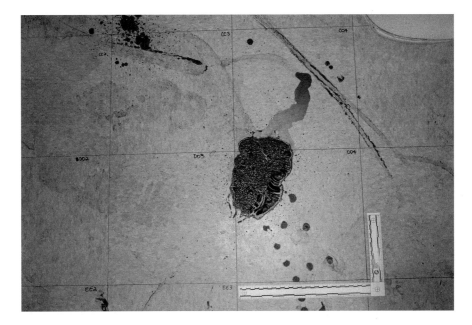

Figure 6.8 Clotted blood.

consistent with alterations to the scene in the form of removing an item or person that had been present during the bloodshed.

6.1.6 Target Surface Differences

Falling blood does not spatter until the surface tension is broken by a physical event such as striking a surface. Blood falling on a smooth surface such as glass, a tile floor, and hard smooth flooring will not spatter. The protuberates of rough surfaces such as raw wood or a cement floor such as driveways or sidewalks rupture the surface tension of blood creating irregular spatter patterns, as illustrated in Figure 6.10a and b.

6.1.7 Directionality and Angle of Impact

Bloodstains falling onto a target at a 90-degree angle are circular in shape. Bloodstains hitting a target surface at an angle of less than 90 degrees are elliptical in shape. The angle of impact is the acute angle formed between the direction of the blood drop and the plane of the surface it strikes. Individual stains within a bloodstain pattern indicate directionality, information that leads to the determination of the area of blood origin. The angle of impact of an elliptically shaped bloodstain can be determined using the mathematical relationship between the width and length of the stain. The analyst measures the width and length of selected stains;

Figure 6.9 Void area.

dividing the width by the length resulting in a ratio less than 1. This ratio is the arc sine of the impact angle. The angle of impact can easily be determined by simple calculation.

$$\frac{\text{Width}}{\text{Length}} = \frac{\text{Opposite}}{\text{Hypotenuse}} = \text{sine of angle } \theta$$

Angle of impact = arc sin W/L

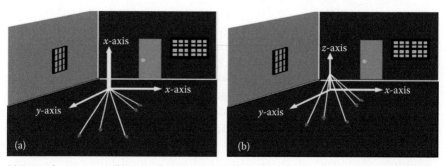

(a) Point of convergence. (b) Area of origin in space. (From James, S., Nordy, J., and Bell, S. (2014). *Forensic Science: An Introduction to Scientific and Investigative Techniques*, 4th ed. CRC Press, Boca Raton, FL.)

(a)

(b)

Figure 6.10 Photos of different target surfaces. (a) Blood on rock and (b) blood on wood.

6.1.8 Areas of Origin

The bloodstain pattern analyst applies physics and geometry to determine the direction of flight of each bloodstain before impacting an object. The edge characteristic of each stain allows the analyst to determine the directionality. Directionality is determined by examining the pointed end of the stain called the tail, as it will always point in the direction of travel. The area of origin is the point on a two-dimensional surface grounded on the presence of several elongated bloodstains showing directionality (James et al., 2014). When drawing a line through the long axis of several select bloodstains, the area of convergence is determined. The area of convergence is the most likely location of the blood source, thus the area of origin of the blood. Through the stringing method, or with computer-aided programs, the analyst can determine the three-dimensional origin of the bloodshed, in other words, the vicinity of the victim when he or she was being assaulted.

6.1.9 Documenting Bloodstains at the Crime Scene

Blood spatter and spatter patterns are present at almost every violent crime scene. Detailed documentation in the form of photographs and notes is of the utmost importance to be able to reconstruct the events that led to the bloodshed.

6.1.9.1 Investigator/Bloodstain Pattern Analyst Safety

Every officer, crime scene investigator, and bloodstain pattern analyst must be aware of the biohazard danger of a bloody crime scene. Airborne pathogens and other biohazards such as hepatitis A, hepatitis B, meningitis, and HIV can be present in the blood. Therefore, always

- Wear protective gear such as gloves, booties, disposable masks, and eyewear.
- Protect your clothing with TyVac suits and dispose of them in biohazard containers after leaving the scene.
- Wash your hands with antiseptic and bacterial hand wash.
- Decontaminate all equipment using a mixture of 10% bleach and water prior to returning in the crime scene vehicle.
- Discard any clothing that has been contaminated.
- Decontaminate the soles of the shoes with the bleach mixture.
- Bandage any cuts or abrasions on the skin and report the exposure to your supervisor.

6.1.9.2 Procedure for Determining the Area of Convergence

The following are basic bloodstain pattern procedures that should be applied to every crime scene where bloodstain patterns are present; see Figure 6.11:

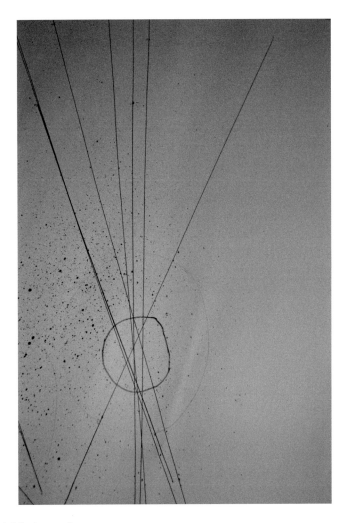

Figure 6.11 Area of convergence.

1. Obtain sufficient overall photographs of the spatter patterns and the areas that contain blood trails, pooled blood, or transfer patterns.
2. Use yellow adhesive scales to outline the overall size of the spatter patterns.
3. Photograph another set of images including the yellow adhesive scales.
4. If multiple spatter patterns are present, apply the road mapping method (as explained below) to document the patterns.
5. Take detailed notes of the size, location, and number of bloodstains.
6. Choose 10 to 15 bloodstains with directionality. These stains are elliptical in shape.

7. Draw a line through the long axis of each selected stain; the area where the lines intersect is the area of convergence.
8. Photograph the area of convergence, as shown in Figure 6.11, and take overall photos to show the relation to other areas of the room for orientation.

6.1.9.3 Stringing Method to Determine the Area of Origin

The area of origin is the three-dimensional area in space where the assault occurred. The stringing method is a manual procedure for approximating the area of origin of an impact at the crime scene.

The string method requires the selection of 10 to 20 stains from a blood-stain pattern, most likely the stains used when we determined the area of convergence, as explained in Section 6.1.7 and illustrated in Figure 6.11. Use the previously selected 10 to 20 stains traveling linearly from the impact point to determine the point of convergence and approximate the elliptical outline of the stain. Do not include the stain's tail in the approximation.

1. Number each stain sequentially and write the number next to the stain.
2. Measure the length and width of each stain in millimeters.
   - Length: eliminate the tail of the stain and measure the length of the ellipse of the stain.
   - Width: measure across the largest point of the stain.

Hint: Small loops with scales are commercially available for a price of less than $10. The loops not only enlarge the stain but the built-in metric millimeter scale allows the analyst to obtain more accurate measurements of the length and width of the stain.

3. Note the measurements for each selected stain, for example,

   Stain 2: 3.5 mm width, 5.6 mm length

4. Determining the angle of impact for each stain requires calculating the length-to-width ration with ratio and applying the following formula:

$$\sin A = \frac{\text{width of bloodstain}}{\text{length of bloodstain}}$$

   A represents the angle of impact, for example, the width of a bloodstain is 11 mm and the length is 22 mm

$$\sin A = \frac{11 \text{ mm}}{22 \text{ mm}} = 0.50$$

Using a scientific calculator with trigonometry functions will calculate that a sine of 0.50 corresponds to a 30-degree angle.

- Using the scientific calculator, type 11/22. The display shows 0.50. Push "second" function and the "sine" key, and the angle will be displayed.

5. Record the angle of impact with the stain number in your log book.
6. Repeat this step for every selected bloodstain.
7. Tape a long piece of string to the area where the stain has hit the surface.
8. Repeat for each selected bloodstain.
9. Ensure tape is holding the string securely.
10. Use a zero edge protractor to track string through the center of the stain's axis along the protractor at the calculated impact angle.
11. Pull the string taut and attach it to the surface, wall, object, floor, etc.
12. Recheck the measurement and angles.
13. Repeat for all selected stains.
14. The area in space where the strings intersect is the area of origin of the blood.
15. Place a yardstick or a ruler to reference the distance from the area of origin to the floor, wall, or ceiling.
16. Take overall and medium range photos including the measurement (as shown in Figure 6.12).
17. Note the measurements and draw a sketch.

Figure 6.12 3D area of origin.

6.1.9.4 Roadmapping

Commonly, there may be several bloodstain patterns present at a scene, especially if different weapons or mechanisms were used, for example, a victim has been beaten and then shot to death. There would be at least two different bloodstain patterns present, an impact pattern from the beating and another impact pattern from the gunshot. Or, alternatively, a victim may have been shot multiple times from different angles. It is necessary to analyze the patterns separately and the road mapping method allows documenting and analyzing multiple blood patterns.

6.1.9.5 Applying the Road Mapping Method

The size of the spatter pattern is important to determine if there is either a presence of multiple spatter patterns or a combination of different mechanisms that created the patterns.

Photography is significant in this procedure to document the different spatter patterns. A set of overall, medium range, and close-up photographs with labels and scales are the minimum documentation required to identify separate spatter groups. Label stains to be used for determination of the point of convergence, as well as the area of origin within the patterns. This method is a systematic approach to document bloodstain patterns while providing graphical illustrations of the relationships between the patterns and other landmarks at the scene. The photo labels and photo scales are used to provide an orientation of the stains and patterns, within larger patterns, similar to directional indicators on a map. They will provide orientation for the scene reconstructionist, independent expert, peer reviewer, and jurors to make an appropriate judgment. The following equipment is required for the road mapping method:

- Yellow adhesive photographic scales
- Adhesive letters such as A, B, C, etc.
- Adhesive scales
- Glue or scotch tape

Impact spatter patterns are most suited for this method; however, the method can be successfully applied to all scenes with multiple spatter patterns.

1. Obtain overall photographs of the different spatter patterns.
2. Surround the pattern, horizontally and vertically, with yellow adhesive scales to show the dimensions of the spatter pattern.
3. Capture with an additional set of overall photos. Confirm to include the scales.
4. Using adhesive letters A, B, C, separate the spatter patterns. Document with overall and medium range photographs.

(a)   (b)

Figure 6.13 Roadmapping on wall (a) and in a room (b). (With permission from Ronald Mueller.)

5. Note the numbers/letters of each pattern in the photo log and categorize the pattern, such as photo 1 cast-off pattern, photo 2-impact pattern, etc.
6. Choose multiple elongated stains with directionality and label as A1, A2, A3, etc. Document with overall, medium range, and close-up photos of each stain.
7. Confirm that the metric side of the scale is placed on the vertical surface. Place a plum line under each stain pointing to the ground and include this line in each close-up photo.
8. Capture another set of overall photos, medium range, and close-up photos of each pattern.
9. Progress with determining the area of convergence and area of origin as it applies to pattern analysis, as illustrated in Figure 6.13a and b.

6.1.10 Computerized Bloodstain Pattern Analysis

6.1.10.1 HemoSpat

HemoSpat is a software program that calculates the area of origin for impact spatter patterns. Physical stringing, measuring selected stains, and applying the mathematical formula are tasks that can be replaced with HemoSpat. The stringing method requires more than one CSI and is very time consuming, whereas the computer-aided analysis can be performed in hours and be included in a report and is suitable for 3D reconstruction software.

6.2 Firearms and Shooting Reconstruction

Crime scenes involving firearms and shooting reconstruction can be a challenge, but with different methods, the CSI can reconstruct the trajectory of the bullets and the location of the spent casings, if any, to help to determine the location of the shooter.

6.2.1 Firearms

Firearms are classified as handguns, such as revolvers and semi-automatic handguns, rifles, such as assault rifles and hunting rifles of different calibers, and shotguns of differing gauges. Handguns are subdivided into two categories: semi-automatic handguns and revolvers.

6.2.1.1 Revolver

A revolver is a handgun that can be held and fired in one hand. A revolver contains a rotating cylinder holding live and spent cartridges. To fire a single-action revolver, the shooter has to manually cock the hammer before pulling the trigger. When cocking the hammer, the cylinder rotates to place

Figure 6.14 Revolver with open cylinder.

one of the chambers under the hammer and cocks the firing mechanism. A single shot revolver fires one round at a time. The revolving cylinder consists of multiple firing chambers. When a shot is fired, the cylinder rotates clockwise or counterclockwise depending on the manufacturer of the weapon. Each cylinder chamber holds one live cartridge that lines up with the barrel when the trigger is pulled and the shot is fired. The spent cartridge has to be manually removed from the cylinder. Several loading mechanisms are available such as top break mechanism, loading gate mechanism, swing-out cylinder, and removable cylinder. Most revolvers have swing-out cylinders swinging out to the side of the weapon to remove and reload cartridges (see Figure 6.14).

"A double action revolver is fired by a long trigger pull that raises the hammer, indexes a firing chamber under the hammer and allows the hammer to drop, firing the cartridge" (Row, 2014, p. 353).

6.2.1.2 Semi-Automatic Handgun

A semi-automatic handgun can also be held in one hand. Semi-automatic handguns, however, contain a magazine holding the live cartridges. In most models, the magazine is located within the grip. To load the handgun, the loaded magazine is inserted; the shooter will pull the slide on top of the gun backward resulting in loading the first round into the chamber. In a breech-loading weapon, the cartridge or shell is loaded into a chamber integral to the rear portion of the barrel. The gases that develop when the cartridge is fired are used to eject the spent cartridge, cock the hammer, and load the next round (see Figure 6.15). A semi-automatic weapon fires one shot per trigger

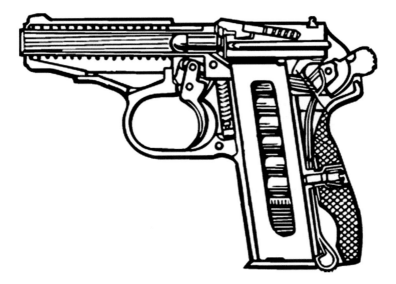

Figure 6.15 Sketch of handgun.

pull, while a fully automatic weapon will continue to fire until the trigger is released or the magazine is emptied (Saferstein, 2011).

6.2.1.3 Rifles and Shotguns

Rifles and shotguns have a long barrel and a stock. Shotguns and rifles are designed to be fired from the shoulder. Rifles have a rifled bore with lands and grooves, whereas shotguns have a smooth bore. The ammunition of rifles and shotguns varies. Shotgun ammunition consists of numerous small lead balls. Shotguns can be single or double barreled, either side-by-side or vertical (see Figure 6.16).

Rifles and shotguns differ in reloading mechanisms. A single shotgun is equal to the revolver, firing one round at a time and the next round has to be manually reloaded (see Figure 6.17). Repeating long guns use a mechanical

Figure 6.16 Shotgun shells.

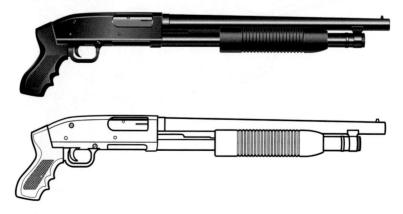

Figure 6.17 Pump action shotgun.

Figure 6.18 Rifles.

instrument to eject spent cartridges, load the next round and cock the hammer after firing a round, equivalent to the mechanism in a semi-automatic handgun, as shown in Figure 6.18. Such mechanisms are lever action, pump or slide action, bold action, and semi-automatic rifles.

6.2.1.4 Cartridges and Shotgun Shells

Cartridges are categorized in caliber and gauge. Caliber is the bullet diameter or bore diameter between the opposite lands. The caliber can be designated in either inches or millimeters (1 mm = approximately 4 caliber). There are several weapons that can load both caliber and mm ammunition, for example, a .357 caliber revolver can also be loaded with a 9-mm cartridge because 9 mm equals .36 calibers.

Shotguns are measured in gauges, such as 12 gauge or 20 gauge. What does that mean? Shotgun gauge stands for the number of round led balls fitting the bore required to make one pound, for example, 12 balls for 12 gauge, 20 balls for 20 gauge.

6.2.1.5 Bullet and Cartridge Comparison

All evidence bears class characteristics, however, it may not possess individual characteristics. Both class characteristic evidence, also called class evidence, and individual characteristic evidence, also called individual evidence, has value. Firearms possess class characteristics as they can be categorized as handguns, rifles, and shotguns, as well as individual characteristics because of the unique characteristics on the bullet after being propelled through the barrel of a firearm. The markings are unique to each firearm allowing matching the spent casing found at the crime scene to the spent casing obtained from the test-fire of the suspect's firearm. The gun barrel is machine produced, resulting in an irregular inner surface. The manufacturer impresses spiral grooves inside the barrel, impacting the spin of a projectile when fired, also known as rifling. The lands are the area between the grooves inside the rifled bore. No two rifled barrels have identical striation markings.

Through a comparison microscope, the firearms examiner can match both casings to determine a positive match. In cases when the firearm is not recovered from the scene or during the investigation, the crime scene investigator can submit the spent casings and projectile to the laboratory for imaging and search in the National Integrated Ballistic Information Network (NIBIN) database maintained by the Department of Alcohol, Tobacco and Firearms (ATF).

6.2.2 Firearm Safety

Gun safety is the cardinal rule every time a firearm is handled. Four additional rules that should be observed at all times are

- Assume all firearms are always loaded.
- Never let the muzzle cross anything that you do not want destroyed, in the event of accidental deployment.
- Always keep your finger off the trigger.
- Be aware and sure of your target and the area beyond.

6.2.2.1 Clearing a Firearm

At shooting scenes, the weapon may have already been secured by the first responding officer and collected as evidence. In other cases, the firearm remains on scene and the crime scene investigator will document, photograph, secure, and collect the firearm. It is essential that every crime scene investigator is familiar with the procedure on how to clear (unload) a firearm.

Caution: Never try to unload a firearm with which you are not familiar. When in doubt, ask a coworker, the police officers securing the scene, or contact a supervisor for advice.

Figure 6.19 Gun with zip tie.

These four steps must be performed in the exact order:

1. Point the weapon in a safe direction.
2. Remove the magazine if the weapon has one.
3. Open the action (cylinder, or breech) and visually and physically inspect.
4. Keep the slide open using a plastic tie, as illustrated in Figure 6.19.

Caution: You cannot clear a revolver while the hammer is cocked.

If a firearm has a nonremovable magazine,

1. Clear the chamber first.
2. Check the chamber visually and physically.
3. Slowly close the action while looking into the chamber ensuring that it is free of ammunition.

Caution: Some firearms may be faulty or of poor unsafe design and may discharge just when picked up or by switching the safety off.

6.2.3 Identifying a Firearm

Globally, there is an abundance of national and international firearm manufacturers producing all different models and calibers of firearms. Multiple laws require markings on each firearm.

Title 27 CFR Para 178.92 requires each licensed American manufacturer since 1968 to do the following:

- Serial number must be on the frame or receiver.
- Name of manufacturer, city and state of manufacturer, model and caliber and gauge must appear on frame/receiver/barrel or slide of each weapon.

In addition to the information required from an American manufacturer, Title 27 CFR para 178.92 additionally requires the name of the importer, and city, state, and country of the gun origin.

At suicide scenes or burglaries where firearms are taken, the crime scene investigator may come across antique weapons. Basic information about firearm markings prior to 1968 may be necessary.

Domestic firearms contain information about the name of the manufacturer, model and caliber, and a serial number. In addition to the model, caliber, and serial number, the name on an imported firearm may be the manufacturer or importer. Firearms produced prior to 1968 when the gun control act was implemented were not required to have a serial number. Firearms found at a crime scene without a serial number may be produced before 1968. Finding the serial number can be more difficult as the number did not have to appear on the frame or receiver.

6.2.4 Identification Markings on Live and Spent Cartridges

The name, initials, or trademark of the manufacturer and the caliber/mm are impressed on the bottom of every live or spent cartridge. The name of the manufacturer of a shotgun shell may be found imprinted on the plastic casings, on the metal ring at the bottom of the shell, whereas the gauge is impressed on the bottom of the shotgun shell (see Figure 6.20). However, many shotgun shells do not contain the manufacturer's information.

6.2.5 Collection and Preservation of Firearms

Many times, we see on TV or in the movies that the detective at a scene will take a pencil and place it inside the gun barrel to pick up the firearm to avoid destroying fingerprints. With this method, the detective disturbs the powder deposits, rust and dirt inside the barrel, and alters the striation marking on test-fired bullets.

Figure 6.20 9 mm luger.

The proper steps for collecting a firearm include:

- Always follow the basic crime scene procedures of documenting, photographing, measuring, and sketching before collecting the firearm.
- Obtain overall, medium range, and close-up photos of the firearm *in situ*.
- Take close-up photographs of the serial number, manufacturer, model number, or any other information. Place a labeled scale next to the barrel to show the overall barrel length. **Do not move the weapon**.

Caution: The first and utmost important rule for collecting firearms from a crime scene is to treat every weapon as being loaded.

- Never place a finger on the trigger.
- Do not handle or pick up weapons with which you are not familiar.
- All weapons should be unloaded before packaging and preserving.
- If a revolver is recovered, mark the chamber position in line with the barrel by making a line with a permanent marker creating a scratch mark on the cylinder.
- Draw a diagram of the cylinder and remove the cartridges from the cylinder.
- In the diagram, list the spent cartridges and live rounds with the corresponding numbers in the sketch.

- Write the corresponding numbers from the sketch on each cartridge.
- Package every round in a separate container.
- Ensure that the surface of the cartridge will not be scratched. Wrapping in cotton or in soft tissue paper before placing in a small cardboard box is recommended.
- If fingerprint recovery is important, the gun should be held on the ripped part of the grip.
- Recovering a semi-automatic handgun or rifle, it is important to note if there had been a live round in the chamber.
- Collect the live round and package and preserve separately.
- Remove the magazine from the weapon and remove all live rounds.
- The magazine and the live rounds can be processed for fingerprints.
- Package the firearm and magazine together, but package all live rounds or spent casings separately.
- If a firearm is recovered in salt or fresh water, the firearm should be placed in a container filled with the same water as the weapon was recovered from. If it was submerged, ensure that the firearm continues to be submerged in water in transit to avoid additional rusting.
- The following information should be placed on the outside of the container of a firearm:
  - Case number
  - Make of firearm
  - Model of firearm
  - Caliber of firearm (either in mm or caliber)

Figure 6.21 Gun with serial number on the bottom of barrel.

- Serial number of firearm (found on the barrel or on the bottom of the grip, as shown in Figure 6.21)
- Make/importer
- If blood is present on the firearm, place a biohazard sticker on the gun box
- Maintain the chain of custody and secure the weapon immediately in the crime scene vehicle for transport to headquarters or the evidence storage facility.

6.2.6 Serial Number Restoration

Offenders will try to avoid the identification of a firearm by scratching, grinding, or punching out the serial number on the barrel of the weapon, just the way car thieves try to alter the serial number of a motor block on a motorcycle or car. Hard steel dies are used to stamp serial numbers onto metal surfaces. When these dies strike the metal plate, each digit sinks into the metal at a determined depth. "Serial numbers can be restored because the metal crystals in the stamped zone are placed under a permanent strain that extends a short distance beneath the original numbers" (Saferstein, 2011, p. 434). The crime scene investigator can choose suitable etching agents based on the surface from which the serial number is to be restored. The serial number restoration consists of the following steps:

- Thoroughly clean the obliterated surface.
- Polish the surface to a mirror-like finish.
- Using a cotton ball, swab the reagent onto the surface.
- The choice of the reagent depends on the kind of metal.
- For a steel surface, a mixture of hydrochloric acid (120 ml), copper chloride (90 ml), and water (100 ml) works best (Saferstein, 2011, p. 434).

6.2.7 Shooter to Target Distance Determination

Ammunition is propelled toward a target caused by the expanding gases produced by the ignition of the smokeless powder inside the cartridge. Every time a firearm is fired, small burned and unburned particles of gunpowder and smoke are propelled out of the barrel. In close range shots, the particles are deposited into the target. These particles allow an assessment of the distance between the handgun and the target. However, the accuracy of the distance determination varies depending on the caliber of the firearm and the circumstances of the case.

Test fires with the same firearm and ammunition as used in the crime are necessary to create standards for comparison with the victim's clothing.

Without the suspect's firearm, the examiner can only examine the characteristics around the bullet hole and provide an estimated distance determination.

6.2.7.1 Characteristics of a Gunshot Fired at a Distance of 1 inch or Less

If the firearm is discharged at a distance of 1 in., there is a high concentration of smoke-like vaporous lead surrounding the bullet entrance. Depending on the material of the clothing, loose fibers and scorch marks may be visible around the bullet hole, while some fibers may show signs of melted fibers around the bullet hole. The blowback of the gases may also produce a star-shaped cut around the bullet hole encircled by a border of smoke-like accumulation of lead particles (see Figure 6.22).

6.2.7.2 Characteristics of a Gunshot Fired at a Distance of 12 to 18 inches

If a ring of vaporous lead is visible around a bullet hole, it is consistent with a shot being fired at a distance between 12 and 18 in. Scattered specks and particles of unburned powder with soot can be seen in cases where the gun was approximately 25 in. to the target. The amount of vaporous lead varies depending on caliber, ammunition, and firearm; for example, lead particles of ball powder ammunition can be propelled up to 6 to 8 ft.

6.2.7.3 Characteristics of a Gunshot Fired at a Distance over 3 feet

Generally, if a firearm has been discharged at a distance of 3 ft or more, there is no deposit of lead or powder residues visible on the target surface or clothing. A bullet wipe, a dark ring around the entrance hole, indicates that a bullet created the defect. Bullet wipe consists of a mixture of carbon, dirt, lubricant, primer residue, and lead. Without the presence of the suspect's firearm, the examiner can only apply the general guidelines for the distance determination and provide approximate firearm to target distances.

6.2.7.4 Distance Determination of Shotguns

As with other firearms such as handguns and rifles, test firing has to be performed with both the suspect's shotgun and the same ammunition used in the crime. If the weapon is not available, the examiner can estimate the muzzle to target distance by measuring the spread of the pellet in the shot pattern. "With close range shots varying in distance up to 4 to 5 feet, the shot charge enters the target as a concentrated mass, producing a hole somewhat larger than the bore of the barrel. As the distance increases, the pellets progressively separate and spread out" (Saferstein 2011, p. 429). In general, the shot pattern of a 12-gauge shotgun increases by 1 in. for each yard of distance to the target. This is only a rule of thumb and provides estimated distance determination.

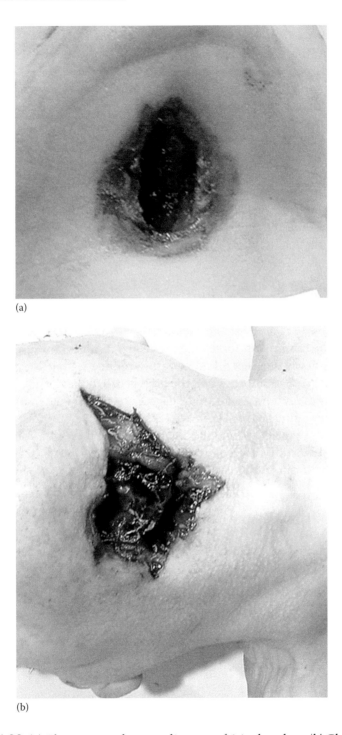

(a)

(b)

Figure 6.22 (a) Close-up gunshot at a distance of 1 inch or less. (b) Close range gun shot.

6.2.7.5 *Collection of Clothing with Powder Residues*

All garments that have been worn by the victim or the shooter should be collected, preserved, and packed separately to avoid cross-contamination and the loss of powder/lead particles on the clothing. In the laboratory, the clothing items will be examined under a microscope for the presence of gunpowder residue. The examiner can perform the Greiss test, which is a method for locating powder residues embedded in surfaces. The method entails pressing chemically treated gelatin-coated photographic paper on the target cloth or clothing item with a hot iron. The particles adhere to the paper and can be visualized using chemicals. Another method is the application of a solution of sodium rhodizonate, followed by multiple sprays with acid solutions to the area around the bullet hole. Due to the chemical reaction, the lead particles will turn pink first, followed by turning a blue-violet color.

6.2.8 Gunshot Residue Kit

Every time a weapon is discharged, gunpowder, primer residues, and lead particles blow back at the shooter's hand.

There are several tests for testing the primer residues on a suspect's hands such as the newly developed ISid2 gunshot residue testing kit, as shown in Figure 6.23. All tests are based on the presence, and the possible amount, of barium, antimony, and lead on the suspect's hands. Unlike in TV or movie dramas, where gunshot residue is evidence of the killer, the presence of gunshot residue is evidence *only* that the person had been in a room where a firearm had been discharged, not necessarily corroborating that they were the individual who discharged it.

Figure 6.23 Gunshot.

6.2.8.1 ISid2—Gunshot Residue SEM Test Kit and Instant Shooter Kit

The new ISid2 is a commercially available binary gunshot residue test kit. This kit consists of two components—the standard scanning electron microscope (SEM) gunshot residue collection for the laboratory and the LET (part of the instant shooter kit) for instant results of the presence of gunshot residue on the suspect's hands. It contains sticky carbon tape particle collection devices to collect the gunshot particles from the shooter's left and right hands and palms for further testing with the SEM. This is commonly used in most state and federal laboratories.

To administer this kit:

- Do not let the person to be tested wash their hands or rub them against clothing or any other surfaces.
- Fill in the information about the suspect, including the whereabouts in the last hour and whether the suspect had been around a firearm, at the gun range, hobbies, and the time expired since the shooting.
- Wear gloves when opening the devices.
- Dab the adhesive side of the device along the suspect's right palm (use the device labeled with right palm). Gunshot residue is not visible to the naked eye.
- Close the device with the plastic lid to avoid loss of particles.
- Continue to the second hand and perform the same evidence collection.
- Fill in the information on the envelope and seal, initial, and date the envelope.

After the SEM sample is collected and sealed for transport to the laboratory, the crime scene investigator swabs the suspect's palms and hands with an LET swab and applies a chemical agent. If a blue reaction occurs on the swab within 5 min or less, it is an indication for the presence of nitrocellulose. This chemical response is consistent with a high probability that the suspect had fired a weapon or was close to the area where a weapon had been fired. These field results can be verified with the SEM test kit in the laboratory.

6.2.9 Trajectory Reconstruction

In crime scenes where shots have been fired and people have been injured or killed, it is necessary to determine the location of the shooter. The shooting scene provides valuable information for the reconstruction of the shooting. If bullet holes are present in the walls or in the ceiling, the crime scene investigator can determine the projectile trajectory to find additional casings and projectiles and place the shooter in a specific area. Bloodstain patterns may show the movements of the victim and the suspect; however, if there is no exit wound, there will be no or only minimal bloodstain patterns. Distance determination can be performed on the victim's clothing as well as from the characteristics of the gunshot wound. However, the most reliable method for determining the shooter's location is by projectile trajectory.

1. Determine an area where the bullet passed through one or two surfaces such as a wall or a door.
2. Bullets travel in relatively straight lines over short distances but have arcs for longer distance shots.
3. The trajectory can be determined by pulling a straight line through the bullet hole. This can be performed with a wooden dowel, ballistic lasers, or a string in conjunction with an angle finder.
4. Project the dowel, string, or laser through the bullet hole to reconstruct the bullet flight path.
5. Obtain medium range and close-up photographs of the trajectory of the bullet path.
6. Measure the straight line to determine the horizontal and vertical angle of the shot.
7. A laser and an angle finder allow reading the vertical angle on the angle finder. It is recommended to take additional measurements of the horizontal angle to confirm the data in the angle finder's vertical angle measurements.
8. Draw a proportional sketch of the scene showing the horizontal, vertical, and depth components of the bullet flight path.
9. After the trajectory has been documented, additional measurements of the location and the size of the bullet hole should be noted, such as
   • Distance from the floor to the bullet hole.
   • Distance to a corner, window, or door or other fixed point in the room.
   • Place an ABO ruler to the bullet hole and note the diameter.
   • If multiple shots have been fired, measure the distance between the bullet holes and the overall size of the shooting pattern, especially if a shotgun was fired.
   • Like in bloodstain pattern analysis, roadmap the bullet holes with letters to differentiate between the patterns.
   • Measure the dimensions of the shotgun pattern for possible distance determination.
10. Collect any piece of drywall or wood that contains the bullet hole.
11. Recover the projectile from the wall, ceiling, or floor. Be sure to obtain sufficient photos of the lodged projectile with and without scale before removing.
12. Carefully remove the projectile to avoid altering the striation on the projectile or the spent cartridge.

24 Bullets in a Crown Victoria

On February 23, 2006, in Fort Myers, Florida, the victim and her boyfriend traveled southbound on Metro Parkway in a 1993 Ford Crown Victoria, when shots were fired upon them by unknown persons. The female driver lost control and the vehicle went off the road onto the embankment where it came to a stop. The female driver died behind the wheel and the passenger had been shot multiple times (see Figure 6.24). He exited the vehicle and collapsed on the east shoulder of Metro Parkway where a passerby saw him and called the Sheriff's Office.

Bullet holes were along the right side of the vehicle, in the right rear window, the right rear door, the right front door and window, the left side of the windshield, and in the right of the hood.

The crime scene team assisted by patrol officers and detectives performed a line search on the embankments and the roadway of the northbound and southbound lanes of Metro Parkway recovering numerous spent shell casings of 7.62 × 39 caliber, consistent with a semi-automatic rifle.

The medical examiner determined that a projectile traveled through the skull and exited behind the left ear. A partially mushroomed projectile that had entered the left shoulder was recovered from the left upper arm. The manner of death was homicide and the cause of death was gunshot wound to the head perforating the brain.

Figure 6.24 Victim in vehicle.

The lead crime scene investigator examined the Ford Crown Victoria that had been secured at the impoundment bay of the Sheriff's Office. According to the crime scene report:

> The right side of the vehicle was riddled with bullet holes from the right front fender, hood, windshield, front door post, right front door, the right rear door window frame, and the right rear window. A single bullet hole was located on the lower left front door panel. The bullet holes were numbered 1 through 24 for identification purposes and do not represent the order in which the bullets struck the vehicle.

Every bullet hole was documented with overall and close-up photos, the location was measured, and the trajectory was marked with wooden dowels, photographed, and sketched. This is an excerpt from the original report:

> Bullet hole number 2 was in the right front fender approximately 31 1/8" to the rear of the right front corner of the vehicle and 33 1/2" off the floor. The bullet traveled through the fender and exited approximately 34 1/2" from the right front corner of the vehicle. The bullet impacted with the plastic radiator overflow container, cutting across the right side. After the bullet exited the container, it struck the wider rear portion of the water reservoir leaving a lead-like deposit on the container.

Figure 6.25 Laser trajectory. (With permission from Tritech Forensics.)

After the documentation, wooden dowels were used to show the trajectory of the projectile. Laser trajectory kits are another method determining the trajectory of the projectile, as shown in Figure 6.25.

6.3 Glass Fracture Match

There are over 700 different kinds of glass. The most common types of glass on vehicles are tempered glass and laminated. Tempered glass is stronger than regular glass through rapid heating and cooling of the glass surfaces. Tempered glass is used as window glass. Window glass does not shatter but rather fragments.

Laminated glass consists of a layer of plastic between two sheets of window glass. Laminated glass is used for the windshield, and side and rear windows of cars.

6.3.1 Glass Fractures

Glass bends when force is applied to any side until the limit of the elasticity is reached and it will fracture. Fractured window glass provides information about the direction of impact and from where the force had been applied. Since the first fractures form on the surface opposite the penetrating force and develops radial fractures, the continued motion of forces places tension on the front surface of the glass, resulting in concentric fractures (Saferstein, 2011). This can allow the crime scene investigator to determine if the window at the burglary scene was broken from the outside inward or from the inside out. In other words, did the burglar break the window to enter the residence or did he break the window to flee from the residence. Always look at the glass fragments and examine for possible blood drops as the suspect could have cut him or herself when breaking the glass.

6.3.2 Glass Fractures Associated with a Gunshot

A common fracture pattern of cracks, radiating outward encircling a hole, is created when a projectile or a stone penetrates a window. The radiating lines are called radial fractures and extend like spokes of a wheel from the point of penetration. The circular lines are called concentric fractures forming a rough circle around the point of penetration (see Figure 6.26).

Caution: It is very difficult to determine the type of propelled item based on the size of the hole in the window glass. Always check for gunpowder residue when determining whether a firearm has caused the damage.

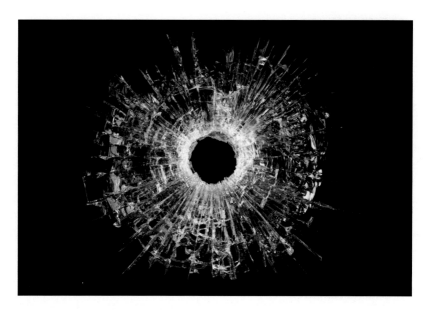

Figure 6.26 Shot fired into window.

6.3.3 The 3R Rule

The 3R rule states that radial cracks form a right angle on the reverse side of the force.

The crime scene investigator can apply this rule to determine from which side the window was broken; however, this rule does not apply to tempered glass.

The 3R rule can be applied to determine which shot has been fired first.

When examining a windshield with two or more bullet holes, the following observations should be made:

- Examine the perpendicular edges of the stress marks as they always face the surface on which the crack originated.
- Examine if the stress marks on the edge of a radial crack near the point of impact as the perpendicular end is always on the opposite side from which the force was applied.
- Examining concentric fractures, the perpendicular end always faces the surface on the side where the force originated, as illustrated in Figure 6.27.

6.3.4 Sequencing Bullet Holes

The basic rule when determining the sequence of multiple bullet holes with glass fractures to apply is

A fracture always terminates at an existing line of fracture.

Figure 6.27 Beveling glass.

Examine the radial fractures (spinning outward from the bullet hole) and look for areas where the fracture lines terminate at the cracks of the former lines. The radial fractures that extend beyond the intersection indicate that this bullet hole was created first.

Hint: When photographing bullet holes and glass fractures of a windshield, placing a brown paper bag, a dark piece of cardboard or paper, or a dark cloth in the background captures more detail of the fracture pattern.

References

James, S., Kish, P., and Sutton, P. (2005). *Principles of Bloodstain Pattern Analysis: Theory and Practice* (Practical Aspects of Criminal & Forensic Investigations), 3rd ed. CRC Press, Boca Raton, FL.

James, S., Nordby, J., and Bell, S. (2014). *Forensic Science: An Introduction to Scientific and Investigative Techniques*, 4th ed. CRC Press, Boca Raton, FL.

Row, W. F. (2014). Chapter in book of James, S., Nordby, J., and Bell, S. (2014). *Forensic Science: An Introduction to Scientific and Investigative Techniques*, 4th ed. CRC Press, Boca Raton, FL.

Saferstein, R. (2011). *Criminalistics, An Introduction to Forensic Science*, 10th ed. Prentice Hall, Upper Saddle River, NJ.

Death Investigation

7

7.1 What Is a Death Investigation?

Throughout the centuries, people have been interested in investigating the causes of death, both natural and human-caused. Ultimately, the roots of forensic science were founded on the investigation of nonnatural, human-caused death. A death investigation is conducted when it is unclear why a person died. The time, manner, and cause of death are determined during the autopsy.

Caution: Not every death investigation is a homicide.

7.1.1 Criminal Investigator versus Medico-Legal Death Investigator

The investigation of any death is a team effort between the law enforcement investigator, crime scene investigator, and the medical examiner's personnel.

The criminal investigator, also called homicide detective or homicide agent, holds the jurisdiction over the crime scene. The detective represents the law enforcement agency and has jurisdiction over the crime scene, whereas the medico-legal death investigator (MLDI) represents the medical examiner's office and has jurisdiction over the body, at least in most states. The detective is responsible for the application of the law when entering the crime scene, and collecting evidence or seizing property. The MLDI collects all property on the body, including but not limited to: wallet, driver's license, money, credit cards, Social Security card, eyeglasses, clothing, jewelry, and any other item the victim carries. The detective interviews witnesses and performs neighborhood canvasses to obtain information about the victim. The MLDI is interested in the victim's medical history and information about family physicians.

7.1.2 Coroner versus Medical Examiner *(James et al., 2014)*

The coroner system was founded in England before the tenth century. British common law was the initial law for the American colonies and later the laws of the states. There were no provisions in the Constitution of the United States

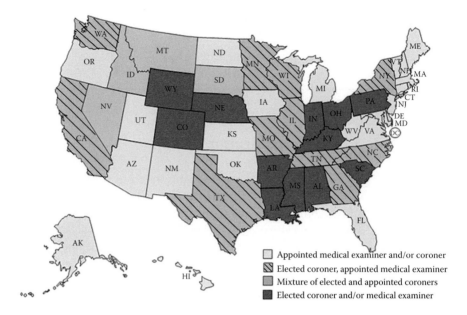

Map 7.1 Map of coroner and medical examiner jurisdictions in the United States. (Retrieved from http://www.cdc.gov.)

and death investigations were considered a local, county, and later state function. Every state maintained its own laws.

Today, in the United States, we still have two systems: the coroner and the medical examiner, as illustrated in Map 7.1.

7.1.2.1 The Coroner (James et al., 2014)

A coroner is an elected official. It is not necessary to have a medical background to become a coroner. In some rural areas, the coroner is the local feed store owner or a farmer. The coroner is responsible for

- Identifying a body
- Notifying the next of kin
- Collecting and returning personal effects from the body to the family
- Signing the death certificate

However, if the nonmedical coroner determines that an autopsy is required, he or she has to contact a medical examiner. The coroner cannot perform autopsies.

7.1.2.2 The Medical Examiner (James et al., 2014)

The medical examiner is a medical doctor; most have specialized training in forensic pathology. The medical examiner is appointed by the governor of the state. Medical examiner districts consist of multiple counties, for example the 21st Medical Examiner's District in Florida consists of Lee, Hendry, and Glades County.

The duties of the medical examiner are to investigate death occurring under suspicious circumstances and perform autopsies to determine the manner, cause, and mechanism of death.

7.2 Autopsy

An autopsy is an after death examination of a body to determine the cause, manner, and mechanism of death. Autopsies are performed on humans and on animals, called necropsy.

7.2.1 What Is an Autopsy?

Every unexpected or unattended death will undergo an investigation and an autopsy. A forensic autopsy differs from a hospital autopsy. In the forensic autopsy, the medical examiner or forensic pathologist does not only determine the cause and manner of death, but will also look at the identification of the deceased, time of death, injuries, and physical evidence from the body. The main reasons for an autopsy are to determine the cause and manner of death. The *cause of death* is, "any injury or disease that produces a physiological derangement of the body that results in death" (Geberth, 2006, p. 632).

7.2.1.1 Cause, Manner, and Mechanism of Death

The cause of death can be an illness or injury leading to the death of a person. A cause of death may be a disease such as cancer, injuries from a car accident, or a gunshot wound to the head.

The *manner of death* is the method in which the cause of death originated. In other words, the manner of death is how the death occurred. Manners of death are categorized as homicide, suicide, natural, accidental, and undetermined.

- *Homicide* is the deliberate and unlawful killing of one person by another. Causes of death include, among others, a gunshot wound, stabbing, or manual asphyxiation.
- *Suicide is* the willful taking of one's own life. The cause of death can include, among others, a self-inflicted gunshot wound, overdose of prescription drugs, drowning, or hanging.
- *Accidental* death is triggered by an accident. The cause of death can include, among others, the injuries sustained from a vehicle accident,

a plane crash, or a work related accident at a construction site or even a lightning strike.

- *Natural death* is a person dying without the involvement of any other force or circumstances. The cause of death can include old age or disease.
- *Undetermined* is a fifth manner of death applied when there is no physical evidence of any circumstances that caused the death, for example, skeletal remains are found in the woods. During the autopsy, the forensic pathologist and the anthropologist cannot find any signs of injuries, bullet holes, cuts, or any indication of force that could have caused the death of that person. Also, if the person is unidentified, the medical history may not be available to determine a natural death.

The *mechanism of death* is the "physiological derangement produced by the cause of death that results in death" (Geberth, 2006, p. 632) such as a gunshot wound or a hemorrhage of a tumor.

7.2.1.2 The Mortis Brothers—The Chemistry of Death

Immediately after death, the body begins to break down. These changes are called livor mortis, rigor mortis, and algor mortis.

7.2.1.2.1 Livor Mortis   Livor mortis begins when the heart stops beating and mixing the blood. The red blood cells are denser and sink, creating a maroon to purple color at the lowest point of the body. The onset of livor mortis begins within 30 minutes up to 2 hours after death.

Important: The discoloration of a body postmortem during livor mortis can indicate whether a body has been moved.

When a person dies, blood is still in the vessels and pressure on a specific area pushes the blood out, called blanching. Blanching can be tested by putting pressure to an area with lividity present. If the lividity discoloration temporarily disappears, lividity has not been set. After time passes, the blood vessels, blood cells, and hemoglobin break down pigments and move out into the tissue. Blanching will stop and the lividity is set. Commonly, lividity sets between 8 and 12 hours. After that time frame, blood begins to congeal within the capillaries resulting in a lack of blanching and the inability for displacement of blood. Pressure from clothing or other constrictive force prevents blood from pooling; there is no discoloration in this area (Dutelle, 2014) (Figure 7.1).

Caution: Do not mistake lividity for injuries or bruising.

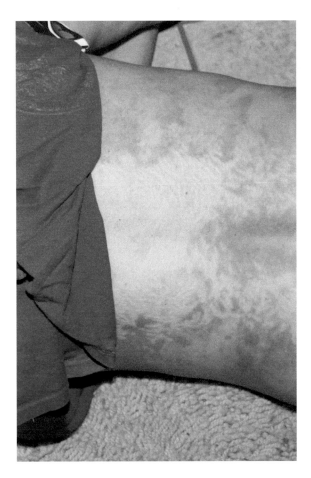

Figure 7.1 Photo of livor mortis.

7.2.1.2.2 Rigor Mortis Rigor mortis is the stiffening of the muscles. The joints begin to stiffen and lock in place. The onset of rigor mortis can be 10 minutes to several hours depending on the environment and the temperature. For example, a rapid cooling of the body can delay the onset of rigor mortis. Rigor mortis disappears within 36 hours.

While living cells need oxygen to burn glycogen, after death there is no oxygen supply to the cells, and the anaerobic glycosis produces lactic and pyruvic acids. The pH level falls, thereby increasing acidity. Acid promotes the reaction between actin and myosin, needed to contract a muscle. The muscle will shorten until all adenosine triphosphate (ATP) and acetylcholine is used up. Rigor mortis ends when the body begins to decompose, breaking down the fibers and relaxing the muscles. The lysosomes release intracellular digestive enzymes at the beginning of the disintegrating of the cells, destroying the muscle fibers.

Caution: Do not confuse rigor mortis with cadaveric spasm. Cadaveric spasm is an immediate rigor at the victim's hands clenching around any object; it is caused by the considerable excitement and tension during death.

7.2.1.2.3 Algor Mortis   Algor mortis is the cooling of the body. The normal body temperature is 98.6°F, and may be higher if the deceased had a fever. Several different environmental conditions influence the cooling of the body:

- Radiation; the higher the original body temperature, the more heat loss.
- Conduction; depending on the surface where the body rested. For example, a body in water will cool faster because of the enhanced contact.
- Convection; for example, wind cools faster.

Important: The cooling rate of a body after death is 1.5°F/hour under normal conditions.

Algor mortis can also be influenced by other factors such as

- Clothing will insulate the body from heat loss.
- Obesity as fat insulates, resulting in a slower drop in temperature.
- Ratio of the surface area to the victim's volume, for example, children and thin people cool faster.
- Water is a better conductor than air, enabling a faster cooling process.

7.2.1.3 Time of Death

The forensic pathologist performs the determination of the time of death during the autopsy.

There are three categories for time of death:

- Physiological time of death is the time when all vital organs of the deceased's body stopped functioning.
- Estimated time of death is a prediction based on available information.
- Legal time of death is the time of recovery and when the person has been pronounced dead. This time will be listed in the death certificate (Claridge, 2015).

Factors that assist in determining the time of death.

Different factors are considered when determining the time of death:

- Livor mortis, the discoloring and settling of blood at the lowest level
- Rigor mortis, the stiffening of the muscles

- Algor mortis, the drop in body temperature
- Vitreous draw
- Appearance of the eyes
- Stomach contents
- Stage of decomposition (Dutelle, 2014, p. 432)

Measuring the body temperature will provide information about the estimated time of death as the body cools by 1.5°F/hour under "normal circumstances" (though this, of course, is a relative term). Commonly, the body temperature of a deceased is taken by using a rectal thermometer. The liver temperature, however, provides a more accurate core body temperature.

Looking at the stiffening of the muscles, especially the small muscles in the face, provides information about the rigor mortis which sets in within 2 hours after death and can last for up to 36 hours.

Measuring the potassium level of the ocular fluid is a recently developed method to determine the post mortem interval (PMI). Upon death, the cells within the inner surface of the eyeball begin to release potassium into the ocular fluid. The analysis of the levels of potassium present can provide data for approximating the time of death.

The earliest signs of decomposition can be observed in the deceased's eyes. Corneal clouding is almost immediately present beginning with a thin film converting to a full clouding conversion within 2 to 3 hours after death. If the eyes are closed, the corneal film development may be delayed and the total cloudiness may take over 24 hours.

The pathologist will also examine the stomach content to determine the level of digestion of the food, providing information when the deceased last ate. What he or she ate may lead the detective, for example, to a special restaurant or otherwise clarify details useful to the investigation.

Important: It may sound silly, but check if the victim has a watch. If it is broken, it most likely was broken at the approximate time of death.

The stage of decomposition is also an indicator of the estimated time of death. Decomposition will usually be visual within 24 to 30 hours.

The following chemical reactions occur between 24 and 30 hours after death:

- Discoloration of the abdomen to a bluish-green color due to the bacteria in the colon and digestive tract.
- The body begins to bloat due to the bacteria breaking down body tissues and organic material in the body, producing methane which causes the body to swell.
- The face discolors, later spreading to the chest and extremities within 36 to 48 hours.

- The separation of the epidermal and dermal skin layers result in gloving (hands) or slippage (feet) (Dutelle, 2014).
- Fluids leak out of the body openings.
- The eyes and other soft tissues liquefy.
- Skin begins to melt.
- In addition to the body bloating with gases, these can sometimes cause abdominal or chest cavities to burst (Norman, 2012).

Caution: There are many variables such as temperature, indoors versus outdoor environment, or whether the person was clothed that can change the rate of decomposition.

Entomology, the study of bugs, can assist in the determination of the time of death. The life cycle of the blowfly/maggots provides valuable information that can help to approximate the time of death. Please find more detailed information in Chapter 5.

Mummification is the stage of dehydrated soft tissue resulting from exposure to high temperatures and low humidity. The skin turns leather-like and tight. Mummification begins at the extremities in the fingertips and toes and progresses to the hands, feet, face, and inward from the extremities.

Forgotten German Tourists

In 1999, two German citizens—a woman and her adult son—spent Christmas at their home in a coastal town in Florida. Shortly after Christmas, the neighbors did not see the mother and son and believed they had gone back to Germany, as they had done every year before. However, that year, they did not return. The mother and son did not have close relatives in Germany and those friends they had in Germany believed that they had stayed in Florida for an extended period of time. The electric bill for the residence was automatically withdrawn from their bank account. The immigration stamp in the passports indicated that they entered the United States on December 10, 1999.

A local resident had managed their home in the United States since 1988 during the times in which they resided in Germany.

In November 2002, this man went to the residence to check on the mother and son as he noticed that the property taxes had not been paid. The tax bill was $4,500.

No signs of forced entry were detected; the lights and air conditioning were on when he entered the residence. He discovered the mother lying on the floor in the living/dining room while her son and the family dog were found decomposing in the bedroom. Prescription medication had been found in the residence and a handwritten note in German was translated to "...Father forgive us what we are doing...." The mother had been partially skeletonized, especially the areas that had been covered with a blue blanket. The legs, exposed to the open air, were mummified, as indicated in Figure 7.2.

The woman's son and the family dog were decomposing in the bedroom. The dog was lying on top of the bed while the son was covered with a blanket, preventing the mummification of his body, as shown in Figure 7.3.

During the autopsy of the mother and son, and the necropsy of the dog, samples of hair and nails were taken for toxicology testing. The toxicology testing exposed high levels of diazepam in the pair as well as the dog. Due to the mummification and advanced stages of decomposition, the pair could not be identified through fingerprints. The skull and teeth were intact and the forensic odontologist was contacted to perform a dental identification. Law enforcement contacted the family in Germany to identify their family dentist who may have recent dental records. Due to German laws similar to HIPPA in the United States, German police and the court had to permit the dentist to release the dental records. The forensic odontologist was able to positively identify the mother and her son as the decedents.

Figure 7.2 The mother's remains.

Figure 7.3 Son and dog in bed.

It remained undetermined if the mother poisoned her adult mentally challenged son or if both agreed to commit suicide. Law enforcement only found one suicide note handwritten by the mother in German.

7.2.2 Purpose of the Autopsy

The forensic autopsy serves the following purposes:

- Identity of the deceased (fingerprints, dental impressions, or identification by relatives, DNA, tattoos, scars, implants, etc.).
- Determine an approximate time when the injury occurred.
- What was the causative agent or object that created the injury.
- The dynamics of the injury such as direction, position, and magnitude.
- Duration between injury and death.
- Time of death.
- Cause of death.
- Manner of death (Table 7.1).

Table 7.1   Cause and Manner of Death

Manner of Death	Cause of Death
Accidental	Person died of the injuries sustained in a car accident, workplace accident, or any other accident.
Natural	Person died of natural causes such as chronic illness or heart disease.
Suicide	Person took his or her own life. Poison, hanging, gunshot wound or cutting the artery can cause death.
Homicide	Person died by the act of another person with the intent to cause bodily harm or death.
Undetermined	This term is used if the cause and manner of death cannot be determined, for example, if the body is skeletonized and no visible signs of injury are present. The medical examiner will also call the cause of death undetermined or pending toxicology results if there is a suspicion of drug use, alcohol, or poison.

7.2.2.1 The Duties of the Medical Examiner and the Medico-Legal Death Investigator

The medical examiner's determination of the cause and manner of death will be based on the information at the death scene, autopsy results, medical history, and medications recovered at the crime scene. If necessary, the medical examiner will contact the victim's family physician for information about the deceased. Many medical examiner jurisdictions employ MLDIs who respond to every death call in their jurisdiction.

7.2.2.1.1 The Medico-Legal Death Investigator at the Crime Scene   The forensic autopsy begins at the crime scene. At every unattended death, the medical examiner's office will be notified and based on the circumstances of the death, an MLDI will respond to the death scene. Upon arrival on scene, the MLDI is briefed by the first officer on scene, the detective, or the crime scene investigator about the specifics of the scene. The MLDI captures overall photographs of the scene and medium-range and close-up photos of the deceased. The MLDI records information about the deceased such as the date, time, and name of the person who discovered the deceased; information when the deceased was last seen alive (if available); any medical history and photographs, and the CSI collects any prescription medication in the deceased's name and signs custody over to the MLDI. Information about the characteristics of the scene such as forced entry, bloodstains, and signs of struggle will assist in the definition of the cause and manner of death, determined by the medical examiner during the autopsy. The MLDI evaluates the deceased for injuries, wounds, and discoloration of the skin, signs of medical issues, and any indications that can assist deciding the preliminary cause of

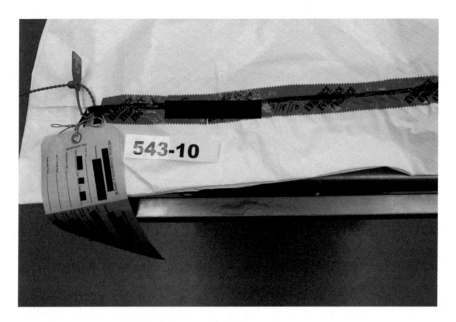

Figure 7.4 Body bag with seal.

death. It is not uncommon that an external examination on scene does not provide a preliminary cause of death and the scene will remain secured until the conclusion of the autopsy.

The MLDI, who has jurisdiction over the body, searches the deceased's clothes and belongings for any form of picture identification such as a driver's license or state identification cards to identify the deceased for death notification for the family. Any of the victim's belongings such as keys, wallets, money, purse, etc. will accompany the victim to the morgue.

Prior to transport to the morgue, both of the victim's hands will be covered with specialized hand bags or, if not available, brown paper bags sealed with evidence tape covering the victim's hands, to avoid loss of trace evidence during transport. The body will be placed in a plastic body bag and sealed with a numbered seal; evidence tape will be taped across the zipper and be initialed by the MLDI or crime scene investigator (Figure 7.4).

7.2.2.1.2 CSI Documenting the Deceased on Scene The CSI arriving on the death scene should follow a series of methodical steps as part of every death investigation. These steps include the following: the basic crime scene procedures of ensuring legal entry, signing the crime scene log, evaluating and observing the scene during the walk-through with the first officer on scene or detective, evaluating and observing the deceased on scene, documentation with photographs, notes, and sketches, establishing and recording decedent profile information, and completing the scene investigation.

The CSI will capture the scene with overall and medium-range photos of the scene and close-up photos of the deceased. A yellow marker number, in most cases number 1, will be assigned to the deceased and placed next to the body. Since the crime scene is the jurisdiction of the law enforcement agency, the CSI is allowed to walk around the deceased; however, the deceased falls under the jurisdiction of the medical examiner's office and cannot be altered in any way.

Photography is noninvasive and can be performed as long as it does not alter the scene prior to the MLDI's arrival. The CSI will visually search for any kind of possible trace evidence such as hairs and fibers on or around the body.

The CSI takes detailed notes about the deceased's position such as

- Sitting on chair, lying on floor, lying on back, stomach, right or left side
- Compass direction of head, hands, and feet
- Note if the hands are open, clenched to a fist, and finger position
- Elbows and knees are straight; if bent, estimate the degrees
- Victim's clothing and shoes
- Describe visible injuries such as gunshot, laceration
- Vomit or any other discharge
- Visible blood and defects on clothing
- Note any smells or insect activity around the body
- If maggots or other insects are present, photograph, note, sketch, and collect samples as explained in Chapter 5

A crime scene sketch will be drawn to show the location of the victim in reference to other items of evidence such as a weapon, point of entry, bloodstain pattern, or other physical evidence.

In most indoor crime scenes, the CSI will apply the triangulation measurement method to obtain measurements of the deceased's location in the room, as shown in Table 7.2.

The CSI will take the same set of photographs as the MLDI. Upon request, the MLDI can sign over custody of government identification or a cellular phone on the deceased to the law enforcement agency for further criminal investigation. If the MLDI requires collecting medication from the scene, the CSI will list the items on a property receipt and sign the chain of custody over to the MLDI.

Table 7.2   Measurements of the Deceased

Deceased	Point A SW Corner of Living Room	Point B SE Corner of Living Room
Head	12'3"	11'6"
Chest	13'5"	12'5"
Torso	14'5"	13'0"
Right elbow	13'7"	12'9"
Right hand	14'6"	13'7"
Left elbow	12'7"	11'4"
Left hand	13'3"	12'6"
Right knee	8'4"	9'2"
Right foot	9'1"	9'7"
Left knee	8'5"	9'3"
Left foot	9'2"	9'6"
Point A to point B	25'0"	

7.2.2.2 Autopsy at the Medical Examiner's Office

The postmortem examination of the deceased consists of the visual/external autopsy when the autopsy technician or MLDI capture numerous different photographs of the victim. The MLDI may use the template as provided in Document 7.1. The CSI attends the autopsy and documents the findings via photographs, notes, and collects physical evidence. Many CSIs use autopsy work sheet as shown in Document 7.2. The internal autopsy is performed by the medical examiner, assisted by the autopsy technician (AT) or MLDI.

7.2.2.2.1 Visual/External Autopsy Upon arrival at the morgue, the AT will assign a case number for the medical examiner's office. This number has to be included in every photograph taken during the external and internal autopsy. The numbers are continuous for each calendar year.

The first step of the external autopsy is to document the victim *in situ*, as found on scene. The AT, as well as the crime scene investigator, will obtain several sets of photographs of overall, midrange, and close-up photos (Figure 7.5).

- Overall photo of the deceased as found at the crime scene (clothed)
- Identification photo of the deceased (ensure that there is no blood visible)
- Close-up photographs of the victim's hands (palm and back of hands)
- Close-up photos with scale of any tattoos and scars
- Close-up photos with scale of injuries (stab wounds, gunshot wounds, cuts and bruises, defense wounds)
- Close-up photos of skin discolorations and bodily fluids such as vomit
- Overall photo of the deceased after being undressed and washed

Death Investigation Form

Case Number: _____   Date: _____

Time Notified: _____   Estimated Time of Death: _____

Notified By: _____

Decedent Name: _____

Decedent Address: _____

Decedent DOB: _____/_____/_____   Decedent SSN: _____

Decedents Drivers License/ID Number: _____   Issued By: _____

Decedent Identified by: _____

Identifying Marks: _____

Location of Body: _____

GPS coordinates (if necessary): N/S _____   W/E _____   Elevation: _____

Cause of Death: ☐ Homicide ☐ Suicide ☐ Accident ☐ Natural ☐ Unknown ☐ Found Dead

If Motor Vehicle Accident: ☐ Driver ☐ Passenger ☐ Pedestrian ☐ Unknown

Pictures Taken: ☐ Yes ☐ No

Autopsy: ☐ Yes ☐ No

Pathologist /s: _____

Transported By: _____

Funeral Home: _____

Immediate Cause of Death: _____

Due to or as a consequence of: _____

_____

Decedent Medical History: _____

_____

_____

Coroner / Medical Examiner: _____

Signature: _____   Date: _____

Document 7.1 Work sheet for the death investigator.   (*Continued*)

Death Investigation Form

Time of Death Determination: ☐ Witnessed Death   Time of Examination: _____

Pronounced By: _____

Outside Air Temperature: _____ F / C   Core Body Temperature: _____F/C   Liver / Rectal

Wind Direction / Temperature: _____/_____   Decedent Body Weight: _____lb/kg

Decedent Clothing: ☐ None ☐ Light ☐ Medium ☐ Heavy   ☐ Wet ☐ Dry

Decomposition: ☐ No Rigor Mortis ☐ Rigor Mortis Developing ☐ Full Rigor Mortis ☐ Rigor Mortis Gone

☐ No Livor Mortis ☐ Faint Livor Mortis ☐ Prominent Livor Mortis (Unfixed) ☐ Fixed Livor Mortis

☐ Corneas Dry (eyes open) ☐ Corneas Dry (eyes closed) ☐ Corneal Collapse (eyes closed)

☐ Corneal Collapse (eyes open) ☐ Skin Decomposition (blue/green) ☐ Corpse Bloating ☐ Skin Marbling

☐ Skin Blistering ☐ Skin Slippage ☐ Purging ☐ Adipocere ☐ Mummification

☐ Known Fever ☐ Radiator Device (sun, heater, etc.) ☐ Known Struggle

Scene Evaluation:

☐ Weapons Found: _____

☐ Blood Spatter: (details): _____

☐ Insects Found

Notes:

_____

_____

_____

_____

_____

_____

_____

_____

_____

_____

_____

_____

Document 7.1 (Continued) Work sheet for the death investigator.   *(Continued)*

Death Investigation Form

Body Examination: (Please Identify All Identified Wounds)

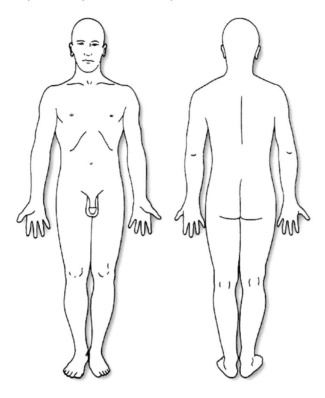

Notes:

_____
_____
_____
_____
_____
_____
_____
_____
_____

Document 7.1 (Continued) Work sheet for the death investigator. (*Continued*)

Death Investigation Form

Formulas***:

Check the Method Used:

☐ Simple Time of Death Calculation Based on Body Temperature

Time of Death = 98.6(F) – Core Body Temperature/ 1.5
Temperature Drops Approximately 1.5 degrees per hour after death for the first 12 hours then drops 1 degree per hour after that up to approximately 18 hours.

☐ To Use Hessnge Nomogram Method please visit the following Web Pages:
http://www.pathguy.com/TimeDead.htm

Approximate Time of Death based on Decomposition***:

Corneal Evaluation:

Corneal Drying
　　　Eyes Open　　　minutes
　　　Eyes Closed　　approximately 2 hours

Corneal Collapse
　　　Eyes Open　　　Approximately 12 – 24 hours
　　　Eyes Closed　　Greater than 24 hours

Corneal Cloudiness
　　　Eyes Open　　　Approximately 2 hours
　　　Eyes Closed　　Approximately 12 – 24 hours

Decomposition:

Blue-Green Skin　　Approximately 24 – 36 hours
Bloating　　　　　Approximately 36 – 48 hours
Marbling　　　　　Approximately 2 – 3 days
Blistering　　　　Approximately 3 days
Skin Slippage　　　Approximately 4 -7 days
Purging　　　　　Approximately 4 -5 days
Adipocere　　　　Months (in wet environment)
Mummification　　Weeks to Years (in dry arid environment)

Rigor / Livor Mortis

Developing Rigor　　　Approximately 30min to 6 hrs
Full Rigor　　　　　　Approximately 6 hours to 24 hours
Rigor Disappears　　　Approximately 12 – 36 hours
Blanching Livor Mortis　Immediate to 2 hours
Fixed Livor Mortis　　　Approximately 8 – 12 hours

***　　All time periods listed above are approximate. Time periods will vary greatly depending on environmental conditions, decedent medical history, and other factors. All estimations are just that estimates and no one factor can accurately determine time of death. Seek professional/expert advice for more detailed determinations. LAPSC will not be held liable for inaccuracies, you may utilize these times at your own risk.

©Louisiana Public Safety Consultants 2009 www.lapsc.com

Document 7.1 (Continued) Work sheet for the death investigator.

Name of Agency   1
Forensics Unit
Crime Scene Investigation

Autopsy Work Sheet

Agency Case Number :

Medical Examiner Case Number :

Location of Medical Examiner's Office

Date and time notified: By:

Date and time of arrival:

Name of Crime Scene Investigators:

Name of Medical Examiner performing
autopsy

Name of Medico Legal Death
Investigator/Autopsy Lab Technician

Name of Detective(s);

Other personnel present:

Name: Agency

Document 7.2 Autopsy work sheet for the CSI.   (*Continued*)

Victim 1 Information
Name:

Address:

Date of Birth:

Place of Birth:

Race: Gender

Height: Weight

Hair color: Eyes

Tattoos:

Scars: Location

Clothes:

Pants
Type   Jeans   Shorts   Slacks   Size
Color   Brand name

Shirt
Long sleeved   short sleeved   Size
Color   Brand name

Shoes
Type: Sneaker   Loafer   Boat Shoe   Sandal
Color: Size   Brand name

Jacket
Long sleeved   short sleeved   Size   Color
Material: Brand name

Hats/Ball caps
Brand name   Logo   Color
Underwear
Type   Brand name
Size   Logo

Document 7.2 (Continued) Autopsy work sheet for the CSI.   (*Continued*)

Name of Agency   3
Forensics Unit
Crime Scene Investigation

Victim 1 Information   continued

Jewelry
Earring   Rings
Metal   Stones
Description of Jewelry and area worn:

Watch
Brand   Color   metal
Digital   Chronomatic
Color of faceplate   Engravings

Victims Injuries:

Document 7.2 (Continued) Autopsy work sheet for the CSI.   (*Continued*)

Gunshot Wounds

Number of Gunshots   Through and Through   Yes   No

Location of entry wound
Location of exit wound
Size of entry wound

Size of exit wound

Gunshot went through clothing   Yes   No

Describe defects in clothing

Projectile   Recovered   Yes   No

Describe shape of projectile

Determination of caliber of projectile

Gunshot Residue Kit performed   Yes   No

Additional Information

Document 7.2 (Continued) Autopsy work sheet for the CSI.   (*Continued*)

Name of Agency   5
Forensics Unit
Crime Scene Investigation

Victims with stab wounds

Number of stab wounds   Location

Size of stab wound

Describe the wounds

Possible weapons identified

Size of possible weapon

Additional Information

Document 7.2 (Continued) Autopsy work sheet for the CSI.   (*Continued*)

Visual Autopsy

Photography
Name of ME Photographer
Name of CSI Photographer

Camera	Digital	35mm		
Flash Assist	Ring flash	Yes	No	
Identification Photo	Yes	No		
Close up Photography of wounds	Yes	No		
Photography of clothing	Yes	No		

Fingernail clippings
Collected by	Date and time

Fingerprints
Set of finger prints	Yes	No
Set of Palm Prints	Yes	No
Collected by	Date and time	

DNA Swabs
Collected by	Date and time
Areas swabs collected from:	
Autopsy Concluded at	

Sexual Assault Evidence Collection Kit
Collected by	Date and time

Body examined for trace evidence
Performed by	Date and time
Alternative Light source	Brand/Wavelength
Findings	

Body examined for fingerprints on skin
Performed by	Date and time		
Method used	Cyancrylite fuming	Yes	No
Fingerprints lifted from:			

Document 7.2 (Continued) Autopsy work sheet for the CSI.

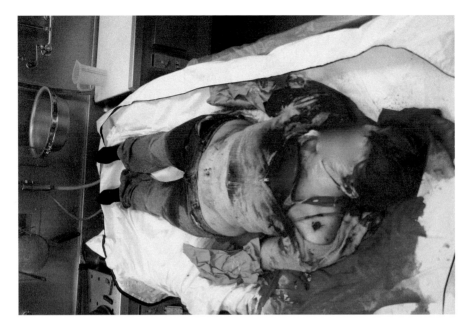

Figure 7.5 Photo of autopsy.

- Overall photo of the victim's
  - Chest
  - Torso
  - Upper and lower legs
  - Feet
  - Upper and lower arms
  - Back
  - Buttocks
- Close-up photos of the victim's clothing with and without scale
- Close-up photos of any defects on the victim's clothing

The AT will measure and weigh the victim. The AT will take X-rays of all gunshot victims and victims with extreme burns. This is very significant in gunshot cases with semijacketed ammunition where parts of the lead core have exited but the jacket might remain in the body (DiMao, 1985). After the photographs and X-rays are taken, the crime scene investigator, with permission from the medical examiner, can perform additional evidence detection and collection as long as they are noninvasive and do not alter the deceased.

Depending on the mechanic of the victim's death such as stabbing, gunshot, strangulation, etc., additional processing is required.

7.2.2.2.2 Stabbing Death   A stabbing victim may have several stab wounds in different sizes. At any time, if the crime scene investigator wants to process the victim to develop additional physical evidence such as the following, permission from the medical examiner is required:

- Photographically documenting the wounds with multiple images with and without scale.
- Sketch the injuries and tattoos on the victim's body. Add the measurements of the wounds and the size of the tattoos. Some wounds may help the MLDI or medical examiner determine the direction of the incision from left to right or right to left.
- Using Mikrosill, create a cast of the wound. The cast will not only show the size but also the jagged edging of the wound. The cast can be used to match any tools or weapons found on scene. Casting a wound with Mikrosill is identical to casting a tool mark impression as described in the tool marks section in Chapter 3.
- If the crime scene or witnesses stated that the victim struggled with the offender, the offender's DNA should be found underneath the fingernails. The fingernails evidence should be collected in a pharmaceutical folder or in a paper envelope. Each hand should be packaged separately as illustrated in Figure 7.6.

Figure 7.6 Decedent's hands bagged for transport. (With permission from Tritech Forensics.)

- If there are any indications of a struggle between the victim and the offender, the crime scene investigator should obtain swabs from the victim's arms, hands, areas around the injuries, and other areas deemed important to the investigation.
  - Wet a sterile cotton swab with sterile water.
  - Swab the area of interest.
  - Air-dry the swab before packaging in a cardboard box. (Special cardboard boxes have a small hole in the box where the swab can be placed during the drying time.)
  - Add necessary information such as case number, date, time, initials of the collector, and description of the swabbed area.
  - Seal with evidence tape, initial and date across the evidence tape and add a biohazard sticker.
  - Repeat for every swab.
- If there are signs or testimony from witnesses that the victim had a sexual encounter with the offender, a sexual assault evidence collection kit is required. However, the sexual assault evidence collection has to be performed by the medical examiner. Some law enforcement agencies require the collection of a sexual assault evidence collection kit from every homicide victim.
- In almost every stabbing, there is close physical contact between the victim and the offender. It might be possible to develop fingerprints from the victim's skin. Please follow the detailed description in Chapter 3, Section 3.1.4.1.1.
- Trace evidence can be found on the victim. The crime scene investigator will use a handheld alternate light source and a set of filter goggles to examine the deceased for hairs and fibers. Wavelengths in the 400 ranges are most successful to depict hairs and fibers. The trace evidence recovered should be packaged separately in an envelope and marked with case number, date and time of collection, initials of the collecting CSI, and description of the location of recovery. The envelope should be sealed with evidence tape, initialed, and dated across the tape.

7.2.2.2.3 Strangulation Death Bruising might be visible around the victim's neck area in cases of strangulation. This also refers to hangings and suicide scenes. Procedures for strangulation death include:

- The photographic documentation is always identical at every autopsy.
- Be sure to take close-up photographs of the knot in the rope and the type of rope.
- In strangulations, it is most likely that the victim struggled with the offender; the offender's DNA can be found underneath the

fingernails. The fingernails should be cut, scraped, and collected in a pharmaceutical folder or in a paper envelope. Each hand should be packaged separately.

- Examine the victim's hands for signs of defense wounds.
- In every manual strangulation case, the crime scene investigator should obtain swabs from the victim's neck area, cheeks, arms, and hands, and other areas deemed important to the investigation.
  - Wet a sterile cotton swab with sterile water.
  - Swab the area of interest.
  - Air-dry the swab before packaging in a cardboard box. (Special cardboard boxes have a small hole in the box where the swab can be placed during the drying time.)
  - Add necessary information such as case number, date, time, initials of the collector, and description of the swabbed area.
  - Seal with evidence tape, initial and date across the evidence tape, and add a biohazard sticker.
  - Repeat for every swab.
- Manual strangulation requires close physical contact between the victim and the offender, and it might be possible to develop fingerprints from the victim's skin. Please follow the detailed description in Chapter 3, Section 3.1.4.1.1.
- Exchanges of trace evidence such as hairs and fibers between the victim and the offender is common. The crime scene investigator should use a handheld alternate light source and filter goggles to examine the deceased for trace evidence. Wavelengths in the 400 ranges are most successful in helping to recover hairs and fibers. The found trace evidence should be packaged separately in an envelope and marked with case number, date and time of collection, initials of the collecting CSI, and description of the location of recovery. The envelope should be sealed with evidence tape, and initialed and dated across the tape.

The AT will look at the victim's eyes, looking for the presence of petechiae. Petechiae on the face and especially in the eyes can be a sign of death by asphyxiation. The appearance of petechiae can vary from very faint to bright red, brown, or purple.

7.2.2.2.4 Gunshot Victims
Gunshot wounds are classified as follows:

- Penetrating gunshot wounds have an entrance and an exit wound. The projectile for every penetrating gunshot wound must be recovered from the body.

- Perforating gunshot wounds have an entrance wound and an exit wound. No projectile will be recovered.
- Perform distance determination.

Gunshot wounds can provide information about the distance between the shooter and the victim. The gunshot wounds are categorized as contact wounds, near contact wounds, and distant wounds.

7.2.2.2.4.1 Contact Wound A contact wound is created when the muzzle of the weapon is pressed against the surface of the body when discharged. A hard contact wound is characterized when the skin envelopes around the muzzle due to the muzzle being jammed against the skin. Hard contact wounds can be identified by the seared edges of the entrance wound caused by the heat of the gases and blackened by the soot. In soft contact wounds, the muzzle is loosely contacting the skin allowing the gases to escape through a gap between the skin and the muzzle, as shown in Figure 7.7 (DiMaio, 2006).

7.2.2.2.4.2 Near Contact Wound A near contact wound lies between contact and intermediate range. The weapon is not contacting the skin, but held at a short distance away. Due to the short distance, the powder grains from the muzzle mark the skin, as they do not have enough room to escape.

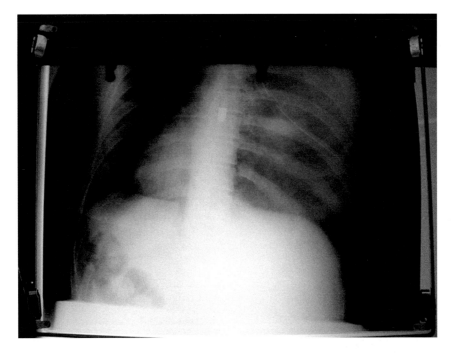

Figure 7.7 X-ray of a projectile.

7.2.2.2.4.3 Intermediate Range Gunshot Wounds   The intermediate range gunshot wound is created when the muzzle of the weapon is held at a dis tance when the weapon is discharged. However, the powder grains from the muzzle together with the projectile produces powder tattooing on the skin. These characteristics are specific characteristics for intermediate range gunshot wounds (DiMaio, 2006).

7.2.2.2.4.4 Distant Gunshot Wounds, Entrance and Exit Wound Characteristics   Distant gunshot wounds are identified by the marks of the bullet when perforating the skin. The entrance wound is always encircled by a reddish ring of abraded skin. This abrasion ring is created when the bullet enters and pierces the skin. The distance from which the shot is fired, close range, medium, or contact, is not significant as all exit wounds have the same characteristics. The exit wound is larger in size and irregularly shaped. Common shapes of exit wounds are stellate, crescent, or circular. Stellate exit wounds on the skull can easily be falsely identified as contact wounds (DeMaio, 2006) (Figure 7.8).

7.2.2.3 Internal Autopsy

The medical examiner begins the internal autopsy with taking notes of the victim's physique, age, race, weight, and height. The AT will undress and wash the victim. At this time, the AT will obtain two sets of inked finger-prints from both of the victim's hands. One set of fingerprints will remain at the medical examiner's office and custody of the second set of fingerprints will be signed over, via property receipt, to the crime scene investigator to maintain the chain of custody. The inked fingerprint standard is used for

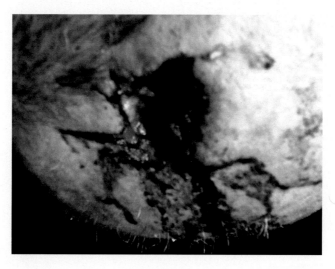

Figure 7.8 Gunshot exit wound on skull.

identification of the victim and for elimination prints for those fingerprints developed and collected from the crime scene. The AT collects fingernail clippings from both of the victim's hands and swabs the area underneath the fingernails for possible DNA from the suspect, especially if the victim and the offender had an altercation or if defense wounds are present.

The medical examiner notes, sketches, and measures any injuries, tattoos, old scars, discoloration of the skin, the appearance of the eyes, and external evidence of disease. The Y-incision is performed to enter the chest cavity to examine and remove organs. The major organs such as the heart, liver, spleen, brain, and kidney are removed and individually weighed and noted for the autopsy report.

In cases of gunshot wounds, the medical examiner determines the path of the projectile and lists all organs that have been penetrated between the entry and exit wound. If lead fragments or jacket pieces are visible on the X-ray, they will be removed and collected as evidence for comparison to recovered firearms and to search in the National Integrated Ballistic Information Network (NIBIN) database. If one or more projectiles are found, it is important to note the condition such as deformed, intact, or fragmented (Figure 7.9). The medical examiner will also examine the victim's clothing to determine if the defects are consistent with the location of any entry and exit wounds. Tissue samples of the major organs are to be collected for toxicology examinations. All findings are documented in notes and close-up photographs.

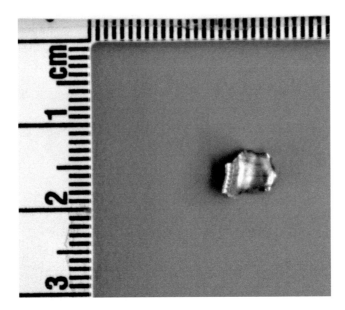

Figure 7.9 Recovered projectile fragment.

The medical examiner then determines the cause and manner of death. The crime scene investigator will document the cause and manner of death as stated by the medical examiner but refrain from including any medical details in the crime scene report as the CSI is not qualified to make pathological statements.

7.2.2.4 Evidence Collection from the Victim

The CSI will attend the autopsy, but the MLDI will collect all physical evidence. Again, the medical examiner/coroner performing the autopsy will sign over custody of the physical evidence to the CSI/law enforcement agency via property receipt while maintaining the chain of custody.

7.2.2.4.1 Blood Standard from the Deceased Victim   During the autopsy, the AT collects a blood sample from the deceased. Until about five years ago, this blood sample would have been collected and stored in a purple-topped blood vial, stored in a refrigerator and shipped with dry ice to the laboratory to avoid temperature changes that could degrade the DNA. Today, since the new PCR and STR DNA testing methods have been adopted, there is no need for liquid blood samples. A bloodstain card with a dried bloodstain is sufficient to establish a profile. The stain card can be stored on the shelf and does not require refrigeration, as illustrated in Figure 7.10.

7.2.2.4.2 Collection of Victim's Clothing and Additional Evidence   The victim's clothing can provide valuable evidence such as the suspect's DNA, fibers, or even fingerprints. After the external autopsy is concluded, the AT will undress and wash the victim. The victim's clothes will be laid out on a clean bedsheet or a clean surface for photographic documentation. When

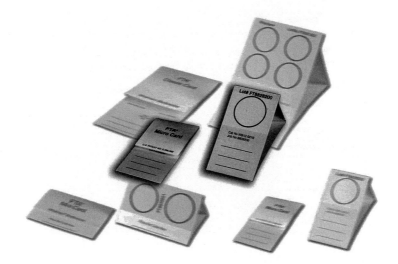

Figure 7.10 Bloodstain card. (With permission from Tritech Forensics.)

photographing any evidence during the autopsy, always include the medical examiner's case label. The procedure includes:

- Capturing an overall photo of all clothing and shoes.
- Obtaining medium range photos of each item of clothing and shoes as shown in Figure 7.11a.
- Marking defects in the clothing with an arrow (Figure 7.11b) and documenting with notes and close-up photos.
- When photographing shoes, ensuring all sides of the shoes, the inside, labels, and the sole pattern are included.
- When photographing a watch, capturing the serial number or information on the inside of the watch and the watchband.
- Photographing any wedding band, which includes any dates, inscriptions, or initials inside the ring.

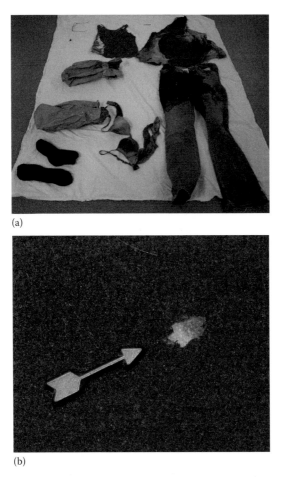

(a)

(b)

Figure 7.11 (a) Photos of a victim's clothing and (b) defect in clothing.

Note specific information such as brand name, style, size, and customized information such as embroidered names or potential gang affiliations.

The AT writes a property receipt listing the following:

- Victim's clothing and shoes
- Jewelry
- Wallet with identification cards, credit cards, and paperwork
- Fingernail clippings
- Sex crimes kit
- Gunshot residue kit
- Swabs obtained during the external and internal autopsy
- Projectiles, fragments, and jacket fragments
- Any physical evidence removed from the victim
- Blood sample from the victim
- Transport sheet from the scene to the morgue

The medical examiner will sign custody of the evidence over to the crime scene investigator. The CSI will package each item separately in paper bags, cardboard boxes, and paper folds, to preserve the quality of the evidence for future laboratory testing.

7.2.3 Lab Submission for Evidence from the Autopsy

After the scene investigation and the autopsy are concluded, the lead detective and the lead crime scene investigator confer to determine which items should be submitted for further analysis to the forensic laboratory. Larger law enforcement agencies such as Miami-Dade, New York City, etc., maintain their own forensic laboratory, while medium and smaller agencies rely on the laboratories of the state police or the FBI. The services of state and federal laboratories are free of charge; however, they routinely have a backlog that may take months before DNA test results are obtained. Private DNA laboratories provide faster service but are costly.

Caution: When consulting a private laboratory for DNA testing, consult with the state laboratory to determine if the DNA results from the private laboratory can be uploaded in the combined DNA identification system (CODIS) database for searches and identification. Private laboratories are not allowed to search in the CODIS database.

In a homicide case, the following evidence should be submitted to the laboratory, as illustrated in Table 7.3.

Caution: Always maintain the chain of custody when submitting evidence to a private, state, or federal laboratory.

Table 7.3 Evidence Submitted to the Forensic Laboratory

DNA	Fingernail clippings	Sexual assault evidence collection kit	Blood standard from victim	Blood standard from suspect	Swabs from victim	Blood from crime scene
Bloodstain pattern analysis	Victim's clothing	Victim's shoes				
Trace evidence	Any hair, fiber found on victim					

7.3 Death Investigations

Death investigations include suicide, accidental, natural, and homicide investigations. Not every death investigation is criminal. In death investigations, we differentiate between *attended* and *unattended deaths*. In an attended death, the victim was under a doctor's care for the medical condition causing his or her death, contrary to an unattended death, where the individual does not have any preconditions causing the death. Every unattended death is investigated by law enforcement and an autopsy is required to determine the cause and manner of death.

7.3.1 Response to Death Investigations

As we learned, the medical examiner determines the cause and manner of death during the autopsy. The MLDI responds to the scene of the death to document the circumstances such as whether it was indoors or outdoors, signs of a struggle, and physical evidence that may inform the medical examiner in efforts to determine the cause and manner of death.

As family members, neighbors, or friends find most of the deceased, these witnesses will provide important information about the victim's physical and mental state. Family members can attest to medical problems and whether the victim had previously attempted suicide.

Caution: Be as thorough in your investigation and do not take it for granted that it is just a suicide because the manner of death can change during the process of the autopsy.

The basic crime scene investigative steps—such as documentation via notes and photographs, marking, measuring, and sketching obvious evidence, sketching the scene and collection, preservation and maintaining the chain of custody—also apply to all death investigations.

The CSI will perform additional tasks including but not limited to the following:

- Take medium range and close-up photographs of the victim's body and location.
- If bloodstain patterns are present, document, photograph, and analyze the spatter pattern to determine
  - Is the pattern consistent with the mechanism of the death?
  - Is the location of the spatter consistent with the final resting point of the victim or had the victim been moved?
  - Examine the inside of the hands for blood, especially in gunshot deaths.

- - Look above the victim and examine the walls and ceiling for cast-off spatter.
  - Visually examine the victim's clothing for bloodstains.
- Search the residence/vehicle for a suicide note.
- Search for a letter to the family and friends.
- Note any medications on scene (the MLDI may collect the medication or ask the CSI to collect all medications).
- Collect any loose pills at the scene and package separately.
- Document the name of the family physician.
- Collect any paperwork containing information about medical conditions.
- Check the calendar for doctor's appointments.
- Note the temperature at the residence.
  - Settings on the A/C thermostat
  - Ceiling fans are on or off
  - Windows are open or closed

Caution: The body is under the jurisdiction of the medical examiner and should under no circumstances be disturbed by law enforcement.

7.3.1.1 Possible Cover-Up Attempt

Sometimes, a murderer is making efforts to disguise his crime, making a homicide appear as an accident or suicide by means of staging a scene. If the victim died of a gunshot wound, it is pertinent to perform background checks on the victim's occupation, hobbies, and interests, especially if he owned a firearm.

7.3.2 Suicide

Suicide is the willful taking of one's own life. The reasons for suicide are manifold ranging from depression, loss of loved one, divorce to financial crisis. In many cases, there are no signs that a person is suicidal, making it very difficult to prevent the act.

Caution: An important rule is to work every death investigation as thoroughly as a homicide.

A reason to treat any death investigation as thoroughly as you would a homicide is based on experience and history of many cases. Some investigations that had been closed as suicide or natural death may be reopened when additional evidence surfaced indicating the death was a homicide.

Popeye

There lived a mentally challenged man in a quiet community, in a coastal Florida city. The children in the neighborhood always made fun of him because he moved his long arms back and forth while walking, so they nicknamed him Popeye. The man was very upset about that but also knew that he could not get back at the kids as they ran faster than him.

There were several 55 and older mobile home communities not far from the man's residence. Aggravated by the children's calling him Popeye and making fun of him, he went to the mobile home community and looked into the windows of several homes, until he found an old lady sitting in her chair knitting and watching TV. He gained entry through the window and smothered the old lady to death with a pillow. She was his first victim.

In the next days, law enforcement performed a well-being check and found the victim deceased in her home. The MLDI contacted her family physician, who stated that she had serious medical conditions, and her death was determined natural without performing an autopsy.

Some time after this, the man and his best friend met a girl and both became fond of her. The man became jealous as he thought his friend would interfere in the friendship with the girl. The man asked his friend to meet him and killed him on a vacant lot near his home. The man left his friend there for a while and returned several days later, to find that his friend's body began to bloat and decompose. The man was afraid that his friend's body would be found so he dismembered him. The man wrapped his friend's head in plastic, took it home and stored it under his boathouse for a long period of time. He buried the rest of the body on the marshy island in a nearby creek. Later, he threw the skull into a creek leading to the river.

Some days later, a 911 call was received at the Lee County Sheriff's Office from a public phone booth. The man on the phone stated that he had just killed a woman and the patrol deputy closest to the phone booth responded and arrested the man in the phone booth.

The Lee County Sheriff's Office crime scene team searched a nearby area where the man indicated he had disposed of his friend's body parts. Weeks of sifting, digging, and searching resulted in the discovery of multiple bones; however, the deceased friend's skull was never recovered. The forensic anthropologist Dr. William R. Maples from the University of Florida in Gainesville, Florida, was contacted to examine the bones and he discovered knife marks on the bones. His examination indicated that the man dismembered his friend's body with a paring knife.

During the interview, the man confessed that he killed his best friend and the old woman.

The man was found incompetent to withstand trial. He was charged with 3 murders, but sentenced to remain in a mental institution for the rest of his life. However, there's no guarantee that he'll remain there forever. If he ever is found sane, he will be tried for his crimes.

7.3.2.1 Suicide through Asphyxiant Gas

About a decade ago, suicide by car exhaust fumes was a common method. The victims would run the car engine in a closed and sealed garage or run a pipe from the exhaust into the cabin of the vehicle. Due to emission control on cars, the CO levels are much lower than previously. Suicide by car requires an older model vehicle—especially in the United States, Australia, and the United Kingdom— and so it has drastically decreased.

7.3.2.1.1 The Effects of Asphyxiant Gases   The group of asphyxiant gases consists of pure nitrogen, helium, neon, argon, sulfur hexafluoride, methane, or other physiological inert gases. The victim inhales such gases and exhales carbon dioxide without resupplying oxygen to the body. These gases are odor-free and tasteless. When inhaling the gases, the victim feels few abnormal sensations, none of the painful feelings of suffocation as when the oxygen levels fall or with other mechanisms of poisoning. The lack of oxygen leads to asphyxiation and death (Willkenfield, 2007). A classic sign of a carbon monoxide poisoning death is the red-cheeked and healthy look of the deceased.

Caution: The cherry-red appearance is not a useful sign to diagnose the cause and manner of death.

7.3.2.1.2 The Suicide Bag   A method of suicide that has become more common is the self-administration of helium in a bag. Between 2001 and 2005, 30 deaths had been reported whereas 79 deaths had been reported between 2005 and 2009. In Australia, helium sale is controlled and two suicides have been reported using the bag mechanism filled with nitrogen gas (Austin et al., 2011).

7.3.2.1.3 Accidental Death by Carbon Monoxide Poisoning   Not every carbon monoxide poisoning death is a suicide. During hurricanes or heavy snowfall in northern climates, people place generators inside the house or in the garage creating high levels of carbon monoxide leading to death. Inhaling the poisonous CO gas from a generator in a closed environment without ventilation causes death within minutes. Likewise, never repair your lawn mower inside the garage while the motor is running. Other fuel burning devices such as camping stoves, fireplaces, gas stoves and heaters, and wood and coal ovens can also cause deadly levels of carbon monoxide. An incomplete combustion of carbon-based fuels such as petroleum, paraffin, oil, wood, and charcoal produces carbon monoxide. CO poisoning causes most of the deaths in a fire.

7.3.2.2 Death Investigation: Asphyxia by Hanging

Asphyxia by hanging is a condition when the body and vital parts are deprived of oxygen. Compression is visible around the victim's neck. While some victims decide to hang themselves from a tree, others use a ceiling fan or a beam in a barn. Hanging is a preferred method of suicide in prisons and jails. Inmates rip a bedsheet into bands, knot them together, place one end around the bars and the other end around their neck, and then simply sit down on the floor and the bands will tighten around the neck cutting off the air supply resulting in strangulation. Others use a rope and knot it over both sides of the doorknobs to hang themselves. Belts and electrical cords may also be used in suicides.

7.3.2.2.1 Specifics of the Crime Scene Investigation The crime scene investigator will perform the basic scene documentation of notes, photographs, and sketches in addition to the following:

- Close-up photography of the hanging mechanism and the type of knot. The knot can provide information about the victim. If a nautical knot is used and the victim does not have any affiliation with the Navy, boating, or any nautical sport, then the death could be staged as a suicide.
- Sketching the hanging mechanism.
- Obtaining measurements of
  - Distance from the victim's feet to the ground.
  - Distance from the ground to where the rope was mounted onto, such as a beam, a tree branch, or a ceiling fan.
  - Length of the body.
- Searching the scene for
  - A chair, stool, ladder, or any item on which the victim was standing before he hangs himself.
  - A ladder or any other items that could have been used to mount the rope over the beam, tree branch, or ceiling fan.
  - Any drag marks on the floor, dirt, or sand and examine the victim's shoes for drag and scuff marks.
  - A handwritten note, or a letter to the family.
  - Medication, doctor's notes.
  - Check the calendar for appointments and notes.

Some victims write detailed instructions about how their property will be separated between friends and family. Suicide notes may also contain information about bank accounts and money markets. If a checkbook is found on scene, document the number of the last check issued and check throughout the checkbook for missing checks. Take a photo of the checks and a checkbook ledger, if applicable.

Caution: Never open the knot of the rope. Cut the rope at an end where the least physical evidence can be destroyed.

Rope over the Door...

Sheriff's deputies responded to an apartment complex in Fort Myers, Florida, to perform a well-being check on a 45-year-old male. He worked in the health profession and had not reported to work for a couple of days. The deputies broke the window of the residence to gain entry finding the victim sitting on the floor in the bedroom. A white towel covered a rope around his neck attached to the doorknob. The rope had been connected to the interior and exterior doorknob to ensure it held the victim's weight. A piece of yellow rope was found on the floor in the hallway. It was determined that the victim had tried to use the yellow rope but it would not support his weight. Prior to his death, he had written letters to his girlfriend, split his belongings, and issued checks to pay his bills until the end of the month. The letters were found on the floor next to his feet. A checkbook and a check ledger were found in the residence (Figure 7.12).

Figure 7.12 Knot over the door.

In this case, it was important to show detailed photos of the hanging mechanism and how the rope was mounted over the door and around his neck. The rope was cut above the knot and transported with the victim to the morgue for the autopsy. The manner of death was determined as suicide.

7.3.2.2.2 Sexual Asphyxia—Autoerotic   In autoerotism, the victim uses a method to become sexually stimulated through internal stimuli generated without another person. In autoerotic asphyxiation, the victim uses a breath control that restricts the flow of oxygen to the brain to achieve sexual arousal. Several mechanisms have been used from a plastic bag over the head to more complicated mechanisms. Once the victim loses consciousness due to partial asphyxia and cannot control the mean of strangulation, the result is death. Signs of autoerotic death are

- Victim is nude and/or genitals are exposed.
- Male victim may be dressed in female clothing.
- Pornographic magazines and movies are present.
- A mirror in front of the asphyxiation mechanism so the victim can watch himself.
- Some mechanisms include a neck padding.
- Always look for a safety mechanism that is used to stop the asphyxiation.

The manner of death is accidental; the cause of death is asphyxiation. In most cases, the hyoid bone is broken.

7.3.2.3 *Death by Power Tools*
Power tools and work tools cause thousands of injuries every year. In 2012, throughout all industries, 712 deaths occurred caused by objects or work equipment. Workplace deaths are reported to law enforcement and the criminal investigator and crime scene investigator respond to the scene.

The Saw

In February of 2010, a 911 call was received by County Sheriff's Office in regard to the death of a 66-year-old white female. Her life partner had found the victim in his wood shed when he returned from shopping. The victim had a long history of depression and had attempted to commit suicide several times before.

The victim was lying on a cement floor in front of a workbench with a mounted table saw. The saw was the suicide mechanism. Hair and tissue were lodged in the saw blade. Passive bloodstains and mist like spatter were on the black saw table. Cast-off spatter was on the wall behind the saw. Blood transfer was on the saw handle.

The victim had several cuts on the back of her skull. During the autopsy, it was determined that the victim had six cuts in her skull created by the saw. She had placed her head underneath the saw and pulled the handle multiple times. Due to the cuts, air had entered the bloodstream and the cause of death was actually a gas embolism to the heart. The manner of death was suicide (Figure 7.13).

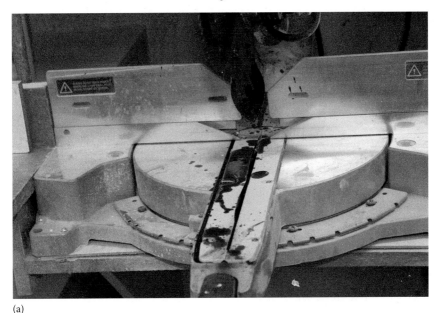

(a)

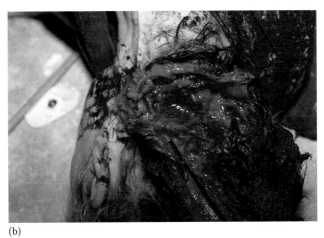

(b)

Figure 7.13 Photo of (a) saw and (b) injuries.

7.3.2.4 Death Investigation: Gunshot

Firearms are one of the preferred mechanisms of suicide. However, there is a fine line between a homicide and a suicide, especially in gunshot deaths. After performing the basic crime scene investigation procedures, the CSI should pay special attention to the following:

- The location of the firearm regarding the victim's location.
- Was the victim right handed or left handed?
- Look at the bloodstain pattern surrounding the victim for
  - Forward spatter on the firearm and on the victim
  - Back spatter on the firearm and the victim
- Are there signs of a struggle?
- If the victim used a rifle or shotgun, measure and determine if the victim could have pulled the trigger.
  - Some victims have used their toes to pull the trigger while the end of the barrel rested in the mouth.
  - Others have used a string to pull the trigger.
- Search the residence for additional evidence such as
  - Gun box
  - Receipt of recent purchase of a firearm
  - Additional ammunition
  - Notes, letters, and medical information
- If the projectile exited the victim, determine the trajectory and recover the projectile.

Together with the MLDI, the CSI will capture additional photos of the victim's injuries by performing the following:

- Examine the entry wound to determine the approximate distance from which the shot had been fired.
- Examine the inside of the hands. Blood inside the hand raises a suspicion as in a suicide; the firearm covered the palm of the hand.
- Inspect both hands for signs of defense wounds.
- Look for an exit wound to determine if the projectile exited the deceased.
- Obtain gunshot residue from the victim's hands using the SEM gunshot residue kit.
- Bag the victim's hands with paper bags or specialized transport bags to avoid contamination and loss of trace evidence.

It is a common practice to secure a gunshot suicide crime scene until the autopsy has been concluded and the medical examiner has determined the cause and manner of death.

Subsequently, after the autopsy and the crime scene have been cleared, the CSI will submit the projectile, spent cartridge, and firearm to the laboratory for ballistics examination to ensure that the bullet had been fired from this firearm.

7.3.2.5 Death Investigation: Poisoning and Overdose

Medications and even over-the-counter supplements, when taken in excessive amounts other than medically necessary, can cause an overdose or poisoning. A drug overdose can be intentional or accidental. Illicit drugs taken to get high result in an overdose if the person's metabolism cannot detoxify the drug fast enough. Exposure to chemicals, plants, or other toxic substances can cause poisoning. The longer the exposure, the more intensive the poisoning, eventually leading to death.

7.3.2.5.1 Drug Overdose   Drug overdoses include a combination of different factors and can be the result from either accident or suicide. Every year, children overdose and die after consuming prescription pills left on a table, believing them to be candy. Elderly citizens intentionally take a large dose of sleeping pills combined with alcohol to commit suicide. While some victims may accidentally mix prescription drugs that put a strain on their already weak body, others mix prescription drugs with alcohol to achieve a high. Mixing alprazolam (Xanax) and oxycodone or oxycontin with alcohol creates a high risk of an overdose.

The death scene of a possible overdose of drugs should be investigated with the same thoroughness of a homicide. In many overdose cases, the medical examiner will define the cause and manner of death pending toxicology. During the autopsy, it is pertinent to take close-up photos of injection marks.

At the crime scene, the CSI adheres to the basic crime scene investigation procedures. Special attention should be paid when searching the scene for

- Any kind of drug paraphernalia
- Packaging material used for drugs such as wax paper for heroin
- Rolling papers
- Razor blades, copper mash, and straws used to snort heroin
- Hypodermic needles, spoons, candle, or cigarette lighter to inject heroin
- Used needles that contain traces of the drug
- Large amounts of money, especially small bills

These items are evidence that the victim has been using illegal drugs for a period of time.

Anna Nicole Smith

On February 8, 2007, Anna Nicole Smith died in a Hollywood, Florida, hotel room of an accidental overdose of nine prescription medications. The Broward County Medical Examiner Dr. Joshua Perper described Anna Nicole as being heavily medicated suffering from overwhelming pressures. Found in her bloodstream were compounds of antidepressants, anti-anxiety drugs, human growth hormones, benzodiazepines, and sleeping pills with choral hydrate. The six-week multi-agency investigation viewed all evidence and concluded that Anna Nicole's death was an accidental overdose with no criminal elements present (http://www.today .com/news/anna-nicole-smith-died-accidental-overdose-2D80555167).

7.3.2.5.2 Poisoning   Since the Middle Ages, poisoning has been a common form of suicide and murder, from Romeo and Juliet to the alleged poisoning of Napoleon with arsenic while on the island of St. Helena. Arsenic and other poisons are not as readily available as they were centuries ago. Today's popular choice of poisonous chemical is bleach and drain cleaners such as Drano. Drinking bleach erodes the throat and stomach lining and continues to the internal organs. It is one of the most painful methods of suicide. Even if the person does not consume enough poison to die, the effects of the poison are irreversible.

At the death scene of suspected poisoning, after performing the basic crime scene investigation procedures, it is essential to collect

- Samples of any liquid at the scene, especially cleaning solutions.
- Check under the sink and in the bathroom for additional bottles of bleach.
- Always fingerprint any bleach bottle on scene.
- Search for any documentation of depression such as
  - Handwritten notes
  - Medication
  - Doctor's appointments
  - Documentation of previous suicide attempt
  - Hate letters from neighbors or other enemies

During the autopsy, the medical examiner will determine the cause and manner of death, and will observe the internal damage caused by the consumption of the poison. The final decision may depend on the toxicology results. If the victim's body is skeletonized or decomposed, several poisons can still be found in the roots of hairs or in the bone marrow.

The Case of Susie

In the mid-1990s, in a small town in Germany, a 24-year-old female called Susie committed suicide in her mother's house. She drank rat poison, and submerged a plugged-in hairdryer in the water of the bathtub in which she sat. She died instantly of electric shock before the rat poison could destroy her stomach and inner organs. Two years earlier, she had tried to commit suicide by slitting her wrists when her boyfriend left her. She had been saved and had moved in with her mother. Susie appeared to be a happy person who used to joke that if she committed suicide again, she would do it right.

A year later, she went on a couple of dates with her old boyfriend creating hope for a reunification. However, he did not plan to reconcile with her. Susie could not overcome a second rejection and killed herself.

Susie was a long friend of this author and is missed very much. Depression is a very hideous illness. I wish Susie had told me that she was sick…

7.3.2.6 Death Investigation: Drowning

Every year, during the summer months, children die from drowning in the family pool or in lakes. Parents fail to watch small children or the pool area is not properly childproofed. Older children can drown in lake or river accidents when jumping off trees or cliffs hitting rocks. The methods can vary widely. Drowning can also occur in a bathtub. The manner of death can range from accidental to suicide to homicide. Decades ago, women used to mix sleeping pills with alcohol to fall asleep in the bathtub. Drowning can also be a homicide if the victim's head is purposefully held under water. In every type of drowning, fluid is aspired into the airways and the lungs fill with water diminishing the oxygen flow. The victim struggles to breathe and water is forced into the sinuses. The lack of oxygen in the blood causes unconsciousness. Drowning victims may have froth around the mouth and nose and there is no difference in this between saltwater and freshwater drowning.

The investigation of the crime scene depends on the locale of the death scene. If the victim is found floating in a lake, river, or stream, it is necessary to require the dive team to assist in the investigation. Most law enforcement agencies in areas with large bodies of water maintain a department dive team. This team consists of certified law enforcement officers who are qualified scuba divers trained in the recovery of evidence and emergency response.

7.3.2.6.1 Vehicle in the Lake The dive team responds to accident scenes of submerged vehicles. In addition, a tow truck is needed to pull the vehicle from the water. The crime scene investigator follows the basic crime scene investigation procedures. If a body is found inside the vehicle, the MLDI is notified and responds to the scene for the preliminary determination of the cause of death. The deceased is removed from the vehicle and transported to the morgue for an autopsy. The CSI issues a property receipt and follows the tow truck carrying the vehicle to the agency's impoundment bay to maintain the chain of custody and to secure the vehicle for later processing. During the autopsy, the medical examiner determines the cause and manner of death. It is difficult to determine if the person died before entering the water or later because a prolonged stay under water will result in water in the lungs as well.

7.3.2.6.2 Victim Floating in the Pool, Lake, or River There are several reasons why a body may float on top of a pool, lake, or river. The cause of death may be accidental, suicide, or homicide. The assistance of the dive team is necessary to remove the body for transport to the morgue for an autopsy. The CSI will apply the basic crime scene investigation procedures and additionally notes:

- Names of the divers on the dive team
- Ask the dive team to search for additional physical evidence such as
  - A vehicle
  - A sunk boat
  - Fishing equipment
  - A firearm
- If additional physical evidence is recovered, use floating markers to depict the location of recovery on the photographs
- Obtain measurements from the river bank to the marker

Caution: If a firearm is recovered from water, seal the weapon in a container filled with the same water.

During the autopsy, the medical examiner will exclude all medical conditions and any other possible causes of death before declaring the cause and manner of death an accidental drowning. It is very difficult to prove if another person was holding the victim under water, unless there are obvious signs of bruising or other injuries (Figure 7.14).

7.3.2.6.3 Death Investigation—Electrocution Death by electrocution has different causes and manners of death ranging from accidental death to suicide. The sources of electricity are either natural such as lightning or manmade. Electricity is measured in volts and amps. High voltage is harmless to the human body, for example, a taser produces 50,000 volts but only 7 watts. Amperage between 100 and 200 mA (milliamps) is fatal.

Figure 7.14 Floater.

7.3.2.6.3.1 Lightning Death According to Jensenius from the National Weather Service (n.d.), between 2006 and 2013, 261 people were struck and killed by lightning in the United States. Two-thirds of the deaths occurred during outdoor leisure activities such as fishing, camping, boating, and golfing.

Signs of lightning death
> Most victims have lightning damage ranging from burns to multiorgan disruption. Skin burns are linear or thermal burns from ignited clothing or heated metal such as a watch or other jewelry. The burns create a smell like burning sulfur or ammonia. Most victims of lightning have an immediate cardiac arrest.

Crime scene response
> The CSI will perform the basic crime scene investigation procedures. Additional attention is required to
> - Document the weather conditions from the Internet, Weather Channel, or local weather service and include that in their final report.
> - Take close-up photographs of the victim's injuries such as
>   - Skin burns
>   - Burned clothing
>   - Melted or burned metal such as jewelry
> - Draw a sketch of the scene including nearby lightning rods

Caution: Crime scene safety is of the utmost importance to ensure that the death is in fact a lightning death and not caused by an electric cable or other forms of electricity being present on scene causing the victim's death.

Always handle every death with the thoroughness of a homicide.

7.3.2.6.3.2 Electrocution   Electrocution occurs when the body is suddenly and involuntary introduced to a large amount of electricity. Many electrocution deaths are results of accidents. Most commonly, electrocutions result from electricians working for power companies repairing high voltage lines on power poles.

Signs of electrocution deaths
Low levels of electric current cause numbness in the limbs lasting from a short moment to a few hours depending on the length of exposure. High levels of electricity can kill instantly as the electricity moves through the body in the shortest path to the ground. The high level shock passing through the body stops the heart from beating resulting in immediate death. Low level currents can cause the heart to skip a beat leading to a cardiac arrhythmia (change of the normal heartbeat).
During the autopsy, the medical examiner will look at
- Burn marks or charring in the area where the electricity entered the deceased
- Blistering and redness of the skin around the area of initial electrocution

Caution: Before the CSI or any law enforcement officer approaches the victim, ensure that the power source for the electricity is unplugged or disconnected. Touching the victim can cause a chain reaction transferring the electric power unless the CSI is grounded with rubber shoes.

CSI response
Always check:
- Electric source is disconnected.
- No wires or cables are laying on the ground.
- Contact the property owner and ask to disconnect the power to the cable.
- If necessary, call the power company to respond to the scene.

After the scene is cleared and safe to enter, perform the basic crime scene investigation procedures. Always sketch the scene and include the distance to the power source (power pole, residence, etc).

In Fort Myers, Florida, a worker for the Florida Power and Light Company was electrocuted while in a cherry picker working on the power lines. In this incident, the CSI measured the distance from the ground level to the height where the incident occurred. In these cases, the CSI should note all information on the transport vehicle including serial number, make, model, and if available maintenance and inspection dates.

Farm Worker Case

In the summer of 2011, in a field off State Road 835 in Hendry County, Florida, a farm worker was spraying the crops when the hydraulic spray-rig caught a power cable. While getting down from the diver's cab, he touched the metal grab handle and was electrocuted. He was propelled from the tractor and his body was found in a 6 to 10 feet deep canal. He was vertically inverted in the water and the soles of his boots were out of the water. The cause of death was electrocution and the manner of death was accidental.

7.3.3 Sudden Infant Death Syndrome

Sudden infant death syndrome (SIDS) is the sudden death of an otherwise healthy infant. Most SIDS deaths occur in newborns up to the age of one year. Commonly, the parents feed the child and place him in the bed only to find it deceased later.

SIDS is a diagnosis of exclusions. The child may have some bloody foam around the nose and mouth and some stains may be found on the bedding and clothing caused by pulmonary edema (fluid in the lungs).

Caution: Do not misinterpret such SIDS blood staining as child abuse.

During the autopsy, the medical examiner will examine the petechial of the thymus, epicedium, and the pleural surfaces as signs of SIDS. The trachea may be congested but the structure should be intact. In many cases, pulmonary edema is present. All those signs are also present in a homicide, so it is important to examine the child for any signs of abuse such as bruises, burns, neglect, and abrasions. The medical examiner will also examine the postmortem lividity for unusual patterns and collect body fluid samples to identify any illness, presence of drugs, poisons, or medication (Document 7.3).

At the crime scene, the CSI will apply the basic crime scene procedures and pay additional attention to the following:

- Note the temperature in the room
  - Note the A/C setting
  - Ceiling fan on or off
  - Humidity in the room
  - Windows open or closed
- Always collect the following items:
  - Baby formula
    - Container with formula
    - Leftover formula

U.S. DEPARTMENT OF HEALTH AND HUMAN SERVICES
Centers for Disease Control and Prevention
Division of Reproductive Health
Maternal and Infant Health Branch
Atlanta, Georgia 30333

CDC

Sudden Unexplained Infant Death Investigation

SUIDI
Reporting Form

INVESTIGATION DATA

Infant's Last Name | Infant's First Name | Middle Name | Case Number

Sex: | Date of Birth: | Age: | SS#:

Race: | White | Black/African Am. | Asian/Pacific Isl. | Am. Indian/Alaskan Native | Hispanic/Latino | Other

Infant's Primary Residence:

Address: | City: | County: | State: | Zip:

Incident Address: | City: | County: | State: | Zip:

Contact Information for Witness:

Relationship to deceased: | Birth Mother | Birth Father | Grandmother | Grandfather

Adoptive or Foster Parent | Physician | Health Records | Other Describe:

Last: | First: | M.: | SS#:

Address: | City: | State: | Zip:

Work Address: | City: | State: | Zip:

Home Phone: | Work Phone: | Date of Birth:

WITNESS INTERVIEW

1 Are you the usual caregiver?

No | Yes

2 Tell me what happened:

3 Did you notice anything unusual or different about the infant in the last 24 hrs?

No | Yes | Specify:

4 Did the infant experience any falls or injury within the last 72 hrs?

No | Yes | Specify:

5 When was the infant LAST PLACED?

Date: | Military Time: : | Location (room):

6 When was the infant LAST KNOWN ALIVE(LKA)?

Date: | Military Time: : | Location (room):

7 When was the infant FOUND?

Date: | Military Time: : | Location (room):

8 Explain how you knew the infant was still alive.

9 Where was the infant - (P)laced, (L)ast known alive, (F)ound (write P, L, or F in front of appropriate response)?

Bassinet	Bedside co-sleeper	Car seat	Chair
Cradle	Crib	Floor	In a person's arms
Mattress/box spring	Mattress on floor	Playpen	Portable crib
Sofa/couch	Stroller/carriage	Swing	Waterbed
Other - describe:			

Document 7.3 SIDS template.

(*Continued*)

WITNESS INTERVIEW (cont.)

10 In what position was the infant LAST PLACED? ☐ Sitting ☐ On back ☐ On side ☐ On stomach ☐ Unknown
Was this the infant's usual position? ☐ Yes ☐ No What was the usual position? _____

11 In what position was the infant LKA? ☐ Sitting ☐ On back ☐ On side ☐ On stomach ☐ Unknown
Was this the infant's usual position? ☐ Yes ☐ No What was the usual position? _____

12 In what position was the infant FOUND? ☐ Sitting ☐ On back ☐ On side ☐ On stomach ☐ Unknown
Was this the infant's usual position? ☐ Yes ☐ No What was the usual position? _____

13 Face position when LAST PLACED? ☐ Face down on surface ☐ Face up ☐ Face right ☐ Face left

14 Neck position when LAST PLACED? ☐ Hyperextended (head back) ☐ Flexed (chin to chest) ☐ Neutral ☐ Turned

15 Face position when LKA? ☐ Face down on surface ☐ Face up ☐ Face right ☐ Face left

16 Neck position when LKA? ☐ Hyperextended (head back) ☐ Flexed (chin to chest) ☐ Neutral ☐ Turned

17 Face position when FOUND? ☐ Face down on surface ☐ Face up ☐ Face right ☐ Face left

18 Neck position when FOUND? ☐ Hyperextended (head back) ☐ Flexed (chin to chest) ☐ Neutral ☐ Turned

19 What was the infant wearing? *(ex. t-shirt, disposable diaper)* _____

20 Was the infant tightly wrapped or swaddled? ☐ No ☐ Yes - describe: _____

21 Please indicate the types and numbers of layers of bedding both over and under infant (not including wrapping blanket):

Bedding UNDER Infant	None	Number	Bedding OVER Infant	None	Number
Receiving blankets			Receiving blankets		
Infant/child blankets			Infant/child blankets		
Infant/child comforters (thick)			Infant/child comforters (thick)		
Adult comforters/duvets			Adult comforters/duvets		
Adult blankets			Adult blankets		
Sheets			Sheets		
Sheepskin			Pillows		
Pillows			Other, specify:		
Rubber or plastic sheet					
Other, specify:					

22 Which of the following devices were operating in the infant's room?
☐ None ☐ Apnea monitor ☐ Humidifier ☐ Vaporizer ☐ Air purifier ☐ Other - _____

23 In was the temperature in the infant's room? ☐ Hot ☐ Cold ☐ Normal ☐ Other - _____

24 Which of the following items were near the infant's face, nose, or mouth?
☐ Bumper pads ☐ Infant pillows ☐ Positional supports ☐ Stuffed animals ☐ Toys ☐ Other - _____

25 Which of the following items were within the infant's reach?
☐ Blankets ☐ Toys ☐ Pillows ☐ Pacifier ☐ Nothing ☐ Other - _____

26 Was anyone sleeping with the infant? ☐ No ☐ Yes

Name of individual sleeping with infant	Age	Height	Weight	Location in relation to infant	Imparement (intoxication, tired)

27 Was there evidence of wedging? ☐ No ☐ Yes - Describe: _____

28 When the infant was found, was s/he: ☐ Breathing ☐ Not Breathing
If not breathing, did you witness the infant stop breathing? ☐ No ☐ Yes

Page 2

Document 7.3 (Continued) SIDS template. *(Continued)*

WITNESS INTERVIEW (cont.)

29 What had led you to check on the infant?

30 Describe the infant's appearance when found.

Appearance	Unknown	No	Yes	Describe and specify location
a) Discoloration around face/nose/mouth				
b) Secretions (foam, froth)				
c) Skin discoloration (livor mortis)				
d) Pressure marks (pale areas, blanching)				
e) Rash or petechiae (small, red blood spots on skin, membranes, or eyes)				
f) Marks on body (scratches or bruises)				
g) Other				

31 What did the infant feel like when found? *(Check all that apply.)*

☐ Sweaty ☐ Warm to touch ☐ Cool to touch ☐ Limp, flexible ☐ Rigid, stif ☐ Unknown

☐ Other - specify:

32 Did anyone else other than EMS try to resuscitate the infant? ☐ No ☐ Yes

Who?   Date: Military time: :

33 Please describe what was done as part of resuscitation:

34 Has the parent/caregiver ever had a child die suddenly and unexpectedly? ☐ No ☐ Yes

Explain:

INFANT MEDICAL HISTORY

1 Source of medical information: ☐ Doctor ☐ Other healthcare provider ☐ Medical record ☐ Family

☐ Mother/primary caregiver ☐ Other:

2 In the 72 hours prior to death, did the infant have:

Condition	Unknown	No	Yes	Condition	Unknown	No	Yes
a) Fever				k) Apnea (stopped breathing)			
h) Diarrhea				e) Decrease in appetite			
b) Excessive sweating				l) Cyanosis (turned blue/gray)			
i) Stool changes				f) Vomiting			
c) Lethargy or sleeping more than usual				m) Seizures or convulsions			
j) Difficulty breathing				g) Choking			
d) Fussiness or excessive crying				n) Other, specify:			

3 In the 72 hours prior to death, was the infant injured or did s/he have any other condition(s) not mentioned?

☐ No ☐ Yes - describe:

4 In the 72 hours prior to the infants death, was the infant given any vaccinations or medications? ☐ No ☐ Yes
(Please include any home remedies, herbal medications, prescription medicines, over-the-counter medications.)

Name of vaccination or medication	Dose last given	Date given Month	Day	Year	Approx. time (Military Time)	comments:
1.						
2.						
3.						
4.						

Page 3

Document 7.3 (Continued) SIDS template.   *(Continued)*

INFANT MEDICAL HISTORY (cont.)

5 At any time in the infant's life, did s/he have a history of?

Medical history	Unknown	No	Yes	Describe
a) Allergies *(food, medication, or other)*				
b) Abnormal growth or weight gain/loss				
c) Apnea *(stopped breathing)*				
d) Cyanosis *(turned blue/gray)*				
e) Seizures or convulsions				
f) Cardiac *(heart)* abnormalities				

6 Did the infant have any birth defects(s)? [ ] No [ ] Yes

Describe: _____

7 Describe the two most recent times that the infant was seen by a physician or health care provider:
(Include emergency department visits, clinic visits, hospital admissions, observational stays, and telephone calls)

	First most recent visit	Second most recent visit
a) Date		
b) Reason for visit		
c) Action taken		
d) Physician's name		
e) Hospital/clinic		
f) Address		
g) City		
h) State, ZIP		
i) Phone number		

8 Birth hospital name: _____ Discharge date: _____

Street address: _____

City: _____ State: _____ Zip: _____

9 What was the infant's length at birth? _____ inches or _____ centimeters

10 What was the infant's weight at birth? _____ pounds _____ ounces or _____ grams

11 Compared to the delivery date, was the infant born on time, early, or late?

[ ] On time [ ] Early - how many weeks? _____ [ ] Late - how many weeks? _____

12 Was the infant a singleton, twin, triplet, or higher gestation?

[ ] Singleton [ ] Twin [ ] Triplet [ ] Quadruplet or higher gestation

13 Were there any complications during delivery or at birth? *(emergency c-section, child needed oxygen)* [ ] Yes [ ] No

Describe: _____

14 Are there any alerts to the pathologist? *(previous infant deaths in family, newborn screen results)* [ ] Yes [ ] No

Specify: _____

Page 4

Document 7.3 (Continued) SIDS template. *(Continued)*

INFANT DIETARY HISTORY

1 On what day and at what approximate time was the infant last fed?

Date: _____ Military Time: ___ : ___

2 What is the name of the person who last fed the infant? _____

3 What is his/her relationship to the infant? _____

4 What foods and liquids was the infant fed in the <u>last 24 hours</u> (include last fed)?

Food	Unknown	No	Yes	Quantity (ounces)	Specify: (type and brand)
a) Breast milk (one/both sides, length of time)					
b) Formula (brand, water source - ex. Similac, tap water)					
c) Cow's milk					
d) Water (brand, bottled, tap, well)					
e) Other liquids (teas, juices)					
f) Solids					
g) Other					

5 Was a new food introduced in the 24 hours prior to his/her death? ☐ No ☐ Yes
If yes, describe (ex. content, amount, change in formula, introduction of solids)
_____

6 Was the infant last placed to sleep with a bottle? ☐ Yes ☐ No - if no, skip to question **9** below

7 Was the bottle propped? (i.e., object used to hold bottle while infant feeds) ☐ No ☐ Yes
If yes, what object was used to prop the bottle? _____

8 What was the quantity of liquid (in ounces) in the bottle? _____

9 Did the death occur during? ☐ Breast-feeding ☐ Bottle-feeding ☐ Eating solid foods ☐ Not during feeding

10 Are there any factors, circumstances, or environmental concerns that may have impacted the infant that have not yet been identified? (ex. exposed to cigarette smoke or fumes at someone else's home, infant unusually heavy, placed with positional supports or wedges)
☐ No ☐ Yes
If yes, - describe: _____

PREGNANCY HISTORY

1 Information about the infant's birth mother:

First name: _____ Last name: _____
Middle name: _____ Maiden name: _____
Birth date: _____ SS#: _____
Street address: _____ City: _____ State: ___ Zip: ___
How long has the birth mother been at this address? Years: ___ Months: ___
Previous Address: _____

2 At how many weeks or months did the birth mother begin prenatal care? ☐ No prenatal care ☐ Unknown
Weeks: ___ Months: ___

3 Where did the birth mother receive prenatal care? (Please specify physician or other health care provider name and address.)
Physician/provider: _____ Hospital/clinic: _____ Phone: _____
Street address: _____ City: _____ State: ___ Zip: ___

Page 5

Document 7.3 (Continued) SIDS template.   (Continued)

PREGNANCY HISTORY (cont.)

4 At how many weeks or months did the birth mother begin prenatal care? [ ] No [ ] Yes
(ex. high blood pressure, bleeding, gestational diabetes)
Specify: _____

5 Was the birth mother injured during her pregnancy with the infant? *(ex. auto accident, falls)* [ ] No [ ] Yes
Specify: _____

6 During her pregnancy, did she use any of the following?

	Unknown	No	Yes	Daily		Unknown	No	Yes	Daily
a) Over the counter medications					d) Cigarettes				
b) Prescription medications					e) Alcohol				
c) Herbal remedies					f) Other				

7 Currently, does any caregiver use any of the following?

	Unknown	No	Yes	Daily		Unknown	No	Yes	Daily
a) Over the counter medications					d) Cigarettes				
b) Prescription medications					e) Alcohol				
c) Herbal remedies					f) Other				

INCIDENT SCENE INVESTIGATION

1 Where did the incident or death occur? _____

2 Was this the primary residence? [ ] No [ ] Yes

3 Is the site of the incident or death scene a daycare or other childcare setting? [ ] Yes [ ] No - If no, skip to question **8**

4 How many children (under age 18) were under the care of the provider at the time of the incident or death? _____

5 How many adults (age 18 and over) were supervising the child(ren)? _____

6 What is the license number and licensing agency for the daycare?
License number: _____ Agency: _____

7 How long has the daycare been open for business? _____

8 How many people live at the site of the incident or death scene?
Number of adults (18 years or older): _____ Number of children (under 18 years old): _____

9 Which of the following heating or cooling sources were being used? *(Check all that apply)*
[ ] Central air [ ] Gas furnace or boiler [ ] Wood burning fireplace [ ] Open window(s)
[ ] A/C window unit [ ] Electric furnace or boiler [ ] Coal burning furnace [ ] Wood burning stove
[ ] Ceiling fan [ ] Electric space heater [ ] Kerosene space heater [ ] Floor/table fan
[ ] Electric baseboard heat [ ] Electric (radiant) ceiling heat [ ] Window fan [ ] Unknown
[ ] Other - specify: _____

10 Indicate the temperature of the room where the infant was found unresponsive:
[ ] Thermostat setting [ ] Thermostat reading [ ] Actual room temp. [ ] Outside temp.

11 What was the source of drinking water at the site of the incident or death scene? *(Check all that apply.)*
[ ] Public/municipal water [ ] Bottled water [ ] Well [ ] Unknown [ ] Other - Specify: _____

12 The site of the incident or death scene has: *(check all that apply)*
[ ] Insects [ ] Mold growth [ ] Smoky smell *(like cigarettes)*
[ ] Pets [ ] Dampness [ ] Presence of alcohol containers
[ ] Peeling paint [ ] Visible standing water [ ] Presence of drug paraphenalia
[ ] Rodents or vermin [ ] Odors or fumes - Describe: _____
[ ] Other - specify: _____

13 Describe the general appearance of incident scene: *(ex. cleanliness, hazards, overcrowding, etc.)*
Specify: _____

Document 7.3 (Continued) SIDS template.   *(Continued)*

SUMMARY FOR PATHOLOGIST

Case Information

1 **Investigator information**   Name: ____   Agency: ____   Phone: ____

	Date	Military time
Investigated:	____	: ____
Pronounced dead:	____	: ____

2 **Infant's information:**   Last: ____   First: ____   M: ____   Case #: ____

Sex: ☐ Male   ☐ Female   Date of Birth: ____   Age: ____

Race: ☐ White   ☐ Black/African Am.   ☐ Asian/Pacific Islander

☐ Am. Indian/Alaskan Native   ☐ Hispanic/Latino   ☐ Other: ____

1 **Indicate whether preliminary investigation suggests any of the following:**

Sleeping Environment

Yes No

Asphyxia *(ex. overlying, wedging, choking, nose/mouth obstruction, re-breathing, neck compression, immersion in water)*
Sharing of sleep surface with adults, children, or pets
Change in sleep condition *(ex. unaccustomed stomach sleep position, location, or sleep surface)*
Hyperthermia/Hypothermia *(ex. excessive wrapping, blankets, clothing, or hot or cold environments)*
Environmental hazards *(ex. carbon monoxide, noxious gases, chemicals, drugs, devices)*
Unsafe sleep condition *(ex. couch/sofa, waterbed, stuffed toys, pillows, soft bedding)*

Infant History

Diet *(e.g., solids introduced, etc.)*
Recent hospitalization
Previous medical diagnosis
History of acute life-threatening events *(ex. apnea, seizures, difficulty breathing)*
History of medical care without diagnosis
Recent fall or other injury
History of religious, cultural, or ethnic remedies
Cause of death due to natural causes other than SIDS *(ex. birth defects, complications of preterm birth)*

Family Info

Prior sibling deaths
Previous encounters with police or social service agencies
Request for tissue or organ donation
Objection to autopsy

Exam

Pre-terminal resuscitative treatment
Death due to trauma (injury), poisoning, or intoxication

Investigator Insight

Suspicious circumstances
Other alerts for pathologist's attention

Any "Yes" answers above should be explained in detail (description of circumstances):

Pathologist

2 **Pathologist information**   Name: ____

Agency: ____   Phone: ____   Fax: ____

Page 8

Document 7.3 (Continued) SIDS template.

- Water used to mix the formula
- Baby bottles with formula
- Check refrigerator for premixed bottles
- Any baby pacifier
- Any baby toys in the bed or sleeping area
- Bedding
- Last used diaper
- Any medication for the baby or medication in the child's room
- Any medical documentation for the child

Hint: A representative sample from the mixed baby formula and the baby water is sufficient.

7.3.3.1 Reconstruction of the Scene

Many medical examiner jurisdictions prefer to reconstruct the last hours of the baby's life on scene. The MLDI will use an anatomic doll and ask the parents, mostly the mother, to lay the doll in bed in the same manner as she did the baby. The reconstruction is videotaped and notes are taken. The CSI should take additional still photos of the reconstruction. The MLDI notes if the mother is using drugs, tobacco, and alcohol or had additional medical conditions that could have led to the baby's death.

The U.S. Department of Health and Human Services has developed an investigative template and guideline for criminal and medico-legal investigations of Sudden Infant Deaths (see Document 7.3).

References

Anna Nicole Smith died of accidental overdose. (March 27, 2007). Retrieved from http://www.today.com/news/anna-nicole-smith-died-accidental-overdose -2D80555167.

Austin, A., Winskog, C., von den Heuvel, C., and Byard, R.W. (2011). Recent trends in suicides utilizing helium. Retrieved from http://www.ncbi.nlm.nih.gov/pubmed /21361949.

Claridge, J. (2015). Estimating the time of death. Retrieved from http://www.explore forensics.co.uk/estimating-the-time-of-death.html.

DiMaio, V. (1985). *Gunshot Wounds*. Elsevier, New York.

DiMaio, V. (2006). *Handbook of Forensic Pathology*, 2nd ed. CRC Press, Boca Raton, FL.

Dutelle, A. (2014). *An Introduction of Crime Scene Investigation*. Jones and Bartlet Learning, Burlington, MA.

Geberth, V.J. (2006). *Practical Homicide Investigation: Tactics, Procedures, and Forensic Techniques*, 4th ed. CRC Press, Boca Raton, FL.

James, S., Nordby, J., and Bell, S. (2014). *Forensic Science: An Introduction to Scientific and Investigative Techniques*, 4th ed. CRC Press, Boca Raton, FL.

Jensenius, J. (n.d.). A detailed analysis of lightning deaths in the United States. Retrieved from http://www.lightningsafety.noaa.gov/.../RecentLightningDeaths.

Norman, T. (2012). 4 Ways to determine the time of death in a dead person. Retrieved from http://skyakes.blogspot.com/2012/01/4-ways-to-determine-time-of-death -in.html.

Wilkenfield, M. (2007). *Environmental and Occupational Medicine*, 4th ed. Lippincott Williams & Wilkins, Philadelphia, PA.

Mixed Cases

8

8.1 Multi-Agency Investigations

The assistance of the crime scene team is also required for multi-agency investigations, for example, drug investigations, human trafficking, and human smuggling. The crime scene team works together with drug task forces, U.S. Coast Guard, Immigration and Customs Enforcement (ICE), as well as task forces consisting of local, state, and federal officers.

8.1.1 Drug Investigations

In June 1973, President Richard Nixon declared a *war on drugs*; in July 1973, President Nixon signed an executive order establishing a single unified command to combat *an all-out global war on drug menace*. The Drug Enforcement Administration (DEA) was founded consisting of 1470 special agents and a budget of approximately $75 million. Today, the DEA employs approximately 5000 special agents with a budget of $2.02 billion. The DEA is the leading drug enforcement agency providing training to municipal, state, and other federal agencies, as well as is the leading agency of drug task forces throughout the country.

8.1.1.1 Marijuana Grow Operations

The hot and humid climate of the southern states such as Florida, Georgia, Alabama, Louisiana, and Texas provides excellent growing conditions for marijuana.

In the 1990s, growers planted marijuana in the midst of wooded areas or cornfields to avoid detection. Law enforcement agencies began to use helicopters and fixed wing airplanes patrolling suspicious areas. Studies on the heat signature given off by marijuana plants allowed law enforcement to identify marijuana fields through infrared detectors mounted onto the helicopters and fixed wing planes. Growers moved the plants in the forest areas to emit the heat from the ground and to disguise the plants. Increased detection from the air was one of the reasons leading growers to move the growing operations indoors. The indoor growing operations also resulted in cultivating stronger tetrahydrocannabinol (THC) level of resin.

8.1.1.1.1 New Options for Grow Houses   Since the fall of the housing market in the mid-2000s, the number of abandoned, foreclosed homes in Florida provided the perfect environment for marijuana growers. The homes are abandoned and owned by the bank. There are minimal traces leading to the growers, as their names are not listed on a rental agreement, mortgage, or lease. The houses are in remote areas with less or no daily traffic. Neighbors are not suspicious, believing that the grower is the new owner/renter of the property.

8.1.1.1.1.1 The Grow Room   Growers convert the residence into a grow operation consisting of a grow room, nursery, and drying rooms, see Figure 8.1. The garage of a residence provides sufficient space for the growing room, for example, pots with plants, a watering system, and air conditioning. In addition, *Cannabis sativa* requires sunlight, water, warmth, and nutrients for an efficient harvest.

Special equipment is required to maintain healthy plants. Most growers use a specialized mixture of fertilizer, nutrients, and soil while others employ hydroponics, a nutrient mixture, instead of soil. Most plants are housed in black plastic buckets connected to a drip watering system to avoid overwatering. In Florida, growers also add dehumidifiers to reduce the humidity, especially in the rainy season. Another important component is sunlight. As not enough sunlight reaches the indoor grow house, artificial lighting in the form of grow lamps with 1000-watt horticulture bulbs is sufficient for 15 to 20 plants.

Figure 8.1 Grow operation.

In the beginning of the grow cycle, the plants are exposed to 16 to 18 hours of light per day; at the end of the cycle, the light exposure is shortened to encourage the plants to flower. This method also encourages the growth for the female plants that produce the valuable buds and increase the overall production. These plants contain higher levels of THC resin. Others seal off the growing environment to avoid outside contamination or use charcoal filter systems or higher CO_2 levels to kill pests.

Most of the equipment necessary to create a grow house for cannabis can be found at the local hardware store, Home Depot, Lowe's, or even Walmart. Horticulture lamps, bulbs, growing media, and chemicals to increase growing can be purchased at the local garden and hydroponics store or online. Several transformers are necessary to supply the growing lamps and dehumidifiers with sufficient electricity. Timers are used to set the hours of lighting.

Using numerous 1000-watt bulbs inside the residence creates a lot of heat and cooling fans and air conditioning units are necessary to maintain a steady temperature for the plants. Special insulation material and aluminum foil are used for additional insulation to maintain the temperature (see Figure 8.2). All this equipment uses a large amount of electricity. The electric companies report customers with extensive electricity usage to law enforcement. Many grow houses have been detected through the extreme electric bill of over $2000/month for a three-bedroom home. Growers compensated and began to hotwire the electricity from the

Figure 8.2 Transformers to distribute power.

electro pole bypassing the meter to avoid detection. Some of the growing installations are detected by the fire department when the growers incorrectly hotwired the electricity to the residence causing a fire that burned down the residence.

8.1.1.1.1.2 The Drying Room   Upon harvesting cannabis, the plant material has to be dried before it can be sold. Like tobacco, growers use clotheslines across rooms to hang the leaves and branches for drying. Expandable laundry drying racks are also used to dry plant material. Live plants tend to mold very easily in humid climates and it is necessary to turn over the plant material on a daily basis.

8.1.1.1.1.3 The Nursery   One room in every grow facility is selected for the nursery for new plants. The nursery consists of numerous plug trays underneath lamps with growing bulbs. The nursery is used to grow new plants from seeds. The nursery is not equipped with an extensive watering system as the plants are transferred into the growing room once they achieve a suitable size, as shown in Figure 8.3.

Caution: Special care is requested for searching a grow house. Be aware of possible traps or even explosives such as hand grenades attached to doors or drawers where money is stored.

Figure 8.3 Smaller plants.

8.1.1.2 Crime Scene Response

The crime scene team will enter the premises of the grow facility after a search warrant is read or the owner provided consent. The crime scene investigator will perform the basic crime scene investigation procedures of documenting, photographing, sketching, and marking of physical evidence.

Always photograph and document

- The power pole next to the residence/facility
- The number on the power pole
- The electric meter outside the residence
- Any damage or broken seal on the meter
- The exterior of the residence for surveillance cameras and search for the recorder inside the residence
- The mailbox
- All garbage cans inside and outside the residence for names and any information leading to the grower and possible customers
- The phone answering system
- Always fingerprint the interior of the residence especially
  - Refrigerator doors
  - Light switches
  - Kitchen counters
  - Doorknobs in every room
  - Tabletops
  - Bathrooms

Check with the prosecuting agency to determine if all growing facility evidence should be collected or only representative samples. If representative samples are sufficient for trial, the CSI or narcotics officers make the equipment unusable on scene. However, always collect every piece of cannabis.

In addition, the CSI always collects the following items as representative samples:

- One sample of the growing media
- One flower pot
- One bucket from the watering system with the connecting pipes
- One transformer
- One grow lamp
- One horticulture bulb
- One fan
- One dehumidifier
- One A/C unit
- Any money and bank account information

- Any ledger, paperwork with names, phone numbers, and addresses
- Surveillance tapes from the surveillance camera
- Any electronic scale
- Any dime bags or other packaging material
- All live plant material

Hint: It may be difficult to find paper bags to package large marijuana trees and bushes. Large cardboard boxes used for cremations provide excellent packaging options for plant material.

8.1.1.3 Maintenance for the Seized Live Plants

Upon arrival of the live plants at the evidence storage facility, open the boxes or bags allowing the plant material to air-dry. Keeping the plants inside the packaging results in growing fungi and mold. An approved method is to cover the floor of an air-conditioned room with brown butcher paper. Place the plants loosely on the paper. It is necessary to turn over the plants every two days to avoid molding and fungi. A representative sample should be sent to the laboratory for testing. Depending on the prosecuting agency, the harvest may be destroyed except for a representative sample.

It is not uncommon that several marijuana grow operations are managed by the same person or group of people. In the mid-2000s, the number of robberies of marijuana grow operations in South Florida increased. Drug dealers robbed grow houses resulting in shootings and murder.

Grow House Robbing Ends in Officer-Involved Shooting

In a rural area in Lehigh Acres, Florida, a single-family residence was converted into a marijuana grow house. The two-car garage was transformed into the grow room, the northeast bedroom served as the drying room, and the closet in the southeast bedroom was utilized for the nursery and the mother plant. The house was equipped with a video surveillance system. The grow operation remained undetected by law enforcement. The house was rented and inhabited by a family of three—husband, wife, and their son.

In the evening hours of October 7, 2007, unknown perpetrators approached the residence and began to fire at the garage door and inside the residence using shotguns and automatic handguns. The residents returned fire, called 911 and the homeowner. The perpetrators fled across the fields.

The homeowner and his wife arrived on scene and fired a handgun at the approaching deputies, who returned fire.

The marijuana grow operation was detected when deputies entered the residence.

The residents were the victims of the shooting, but also charged with cultivating marijuana and arrested. The homeowner was arrested and charged with two counts of attempted murder on a law enforcement officer.

The on-call CSI responded to the scene, took notes and overall night photographs of the scene. The CSI marked, photographed, sketched, and collected two spent cartridges found on the street that could easily have been lost if not collected immediately. It was dark and poor lighting conditions resulted in securing the scene overnight by members of the patrol division.

Depending on the agency's policy, the police officers' handguns used in the officer-involved shooting will be documented and collected by the supervisor of the agency's training department. The firearms will be submitted to the laboratory for functionality test and comparison to the recovered spent cartridges.

The next morning, the CSI team returned to the scene and a search warrant was served to allow legal entry to the residence. This crime scene consisted of two scenes—the officer-involved shooting/attempted murder of a law enforcement officer and the marijuana grow house.

CRIME SCENE 1: OFFICER-INVOLVED SHOOTING SCENE

The officer-involved shooting occurred on the roughly paved road with grass areas and bushes bordering both sides of the road. A single-family residence and a construction site were on the north side and a single family home on the south side of the road.

The CSI team photographed, sketched, and measured the locations of the three patrol vehicles and the suspect's white Mercedes. In addition, aerial photographs from the agency's helicopter were captured to show the location of the vehicles.

The distances between the vehicles are important for a later reconstruction and additional measurements were obtained, such as

- Distances between front bumpers of each vehicle to fixed points A and B (electro poles on the street, remember to note the numbers edged in the poles).
- Distances between the rear bumpers of each vehicle to fixed points A and B.
- Distance between points A and B.
- Distance between the front centers of the front bumpers to the center of the rear bumpers of all involved vehicles.

These measurements became very important in the later trial and reconstruction of the shooting event.

A line search on the road and on both sides of the road led to the discovery of spent .40 caliber cartridges on the south side of the road next to a patrol vehicle. A 9-mm Luger spent cartridge on the north side of the road, and an additional four 9-mm Luger spent casings were found on the south side of the road. An automatic handgun, a loaded ammunition belt, and a shotgun were secured and placed on the roof of the Mercedes by the first responding officer during the night. Another 9-mm Luger spent casing was found in the grass next to the passenger's side of the Mercedes.

Every item of evidence was

- Marked with yellow number markers in a continuous order.
- Photographed with overall, medium range, and close-up photographs with and without yellow number markers with scale.
- Triangulated measurements were obtained using the electro poles as fixed points. (Remember to note all information on the pole such as numbers, name of company, etc.)

After the officer-involved shooting scene was concluded, the investigation continued to the premises of the residence to document the shooting and the marijuana grow operation.

CRIME SCENE 2: THE GROW HOUSE

The residence was located on the south side of the road. All windows, except the north side windows, were covered with metal hurricane shutters. A chain-link fence bordered the residence; a gate allowed entry to the northwest side of the house. Spent cartridges were recovered from the driveway while bullet holes were discovered in the closed garage door. Multiple spent shotgun shells and .40 caliber spent cartridges were found in the grass and on the pathway leading to the front porch. The living room window was broken and birdshot shotgun patterns were visible on the mini blinds and the window frame. Ricochet marks were found on the front porch wall, numerous spent shotgun shells were in the grass underneath the bedroom window at the northeast side of the residence. The lock system of the front door contained seven bullet holes from a shotgun shell propelling the dead bolt on the floor behind the door.

Bullet holes were found in the furniture in the living room. Multiple .22 caliber spent cartridges were found on the kitchen floor consistent with the residents shooting back at the robbers.

Inside the laundry room, numerous bottles and plastic containers of growing media were found. In the garage, rows of potting marijuana plants covered the floor. A specialized water system serviced each plant. Timers, transformers, and electrical circuit boards covered the walls. Rows of growing lamps were mounted on the ceiling above the plants to provide sufficient lighting. An additional air conditioning unit was in the corner of the garage.

In the southeast bedroom, a large mother marijuana plant was placed underneath a growing lamp mounted onto the ceiling, as shown in Figure 8.4. The lamp was connected to a timing device to control the exposure to light. The wall closet contained additional growing chemicals.

In the closet of the northeast bedroom, a plastic tray with several baby marijuana plants underneath a growing lamp was discovered.

Figure 8.4 Mother plant.

The CSI team photographed the scene with overall, medium range, and close-up photographs with and without scale of each item of evidence. All evidence was marked with yellow number markers.

Hint: In this case, the CSI team marked over 100 items and had to improvise such as item 101 with marker 10 and 1, and so on.

The lead CSI assigned a CSI to draw detailed sketches of the premises including all discovered evidence. Every item of evidence was measured before collecting and packaging. The trajectory patterns such as the two shotgun blasts on the living room window were examined and marked in alphanumerical order. Multiple shooting patterns were examined, photographed, measured, and sketched. During a walk around the residence, a possible illegal hookup of a telephone to the residence was detected and documented.

The CSI team performed a zone search of each room of the residence. The lead CSI assigned a room to each team member. In the kitchen, unknown pills were found in an Ibuprofen container and US currency in the dining room. The metal-detector search revealed additional spent cartridges in the front yard.

The CSI team collected the following samples from the grow operation:

- One sample of green leafy substance from closet in northeast bedroom
- One sample of green leafy substance from southeast bedroom
- One sample of green leafy substance from garage
- One sample of green leafy substance from plastic bags in garage
- One light hood with bulb from garage
- One ballast from garage
- One fan from garage
- One circuit panel from garage
- One bag of live marijuana plants (originally in three plastic bags) from garage
- One marijuana mother plant from southeast bedroom
- Seven marijuana baby plants from northeast bedroom
- 42 live marijuana plants from garage

8.1.1.4 Methamphetamine

Methamphetamine (meth), also called meth, ice, crystal, or crank is a homemade chemical drug affecting the nervous system, as shown in Figure 8.5. Meth creates a rush of intense feeling of pleasure lasting longer than cocaine. Meth can be smoked, inhaled, or injected. Users experience high

Figure 8.5 Methamphetamine.

energy, rapid speech and breathing, and increased blood pressure; however, long-term users are prone to depression, paranoia, insomnia, and delusions. Violent behavior has been connected to meth use. Long-term use leads to loss of teeth, fast aging, and heart problems. Even though most meth is produced in super labs in Mexico, the number of homegrown laboratories is on the rise.

8.1.1.4.1 Ingredients of Methamphetamine The production of methamphetamine consists of several items that can be found in every household and purchased at any Walmart or supermarket. The basic elements for the production of meth are as shown in Figure 8.6.

Figure 8.6 Meth supplies.

- Ephedrine or pseudoephedrine in pure powder form, obtained from cold medication such as Sudafed. (Have you noticed you need to show your I.D. to buy Sudafed at the pharmacy?) The cold medicine tablet is a mixture of pseudoephedrine and a solvent. By filtering and exposure to low temperatures the components are separated and the inert material of the tablet is removed, leaving the pure pseudoephedrine.
- Acetone found in nail polish and paint thinner
- Lithium found in batteries
- Toluene found in brake fluid
- Hydrochloric acid found in acid toilet bowl cleaners
- Red phosphorus found on the tip of matches
- Sodium hydroxide found in drain cleaners
- Sulfuric acid or battery acid
- Anhydrous ammonia
- Freon
- Paint thinner
- Iodine crystals
- Sodium and lithium
- Ether or starting fluid

8.1.1.4.2 Identify a Methamphetamine Laboratory   The location of the methamphetamine laboratory varies from a residence to a hotel room or the truck bed of a pickup truck. Drug users trying to cook the drug based on the information from the Internet rather than scientists run methamphetamine laboratories. The chemicals used in the production of meth are highly flammable and combined in a mixture may be toxic or highly explosive.

Special equipment is required to filter chemicals. The equipment may consist of

- Propane tanks with fittings (fittings turned blue)
- Large amount of cold medication containing ephedrine or pseudoephedrine
- Glass jars such as large pickle jars with liquids and crystals on the bottom of the jar
- Coffee filters with white or red sludge or crystals
- Bottles containing different acids
- Bottles or jars with rubber tubing attached
- Glass cookware with a powdery residue
- Large amount of stripped batteries
- Large containers of camp fuel, paint thinner, muriatic acid, acetone, and other chemicals

8.1.1.4.3 Response to a Methamphetamine Laboratory Special caution is required when entering a meth lab. Some meth labs are booby trapped with hand grenades or other firearms and explosives to avoid detection.

Two distinct signs of a meth lab are

- Occupants of the residence or hotel room go outside to smoke a cigarette.
- The presence of a strong smell of urine or chemicals such as ammonia, acetone, or ether.

Caution: If the CSI is not trained in the collection and preservation of a meth laboratory, additional personnel with meth laboratory cleanup training and experience should be consulted.

Under no circumstances should anybody at the scene

- Touch or sniff any container.
- Turn any electrical power switches on or off.
- Open or move any container with unknown chemicals.
- Eat, drink, or smoke anywhere near the meth lab.

If you come in contact with a meth lab,

- Decontaminate your clothing.
- Wash your hands and face (www.dea.gov).

The cleanup of a meth lab requires breathing apparatus such as masks with filters for clean air. Many of the chemicals can be harmful and cause health problems such as breathing problems, skin and eye irritation, headaches, nausea, and dizziness. High exposure can lead to lung damage and even death (http://www.deq.state.ok.us/LPDnew/methlabs/meth.htm).

The CSI should perform the basic crime scene investigation procedures such as notes, photos, sketch, and marking and photographing evidence; however, the packaging, preservation, and collection as well as the transport of the evidence should only be performed by a professional trained in meth laboratory evidence collection. The Drug Enforcement Agency provides training in meth lab investigations.

8.1.1.4.4 DEA Basic Clandestine Laboratory Certification School Every law enforcement agency should have several CSIs and law enforcement officers trained in the recognition of clandestine narcotics laboratories. The DEA Basic Clandestine Laboratory Certification School is the most widely recognized clandestine laboratory training course that meets Occupational Safety and Health Administration (OSHA) standards. The training is available to special agents from the DEA and state and local law enforcement officers in the United States and abroad. The DEA clandestine laboratory unit also provides advanced site safety training. The presence of a certified clandestine laboratory site safety officer at every clandestine laboratory site is a requirement of OSHA (http://www.dea.gov/ops/Training/Clandestine.shtml). For more information, contact the Drug Enforcement Administration Office of Training, P.O. Box 1475, Quantico, VA 22124-1475, Phone 703-632-5000.

8.1.2 Aviation Accidents

Commercial airplane accidents are always reported by the mainstream media, such as the disappearance of Malaysia Airlines Flight 370 on March 8, 2014. Unfortunately, there are a number of private airplane crashes taking the lives of the pilots and the passengers that are only reported in the local newspaper or the local news stations.

8.1.2.1 The National Transportation and Safety Board (NTSB)

The NTSB is responsible for determining the probable cause of transportation accidents, promoting transportation safety, and assisting victims of transportation accidents and their families. In 2013, the NTSB investigated 1222 aircraft accidents where 221 were fatal (http://www.ntsb.gov/Pages/default.aspx).

8.1.2.1.1 Response to an Aviation Accident   The NTSB maintains several Go Teams consisting of aviation experts. The purpose of the team is to respond to the scene of a major accident as quickly as possible to assess the need for technical expertise required to solve complex transportation safety problems. The team consists of three or four specialists assigned on a rotational basis to respond to scenes, for example, a Go Team is located in Miami, Florida. The team will travel either by commercial airline or government aircraft depending on the circumstances. The teams also investigate rail, highway, marine, and pipeline accidents.

Members of the Go Team must be available 24 hours a day by phone or pager while on-call. Most Go Team members maintain a bag packed with the tools necessary for the investigation including hand tools, camera, flashlights, and digital recorders, similar to the basic crime scene documentation equipment.

The investigator in charge is a senior investigator with years of industry experience and seniority in the NTSB. Aviation specialists are responsible for

- Collecting information on the accident flight and crewmembers' duties for as many days prior to the crash as relevant.

- Documenting the airframe wreckage, the accident scene including the determination of the impact angles to reconstruct the plane's pre-impact course and altitude.
- Examining the engine and propeller and engine accessories.
- Examining the plane's hydraulic, electrical, and pneumatic systems as well as the instruments and flight control system.
- Reconstructing the information given to the plane by the air traffic service including Air Traffic Control (ATC) radar data and the transcripts of the pilot-controller transmission.
- Documenting the weather data from the National Weather Service and from local TV stations.
- Investigating the crew performance including all before the accident factors to determine if human error, fatigue, alcohol, drugs or medical problems, or lack of training and experience caused the accident.
- Documenting the impact of the accident on the community and the fire rescue efforts.
- One of the team members is assigned to update the media on a daily basis if the investigation lasts over a longer period of time such as a commercial airliner accident.

The scene investigation may last from one or two days to a week or longer, depending on the dimension of the accident scene. The NTSB officer applies the basic crime scene investigation procedures of documenting, photographing, mapping, collecting, and preserving any evidence found at the scene. The most important pieces of evidence to recover are the cockpit voice recorder and the flight data recorder, also called the black box. Both devices are constructed to survive extreme impacts. The flight data recorder and the cockpit voice recorder are evaluated at headquarters to reconstruct the causes of the accident. Because of the large amount of evidence, the NTSB investigator will not speculate. The investigation may take months as the NTSB investigators reconstruct the plane to determine the reasons for the crash.

8.1.2.1.2 The NTSB Investigative Party   The NTSB investigates approximately 2000 aviation accidents annually and over 500 other modes of transportation accidents. The Board only employs 400 specialists and works together with other organizations or companies to accomplish the investigations. Other than the Federal Aviation Agency (FAA), it is up to the discretion of the NTSB to designate other organizations to the investigation. Every organization has to be able to provide expertise in a specialized field to serve in the investigation. The group chairman prepares the factual report while each group member verifies the accuracy of the report. These factual reports can be found in the public docket.

If criminal activity is involved in the aviation or transportation investigation, the NTSB does not investigate the criminal activity and the FBI will become the leading federal agency assisted by the NTSB.

8.1.2.2 Local Response to an Aviation Accident Site

Local law enforcement officers are the first responders at most aviation accident sites. The local law enforcement agency may receive multiple 911 calls from witnesses reporting that a plane was flying low before they heard a loud bang and saw a fireball in the distance. The communications supervisor will notify emergency medical personnel and the fire department as well as dispatch police officers to the scene as well as report the plane crash to the NTSB Regional Operations Center (ROC). Depending on the information received from the 911 call, the communication supervisor may dispatch a police officer to respond to the scene to verify the incident and the location before notifying other agencies, for example, if only one 911 call is received reporting that a plane was flying low over a house and there may have been a problem, but no further loud bang or fire has been witnessed, there is a possibility that the witness saw a crop duster plane spraying insecticides. In this scenario, the officer will respond to the scene to assess the situation and report back to the communication supervisor.

The NTSB notification procedures may vary depending on local and state policies. In some areas, local law enforcement will notify airport police who reports the aviation accident to the NTSB ROC.

Under federal regulations, operators are required to notify the NTSB immediately after aviation accidents or certain incidents. The watch commander, officer in charge, or communication supervisor, depending on department policy, contacts the NTSB ROC reporting the incident providing the following information:

- Type, nationality, and registration of the aircraft
- The name of the owner and operator of the aircraft
- Name of the pilot in command
- Date and time of the incident
- Last point of departure and intended landing point
- Geographical point of the position of the aircraft
- Number of passengers (including the number of injured and killed)
- Nature of the incident
- Weather conditions and extent of the damage to the plane
- Description of any explosives, radioactive material, or other dangerous cargo on the plane

8.1.2.2.1 Incident Command   In the event of a plane crash, the first officer on scene will become the incident commander. Saving lives is the first responsibility; however, the officer has to evaluate possible dangers of spilled gasoline or other fluids that could cause an explosion. The first responding officer on scene may hold the rank of a captain; however, if tactical or specialized trained response is required, the even lower ranking specialist will become the incident commander. Multiple agency responses to large scenes are managed through the Incident Command System (ICS). All law enforcement, Emergency Medical Service (EMS), and fire personnel should be well trained in ICS protocol.

ICS provides guidance for standard management procedures for temporary incident response of any size. Aviation crash sites can vary in size from a small area where the plane hit the ground to a crash site extending over 1 or 2 miles and multi-agency response is required to secure the scene. ICS also provides procedures for temporary management hierarchies for personnel, facilities, equipment, and communication. Personnel are assigned based on established standards and procedures as sanctioned by the participating authorities/agencies. ICS is applied from the time the incident occurs until the requirements for management and operations are no longer required.

Caution: Local law enforcement is responsible for saving lives, and the safety and the security of the scene. The NTSB investigator leads the investigation.

8.1.2.2.2 CSI Response   The investigation of an aviation accident at a larger scene is a team effort and all CSI personnel will be called out to assist in the investigation.

Caution: Before entering the inner perimeter of the scene, check with the fire department that the scene is safe and that there is no leaking fuel or other accelerant that could result in a combustion igniting a fire or explosion.

After being briefed by the first responder on scene, request if the NTSB has been notified and if an investigator will respond. If the investigator is responding, await his or her arrival before performing any intrusive actions such as marking evidence. The CSI team can obtain overall, medium range, and close-up photos of the scene while awaiting the arrival.

The lead CSI manages the team and assigns

- One CSI member to capture all scene photographs.
- One CSI member to sketch the scene and the evidence.
- One or two CSI members will be responsible for the evidence collection, packaging, and preservation.

If available, aerial photographs of the scene should be taken to show the dimensions and impact of the crash. Always take close-up photographs of any gauges, serial numbers including, but not limited to, plane identification number, engine numbers, and any placards with information about the plane.

The lead investigator maintains notes and writes the final report. In addition to the basic scene documentation, special information from the airplane wreckage should be obtained. A template, as shown in Document 8.1, assists in the documentation of the plane.

Caution: The NTSB investigator is in charge of the investigation and the CSI team assists in searching, documentation through photographs, evidence identification, mapping, collection, and preservation; however, the NTSB investigator is in control of the evidence.

According to Policy 49 CFR 830.10 preservation of aircraft wreckage, mail, cargo and records, requires that the operators will preserve the aircraft wreckage, recorders, any documents, and other items of evidentiary value for such time until the authorized representative of the NTSB takes custody of the items. However, first responders such as EMS, fire department, and law enforcement officers may disturb the wreckage to remove injured or trapped persons, protect the wreckage from additional damage, or to protect the public from being injured. The NTSB investigator in charge will decide if he wants to take custody of the wreckage or may release the entire wreckage for transportation from the accident site.

Caution: If there are any questions about moving the wreckage from the accident site, always contact the NTSB investigator assigned to the case or the NTSB ROC.

```
┌─────────────────────────────────────────────────────────────────┐
│                      AVIATION ACCIDENT                            │
│                       FIELD NOTES                                 │
└─────────────────────────────────────────────────────────────────┘
```

AIR CRAFT DESCRIPTION					
MARKER #		VICTIM		PERPETRATOR	OTHER

TYPE OF AIRCRAFT	FIXED WING		HELICOPTER		ULTRA LIGHT		OTHER	

MAKE		MODEL		YEAR	

SERIAL NUMBER		TAIL #	

COLOR	
MARKINGS	

CONSTRUCTION	FABRIC		METAL		WOOD FRAME		METAL FRAME		OTHER	

BODY TYPE	HIGH WING		LOW WING			TANDEM SEAT	
	SIDE BY SIDE		FOUR PLACE		MULTIPLE SEATS		
	FIXED LANDING GEAR		RETRACTABLE LANDING GEAR		TRICYCLE GEAR		
OTHER							

NUMBER OF SEATS	

NUMBER OF ENGINES	SINGLE		TYPE OF ENGINE	PISTON		JET	TURBO PROP	RADIAL		OTHER	
	TWIN										
	MULTIPLE ENGINES										

ENGINE MANUFACTURER					

ENGINE SERIAL NUMBER			

PROPELLER MANUFACTURER		TYPE OF PROPELLER		VARIABLE PITCH		FIXED	

NOTES

1

Document 8.1 Aviation accident/aircraft description.

In most aircraft accidents, the NTSB investigator takes custody of the wreckage. The airplane wreckage will be transported to the nearest NTSB facility for additional examinations determining what caused the accident.

Additional collected evidence may remain with the local law enforcement agency.

The lead CSI will write the final report including all evidence collected and list the items that were taken into custody by the NTSB.

Cross Creek Plane Crash

On December 6, 2002, at 3:55 pm, a twin engine Beechwood Baron 58 private airplane crashed into two houses in the Cross Creek subcommunity in South Fort Myers, Florida. According to the report from the NTSB, the plane left from St. Joseph, Missouri and was low on fuel when attempting to land at the municipal Page Field airport. The poor weather conditions hindered the pilot to land the plane and he attempted to land at Southwest Florida International Airport. However, he did not have enough fuel to reach the airport and crashed on approach to SWFIA (see Figure 8.7).

The plane crashed through the roof of a residence and a palm tree before the propeller separated and was projected through the roof of the house across the street, as illustrated in Figure 8.8.

The homeowner had been sitting in a recliner in the living room watching TV. He got up and went to the restroom. Seconds later, the propeller from the plane crashed through the ceiling and the propeller blade embedded in the recliner. He would have been killed if he had sat in that chair, as shown in Figure 8.9.

The plane continued to break apart on the journey along the road. Larger and smaller pieces of the plane and its contents were found along the road, in the grass, trees, and in a nearby lake. Overall, the scene extended over one block in dimension; see Figure 8.10.

A mobile command center was established and the American Red Cross provided shelter, food, and water for the search teams. The NTSB investigator was in charge of the scene and briefed all personnel about

Figure 8.7 Aerial of crash site.

Figure 8.8 First impact in the roof of the house.

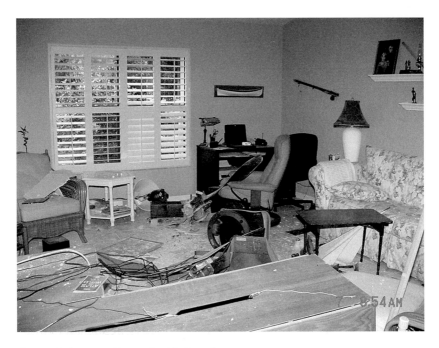

Figure 8.9 Propeller embedded in chair.

Figure 8.10 Dimension of the scene.

the specifics of the incident and explained what type of evidence to search for.

The search of the scene was not only for technical evidence but also the body parts of the people and the dog on the plane. The search was a multi-agency effort between the Lee County Sheriff's Office, Florida Department of Law Enforcement, Fort Myers Police, and the Medical Examiner's Office. Law enforcement officers, MLDIs, CSI personnel, and forensic personnel from the Florida Department of Law Enforcement assisted in the line searches that were performed along the street and in the grass areas.

The lead CSI of the sheriff's office documented the scene, and assigned additional CSI personnel to take photographs and assist in the recovery and collection of evidence.

The multi-agency search teams marked the items of evidence with red metal flags. Members of the sheriff's office CSI team assigned to evidence collection followed the search teams and marked the flagged evidence with continuous yellow number markers, photographed with overall, medium range, and close-up photos, and mapped each item before physically collecting and packaging.

The search lasted for approximately 10 hours. The dog and most of the victims' body parts were recovered and transported to the morgue.

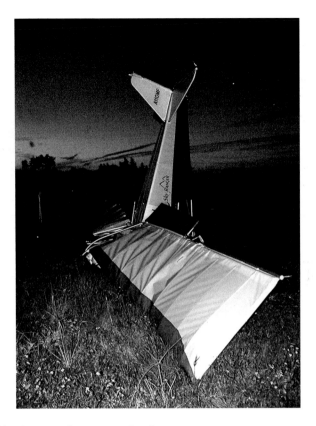

Figure 8.11 Plane crash in Pine Island.

Large items of evidence such as motor parts, etc., were transported to the hangar of the Lee County Sheriff's Office aviation unit. The NTSB officer took custody of the plane wreckage and all evidence with technical value for his investigation.

Not every plane crash extends over a large area, however, it can be as fatal. The pilot and co-pilot of a small private plane encountered problems over Pine Island, Florida. The pilot tried to land the plane in a field when the head dived into the ground, as shown in Figure 8.11.

8.1.3 Human Trafficking and Human Smuggling

The numbers of people falling victim to human trafficking and human smuggling are on the rise. Human trafficking and human smuggling is a form of organized crime promising fast cash and power with less risk involved.

8.1.3.1 *Human Trafficking*

Human trafficking is trading humans for sexual slavery, forced labor, or sexual exploitation. Commonly, women and children are the victims; however, men are also traded. People are sold, bought, and smuggled like modern-day slaves. The victims come from third-world countries and are smuggled into Western countries. Children are sold to the traffickers so parents can pay their debts or for the other family members to survive. The victims are transported in cargo ships or land routes to the designated countries where they work as prostitutes, in sweat shops, in households, or restaurants without pay or with minimum pay. Their passport and identification documents are held by the trafficker to prevent fleeing. Victims are beaten and starved and threatened that their family members will be hurt or killed if they do not follow orders.

Teens Trafficked for Sex Slavery

Human trafficking is very difficult to investigate, as the victims are too scared to talk to the police. Most of the victims are teens and young girls who do not speak English.

In an interview, a counselor from the school board in Lee County, Florida, stated that she worked several cases of human trafficking of young girls. The traffickers act as the parents and send the girls to school. The girls barely speak English and are scared to talk to the teacher or any other authority person about the abuse. The girls show bruises and when asked say that they fell and it was their own fault. The girls are forced into prostitution. One girl stated that she had to serve 5 men in one afternoon; otherwise, her family in Mexico would be hurt or killed. Another victim, a 15-year-old girl with a 1-year-old baby, was threatened that her baby would be taken away if she did not do what was expected of her, to make money in prostitution.

8.1.3.2 *Human Smuggling*

Human smuggling is the transport of people into a country via deliberate evasion of immigration laws. The law includes bringing, harboring, and transportation of illegal aliens into the country (www.ice.gov).

In Florida, the number of human smuggling cases increased over the last decade. The 90-mile distance between Florida's southern point in Key West and the northern coast of Cuba provides excellent opportunities for human smuggling. Human smuggling is a very profitable illegal activity. The current estimated charge per person being smuggled from Cuba to Florida is approximately $15,000, for a 12-hour boat ride.

8.1.3.2.1 Why Do Cubans Pay to Be Smuggled to the United States?

Immigrants from Cuba receive special treatment from the United States.

The wet-foot, dry-foot policy puts Cubans in reach of U.S. soil and permanent residence. This policy was implemented in 1995 as an amendment to the 1966 Cuban Adjustment Act passed by Congress during the Cold War tensions.

The practical application of the amendment is when a Cuban migrant reaches U.S. soil, he can claim dry feet, qualifying for legal residency and U.S. citizenship. If the migrant is caught in the waterways between the two countries, it is considered wet feet, and he or she will be sent back to Cuba. The only exception is if a Cuban can prove that he or she will be prosecuted when sent back; then asylum may be granted based on the provided evidence.

The intentions of the wet-foot, dry-foot law was to discourage Cubans from fleeing Cuba; however, the Coast Guard reported capturing over 35,000 Cubans in the oceans in 1995 when the law was implemented. Refugees from the Dominican Republic or Haiti coming in boats with Cubans will be deported back to their home country; only Cubans fall under the jurisdiction of the wet-foot, dry-foot law.

Beached in Sanibel Island

On Sunday evening on July 22, 2007, a task force consisting of the U.S. Coast Guard, officers from Florida Fish and Wildlife officers, Sanibel Police Department, and the Lee County Sheriff's Office received information about a speedboat containing 27 Cuban migrants near Sanibel Island's beach. The high-speed chase between the boats exceeded 40 knots. The smugglers beached the Wellcraft Scarab boat with the migrants on the beach of Sanibel. All passengers were healthy and the Cubans were transported the next day to the detention center in Miami for processing.

The smugglers used to approach the east coast of Florida, but changed to approach the west coast area that was less patrolled by the U.S. Coast Guard. This was the fourth landing within 18 months and is becoming a growing problem.

8.1.3.2.2 How Do the Human Smuggling Rings Work? A commonly used method of operation for human smuggling is the two-boat approach. One speedboat leaves the northern coast of Cuba loaded with migrants, while another boat with spare gasoline tanks leaves the coast of Southwest Florida. The Cuban Coast Guards are bribed to patrol a different area that night. The two boats meet in the Gulf of Mexico. This rendezvous of the boats in the ocean is necessary, as the boat carrying 25 to 27 Cubans cannot hold the weight of the gasoline necessary for the entire trip to the coast of Florida. Both boats travel in a convoy formation. The boat holding the gasoline tanks has the navigation lights on, while the boat carrying the Cubans is blacked out. The blacked out boat will change course if an unidentified boat approaches in the distance to avoid being captured by law enforcement or the US Coast Guard.

The Same Boat

In spring of 2008, a disabled boat was discovered in the Gulf of Mexico near Sanibel Island in Southwest Florida; see Figure 8.12. The passengers in the boat were Cubans being smuggled to the coast of Florida. The US Coast Guard worked together with officers from ICE and the Lee County Sheriff's Office Marine Patrol Division. CSIs documented and processed the boat. The hull numbers and motor numbers of the outboard motors were documented. In early fall of 2008, a speedboat with smuggled Cubans reached the land of a gated community along the coastline of Lee County, Florida. The Cubans were transported to the processing station and the CSI unit was notified to document and process the boat for any type of evidence leading to the identification of the smugglers.

When writing the crime scene report, the CSI noticed that the hull number and motor number appeared familiar. The same boat and outboard motor had been used, except for this excursion a second outboard motor had been added. The CSI informed the lead ICE investigator.

During the investigation, it became relevant that the registered owner of the boat called the authorities reporting the boat as stolen. Following the law, the boat was returned to the owner in Miami. At that time, it was not known to law enforcement that the boat owner was the leader of the human smuggling ring.

Figure 8.12 Cubans smuggled to the coast of Florida.

Hint: Always document the serial number of the hull, outboard motors, trolling motors, and inboard motors with notes and photographs. If several human trafficking or human smuggling cases occur in the area, compare the serial numbers of the hulls and motors to combine crimes most likely being committed by the same human smuggling ring.

Unfortunately, many Cubans cannot afford to pay smugglers to bring them to the United States and build homemade rafts or use 50-gallon drums tied together to cross the 90 miles of waterway between Cuba and Florida. Sadly, many immigrants cannot withstand the extreme environmental conditions of heat, storms, and other dangers during the journey on a small raft.

8.1.3.3 Crime Scene Response to Human Trafficking and Human Smuggling

The CSI responding to the human trafficking/smuggling scene will perform the basic crime scene investigation procedures. In these cases, the boat is the crime scene.

It is important to thoroughly document all serial numbers of the boat and the motors.

The template shown in Document 8.2 is a great reminder of where to find all numbers and information.

After extensive photography of the exterior and interior of the boat with overall, medium range, and close-up photos, the following processing methods should be applied on the interior and exterior of the boat:

- Fingerprinting
  - All railings on the boat
  - All metal surfaces
  - Gas tank
  - Lids of coolers
  - Steering wheel and any radio knobs, shifter (visually check for prints, if none are detected, swab for DNA instead)
  - Door to the cabins
  - Any surfaces inside the cabins
- DNA swabs
  - Boat seats, steering wheel, and shifter (if not already fingerprinted, however, check with the DNA laboratory if fingerprinted swabs are acceptable. The fingerprint powder can be extracted; however, some state laboratories will not accept DNA swabs of items that have been fingerprinted).
  - Check for any food that had been half eaten.
  - Swab any empty bottles and containers.
  - Collect samples of vomit or other body fluids.

CRIME SCENE UNIT FIELD NOTES		

BOAT DESCRIPTION				
MARKER #		VICTIM	PERPETRATOR	OTHER

MAKE	MODEL	YEAR

SERIAL NUMBER		BOW # & STATE	

COLOR	
MARKINGS	

CONSTRUCTION	WOOD	METAL	FIBER GLASS	PLASTIC	OTHER

TYPE		SAIL BOAT	POWER BOAT	YACHT	
SPEED BOAT		CABIN CRUISER	HOUSE BOAT	PONTOON BOAT	
COMMERCIAL BOAT		JET SKI	CANOE	JOHN BOAT	
BASS BOAT		KAYAK	OTHER		

NUMBER OF ENGINES	SINGLE	TWIN	MULTIPLE

TYPE OF ENGINE	OUTBOARD	INBOARD	INBOARD/OUTBOARD	OTHER

ENGINE MANUFACTURER				

ENGINE SERIAL NUMBER			

NOTES

1

Document 8.2 Boat identification template.

All evidence will be collected and transported to the evidence section for storage. The CSI will write a report and, upon request, a copy may be sent to the Coast Guard investigator or ICE agent in charge of the case.

Human trafficking/smuggling cases are tried in federal court and the CSI will be subpoenaed to testify in the trial.

8.1.4 Officer-Involved Shooting

Every time a police officer signs in for duty, there is a chance he or she may become involved in a use-of-force encounter. The officer has to make a split second decision to evaluate the situation, the danger for himself, the victim, the suspect, and bystanders when choosing between a nonlethal or lethal weapon response.

On August 9, 2014, in Fergusson, Missouri, white police officer Darren Wilson shot and killed African American Michael Brown in a use-of-force incident. The shooting prompted an outcry in the black community followed by protests, looting, and setting stores on fire in Fergusson. The case was brought before a grand jury that decided on November 24, 2014 not to indict Officer Wilson.

Cases like the Michael Brown officer-involved shootings are high profile cases with extensive media attention. Law enforcement agencies and the officer may be held criminally or civilly liable.

8.1.4.1 Who Should Investigate the Officer-Involved Shooting?

Who should investigate an officer-involved shooting? This question has been the topic for many discussions. While some police chiefs and sheriffs argue that their own criminal investigation and crime scene investigators should investigate the case and collect and examine the evidence, others argue that an independent agency should investigate officer-involved cases. Many law enforcement agencies maintain a specialized investigative team with high levels of expertise in ballistics, weapons, human performance, tactics, deadly force, and department policy. The team should also include detectives, an assistant state attorney or state attorney's office investigator or US attorney and US attorney's office investigator, forensic personnel as well as subject matter experts depending on the specifics of the case.

8.1.4.2 CSI Response to Officer-Involved Shooting

Investigating an officer-involved shooting is a team effort and requires at least two CSIs. The first officer on scene or lead investigator briefs the CSI team about the specifics of the incident during the walk-through of the scene.

The basic crime scene procedures such as continuous documentation, overall, medium range, and close-up photographs, mapping and evidence collection and preservation apply in addition to:

- Videotaping the scene including (if no video camera is available, ask to use the dash camera in the patrol vehicle).
  - Onlookers at the scene to
    - Confirm statements from witnesses about their positioning during the incident
    - Prove that certain people who come forward as witnesses were actually present on scene
    - People may claim not to be at the scene when in fact they had been there

  - Lighting conditions on scene
  - Weather conditions
  - Integrity of the scene in the form of barrier tape and scene security
  - Aerial photographs and videotaping is recommended for possible grand jury or court presentation
- Photographing and videotaping from the officer's location toward the subject and the subject's location toward the officer.
- Photographing all officers involved in the shooting being separated from each other to avoid scrutiny of testimony and allegations of collusion.
- Asking the officer involved to provide a walk-through of the scene (only if it is a one-officer incident).
- Seizing the officer's weapon and duty gear is policy in many agencies. The weapon will be signed over to a sergeant or duty officer of the training division.
- Photographing the officer's clothing paying special attention to
  - Cuts and other defects in the clothing as signs of struggle
  - Blood on the clothing
- Searching for all spent cartridges for the shots fired. It is imperative that all fired cartridges and spent projectiles are recovered.
- Search for any evidence of a struggle between the subject and the officer.
- Mapping the location of the subject and officer.
- Mapping the location of the subject and officer's vehicle in an outdoor shooting.
- Determining the trajectory of the rounds fired
  - From the subject to the officer
  - From the officer toward the subject
- In outdoor shooting scenes, additionally
  - Mapping of the officer's vehicle and the subject's vehicle
  - Sketching of the location of all vehicles involved
  - Obtaining additional measurement between the vehicles
    - Police vehicle to police vehicle
    - Police vehicle to subject vehicle
    - All police vehicles to subject vehicle
- Maintaining the chain of custody from the recovery to the courtroom is of the utmost importance.

Dexter Copycat

On May 16, 2014, at the Inn at the Springs in Bonita Springs, Florida, Craig Spitz, a former hotel worker, waited in the hotel office for the arrival of the night concierge, Tony Almeida. In the office, Spitz overpowered him, handcuffed Almeida behind his back, placed a black gag in his mouth, and put shackles on his feet (see Figure 8.13). Almeida was able to escape and, while running through the lounge door to the pool area, Spitz fired two rounds hitting Almeida's right and left shoulders. Spitz fled the pool area.

Witnesses heard the shooting and notified the sheriff's office. The victim was taken to the hospital with non-life-threatening injuries.

Witnesses told the officer that the suspect fled in a silver-colored sedan. Spitz was identified as the offender and the owner of the vehicle. Deputies were dispatched to search the vicinity of Spitz's home on Morton Avenue in Bonita Springs, Florida.

Spitz arrived and deputies tried to conduct a traffic stop, but Spitz led them on a pursuit.

A deputy performed a pit maneuver forcing Spitz's vehicle in the ditch on Morton Street. Three other deputies responded to Morton Street. When one of the deputies approached Spitz's vehicle in the ditch, he discovered that Spitz had a firearm in his hand. Upon approach of the deputy, Spitz ignored the command to drop the weapon and slightly lowered the barrel toward the officer. The deputy fired a shot and the other officers engaged in the shooting. Spitz died on scene.

The investigation by the State Attorney's office determined that the shooting was a justified use of force and no charges were filed. During the investigation, it was revealed that Spitz had planned to kidnap Almeida, torture him, and kill him. Spitz had rented a room at a Motel 6 for one

Figure 8.13 Gag, shackles, and towel.

week under a fictitious name and items found inside his vehicle indicated that he was well prepared for his venture.

RESPONSE BY THE CSI TEAM

AT THE HOTEL

The CSI responded to the Inn at the Springs and documented the crime scene with photographs and sketches. In the office, multiple clear plastic gloves and two cotton balls, and a black canvas bag with duct tape, thumb cuffs, finger light, cotton balls, diaper, lock-picking tools, homemade device, ACE wrap, scissors, gag, GPS, hole punch, and a bottle of hydrocodone pills from a desk in the office were found. A pair of silver-colored shackles, a black gag, and a bloody towel had been found outside the door leading to the pool area. The CSI documented, marked, obtained triangulated measurements, and sketched all evidence before collecting and packaging.

While finishing the collection of the last item of evidence, the CSI was notified about the officer-involved shooting and requested to respond to the scene.

ON MORTON STREET

The CSI responded to the shooting scene and was briefed by the captain of the forensics unit about the specifics of the incident. The CSI was advised that the suspect's revolver had been secured for collection. The scene was cordoned off with yellow barrier tape, and a crime scene log was maintained listing all personnel entering and leaving the scene (see Figure 8.14).

Morton Avenue is a paved, single-lane road running north and south. Grass and shrubs were west of the road and a ditch with water, also bordered by grass and shrubs, was east of the road. Four patrol vehicles had been parked on the road, facing south. A gray Saturn was in the ditch east of the road, facing west. The emergency lights on all patrol vehicles were on and the spotlights pointed toward the vehicle in the ditch.

It was night and the road was poorly lit.

After the initial notes, the CSI began with the photographic documentation of the scene including:

- Overall photographs
  - View from each patrol vehicle toward the suspect vehicle
  - View from the suspect vehicle toward the patrol vehicles
  - Overall view of the road from different viewpoints (use compass directions)
  - Any type of tire marks on and off the road
- Medium range photos

Figure 8.14 Aerial photo of the scene.

- Patrol vehicles including
  - All four sides of vehicle including license plate
  - Patrol vehicle number (on roof and trunk lid)
  - Open doors, windows
  - Any damage (interior and exterior)
- Suspect vehicle
  - All four sides of the vehicle including the license plate
  - Open doors, windows
  - Any damage (interior and exterior)

A videographer from the video production unit of the sheriff's office responded to the scene and videotaped the scene.

In the meantime, an additional CSI was notified and responded to the Bonita Springs substation where the four deputies involved in the incident remained. The CSI obtained close-up photos of the officers' nameplates, uniforms, service weapons, magazines, and ammunition.

Back at the scene on Morton Street, the lead CSI exposed another set of photographs during daylight and sketched the location of all vehicles involved. Utilizing the department helicopter, aerial photos of the scene had been exposed. The lead CSI documented the information and listed the condition and content of each patrol vehicle.

The CSI team, consisting of a lead CSI and the additional CSI arriving from the substation, obtained baseline measurements to map the location and distances between all vehicles, and the width of the pavement of the road.

The medico-legal death investigator (MLDI) arrived on scene and examined the deceased. While the lead CSI used a gunshot residue evidence collection kit to collect samples of the deceased's hands, she discovered a spent projectile on the floorboard of the deceased's vehicle. The projectile was photographed, measured, and collected as evidence. Exigent circumstances existed to collect the projectile without a search warrant as the projectile could have been lost during transport to the Sheriff's Office Impoundment Bay. The suspect's vehicle is shown in Figure 8.15.

After the body was removed, the vehicle was towed on a flatbed tow truck to the impoundment bay of the sheriff's office. A deputy sheriff followed the tow truck to the Sheriff's Office Impoundment Bay and maintained the chain of custody on the property receipt issued for the silver-colored Saturn sedan.

Meanwhile, the CSI team searched the street, the grass area, and the bushes along both sides of the road for the spent cartridges and projectiles (see Figure 8.16). Seven spent .40 caliber cartridges were recovered, photographed, measured, sketched, collected, and packaged.

Hint: The baseline measuring method is most suited for outdoor scenes by placing the measuring tape in the center of the road.

The crime scene team cleared from the scene and all evidence was transported to the forensic center and subsequently turned over to the evidence section.

SEARCHING THE SATURN

On May 17, 2014, at the Sheriff's Office Impoundment Bay, the lead detective read and served a search warrant on the 1996 Saturn. The lead CSI

Figure 8.15 Suspect's vehicle.

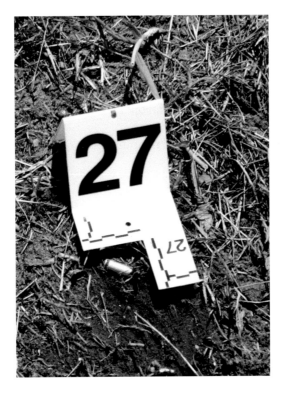

Figure 8.16 Spent cartridge.

noted the vehicle information, for example, mileage, open doors, windows, interior and exterior damage, and bloodstain pattern in the vehicle.

The CSI captured overall, medium range, and close-up images of the vehicle. A thorough search of the vehicle was performed and all items found inside the vehicle had been photographed with medium range photographs where the items were found and close-up photos.

Hint: Placing the evidence on a table covered with brown butcher paper provides a good background for the close-up photos.

A plastic bin on the rear seat attracted the CSI's attention. The bin contained a box of 20 Good Sense trash bags, empty box of handcuffs, Dirt Devil vacuum cleaner, Velcro band, one large bottle of hydrogen peroxide, one set of ear protection with green rubber band, one bottle of all-purpose citrus cleaner, one black camera bag with JVC video camera and two 8-mm tapes, one surgical dressing, one box of sleep aid with 12 pills, one large black plastic liner, scoop-away bucket with one oven cleaner spray, one box of Epsom salts, one bottle of Mister Plumber, one bottle of Sno Bol toilet cleaner, one base for Hamilton Beach blender, and one bottle of hydrogen peroxide. In the trunk, the following items created suspicion about what Spitz planned for Almeida, as illustrated in Figure 8.17.

- Black bag with Welch Alyn Tyco's blood pressure meter with 3 cuffs
- One box with one pair of Playtex Living Gloves in size L
- One Grant's Atlas of Anatomy
- One orange-and-black telescoping Fiskars branch cutter, SN EA1009
- One green bath towel
- Five blue surgical booties
- One clean diaper
- One Sky King plastic bag
- One bag with AJM Giant size lunch bags
- One black Coleman Powermate drill with battery pack

Figure 8.17 Items in Saturn.

- One brown-handled Rug Crafters shag cutter
- One Tyco stethoscope with name Craig Spitz engraved
- One "The Shower Massager" shower head
- One water pick with hose and connector
- Five face masks
- Two metal strainers
- One metal handsaw in blue bootie
- One Makita saw with blue bootie at saw blade in plastic basket
- One 18-volt charger for drill
- Two clear plastic bags
- Open package of multi-colored zip ties
- Seven plastic bags
- One Dura-built China spatula with red-and-black handle
- Two black plastic pads
- One white plastic strainer and one metal strainer
- Clear plastic gloves
- One black-handled Erretschu garden scissors, Patent # 4,156,311
- 1 face mask

All items were documented, photographed, and collected as evidence. A property receipt was issued listing all evidence and the chain of custody was maintained. A copy of the search warrant and the property receipt remained in the vehicle, while another copy was sent to the detective to return to the judge.

BULLET TRAJECTORY

The lead CSI took additional photographs, with and without scale, of the windshield and the driver's window. The letters A through F were used to mark the six bullet holes in the driver's window. A detailed trajectory determination of those bullet holes was not possible due to the broken glass.

Three bullet holes in the windshield were marked with letters G through I. Marker G was in the center of the windshield, while markers H and I were on the passenger's side with a general directionality toward the driver's seat. A direct trajectory examination was not possible due to the broken glass. The projectile that had entered marker G had continued through the back of the driver's seat (G1 and G2), embedding itself in the outer wall of the blue-and-white cooler (G3) on the driver's side of the rear bench seat, as shown in Figure 8.18a and b.

Hint: Using the road mapping method as explained in Chapter 6, crime scene reconstruction can be applied when documenting multiple bullet holes in a window or windshield.

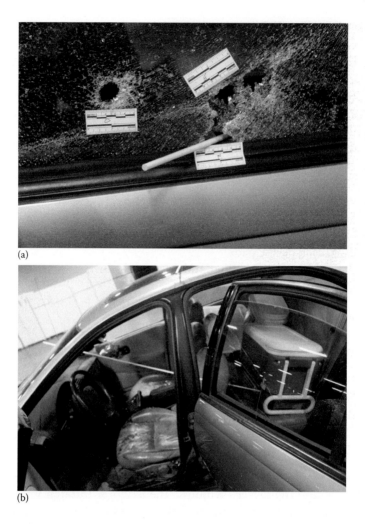

Figure 8.18 Projectile trajectory. (a) Bullet holes in driver's side window. (b) Trajectory of the projectile through the windshield, driver's seat into the cooler on the rear driver's bench.

MOTEL 6

During the investigation, it was revealed that Spitz had rented room #132 at Motel 6, paying cash for a week in advance and under a fictitious name of Carl Sinclair Spitz. He planned to kidnap Almeida, bring him to the hotel room, and torture him for some time before he would kill him.

The lead detectives and the CSI conducted a walk-through of the hotel room. The CSI took notes and photographed the room with overall, medium range, and close-up photographs. During the search, the following items of interest were recovered that concurred with Spitz's plans.

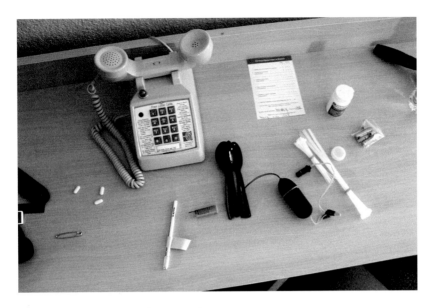

Figure 8.19 Items found in Motel 6.

- One medium-sized, clear plastic, zip lock bag, one orange cable cuff, one roll of electrical tape, wire, one superglue tube
- Wire cutters and carpet knives
- Unknown pills
- Batteries and electronic connector "12"
- Odor annihilator
- Rolls of duct tape
- Black strap with metal rings
- Camera

Every item of evidentiary value was photographed, marked, sketched, and collected as evidence; see Figure 8.19.

CONCLUSION

The victim Almeida was fortunate to be able to escape. He suffered two gunshot wounds; however, there is a mere suspicion that he would have been tortured and killed by Spitz.

Appendix A: Forensic Databases

A.1 Integrated Automated Fingerprint Identification System (IAFIS)

The IAFIS database is maintained by the Federal Bureau of Investigation and contains fingerprints and palm prints from

- Fingerprints of arrested suspects by municipal, state, and federal law enforcement
- Fingerprints collected through background checks for employment, licenses such as real estate license, kindergarten, etc., or other non-criminal purposes
- Latent prints recovered from crime scenes

In IAFIS, the latent print examiner can search and compare unknown latent impressions from neighboring agencies, statewide and nationwide (James and Nordby, 2005). In the United States, each state maintains its own Automated Fingerprint Identification System (AFIS) that is linked to the FBI's IAFIS. If a latent fingerprint obtained from the crime scene has the sufficient ridge detail for submission for an IAFIS search, prior to the submission, the latent examiner creates a digital image of the print using a scanner. Using a coder allows marking of the points on the print for search in the computer database. Through a secured T1 internet connection, the print will be electronically submitted to IAFIS. The comparison of the scanned fingerprint against all fingerprint images in the database can be performed within minutes. For more information, please visit http://www.fbi.gov/about-us/cjis /fingerprints_biometrics/iafis/iafis.

A.2 Integrated Ballistics Identification System (IBIS)

The Bureau of Alcohol, Tobacco, Firearms and Explosives maintain the IBIS database. The database contains images of cartridges and casings collected from crime scenes and test fired in the laboratory. The database has one limitation: that a suspected firearm has to be submitted for comparison as the database is limited to information of bullets and casings, but not firearms. The database can compare the images of test-fired bullets to the images of a known firearm. It can match the images of a known firearm to the images of a bullet found at the crime scene, but cannot link the images of a bullet to an unknown firearm (www.nij.gov).

A.3 TreadMate, TreadMark, and SoleMate

At crime scenes, multiple shoe impressions can be present making the process of impression recovery and identification very time consuming. TreadMark is a commercial product using four characteristics to identify individual outsole impressions, such as pattern, size, damage, and wear pattern. These characteristics can be matched to the shoe imprint data from the suspect's shoes and are evidence that the suspect was present at the crime scene. A match in the database can provide the name, date of birth, criminal record number, and similar offenses for possible suspects (Bowen and Schneider, 2007). TreadMark and SoleMate aid the shoe impression examiner by searching large repositories of shoes to identify possible suspects through their shoe impressions left at the crime scene. The TreadMate database assists the tire impression examiner with information of over 5000 vehicles' tire tread patterns. The match of the tread patterns found at the crime scene to the database can lead to the identification of possible suspects (Bowen and Schneider, 2007) (http://www.fosterfreeman.com/index.php/latest-news/484-solemate-50).

A.4 National Automotive Paint File

The Federal Bureau of Investigation (FBI) maintains the National Automotive Paint File, a database that maintains over 40,000 samples of automotive paint used by different national and international manufacturers. The database allows the examiner to compare paint chips from the crime scenes or accident scene to the paint standards in the database to positively identify the year, make, and model of the vehicle used in the offense. For more information and lab submission requests please contact the FBI's Laboratory at 202-324-3000.

A.5 Combined DNA Index System (CODIS)

In 1990, the FBI laboratory implemented the CODIS software project serving 14 states and local laboratories. It was not until 1994 that the DNA

Identification Act was enacted requesting the FBI to create and maintain a National DNA Index System (NDIS) for law enforcement purposes. Today, over 190 public law enforcement laboratories in the United States and more than 70 law enforcement laboratories in over 40 countries participate in NDIS using CODIS software. However, the international laboratories do not have access to the United States CODIS system (www.fbi.gov).

All convicted offenders in municipal, state, and federal prisons are requested by law to provide a buccal swab and their DNA profile in CODIS. The DNA profiles of missing persons and blood samples recovered at crime scenes are stored in CODIS, available for searches. Local, state, and national crime laboratories are permitted to electronically search and upload DNA profiles. CODIS is an excellent resource for investigative leads in cases with biological evidence. Searches in CODIS reveal positive matches based on 13 core CODIS STR loci. This process does not only allow the identification of possible serial killers but can also link crime scenes together (Saferstein, 2011) (http://www.fbi.gov/about-us/lab/codis/codis).

A.6 National Integrated Ballistics Information Network (NIBIN)

NIBIN is an automated ballistics evaluation program maintained by the Bureau of Alcohol, Tobacco, Firearms and Explosives (ATF). Firearms examiners acquire, digitize, and compare markings created by a specific firearm onto bullets and cartridge cases collected at the crime scene or test firing in a known weapon. NIBIN consists of a microscope and a computer that captures the image of the markings on the bullet or cartridge. Once the images are forwarded to the regional server, they will be stored and compared to other images in the database (Saferstein, 2011). NIBIN partners can submit casings and cartridges for analysis free of charge (https://www.atf.gov/user?destination=content/Firearms/firearms-enforcement/NIBIN/NIBIN-user-area).

A.7 RxList

At crime scenes, the crime scene investigator might find loose pills that have either a letter or a number indented, but no further marks for identification. The RxList is a free Internet database of prescription drugs that allows searching for the name of the medication based on the markings on the pills and provides data about the side affects and interactions, information that can be very important in overdose or suicide cases (www.rxlist.com).

A.8 International Ink Library

Why would a crime scene investigator look for an ink library? Even in our time of e-mails and texting, important documents are still signed with an ink pen such as contracts and most important last will and testaments. Handwriting and ink examination can become a very important aspect of the authentication of a signature.

According to the National Institute of Justice (n.d.), the U.S. Secret Service and the Internal Revenue Service maintains a collection of over 9500 inks, dating back to the 1920s. Every year, ink manufacturers provide samples of new inks that, after chemical testing, will be added to the reference collection. Ink identification can assist in determining the earliest possible time when a document had been signed by chemically analyzing the sample ink and comparing it to the library specimens. The U.S. Secret Service will provide such services to law enforcement agencies (202-406-5708).

A.9 Forensic Information System for Handwriting (FISH)

The FISH database is maintained by the U.S. Secret Service. FISH is a collection of every threatening correspondence received by federal agencies and other government agencies. The scanned digitalized text writing samples are plotted as arithmetic and geometric values before being stored in FISH. FISH also maintains a database for the letters submitted by the National Center for Missing and Exploited Children (NCMEC). FISH contains approximately 12,000 samples of threatening letter to governors, senators, and protectees as well as 4000 samples in the NCMEC file. Law enforcement agencies can send in documents through the local U.S. Secret Service field offices for analysis. The service is free of charge (NIST.gov). For more information visit www .secretservice.gov/forensics.shtml.

A.10 Glass Evidence Reference Database

The glass evidence reference database contains more than 700 glass samples collected from different glass manufacturers, distributors, and vehicle junkyards. The database is housed with the Technical Support Working Group, an interagency group that includes the U.S. Department of State and the U.S. Department of Defense. Although a match in the database cannot definitely determine the accurate source of unknown glass samples, it provides the relative frequency of two glass samples from different sources having the same elemental profile. In other words, the database contains the results of two plasma mass spectrometers performing an elemental analysis of glass (National Institute of Standard and Technology, n.d.). For more information, please visit isfsubgroup@tswg.gov.

A.11 Automated Counterfeiting Identification Database (ACID)

The ACID database contains check images and is used to identify counterfeit checks based on printing processes and check formats. The database contains about 2000 images. Outside law enforcement agencies cannot access the database. Please send your possible counterfeit checks to the FBI Questioned Document Examination unit for analysis free of charge (www.nist.gov). For information, please contact Antoine Frazier, Federal Bureau of Investigation, FBI Laboratory, 703-632-7293, Antoine.frazier@ic.fbi.gov.

A.12 Texas Missing Person DNA Database (UNTCHI)

In 2001, the Texas Missing Persons DNA database was founded at the University of North Texas Health Science Center campus. This was the first missing persons DNA database capable of analyzing both mitochondrial and STR systems and to participate in the federal database for missing persons maintained by the FBI. This database allows municipal, state, and federal crime laboratories to exchange and compare DNA profiles of missing persons and unidentified remains. Medical examiners, coroner's offices, the National Center of Missing Adults, the National Center for Missing and Exploited Children, and law enforcement agencies throughout the United States can request assistance with the submission, collection, and analysis of missing person's samples. The services are free of charge for the family of the missing person as well as for law enforcement.

A.13 Soil Databases

Soil is a type of trace evidence whose value is easily overlooked. Through soil, we can determine if the victim had been killed at another location and transported to the area where the body had been recovered. Soil components can determine the area in the United States, even in the world. The Web Soil Survey provides soil data and information obtained from the National Corporative Soil Survey. Web Soil Survey is operated by the USDA Natural Resources Conservation Service (NRCS) and allows access to the largest natural resources information system worldwide. Information of more than 95% of the nation's counties are included in the soil maps and data available online. Please contact your local USDA Service Center or the NRCS State Soil Scientist for questions and submission of soil samples for identification. The Department of Agriculture, USDA, Natural Resources Conservation Services maintain a database for soil survey by state, soil geography by state, and other important information about the different soils. More information is available at http://www.nrcs.usda.gov/wps/portal/nrcs/site/soils/home/ and at http://websoilsurvey.sc.egov.usda.gov/App/HomePage.htm.

A.14 Entomology Database

Forensic entomology refers to the insects found around and on a deceased. The forensic entomologist can determine the approximate time of death based on the developed stages of the different insects. Some insects are only present in specific areas of the United States. The Department of Entomology houses more than 35 million specimens, the largest entomology collection in the world. Almost 300,000 records are available in the online catalog, as well as the illustration archive records including images and data about published scientific illustrations (http://collections.nmnh.si.edu/search/ento). This database provides an excellent resource for insect identification, information that might lead to the area where the victim lived or where the victim had been murdered. Please visit http://collections.nmnh.si.edu/search/ento for more information and how to submit evidence.

References

Bowen, R. and Schneider, J. (2007). Forensic databases: Paint, shoe prints, and beyond. Retrieved from http://www.nij.gov/journals/258/pages/forensic-databases.aspx.
James, S. and Norby, J. (2005). *Forensic Science: An Introduction to Scientific and Investigative Techniques*. CRC Press, Boca Raton, FL.
National Institute of Justice. Retrieved from www.nij.gov.
National Institute of Standard and Technology. Retrieved from www.nist.gov.
Saferstein, R. (2011). *Criminalistics: An Introduction to Forensic Science*, 10th ed. Prentice Hall, Upper Saddle River, NJ.

Appendix B: Violent Crimes and Homicide Field Notes

CRIME SCENE UNIT
FIELD NOTES

Case #	

TYPE CRIME/INCIDENT	DEATH INVESTIGATION		DAY OF WEEK	MON	TUE	WED	THU	FRI	SAT	SUN

TIME & DATE NOTIFIED		TIME & DATE ARRIVED			TIME & DATE CLEARED	

NOTIFIED BY	COMMUNICATIONS SUPERVISOR		CSM		CPT		SGT		OTHER	

LOCATION OF SCENE	

NAME OF BUSINESS/ DEVELOPMENT	

ENVIRONMENTAL CONDITIONS

ENVIRONMENTAL CONDITIONS OUTSIDE (AT TIME OF ARRIVAL)	TEMPERATURE:	HUMIDITY:

ENVIRONMENTAL CONDITIONS INSIDE (AT TIME OF ARRIVAL)	TEMPERATURE:

BRIEFING AND WALK THROUGH OF SCENE

BRIEFING AT SCENE GIVEN BY		CASE AGENT	
WALKTHROUGH OF SCENE BY			
SYNOPSIS OF WHAT HAPPENED			

SEARCH WARRANT INFORMATION

SEARCH WARRANT REQUIRED	YES	NO	SEARCH WARRANT READ BY	
DATE/TIME SEARCH WARRANT SERVED				

345

CRIME SCENE UNIT FIELD NOTES

MEDICAL EXAMINER INFORMATION

MEDICAL EXAMINER INVESTIGATOR	YES	NO	NAME OF INVESTIGATOR	HARDING JOHNSON GLEASON STRASSEL OTHER:
TIME & DATE ME ARRIVED			TIME BODY REMOVED TO MEDICAL EXAMINERS OFFICE	
TRANSPORT PERSON(S)				
BODY BAG SEAL #		OTHER INFORMATION		

VICTIM INFORMATION

VICTIM'S NAME	

AGE		DOB		SEX	MALE FEMALE	RACE	WHITE BLACK HISPANIC OTHER

VICTIM'S ADDRESS	

VICTIM DECEASED	Yes No	VICTIM AT THE SCENE	Yes No

VICTIM'S INJURIES	

CLOTHING WORN	

CONDITION OF CLOTHING

DISHEVELED	YES	NO	PENETRATED OR OPEN	YES	NO	STAINED (BLOOD SEMEN ETC)	YES	NO
TORN	YES	NO	CUT	YES	NO	PUNCTURED	YES	NO	FASTENED	YES	NO

DOES IMPERFECTION IN CLOTHING CORRESPOND TO WOUNDS ON BODY?	YES	NO

IS CLOTHING APPROPRIATE FOR THE LOCATION AND CIRCUMSTANCES?	YES	NO

NOTES	

BODY POSITION	

CRIME SCENE UNIT FIELD NOTES

CONDITION

FRESH		BLOAT		ACTIVE DECAY		ADVANCED DECAY			
SKELETON		MUMMIFICATION		DISMEMBERMENT		INSECT ACTIVITY	YES	NO	

RIGOR:
LAVIDITY:
FROTH AT NOSE AND MOUTH:
NEEDLE MARKS:
WOUNDS, CUTS, SCRATCHES"

	HOMICIDE	SUICIDE	ACCIDENTAL	NATURAL	UNKNOWN	

\PERPETRATOR INFORMATION (LEAVE BLANK IF UNKNOWN)

PERPETRATOR'S NAME	

AGE		DOB		SEX	MALE FEMALE	RACE	WHITE BLACK HISPANIC OTHER

PERPETRATOR'S ADDRESS	

PERPETRATOR DECEASED	Yes No	PERPETRATOR AT THE SCENE	Yes No

PERPETRATOR'S INJURIES

CLOTHING WORN

CONDITION OF CLOTHING

DISHEVELED	YES	NO	PENETRATED OR OPEN	YES	NO	STAINED (BLOOD SEMEN ETC)	YES	NO
TORN	YES	NO	CUT	YES	NO	PUNCTURED	YES	NO	FASTENED	YES	NO

DOES IMPERFECTION IN CLOTHING CORRESPOND TO WOUNDS ON BODY?   YES   NO

IS CLOTHING APPROPRIATE FOR THE LOCATION AND CIRCUMSTANCES?   YES   NO

NOTES

CRIME SCENE UNIT FIELD NOTES

BODY POSITION	

CONDITION			
FRESH	BLOAT	ACTIVE DECAY	ADVANCED DECAY
SKELETON	MUMMIFICATION	DISMEMBERMENT	INSECT ACTIVITY	YES	NO

RIGOR:
LAVIDITY:
FROTH AT NOSE AND MOUTH:
NEEDLE MARKS:
WOUNDS, CUTS, SCRATCHES"

MANNER OF DEATH	HOMICIDE	SUICIDE	ACCIDENTAL	NATURAL	UNKNOWN
PRELIMINARY CAUSE OF DEATH					

ADDITIONAL NOTES:

CRIME SCENE UNIT FIELD NOTES

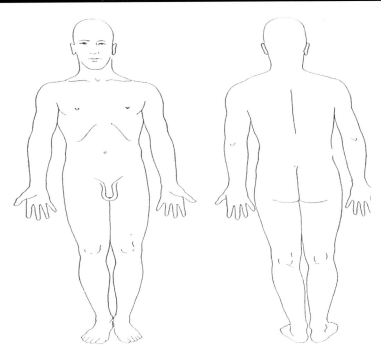

CRIME SCENE UNIT FIELD NOTES

Measurement chart (Body TRIANGULATION)

BODY MEASUREMENTS ITEM	Marker #	A	B			
HEAD						
RIGHT SHOULDER						
LEFT SHOULDER						
RIGHT ELBOW						
LEFT ELBOW						
RIGHT HAND						
LEFT HAND						
LOWER ABDOMEN OR CENTER OF BODY						
RIGHT KNEE						
LEFT KNEE						
RIGHT FOOT						
LEFT FOOT						

DISTANCE FROM TO	DISTANCE FROM TO
DISTANCE FROM TO	DISTANCE FROM TO
DISTANCE FROM TO	

CRIME SCENE UNIT FIELD NOTES

SCENE LOCATION TYPE

BUSINESS	INDUSTRIAL	RESIDENTIAL	CONSTRUCTION SITE	GOVERNMENT	PARK/RECREATION

GATED COMMUNITY	RURAL	FARM/AGRICULTURAL	OTHER

WATERWAY	RIVER	CANAL	POND	LAKE	BAY	GULF	FLOODED	N/A	WOODS	FIELD

OTHER

NOTES
_____
_____
_____
_____

ROADWAY INFORMATION

HIGHWAY NAME / NUMBER

ROADWAY CHARACTERISTICS	SINGLE LANE TWO LANE MULTIPLE LANES	# LANES RIGHT		# LANES LEFT		ROAD MARKED	YES NO

ROADWAY CONSTRUCTION	ASPHALT CONCRETE DIRT GRAVEL BRICK OTHER	ROADWAY IS	STRAIGHT OTHER	CURVED	FLAT	HILL

MEDIAN	YES NO	MEDIAN TYPE	NOT APPLICABLE GRASS CONCRETE GUARD RAIL OTHER

CURB		SHOULDER IS	GRASS	DIRT	PAVED	SIDEWALK	DITCH	CANAL	OTHER INFORMATION:

HIGHWAY NAME / NUMBER

ROADWAY CHARACTERISTICS	SINGLE LANE TWO LANE MULTIPLE LANES	# LANES RIGHT		# LANES LEFT		ROAD MARKED	YES NO

ROADWAY CONSTRUCTION	ASPHALT CONCRETE DIRT GRAVEL BRICK OTHER	ROADWAY IS	STRAIGHT OTHER	CURVED	FLAT	HILL

MEDIAN	YES NO	MEDIAN TYPE	NOT APPLICABLE GRASS CONCRETE GUARD RAIL OTHER

CURB		SHOULDER IS	GRASS	DIRT	PAVED	SIDEWALK	DITCH	CANAL	OTHER INFORMATION:

ACCESS TO THE SCENE

CRIME SCENE UNIT FIELD NOTES

ACCESS TO THE SCENE CONTINUED:

STRUCTURE TYPE

SINGLE FAMILY RESIDENCE		DUPLEX		APARTMENT		CONDOMINIUM		MANUFACTURED HOME/TRAILER		TENT	

GARAGE		SHOPPING CENTER/STRIP MALL		BARN		WAREHOUSE		FACTORY		RESTAURANT		STORE	

BUSINESS		OFFICE BLDG		HOTEL/MOTEL		MEDICAL/HOSPITAL		SCHOOL		GOV BUILDING		CHURCH/SYNAGOGUE	

CONSTRUCTION SITE		FENCED COMPOUND		BOAT DOCK		MOTOR HOME		AIRCRAFT	

CAR SALES LOT BOAT SALES LOT		BRIDGE		VEHICLE (CAR BUS, TRUCK, ETC)		BOAT	

OTHER	

BUILDING CONSTRUCTION

CBS		WOOD FRAME		METAL FRAME		CONCRETE PANEL		VINYL SIDING		BRICK OR BRICK SIDING		WOOD SIDING	

METAL & CONCRETE BLDG		ALUMINUM SIDING		SHEET METAL		OTHER DESCRIBE	

BUILDING COLOR	

TRIM COLOR	

ROOF TYPE

MANSARD (GABLE WITH FLAT TOP)		FLAT		GABLE (TRIANGLE)		CROSS GABLE 2 PARTS THAT CROSS		HIPPED		CROSS HIPPED 2 PARTS THAT CROSS		PYRAMIDAL HIPPED FORMS PYRAMID		GAMBREL (DELL SHAPE OLD BARN ROOF	

SHED		SALT BOX NOT SYMMETRICAL		OTHER		DESCRIBE:	

ROOF CONSTRUCTION	ASPHALT SHINGLE		TILE		METAL		GRAVEL		ROLLED ASPHALT		OTHER	

ROOF COLOR	

CRIME SCENE UNIT FIELD NOTES

BUILDING FACES		NUMBER OF STORIES		# OF BEDROOM & BATH ROOMS	

DRIVEWAY/PARKING LOT LOCATED AT							
DRIVEWAY CONSTRUCTED OF	CONCRETE	DIRT	ASPHALT	BRICK	GRAVEL	OTHER	

LANDSCAPE INFORMATION

CRIME SCENE UNIT FIELD NOTES

WINDOW TYPES

TYPE	X	LOCATION
UP & DOWN DOUBLE HUNG (SINGLE WINDOW)		
UP & DOWN DOUBLE HUNG (TWO WINDOWS SIDE BY SIDE)		
SLIDER (TO LEFT OR RIGHT)		
CASEMENT (SWING OUT FROM SIDE)		
AWNING WINDOW		
JALOUSIE		
DORMER WINDOW (STICK OUT OF ROOF WITH ROOF OF THEIR OWN)		
FANLIGHT (SEMI CIRCLE WINDOW OVER DOOR OR WINDOW)		
SIDELIGHT (WINDOWS BESIDE DOOR)		
FIXED PANEL (PICTURE WINDOW OR SIDE-LIGHT)		
ARCHITECTURAL SHAPE CURVED /ANGLED		
TRANSOM (WINDOW OVER DOOR)		
DORMER WINDOW (GABLED OR ARCHED ON ROOF)		
SCREENS		

FLOOR TYPE

TYPE	X	LOCATION
TILE		
CARPET		
LINOLEUM		
WOOD		
CONCRETE		
DIRT		
METAL		
OTHER		

DOOR TYPE		
TYPE	X	LOCATION
WOOD		
GLASS		
SLIDING GLASS		
OVERHEAD GARAGE TYPE		
FRENCH DOOR		
LOUVRE DOOR		
BIFOLD DOOR (2-4 SECTIONS		
POCKET DOOR		
METAL		
METAL SLIDING		
SCREEN		
WOOD WITH GLASS		
METAL WITH GLASS		
METAL SLIDING DOOR		

INTERIOR WALL INFORMATION	
PAINTED	
WALL PAPER	
TILE	
WOOD	
METAL	
CONCRETE	
OTHER	

CRIME SCENE UNIT FIELD NOTES

WEAPON INFORMATION

WEAPON INVOLVED	YES	N0	TYPE OF WEAPON	FIREARM CUTTING STABBING BLUNT FORCE OTHER

FIREARM TYPE	CUTTING TYPE		BLUNT FORCE TYPE	
REVOLVER	KNIFE, FIXED BLADE		BALL BAT	
SEMI AUTO PISTOL	KNIFE FOLDING BLADE		STICK	
RIFLE BOLT ACTION	KNIFE LOCK BLADE		CLUB	
RIFLE SEMI AUTO	SWORD		TOOL HANDLE	
RIFLE SINGLE SHOT	MACHETE		TOOL (HAMMER, ETC)	
SHOTGUN PUMP	BROKEN GLASS		MOTOR VEHICLE	
SHOTGUN SEMI AUTO	SHARP TOOL (SCREW DRIVER, ICE PICK ETC)		PIPE	
SHOTGUN DBL BARREL	BROKEN BOTTLE		BOTTLE	
SHOTGUN SINGLE BARREL				
OTHER	OTHER		OTHER	
IF OTHER DESCRIBE				

MAKE		MODEL		CALIBER	
SERIAL NUMBER					
DESCRIPTION OF WEAPON					
LOCATION OF WEAPON				PLACARD #	

MAKE		MODEL		CALIBER	
SERIAL NUMBER					
DESCRIPTION OF WEAPON					
LOCATION OF WEAPON				PLACARD #	

MAKE		MODEL		CALIBER	
SERIAL NUMBER					
DESCRIPTION OF WEAPON					
LOCATION OF WEAPON				PLACARD #	

CRIME SCENE UNIT FIELD NOTES

CARTRIDGES IN WEAPON					
REVOLVER			**MAGAZINE FED FIREARM**		
WEAPON DESCRIPTION & PLACARD #	# LIVE ROUNDS IN CYLINDER	# OF FIRED CASINGS IN REVOLVER	WEAPON DESCRIPTION & PLACARD #	# LIVE ROUNDS IN MAGAZINE	ROUND CHAMBERED YES OR NO

POSITION SKETCH OF FIRED AND LIVE ROUNDS IN REVOLVER

AMMUNITION FOUND AT THE SCENE					
BRAND OF AMMO	CALIBER	# OF LIVE ROUNDS	# OF CASINGS	# OF SPENT PROJECTILES	LOCATION OR PLACARD NUMBER

CRIME SCENE UNIT FIELD NOTES

VEHICLE INFORMATION
VEHICLE #1 DESCRIPTION

MARKER #		VICTIM		PERPETRATOR		OTHER	

MAKE		MODEL			YEAR			BODY	

COLOR			TAG #			STATE	

V.I.N. COPY FROM VEHICLE													

VEHICLE INTERIOR

FRONT SEAT	MIDDLE SEATS	REAR SEAT	FLOOR	UPHOLSTERY	COLOR		
BENCH	BENCH	BENCH	VINYL	LEATHER			
BUCKET	BUCKET	CPT CHAIR	CARPET	CLOTH	TRIM COLOR		
SPLIT BENCH	SPLIT BENCH	FOLDING BENCH	OTHER	VINYL			
CPT CHAIR	CPT CHAIR	OTHER			CENTER CONSOLE	YES	NO
CUSTOM	CUSTOM		TRANSMISSION TYPE	MANUEL SHIFT	AUTOMATIC SHIFT	FLOOR	STEERING COLUMN

ODOMETER READING		LEFT FRONT SEAT MEASUREMENT FROM FIREWALL TO LOWER EDGE OF SEAT		RIGHT FRONT SEAT MEASUREMENT FROM FIREWALL TO LOWER EDGE OF SEAT	
TRIP METER READING		TOP LEFT FRONT SEAT MEASUREMENT FROM HEAD REST TO DASH		TOP RIGHT FRONT SEAT MEASUREMENT FROM HEAD REST TO DASH	
RADIO SETTING		**FUEL AMOUNT**			

VEHICLE #2 DESCRIPTION

MARKER #		VICTIM		PERPETRATOR		OTHER	

MAKE		MODEL			YEAR			BODY	

COLOR			TAG #			STATE	

V.I.N. COPY FROM VEHICLE													

VEHICLE INTERIOR

FRONT SEAT	MIDDLE SEATS	REAR SEAT	FLOOR	UPHOLSTERY	COLOR		
BENCH	BENCH	BENCH	VINYL	LEATHER			
BUCKET	BUCKET	CPT CHAIR	CARPET	CLOTH	TRIM COLOR		
SPLIT BENCH	SPLIT BENCH	FOLDING BENCH	OTHER	VINYL			
CPT CHAIR	CPT CHAIR	OTHER			CENTER CONSOLE	YES	NO
CUSTOM	CUSTOM		TRANSMISSION TYPE	MANUEL SHIFT	AUTOMATIC SHIFT	FLOOR	STEERING COLUMN

ODOMETER READING		LEFT FRONT SEAT MEASUREMENT FROM FIREWALL TO LOWER EDGE OF SEAT		RIGHT FRONT SEAT MEASUREMENT FROM FIREWALL TO LOWER EDGE OF SEAT	
TRIP METER READING		TOP LEFT FRONT SEAT MEASUREMENT FROM HEAD REST TO DASH		TOP RIGHT FRONT SEAT MEASUREMENT FROM HEAD REST TO DASH	
RADIO SETTING		**FUEL AMOUNT**			

CRIME SCENE UNIT FIELD NOTES

CONDITION OF THE SCENE

CRIME SCENE UNIT FIELD NOTES

CONDITION OF THE SCENE

CRIME SCENE UNIT FIELD NOTES

CONDITION OF THE SCENE

CRIME SCENE UNIT FIELD NOTES

CONDITION OF THE SCENE

CRIME SCENE UNIT FIELD NOTES

Measurement chart **(EVIDENCE TRIANGULATION)**

ITEM	Marker #	A	B	C	D	E

DISTANCE FROM	TO		DISTANCE FROM	TO	
DISTANCE FROM	TO		DISTANCE FROM	TO	
DISTANCE FROM	TO		DISTANCE FROM	TO	

CRIME SCENE UNIT FIELD NOTES

ITEM	Marker #					

Measurement chart *(EVIDENCE TRIANGULATION)*

DISTANCE FROM	TO		DISTANCE FROM	TO
DISTANCE FROM	TO		DISTANCE FROM	TO
DISTANCE FROM	TO		DISTANCE FROM	TO

CRIME SCENE UNIT FIELD NOTES

Measurement Chart

CHART DEPICTING DISTANCE BETWEEN PIECES OF EVIDENCE OR ITEMS OF INTEREST			
ITEM	PLACARD #	DISTANCE FROM BODY OR KEY POINT OF INTEREST	DIRECTION OR COMPASS HEADING

CRIME SCENE UNIT FIELD NOTES

CRIME SCENE PROCESSING INFORMATION
LATENT PROCESSING   (AREA OR ITEMS PROCESSED)

TYPE OF EXAMINATION	BRUSH AND POWDER	MAGNA BRUSH	NINHYDRIN	PHOTOGRAPHED	SUPER GLUE
PERSON DOING PROCESSING					

TYPE OF EXAMINATION	ALTERNATE LIGHT SOURCE	FLUORESCENT POWDERS	OTHER CHEMICAL PROCESSING
PERSON DOING PROCESSING			

NUMBER OF LATENT LIFTS			

CRIME SCENE UNIT FIELD NOTES

PHOTOGRAPHY DETAILS

PHOTOGRAPHS TAKEN	YES	NO	EXTERIOR	YES	NO	TAKEN BY		INTERIOR	YES	NO	TAKEN BY	
AERIALS	YES	NO	TAKEN BY		VIDEO OF SCENE	YES	NO	DONE BY				

CAMERA TYPE	CANNON REBEL T1i DIGITAL		CANNON REBEL XTi DIGITAL		CANNON REBEL DIGITAL	
CAMERA TYPE	OTHER					

LENS	MACRO 28-90MM	28-80MM	18-55MM	Other lens	MEDIA	COMPACTFLASH	SANDISK 8GB	

INSIDE LIGHTING CONDITIONS	ELECTRIC LIGHT	FLASH ASSIST USED	NO LIGHTING	OTHER	

OUTSIDE LIGHTING CONDITIONS	SUNLIGHT	DARK	FLASH ASSIST USED	ELECTRIC LIGHT	OTHER	

PHOTO PLACARDS USED (YES) (NO)	NUMBERS FROM	LETTERS TO	NUMBERS FROM	LETTERS TO	NUMBERS FROM	LETTERS TO

# Of exposed Photographs		OTHER	

OTHER PROCESSING:

BLOODSTAIN SWABS	OTHER DNA SWABS	NINHYDRIN	LUMINAL EXAMINATION	OTHER	
PERSON CONDUCTING TEST	PERSON CONDUCTING TEST	PERSON CONDUCTING TEST	PERSON CONDUCTING TEST	PERSON CONDUCTING TEST	

NOTES:

CRIME SCENE UNIT FIELD NOTES

OTHER PROCESSING:

VACUUM	ACID PHOSPHATES TEST	GSR	BLOOD TEST (LIST TYPE OF TEST USED)	ALTERNATE LIGHT SOURCE	LASER TRAJECTORY
PERSON CONDUCTING TEST	PERSON CONDUCTING TEST	PERSON CONDUCTING TEST	PERSON CONDUCTING TEST	PERSON CONDUCTING TEST	PERSON CONDUCTING TEST

NOTES:

TRAJECTORY RODS	METAL DETECTION		EXTENDED SEARCHES	MEASUREMENTS	
PERSON CONDUCTING TEST	PERSON CONDUCTING TEST	PERSON CONDUCTING TEST	PERSON CONDUCTING TEST	PERSON CONDUCTING TEST	

NOTES:

CRIME SCENE UNIT FIELD NOTES

OTHER PROCESSING:

PLASTER CASTING		RUBBER CASTING		OTHER CHEMICAL EXAMINATION: DESCRIBE		OTHER PROCESSING: DESCRIBE	
PERSON CONDUCTING TEST		PERSON CONDUCTING TEST		PERSON CONDUCTING TEST		PERSON CONDUCTING TEST	

NOTES:

OTHER PROCESSING NOTES:

CRIME SCENE UNIT FIELD NOTES

	PHOTOGRAPHIC PLACARDS AND EVIDENCE LOCATION (SUPPLEMENT TO SKETCH) LIST ALL MARKERS		
ITEM #	ITEM DESCRIPTION AND LOCATION COLLECTED FROM	PHOTO MARKER #	TIME COLLECTED

CRIME SCENE UNIT FIELD NOTES

PHOTOGRAPHIC PLACARDS AND EVIDENCE LOCATION (SUPPLEMENT TO SKETCH) LIST ALL MARKERS			
ITEM #	ITEM DESCRIPTION AND LOCATION COLLECTED FROM	PHOTO MARKER #	TIME COLLECTED

CRIME SCENE UNIT FIELD NOTES

ROUGH SKETCH

CRIME SCENE UNIT FIELD NOTES

ROUGH SKETCH

CRIME SCENE UNIT FIELD NOTES

ROUGH SKETCH

Index

Page numbers followed by f, t, d, and m indicate figures, tables, documents, and maps, respectively.

A

Accessory lights, 25
Accident scene photography, 60–62
  hit-and-run, 61–62
Accidental death, 241–242, 249t; *see also*
      Death; Manner of death
  carbon monoxide poisoning, 277–278
ACID, *see* Automated Counterfeiting
      Identification Database (ACID)
Acid phosphatase (AP) kit, 15, 15f
Adhesion of liquid, 197
Adobe Photoshop, 57, 64
Adult age indicators, 179
AFIS, *see* Automated Fingerprint
      Identification System (AFIS)
Age, estimation of, 178–180
  sexual dimorphism and, 179
  skeletal development and, 178–179
  stature and, 180
  teeth development and, 179
Aircraft accidents, *see* Aviation accidents
Algor mortis, 244
Allometry, 180
Almeida, Tony, 328–337
Altered bloodstain patterns, 199t, 207,
      208t, 209–210; *see also* Bloodstain
      pattern analysis
Aluminum Black solution, 86–88, 88t
Amido Black, 23, 84–85, 85f
Amino acids, and DFO, 84
Angle, flash units, 39; *see also* Flash
Angle of impact, bloodstain pattern
      analysis, 209–210
Anthropology
  age estimation, *see* Age, estimation of
  case, 180
  categories, 177

cause and manner of death, 180
concept, 177
human remains and, 177
report, 180
sexual dimorphism, 179
skeletal development, 178–179
stature and, 180
taphonomic assessment, 177–178
teeth development, 179
Aperture priority, 38–39; *see also*
      Photography
Archaeology, 177
Arch fingerprint patterns, 67, 68f
Area of convergence, bloodstain pattern,
      212–214, 213f
Areas of origin, bloodstain pattern analysis,
      212
  string method for, 214–215
Arrival on scene, 108
Asphyxia
  by hanging, 278–280
  sexual, 280
Asphyxiant gases
  effects of, 277
  inhalation of, 277
  suicide through, 277
Attended *vs.* unattended death, 274
Autoerotic asphyxiation, 280
Autoerotic death, 280
Autofocus equipped cameras, 30–31
Automated Counterfeiting Identification
      Database (ACID), 343
Automated Fingerprint Identification
      System (AFIS), 89, 339
Autopsy; *see also* Death investigation
  algor mortis, 244
  asphyxia by hanging, 278–280
  autoerotic death, 280

cause of death, 241
concept, 241
drowning victims, 285–287
German tourists case, 246–248
gunshot deaths, 282–283
gunshot wounds, 266–268
internal, 268–270
lab submission for evidence from,
    272–273, 273t
livor mortis, 242, 243f
manner of death, 241–242
mechanism of death, 242
purpose of, 248–272
rigor mortis, 243–244
sexual asphyxia, 280
SIDS, 289–297
visual/external, 252, 263
Aviation accidents, 312–321; see also
        National Transportation and
        Safety Board (NTSB)
    aircraft description, 317d
    Cross Creek plane crash, 317–321
    CSI response, 315–317
    incident command, 314–315
    local response to, 314–317

B

Baseline mapping, 131–133, 131f–132f
Basic Clandestine Laboratory Certification
        School (DEA), 311–312
Beechwood Baron 58 crash, in Cross Creek,
        South Fort Myers, Florida, 317–321
Bio-Foam, 97, 97f; see also Three-
        dimensional shoe impressions
Biohazard materials, 5
Birchwood Casey Brass Black, 86–87
Bird's-eye view/overview sketch, 124, 125f;
        see also Sketching
Black powder, see Carbon powder
Blood
    anatomical aspects, 196–197
    detection kit, 18–23
    evidence collection kit, 8–9, 9f
    fingerprint processing in, 84–85
    physical properties, 197–198
    surface tension, 197, 198
Blood sample, from deceased victim, 270
Bloodstain card, 270, 270f
Bloodstain pattern analysis, 195–218
    altered patterns, 199t, 207, 208t, 209–210
    angle of impact, 209–210

area of convergence, determining,
        212–214, 213f
    areas of origin, 212
    computerized, 217–218
    concept, 195
    directionality, 209–210
    documentation, 212–217
    factors to be determined by, 195–196
    levels of, 198
    passive/gravity pattern, 198, 199t,
        200–202
    safety of analysts/investigators, 212
    spatter patterns, 199t, 202, 203t, 204t,
        205–207
    target surface differences, 209
    tool kit, 17–18, 17f
Bloodstains
    classification of, 198
    documenting, 212–217
Blowfly/maggots, life cycle of, 246; see also
        Time of death
Blue filters, 31
Bluestar, 22–23
    photography, 41
Blunt force trauma, 180
Boat
    for human smuggling, 322–325
    identification template, 326d
Body boxes, 148
Body Farm, see Southeast Texas Applied
        Forensic Science Facility
Body panorama photos, 58–59
Body search warrant, 117–118
Body temperature, and time of death
        estimation, 245
Boiling water method, 72
Bollinger, Susan A., 182
Bolton, Susan, 191
Bone density, 179
Bones; see also Age, estimation of;
        Anthropology; Skeletal
        development
    changes, 178
    development, 178–179
    recovering, 161
Bonita Springs, Florida, 120
Booties, 5
Botany, 190–192; see also Plants
Brass Black solution, 86–88, 88t
Brumit, Paula C., 182
Bugs, see Entomology; Insects
Bullet holes

glass fractures, 236–237
    radial fractures, 237
    windshield, 236, 237f
Bullet trajectory, 1
    case, 233–235
    reconstruction, 231–232
Bullet *vs.* cartridges, 222
Bureau of Alcohol, Tobacco, Firearms and
        Explosives (ATF), 339, 341
Burglar in attic case, 104
Bytheway, Joan, 180

C

Caliber, 221; *see also* Cartridges
Camera(s)
    autofocus equipped, 30–31
    batteries, 30
    digital, 29–30
    equipment, 29–33, 30f
    filters, 31–32
    flash, 34
    lenses, 30–31
    storage media, 30, 32–33; *see also*
        Memory cards
Camera Armor, 30
Camera kit, 3, 4f
Cannabis sativa, 300; *see also* Marijuana
        growing operations
Capillarity of liquid, 197
Carbon monoxide (CO) poisoning
    accidental death by, 277–278
    suicide by, 277
Carbon powder, 78; *see also* Powder for
        fingerprints
    shoe impression with, 90–92
    steps for fingerprinting using, 79–80
Car exhaust fumes, suicide by, 277
Cartridges, 221; *see also* Firearms
    bullet *vs.*, 222
    caliber, 221
    categories, 221
    gauges, 221
    identification markings on live or spent,
        224
Cause of death, 241, 249t; *see also* Autopsy;
        Death
Checklist, for photography, 65–66
Children, trafficking of, 322
Clandestine graves/gravesites, 164–174
    body removal/remains transportation,
        173–174

clearing from, 174
    condition of body, 173
    excavation, 167–168
    insects/bugs, 174
    outer and inner perimeter, 165
    plant material, 174
    recovery of body, 168–172
    searching for, 164, 165f
    setting up a grid, 167
    7-year-old boy, 171–172, 172f
    surface evidence collection, 165–166
Close-up photographs, 55–57
    Adobe Photoshop and, 57
    altered, 57–58
    with labeled scale, 57f
Clothing with powder residues, 230
CODIS, *see* Combined DNA Index System
        (CODIS)
Cohesion of liquid, 197
Combined DNA Index System (CODIS),
        272, 340–341
Commercial airplane accidents, *see*
        Aviation accidents
Compact Flash (CF) memory card, 33
Compass method, *see* Four corners or
        compass method
Computerized bloodstain pattern analysis,
        217–218
Concentric fractures, 235, 236, 236f, 237f;
        see also Glass fractures
Consent, searches with, 118–119, 119d
Contact wound, 267; *see also* Gunshot
        wounds
Containers
    cardboard boxes, 145, 146–147
    paper bags, 145, 146
    plastic and metal, 147–148
    plastic bags, 147, 147f
Contamination, 4–5
    first responders and, 104–105
    prevention, 5
    protective gear, 5, 6f
Corneal clouding, 245; *see also* Time of
        death
Coroner
    description, 240
    responsibility, 240
    vs. medical examiner, 239–240, 240m
Cover-up attempt, 275
Crime scene
    contamination, *see* Contamination
    documentation, *see* Documentation

investigations, sequence of, 122t
   process, 121
   reconstruction, *see* Reconstruction of
     scene
   searches, *see* Searches
   sketching, *see* Sketching
Crime scene investigator (CSI)
   arrival on scene, 108
   autopsy work sheet for, 257d–262d
   aviation accidents and, 315–317
   documenting deceased, 250–251, 252t
   duties of, 1
   electrocution deaths, 288
   and excavations, 163–164
   gunshot victims, 282–283
   initial call for, 107–108
   officer-involved shooting, 327–328
   SIDS, 289, 297
   work sheet template for, 257d–262d
Crime scene log, first responders, 106, 107d
Criminal investigator
   defined, 239
   vs. MLDI, 239
Cross Creek plane crash, 317–321
Cross-protection sketch, 125, 127f; *see also*
     Sketching
CSI, *see* Crime scene investigator (CSI)
Cuba, 322–325; *see also* Human smuggling
Cuban Adjustment Act of 1966, 323
Cuban Coast Guard, 323
Cubans, human smuggling of, 322–325
Cyanoacrylate fuming methods, *see*
     Superglue fuming

D

Dadmun, Mark D., 75–76
Database(s)
   ACID, 343
   entomology, 344
   FISH, 342
   glass evidence reference, 342–343
   IAFIS, 339
   IBIS, 339–340
   ink library, 342
   NIBIN, 269, 341
   prescription drugs, 341
   RxList, 341
   soil, 343–344
   SoleMate, 340
   Texas Missing Persons DNA database, 343
   TreadMark, 340
   TreadMate, 340
Daylight, 33–34; *see also* Sunlight
DEA, *see* Drug Enforcement
     Administration (DEA)
Death
   accidental, *see* Accidental death
   attended *vs.* unattended, 274
   autoerotic, 280
   cause of, 241, 249t
   homicide, 241, 249t
   manner of, 241–242, 249t
   mechanism of, 242
   natural, 242, 249t
   power tools, 280–281, 281f
   sexual asphyxia, 280
   suicide, *see* Suicide
   time of, 244–246
   undetermined, 242, 249t
Death investigation; *see also* Autopsy
   asphyxia by hanging, 278–280
   coroner *vs.* medical examiner, 239–241,
     240m
   criminal investigator *vs.* MLDI, 239
   defined, 239
   drowning, 285–286
   drug overdoses, 283–284
   electrocution, 286–289
   gunshot, 282
   gunshot victims, 282–283
   poisoning, 284–285
   response to, 274–275
   sexual asphyxia, 280
   suicide, *see* Suicide
Deceased person, blood sample from, 270
Deceased person, inked fingerprints from,
     70–74
   boiling water method, 72
   fluid injection method, 72
   peeled skin method, 72
   processing method, 71
Decomposition of dead body, 245–246;
     see also Time of death
Dehumidifiers, 300
Dental identification, 181–183
   grin line or GLID technique, 182–183
Department of Agriculture (USDA)
   NRCS, *see* Natural Resources
     Conservation Service (NRCS)
   Service Center, 344
The Department of Entomology, 344
Department of Health and Human Services
   SIDS template, 290d–296d, 297

Depth of field (DOF), 36–37, 36f; *see also* Photography
  aperture priority, 38
  f/2, 36
  f/22, 36, 37
  f/stop, 36, 37
DFO
  amino acids and, 84
  fingerprint processing on porous surface, 84
Diaphysis, 178
Digital cameras, 29–30; *see also* Camera(s)
Digital single lens reflex camera (DSLR), 29
Dirt, casting tire impression in, 97
Distance determination, 227–230
  gunshots fired at 1 inch or less, 228, 229f
  gunshots fired at 12 to 18 inches, 228
  gunshots fired at distance over 3 feet, 228
  shotguns, 228
Distant gunshot wounds, 268; *see also* Gunshot wounds
DNA Identification Act, 340–341
DNA testing, 272
  seedpods, 191
  sexual assault cases, 157
Documentation, 1–4
  mapping, *see* Mapping
  motor vehicles used in crime, 152, 153d–154d
  note taking, 2; *see also* Note taking
  photographic, *see* Photography
  sketching, *see* Sketching
  tools, 1–4
DOF, *see* Depth of field (DOF)
Double murder case, in Florida, 140–143
Drowning
  death investigation, 285–286
  vehicles, 286
  victims floating in pool, lake, or river, 286
Drug Enforcement Administration (DEA), 299
  Basic Clandestine Laboratory Certification School, 311–312
Drug investigations, 299–312
  marijuana growing operations, 299–308
  methamphetamine, 308–312, 309f
Drug overdoses
  case of Anna Nicole Smith, 284
  death investigation, 283–284

Drug testing kit, 11, 12f
DSLR, *see* Digital single lens reflex camera (DSLR)
Duties, of CSI, 1

E

Earth's orbit, satellites, in, 134; *see also* Global positioning system (GPS)
Electricity, death by, *see* Electrocution
Electrocution
  crime scene response, 288
  death investigation, 286–289
  farm worker case, 289
  signs, 288
Electromagnetic spectrum, 41, 42f
Electrostatic dust lifting (ESDL), 93, 94f
Electrostatic dust print-lifting device, 93
Elevation sketching, 124, 126f; *see also* Sketching
Elimination fingerprints, 69–70
  kit, 69, 70f
  steps to be followed, 69–70
  suspect fingerprints, 70
Emergency operations center (EOC), 34
Entering crime scene, legalities for, 108–120
Entomology, 183–190, 246
  database, 344
  defined, 183, 344
  evidence collection kit, 9–10, 10f
  medico-legal, 183
  specimens/sample collection on scene, 187, 188d–189d
  time of death and, 183–184, 246
Entrance wounds, 268; *see also* Gunshot wounds
EOC, *see* Emergency operations center (EOC)
Epiphyses, 178
Equipment
  excavations, 161–163
ESDL, *see* Electrostatic dust lifting (ESDL)
Evidence collection; *see also* Searches
  autopsy, 270–272
  blood sample, 270
  clothes/clothing, 270–272
  crime scene search and, 143–144
  paper listing, 150
  property receipt, 150, 151d
  sequence of, 149–150
  steps of, 145t
  tools, 4–15

Excavation kit, 25
Excavations, 161–176
    basic crime scene rules, 161
    CSI team and, 163–164
    equipment, 161–163
    legal implications, 161
    prisoners and, 163
    site information, 163
Exigent circumstances, 119–120
Exit wounds, 268; see also Gunshot wounds
Expert witness, 63
Exploded view sketch, see Cross-protection
    sketch
External autopsy, 252, 263

F

F/2, and DOF, 36
F/22, and DOF, 36, 37
Face mask, 5
Facial reconstruction, 181
Farm worker case, 289
FBI, see Federal Bureau of Investigation
    (FBI)
Federal Aviation Agency (FAA), 313
Federal Bureau of Investigation (FBI), 340
    CODIS software, 340–341
    IAFIS, 339
    missing persons database, 343
    National Automotive Paint File, 340
    Questioned Document Examination
        unit, 343
Female pelvis, 179
Fibers
    motor vehicles used in crime and, 158
Film plane, keeping parallel to surface, 38
Filters, 31–32
    blue, 31
    defined, 31
    orange, 31
    polarizing, 31
    red, 31, 32
Fingerprint(s), 67–89
    in blood, 84–85
    categories, 72–73
    chemical processing on porous surfaces,
        81–84
    detection kit, 16–17, 16f
    elimination, 69–72
    inked, see Inked fingerprints
    latent, 72, 73–78
    motor vehicles used in crime, 158

    on nonporous surfaces, 73–76; see also
        Superglue fuming
    powder processing, 78–81
    special processing methods, 85–89
    superglue method, see Superglue
        fuming
Fingerprint patterns
    arch, 67, 68f
    loop, 67, 69f
    whorl, 67, 68f
Firearms
    bullet, 222
    cartridges, 221, 222; see also Cartridges
    classification, 218
    clearing, 222–223
    collection and preservation, 224–227
    gunshot death investigation, 282–283
    gunshot residue kit, 230–231
    identifying, 224
    packaging, cardboard boxes, 146
    revolver, 218–219, 218f
    rifles, 220–221, 221f
    safety, see Safety of firearms
    semi-automatic handguns, 219–220,
        219f
    serial number restoration, 227
    shotguns, 220–221, 220f
    shotgun shells, 221
    suicide and, 282
    target distance determination, 227–230
    trajectory reconstruction, 231–235
First responders, 103–106
    crime scene contamination and,
        104–105
    crime scene log, 106, 107d
    defined, 103
    safety, 103–104
    securing scene, 104
    setting inner and outer perimeter,
        105–106
FISH, see Forensic Information System for
    Handwriting (FISH)
Flash; see also Photography
    angle, effect of, 39
    camera, 34, 39; see also Painting with
        light
    DSLR digital cameras, 39
    image quality, 39
Florida Power and Light Company, 288
Fluid injection method, 72
Fluorescent powders, 78, 79t; see also
    Powder for fingerprints

Footwear impressions, 62–63, 63f
Forensic entomology, *see* Entomology
Forensic Information System for Handwriting (FISH), 342
Forensic photography, *see* Photography
Four corners or compass method, 54, 55f
Fourth Amendment, 108, 111
Freezing movement, shutter speed for, 37
F/stop, and DOF, 36, 37
Fume-A-Wand, 78

G

Gauges, 221; *see also* Cartridges
German tourists, autopsy of, 246–248
Girls, trafficking for sex slavery, 322
Glass
    evidence reference database, 342–343
    laminated, 235
    pieces for packaging, 147–148
    tempered, 235
Glass fractures
    bullet holes, 236–237
    gunshot, 235, 236f
    matching, 180, 235–237
    3R rule, 236
GLID technique, 182–183
Global positioning system (GPS), 134
Gloves, 5
Go Teams, of NTSB, 312
GPS, *see* Global positioning system (GPS)
Greiss test, 230
Grid search pattern, 139, 140f; *see also* Outdoor crime scene searches
Grin line identification, 182–183; *see also* Dental identification
Gulf of Mexico, 323, 324; *see also* Human smuggling
Gun boxes, 145
Gunpowder residues
    clothing with, 230
    Greiss test, 230
Gunshot, glass fractures and, 235
    concentric fractures, 235, 236f
    radial fractures, 235
Gunshot deaths, autopsy, 282–283
Gunshot residue kit, 14–15, 14f, 230–231
    ISid2, 230, 231
Gunshots
    distance determination, 227–230
    projectile trajectory, *see* Bullet trajectory

Gunshot wounds, 180, 266–268
    classification, 266–267
    contact wound, 267
    distant, 268
    entrance, 268
    exit, 268
    intermediate range, 268
    near contact wound, 267

H

Hairnet, 5
Hairs
    mitochondrial DNA in, 5
    motor vehicles used in crime and, 158
Handguns; *see also* Firearms
    revolvers, 218–219, 218f
    semi-automatic, 219–220, 219f
Hand tools, 24
Hanging, asphyxia by, 278–280
    case, 279–280
Hard contact wound, 267
Hard steel dies, 227
Hauptmann, Bruno, 190
Helentjaris, Tim, 191
Helium bag mechanism, for suicide, 277
HemoSpat, 217–218; *see also* Bloodstain pattern analysis
Hendry County, Florida, 289
Hexagon OBTI presumptive test, 19–20, 20f
Hinton, Robert, 180
Hit-and-run accident photography, 61–62
Homicide, 241, 249t; *see also* Death; Manner of death
    case of Bonita Springs, Florida, 120
Human remains; *see also* Anthropology; Excavations
    anthropologists and, 177
    categories, 161
    prehistoric, 161
    reasons for recovering, 161
    recent, 161
Human smuggling, 321, 322–325
    crime scene response to, 325–326
    operational method of, 323–324, 325
    two-boat approach, 323–324
Human trafficking, 321–322
    crime scene response to, 325–326
    sex slavery, 322
Hyper focal focus, 37; *see also* Depth of field (DOF)

I

IAFIS, *see* Integrated Automated Fingerprint
    Identification System (IAFIS)
IBIS, *see* Integrated Ballistics Identification
    System (IBIS)
ICS, *see* Incident Command System (ICS)
Identification photographs, 44–45, 44f
    color photos, 45
Iliac auricular surface, 179
Illicit drugs, 283; *see also* Drug overdoses
Impression evidence kit, 26–27, 27f
Impression pattern evidence
    fingerprints, *see* Fingerprint(s)
    shoe impression, *see* Shoe impressions
    tire impressions, *see* Tire impressions
Incident command, aviation accidents,
    314–315
Incident Command System (ICS), 315
Indoor crime scene searches, 135–138, 143
    managing, 143
    pie search pattern, 136, 137f
    spiral search pattern, 136
    wheel search pattern, 136, 137f
    zone search pattern, 136, 137, 137f
Infrared photography, 43–44
Initial call for CSI, 107–108
Injuries, photographing, 59
Inked fingerprints
    boiling water method, 72
    deceased, 70
    fluid injection method, 72
    peeled skin method, 72
    processing method, 71
    suspect, 70
    victim's, 70
Inked shoe impression from sole, 92–93
Ink library, 342
Inn at the Springs, in Bonita Springs,
    Florida, 328–337
Insects, 183–190; *see also* Entomology
    life cycle of, 185, 186f
    note taking at death scene, 187, 189–190
    specimens/sample collection on scene,
        187, 188d–189d
    toxicology and, 186
Instant shooter kit, 231
Integrated Automated Fingerprint
    Identification System (IAFIS), 339
Integrated Ballistics Identification System
    (IBIS), 339–340
Intensity of light, 33

Intermediate range gunshot wounds, 268
Internal autopsy, 268–270
Internal Revenue Service, 342
Inward spiral search, 136
Iodine fuming, 81–82; *see also* Porous
    surfaces, chemical processing of
    fingerprints on
ISid2, 230, 231; *see also* Gunshot residue kit
    instant shooter kit, 231
    SEM test kit, 231

J

*Journal of the American Academy of
    Forensic Science*, 182

K

Kastle Meyer test kit, 18–19, 19f

L

Labeling evidence, 148–149
Laboratory, methamphetamine, 310–311
    identifying, 310
    response to, 311
Lab submission for evidence from autopsy,
    272–273, 273t
Laminated glass, 235
Larva Diptera, 183
Laser trajectory kit, 25–26, 26f
Latent fingerprints, 72
    developing methods, 73–78
    magnetic powder processing, 80–81
    metal surfaces, 86–88
    nonporous surfaces, 73–76; *see also*
        Superglue fuming
Latent impressions, 90; *see also* Shoe
    impressions; Tire impressions
Legal challenges, for photography, 64–65
Legal searches, Fourth Amendment and,
    108, 111
Lehigh Acres, Florida, 304–308
Lenses, camera, 30–31
    macro, 31
    normal, 30
    telephoto, 30
    wide-angle, 30
Light
    concept, 33
    daylight, 33–34
    intensity of, 33

night photography, 34
painting with, 34, 35f
types of, 33
ultraviolet, 41
Lightning death, 287
crime scene response, 287
signs, 287
Lindbergh kidnapping, 190
Line, strip, or parallel search pattern, 138,
139f
Liquid
adhesion, 197
capillarity, 197
cohesion, 197
physical properties, 197
surface tension, 197t
Liver temperature, 245
Livor mortis, 242, 243f, 244
Locard's principle
biological evidence, 146
of exchange, 190
Long wave UV, 41
Loop fingerprint patterns, 67, 69f
Luminol, 20–22, 21f
photography, 39–41
processing scene with, 21–22
and sterile water, 39

M

Macro lenses, 31; *see also* Lenses, camera
Macro photography, *see* Close-up
photographs
Maggot motel, 187
Maggots, life cycle of, *see* Blowfly/maggots,
life cycle of
Magnetic powder, 78, 79t
latent fingerprints with, 80–81
shoe impression with, 90–92, 91f
Malaysia Airlines Flight 370, 312
Manner of death, 241–242, 249t; *see also*
Autopsy; Death
accidental death, 241–242
homicide, 241
natural death, 242
suicide, 241
undetermined death, 242
Mapping, 128, 131–134
baseline, 131–133, 131f–132f
GPS, 134
polar/grid coordinate, 134, 135f
rectangular coordinate, 133, 134f

triangulation method, 133, 134f
Maricopa County, 191
Marijuana growing operations
artificial lighting, 300, 301
case, 304–308
crime scene response, 303–304
dehumidifiers, 300
drying room, 302
female plants, 301
grow houses/rooms, 300–302
housing market and, 300
indoor, 299
insulation material, 301
nursery, 302
seized live plants maintenance, 304
temperature, 301
THC resin, 299, 301
Marked evidence, sketch with, 128, 129f
Markers for identifying physical evidence,
6–7
Measurements, sketch with, 128, 130f;
see also Sketching
Measuring devices, evidence, 7
Mechanism of death, 242; *see also* Autopsy
Medical examiner
autopsy at office of, *see* Autopsy
description, 240–241
duties of, 241
SIDS autopsy, 289
vs. coroner, 239–241, 240m
Medico-legal death investigator (MLDI)
criminal investigator *vs.*, 239
defined, 239
duties of, 249–250
gunshot victims, 282
reconstruction of SIDS scene, 297
work sheet template for, 253d–256d
Medico-legal entomology, 183
Medium distance photos, *see* Midrange
photographs
Medium wave UV, 41
Memory cards, 32–33; *see also specific*
Memory card
Metal containers for packaging, 147–148
Metal detector, 24
Metal surfaces, latent fingerprints on, 86–88
Birchwood Casey Brass Black, 86–87
Brass Black or Aluminum Black
solution, 86–88, 88t
Methamphetamine, 308–312, 309f
clandestine laboratory training course,
311–312

ingredients of, 309–310, 309f
laboratory, 310–311
Micro SD memory cards, 33
Midrange photographs, 54–55
MLDI, *see* Medico-legal death investigator
    (MLDI)
More Hits, 64
Mortis
    algor, 244
    livor, 242, 243f
    rigor, 243–244
Morton Avenue, 330–332
Motel 6, 336–337
Motor vehicles used in crime, 151–158
    DNA evidence, 157
    documentation, 152, 153d–154d
    fingerprinting, 158
    general procedures, 152–157
    photographing, 152, 155
    recovering additional evidence, 157–158
    releasing, 159
    searching, 157
    sketching, 155–156
    transporting, 156
    zone search pattern, 157
Mueller, Ron, 93
Mug shots, *see* Identification photographs
Multi-agency investigations
    aviation accidents, *see* Aviation accidents
    drug investigations, *see* Drug
        investigations
    human smuggling, 321, 322–325
    human trafficking, 321–322
    officer-involved shooting, 326–337
Mummification, 246
Murder trial in Florida, 64–65

N

National Automotive Paint File, 340
National DNA Index System (NDIS), 341
National Institute of Justice, 342
National Integrated Ballistics Information
    Network (NIBIN), 269, 341
National Transportation and Safety Board
    (NTSB), 312–314
    aviation specialists responsibilities,
        312–313
    Go Teams, 312
    investigative party, 313–314
    notification procedures, 314
    Regional Operations Center (ROC), 314

response to aviation accident, 312–313
National Weather Service, 287
Native American Grave Protection and
    Repatriation Act, 161
Natural death, 242, 249t; *see also* Death;
    Manner of death
Natural Resources Conservation Service
    (NRCS), 343–344
NDIS, *see* National DNA Index System
    (NDIS)
Near contact wound, 267; *see also* Gunshot
    wounds
NIBIN, *see* National Integrated Ballistics
    Information Network (NIBIN)
Night photography, 34; *see also* Light
Ninhydrin, 82–83, 82f
Nixon, Richard, 299
Normal lenses, 30; *see also* Lenses, camera
Note taking
    crime scene documentation, 2
    at death scene, with insect activity, 187,
        189–190
NRCS, *see* Natural Resources Conservation
    Service (NRCS)
Nuclear DNA testing, hair root for, 5

O

Ocular fluid, potassium level of, 245
Odontology, 181–183; *see also* Dental
    identification
Officer-involved shooting, 326–337
    CSI response to, 327–328
    dexter copycat case, 328–337
    investigation responsibility, 327
    marijuana grow house robbing and,
        304–308
Officer safety during searches, 144
On-call CSI personnel, 107–108
Orange filters, 31
Osteology, 177
Outdoor crime scene searches, 138–143
    grid search pattern, 139, 140f
    line, strip, or parallel search pattern,
        138, 139f
    managing, 139–140
Outward spiral search, 136
Overall photography, 48–54
    exterior, 49–51, 50f
    four corners or compass method, 54
    interior, 51
    360-degree method, 51–52, 52f, 53f

wall-to-wall method, 52, 54, 54f
Overdose, *see* Drug overdoses
Overview sketch, *see* Bird's-eye view/
    overview sketch

P

Packaging
    bedsheets for, 148
    body boxes, 148
    cardboard boxes for, 145, 146–147
    materials, 7–8, 7f
    optional, 148
    paper bags for, 145, 146
    plastic and metal containers for, 147–148
    plastic bags for, 147, 147f
Painting with light, 34, 35f
Palo Verde tree, 191
Passive/gravity bloodstain pattern, 198,
    199t, 200–202; *see also* Bloodstain
    pattern analysis
Patterns, fingerprint, *see* Fingerprint
    patterns
Patton, Richard, 89
Peeled skin method, 72
Pelvic joint morphology, 179
Perimortem trauma, 180
Perper, Joshua, 284
Photographer, as expert witness, 63
Photography
    accident scene, 60–62
    aperture priority, 38–39
    basics, 33–39
    Bluestar, 41
    body panorama photos, 58–59
    checklist for, 65–66
    close-up, 55–58
    depth of field, 36–37, 36f
    expert witness, 63
    filling the frame, 35
    flash, 39
    flash angle effect, 39
    infrared, 43–44
    injuries, 59, 59f
    keeping film plane parallel, 38
    legal challenges, 64–65
    light and, 33–34
    Luminol, 39–41
    midrange, 54–55
    motor vehicles used in crime, 152, 155
    overall, 48–54
    purpose of, 29

shutter priority, 37
shutter speed, 37
ultraviolet, 41–43
Photo identifier, 45–47
Photo log, 47–48
    labeled scale, 47–48, 48f
Physical developer
    description, 83
    fingerprint processing on porous
        surface, 83
Pie search pattern, 136, 137f
Plants, 190–192
    material, collection of, 191–192
Plastic bags for packaging, 147, 147f
Plastic containers for packaging, 147–148
Plastic impressions, 90; *see also*
        Shoe impressions; Tire
        impressions
Poisoning
    carbon monoxide (CO), 277–278
    death investigation, 284–285
Polar/grid coordinate mapping, 134, 135f
Polarizing filters, 31
Policy 49 CFR 830.10, 316
Popeye, 276–277
Porous surfaces, chemical processing of
        fingerprints on, 81–84
    DFO, 84
    iodine fuming, 81–82
    ninhydrin, 82–83, 82f
    physical developer, 83
Potassium level of ocular fluid, 245
Powder for fingerprints, 78–81
    carbon powder, 78, 79–80
    fluorescent powder, 78, 79t
    latent powder, 78
    magnetic powder, 78, 79t, 80–81
    powdering process, 79–80
Power tools, death by, 280–281, 281f
Prehistoric human remains, 161
Prescription drugs database, 341; *see also*
        RxList
Prisoners, and gravesite, 163
Projectile trajectory, *see* Bullet trajectory
Property receipt, 150, 151d
Protective gear, 5, 6f
Pubic symphysis, 179

R

Radial fractures, 235, 237; *see also* Glass
        fractures

Radial loop fingerprint patterns, 67
Randomly amplified polymorphic DNA
    (RAPD), 191
RAPD, see Randomly amplified
    polymorphic DNA
Recent human remains, 161
Reconstruction of scene
    bloodstain pattern analysis, see
        Bloodstain pattern analysis
    firearms and shooting, 218–235
    glass fracture match, 235–237
    overview, 195
    SIDS, 297
Rectal thermometer, 245
Rectangular coordinate mapping, 133, 134f
Red filters, 31, 32
Reflected ultraviolet imaging system
    (RUVIS), 88
Regional Operations Center (ROC), 314;
        see also National Transportation
        and Safety Board (NTSB)
Revolvers, 218–219, 218f; see also Firearms
Rifles, 220–221, 221f; see also Firearms
Rigor mortis, 243–244
Rinsing solution, Amido Black, 23
Road mapping method, for bloodstain
        pattern analysis, 216–217, 217f
RUVIS, see Reflected ultraviolet imaging
        system (RUVIS)
RxList, 341

S

Safety of bloodstain analysts/investigators,
        212
Safety of firearms, 222–227
    clearing firearm, 222–223
    identification markings on cartridges,
        224
    identifying firearm, 224
Safety of first responding officers, 103–104
    burglar in attic case, 104
Sand, casting tire impression in, 97
Sanibel Island in Southwest Florida, 323,
        324
Satellite-based navigation system, see
        Global positioning system (GPS)
Scanning electron microscope (SEM) test
        kit, 231
Schrader, Bruce A., 182
Searches
    with consent, 118–119, 119d

double murder case, 140–143
evidence, 143–144
exigent circumstances, 119–120
Fourth Amendment and, 108, 111
grid search pattern, 139, 140f
indoor crime scene, 135–138, 143; see
        also Indoor crime scene searches
line, strip, or parallel search pattern,
        138, 139f
managing, 139–144
officer safety during, 144
outdoor crime scene, 138–143; see also
        Outdoor crime scene searches
pie search pattern, 136, 137f
reasonable, justification of, 111–112
spiral search pattern, 136
wheel search pattern, 136, 137f
zone search pattern, 136, 137, 137f
Search warrant, 112
    body, 117–118
    serving, 112
    on vehicle, serving, 117
Secret Service, 342
Secure Digital High Capacity (SDHC)
        memory card, 32
Secure Digital (SD) memory card, 32
Secure Digital 'Xtra Capacity (SDXC)
        memory card, 32–33
Seedpods, 191
SEM, see Scanning electron microscope
        (SEM) test kit
Semen testing kit, see Acid phosphatase
        (AP) kit
Semi-automatic handguns, 219–220, 219f;
        see also Firearms
Senn, David R., 182
Serial number restoration of firearms, 227
7-year-old boy, excavation of, 171–172, 172f
Sex slavery, human trafficking for, 322
Sexual asphyxia, 280
Sexual assault cases, DNA testing in, 157
Sexual assault evidence collection kit,
        11–13, 12f
    for suspect, 13
    for victim, 13
Sexual dimorphism, 179
Sharp force trauma, 180
Shoe impressions; see also Tire
        impressions
    carbon powder and, 90–92
    classification, 90
    electrostatic dust print-lifting device, 93

evidence kit, 26–27
identification of, 99
inked impression from sole, 92–93
magnetic powder and, 90–92, 91f
processing methods, 90–97
three-dimensional, 93, 95–97
Shooting reconstruction, 218–235; see also
        Firearms
Short wave UV, 41
Shotguns, 220–221, 220f; see also
        Firearms
    distance determination of, 228
    gauge, 221
    shells, 221
Shutter priority, 37
Shutter speed, 37; see also Photography
    aperture priority, 38
    freezing movement, 37
    higher, 37
    slower, 37, 38f
Silverthorne Lumber Co. v. United States,
        108
Skeletal development, 178–179
Sketching
    bird's-eye view/overview, 124, 125f
    cross-protection, 125, 127f
    documenting crime scene, 124–128
    elevation, 124, 126f
    kit tool, 2, 3f
    with marked evidence, 128, 129f
    with measurements, 128, 130f
    motor vehicles used in crime, 155–156
    perspective, 125
    types, 124–128
Small particle reagent (SPR), 85–86
Smith, Anna Nicole, drug overdose case of,
        284
Social Security Administration, 171
Sodium rhodizonate solution, 230
Soft contact wound, 267
Soil
    database, 343–344
SoleMate, 340
Sole Mate database, 99
Southeast Texas Applied Forensic Science
        Facility, 180
Southwest Florida International Airport,
        318
Spatter patterns, 199t, 202, 203t, 204t,
        205–207; see also Bloodstain
        pattern analysis
Spiral search pattern, 136, 136f

Spitz, Craig, case of, 328–337
SPR, see Small particle reagent (SPR)
Stabbing death, 264–265
Staining solution, Amido Black, 23
Standard operating procedures (SOP)
    with digital imaging investigation,
        64–65
Stature
    allometry, 180
    estimation of, 180
Sterile water, luminol and, 39
Storage media, 30, 32–33; see also Memory
        cards
Strangulation death, 265–266
    manual, 266
    procedures for, 265–266
String method, for areas of origin, 214–215;
        see also Bloodstain pattern
        analysis
Styrofoam blocks, 147
Sudden infant death syndrome (SIDS),
        289–297
    reconstruction of scene, 297
    template, 290d–296d
Suicide, 241, 249t; see also Death; Manner
        of death
    carbon monoxide poisoning, 277
    by car exhaust fumes, 277
    firearms and, 282
    hanging, 278–280
    helium bag mechanism and, 277
    through asphyxiant gas, 277
Suicide bag, 277; see also Helium bag
        mechanism, for suicide
Sunlight, 33–34
Superglue fuming
    at crime scene, 78
    cyanoacrylate fuming, 76–78
    to deceased person, 76–77
    fuming wand, 78
    homemade chamber, 78
    methods, 74–75
    nonporous surfaces with, 73–76
    quality and efficiency, 75–76
Superior Court of Maricopa County, 191
Surface tension
    defined, 197
    liquid, 197t
Susie, case of, 285
Suspect fingerprints, 70
Suspect's sexual assault evidence collection
        kit, 13

T

Taphonomic assessment, 177–178
Taphonomy, 177
Target distance determination, of gunshots, 227–230
Teeth; *see also* Dental identification
  determining age and sex, 179
  development, 179
Tempered glass, 235
Texas Missing Persons DNA database, 343
Threadmate database, 99
3R rule, glass fractures, 236
Three-dimensional shoe impressions, 93, 95–97
  equipment required, 95
  processing method, 96–97
360-degree method, 51–52, 52f, 53f
Time of death, 244–246; *see also* Autopsy; Death investigation
  body temperature and, 245
  categories, 244
  decomposition and, 245–246
  entomology and, 246
  factors determining, 244–245
  mummification and, 246
  ocular fluid potassium and, 245
Tire impressions; *see also* Shoe impressions
  classification, 90
  dirt and sand, 97
  evidence kit, 26–27
  identification of, 99
  lifted from tire, 98–99
Toolbox, 24
Tool mark impressions, 99–100
  Accutrans casting, 100
  Mikrosil casting, 100
  processing method, 100
Tools
  developing evidence, 16–27
  evidence collection, 4–15
  scene documentation, 1–3
Toxicology and insects, 186
Trace evidence
  collection, 10–11
  macro lenses for, 31
Traditional powder, *see* Carbon powder
Trajectory reconstruction, *see* Bullet trajectory
Transporting
  motor vehicles used in crime, 156
Trauma

blunt force, 180
  perimortem, 180
  sharp force, 180
TreadMark, 340
TreadMate, 340
Triangulation mapping method, 133, 134f
Tripod, 51, 52, 59
Two-boat approach, to human smuggling, 323–324

U

Ulnar loop fingerprint patterns, 67
Ultraviolet light, 41
Ultraviolet photography, 41–43
  applications, 43
Unattended *vs.* attended death, 274
Undetermined death, 242, 249t; *see also* Death; Manner of death
University of North Texas Health Science Center, 343
US Coast Guard, 323, 324
USDA, *see* Department of Agriculture (USDA)

V

Vehicle drowning, death by, 286
Victims
  drowning, *see* Drowning
Victim's sexual assault evidence collection kit, 13
Visible impressions, 90; *see also* Shoe impressions; Tire impressions
Visual/external autopsy, 252, 263

W

Walk-through of scene, 120–121, 158–159
War on drugs, 299
Warrantless search, *see* Exigent circumstances
Web Soil Survey, 343–344
Wetwop, 86
Wheel search pattern, 136, 137f
Whorl fingerprint patterns, 67, 68f
Wide-angle lens, 54
Window glass
  fractured, 235
  tempered glass as, 235
Windshield
  bullet holes, 236, 237f